# THE EFFECTIVENESS OF INTERNATIONAL SUPERVISION

## Thirty Years of I.L.O. Experience

AUSTRALIA
The Law Book Co. Ltd.
Sydney: Melbourne: Brisbane

GREAT BRITAIN
Stevens & Sons Ltd.
London

INDIA
N. M. Tripathi Private Ltd.
Bombay

ISRAEL
Steimatzky's Agency Ltd.
Jerusalem: Tel Aviv: Haifa

NEW ZEALAND
Sweet & Maxwell (N.Z.) Ltd.
Wellington

NORTH AND SOUTH AMERICA
AND THE PHILIPPINES
Oceana Publications Inc.
Dobbs Ferry, New York

PAKISTAN
Pakistan Law House
Karachi

# THE EFFECTIVENESS
# OF
# INTERNATIONAL SUPERVISION

## Thirty Years of I.L.O. Experience

by

## E. A. LANDY

LONDON · STEVENS & SONS
DOBBS FERRY, NEW YORK · OCEANA PUBLICATIONS, INC.
1966

*Published in 1966 by*
*Stevens & Sons Limited of*
*11 New Fetter Lane, London*
*and*
*Oceana Publications, Inc.*
*of Dobbs Ferry, New York*

*Printed in Switzerland*
*by Imprimeries Populaires, Geneva*

*Library of Congress Catalog*
*Card No. 66-11877*

*To the Memory of
my Father*

# TABLE OF CONTENTS

# LIST OF TABLES

# LIST OF ABBREVIATIONS OF TITLES
## OF PUBLICATIONS OF THE INTERNATIONAL LABOUR OFFICE [1]

R.P.  Record of Proceedings of the International Labour Conference.[2]

P.R.  Provisional Record of the International Labour Conference.[3]

D.R.  Report of the Director-General of the International Labour Office to the International Labour Conference.[4]

Report  Report on a subject included in the agenda of the International Labour Conference.[5]

R.C.E.  Report of the Committee of Experts on the Application of Conventions and Recommendations.[6]

S.R.  Summary of Reports on Ratified Conventions, submitted to the International Labour Conference.[7]

G.B.  Minutes of the Governing Body of the International Labour Office.[2]

O.B.  Official Bulletin of the International Labour Office.[8]

---

[1] Whenever an I.L.O. document only exists in roneoed rather than printed form, this is indicated in the reference.

[2] In citations the number preceding the letters is that of the session; the numbers following are page numbers.

[3] The number preceding the letters is that of the session; the number and pages of the Provisional Record follow the letters.

[4] The number preceding the letters is that of the session; the numbers following are page numbers. Until 1932 inclusive, the Director's Report was published both as part of the Conference Record of Proceedings and separately; the references here are to the separate editions.

[5] The number preceding the term "Report" is that of the session; the citation also includes the subject title of the report; the numbers following this title are page numbers.

[6] The number preceding the letters gives the year of the Committee's session; the numbers following are page numbers; the Explanatory Note to Appendix II (pp. 217-218 below) indicates how the Committee's Report has been published over the years.

[7] The number preceding the letters is that of the session; the numbers following are page numbers; the Explanatory Note to Appendix II indicates how the Summary has been published over the years.

[8] The number preceding the letters is that of the volume; the numbers following are page numbers.

# PREFACE

The time has passed when meaningful international supervision could be dismissed as a fantasy, a theoretical notion or a catchword. The need for tangible progress in this field is all too obvious by now. But there is a parallel need to know more about actual experience and results, so that the problems, implications and prospects of international supervision can come more clearly into focus.

It was with this practical purpose in mind that the present study was conceived and carried out. Rather than dealing in generalities, an initial attempt has been made here to determine on the basis of a working model whether systematic arrangements for international supervision have helped to promote compliance with treaty obligations. In terms of time span, variety of standards and extent of their ratification, the International Labour Organization seemed to provide a promising subject of inquiry. Other models may require different methods of evaluation and may yield different results but a beginning had to be made.

The credit for persuading the author to carry through this task goes to Professor Jacques Freymond, Director of the Graduate Institute of International Studies at the University of Geneva. I am equally indebted to Dr. Michel Virally, Professor at the Graduate Institute and the University of Geneva, whose advice and guidance proved invaluable. My sincere thanks also go to Professor Ernst B. Haas of the University of California, to Professor Jean Siotis of the Graduate Institute, and to Professor Lincoln Bloomfield of the Massachusetts Institute of Technology who read the manuscript and made many pertinent suggestions. The expert assistance of Mr. M. L. Lowenthal Jr. of *The New York Times* in editing the manuscript is especially appreciated.

The completion of this study would have been much delayed without a leave of absence from my regular duties at the International Labour Office, authorized by its Director-General, Mr. David A. Morse. Nor would this leave have been materially possible without the generous assistance of The Rockefeller Foundation.

With the study thus prepared on my own time and responsibility, it is hardly necessary to emphasize that the findings and conclusions it contains exclusively reflect the views of the author.

E. A. L.

Pregny-Chambésy,
October, 1965.

# INTRODUCTION

Future historians may remember the Twentieth Century not only as an era of total war and scientific revolution but also as the period when the problems of peace and world order were tackled for the first time on a truly global scale. The system of international organization which has gradually taken shape over the past 50 years now possesses sufficient weight and momentum to constitute an independent factor in inter-State affairs. And even if its early high hopes have yet to be fulfilled, this new instrument has already begun to leave a permanent imprint on the Community of States which created it.

The basic tool used in building this new system is the law-making treaty.[1] From the Geneva Convention of 1864 to the codification of the Régime of the High Seas in 1958, from the Hague Conventions of 1899 and 1907 to the Moscow Treaty banning nuclear weapons tests in the atmosphere, in outer space and under water, agreements have been negotiated to lay down the rules which the growing complexity and interdependence of the modern world require. As a result "international legislation" [2] is becoming as essential an element in the life of nations as municipal law has been for many centuries in the life of individuals.[3]

It is hardly surprising that, with this steady extension of the treaty as the main-stay of international organization, the question of actual performance should also have been raised with increasing insistence. For the adoption of international legislation and its formal acceptance by a growing number of countries cannot, by themselves, add to the stability of inter-State relations, unless there also exists some degree of assurance that the contracting parties really comply with their treaty obligations. This

---

[1] J. L. Brierly defines this as "the class of treaties which... a large number of States have concluded for the purpose either of declaring their understanding of what the law is on a particular subject, or of laying down a new general rule for future conduct, or for creating some international institution" (*The Law of Nations*, Sixth Edition (Oxford: Clarendon Press, 1963), p. 58).

[2] In the Introduction to his "collection of the texts of multipartite instruments of general interest", Judge Manley O. Hudson explained that this term refers to "both the process and the product of the conscious effort to make additions to, or changes in, the law of nations" and that "it seems to describe more accurately than any other, the contributions of international conferences at which States enact a law which is to govern their relations" (*International Legislation*, Vol. I, 1919-1921 (Washington: Carnegie Endowment for International Peace, 1931), pp. XIII-XIV).

[3] Among many recent statements recognizing this development, cf. in particular Wolfgang Friedmann, *The Changing Structure of International Law* (London: Stevens & Sons, 1964), pp. 123-125.

concern that governments respect their pledged word thus emerges as a crucial problem of the contemporary world.

States are of course expected to carry out their obligations in good faith and the principle *pacta sunt servanda* has long been considered as a fundamental rule of international law. But mere reliance on this rule, however generally it may be accepted,[1] still represents a rather frail basis on which to found a durable system of global rights and duties. As the system has grown in complexity, therefore, procedures have had to be developed in order to verify governmental compliance with ratified treaties. Starting with the end of the First World War, the question of international supervision thus gradually lost its largely theoretical character to become one of the practical measures through which it was hoped to achieve a more stable world order. Yet it must be admitted that concrete achievements have been very much slower to materialize in this field than in the sphere of treaty-making.

The limited initiatives of the League of Nations, such as the Mandates Commission and the control of narcotic drugs, have been continued in modified form by the United Nations. The International Labour Organization has been able, over the past 40 years, to maintain and expand its procedures for following up the effect given to its Conventions. Some measure of control has been exercised, intermittently, over the production and exchange of certain commodities like sugar, wheat, coffee and tin. A system to protect human rights, first attempted in Upper Silesia during the inter-war period, now operates with some success within the framework of the Council of Europe, which has also drawn up a Social Charter. The International Atomic Energy Agency and Euratom have instituted special safeguards to ensure that fissionable materials are used only for peaceful purposes. Even in the military field, regional treaties covering Western Europe and Antarctica provide for a measure of actual inspection.

But in other important areas little or no progress has been possible.[2] The United Nations has not yet completed the framing of its Human Rights Covenants which it has been discussing for a decade and a half and which are to provide for measures of implementation. More vital still, in the sphere of disarmament it is precisely the question of supervision which seems to represent the principal stumbling block to an accord. This danger that the negotiation of essential treaties may be impeded because no agreement can be reached on controlling their implementation adds further urgency to the whole problem of international supervision.

---

[1] Cf. Paul Guggenheim, *Traité de Droit International Public* (Geneva: Librairie de l'Université, 1954), Vol. I, pp. 6-11. Professor Hans Kelsen calls the rule *pacta* "the relatively top-most stratum" of "customary international law" (*Théorie Pure du Droit* (Paris: Dalloz, 1962), p. 425). Lord McNair affirms that "no government would decline to accept the principle *pacta sunt servanda*" (*Law of Treaties* (Oxford: Clarendon Press, 1961), p. 493).

[2] The need for supervision machinery in the implementation, e.g., of the international Conventions on the abolition of slavery was stressed forcefully by Viscount Maugham in a debate in the British House of Lords in 1960: "International Conventions are useless unless they have the machinery for supervising their application. An international Convention is a mere piece of paper if no agency exists for translating its terms into action" (Parliamentary Debates, House of Lords, 14 July 1960, *Hansard*, Vol. CCXXV, col. 346).

It would be tempting to look for solutions based on national experience but, whereas governments usually have competence to enforce their laws, no corresponding power yet exists in regard to international legislation. The implementation of international standards can therefore only be promoted through methods appropriate to the present degree of organization and integration of the Community of Nations. The task of supervision thus implies a constant compromise between the independence of States on the one hand and the co-ordination of their activities on the other. In the pursuance of this objective the supervisory procedures must principally rely on a combination of fact-finding and persuasion. Although certain systems may contain elements of judicial control and on-the-spot inspection, the main emphasis is always on ascertaining the extent of compliance with treaty obligations rather than on coercive measures to remove violations.

Depending on the type of treaty to be supervised and on the machinery available for this purpose, supervision can be organized on an occasional or on a systematic basis. In the former case a charge of non-compliance is, as a rule, examined by an independent commission of inquiry or a similar body. In the latter case a regular procedure exists under which the parties to a treaty report periodically on its application and this information is subjected automatically to technical verification and sometimes also to political discussion. Both the intermittent and the automatic types of supervision can operate most easily within the permanent framework of international organizations which use them to administer the norms negotiated under their aegis.

The fact that international supervision is of fairly recent origin and that such experience as has been acquired comes from a variety of fields and systems probably accounts for the relative dearth of studies exploring this subject from a general point of view. Only a few books and articles have so far attempted to deal in depth with the problems and prospects of verifying the implementation of treaty obligations.[1] Another, closely related topic, the effectiveness of international supervision, has received even less attention thus far. Yet this question of the actual impact of existing supervisory procedures represents the crux of the whole matter because

---

[1] The list includes three books: V. N. Kaasik, *Le Contrôle en Droit International* (Paris: Pédone, 1933); Erwin Bernarth, *Die Internationale Kontrolle* (Zurich: Ernst Lang, 1935); Paul Berthoud, *Le Contrôle International de l'Exécution des Conventions Collectives* (Geneva: Imprimerie de Saint-Gervais, 1946); a short course at the Hague Academy of International Law: L. Kopelmanas, *Le Contrôle International* (Recueil des Cours de l'Académie de Droit International, 1950, Vol. II, pp. 59-149); and four articles: Hugo J. Hahn, "Internationale Kontrollen", *Archiv des Völkerrechts* (Vol. 7 (1958), pp. 88-112); Marcel Merle, "Le contrôle exercé par les organisations internationales sur les activités des Etats Membres", *Annuaire Français de Droit International*, Vol. V (1959), pp. 411-431; F. M. van Asbeck, "Quelques aspects du contrôle international non-judiciaire de l'application par les gouvernements de conventions internationales", *Nederlands Tijdschrift voor International Recht*, Volume en l'honneur du professeur François (Leyde: A. W. Sijthoff's, 1959, pp. 27-41); Nicolas Valticos, "Aperçu de certains grands problèmes du contrôle international (spécialement à propos des Conventions internationales du Travail)", *Eranion en l'honneur de G. S. Maridakis* (Athens: Klissiounis, 1964), Vol. III, pp. 543-586. The absence of any such general studies in English is all the more surprising in the light of the many analyses of the military aspects of international supervision which have appeared of late in the United States and in Britain.

the contribution which such procedures can make in strengthening international confidence and co-operation largely depends on the influence they are able to exert on the behaviour of States. But any attempt to measure this influence with some degree of accuracy soon encounters serious difficulties: very few systems of supervision have operated over a sufficiently long span of time and have covered a sufficiently large number of international obligations to permit significant conclusions to emerge; even where a sizable body of information is available for inquiry, a clear connection must be established between the promptings of the supervisory organs and the action governments have taken in response; the availability of full and reliable documentary evidence constitutes a further prerequisite.[1]

If, despite these difficulties, an attempt can be made to measure the effectiveness of supervisory arrangements in at least one area of world organization, this may help to provide a better insight into the working and potentialities of international supervision. The present study represents such an attempt. Because of the various complicating factors mentioned above, the International Labour Organization was selected as a suitable subject of inquiry. During its almost half a century of existence the I.L.O. has been able to formulate over a hundred separate Conventions on labour and social questions. These international labour standards —as they are commonly called—have been ratified on such a scale that the network of international obligations assumed by the member States currently exceeds 4,000. Reports on the effect given to these instruments are required under the I.L.O. Constitution and form the basis of an annual cycle of expert and mutual supervision which has by now been in full operation for over three decades. The findings of these two supervisory committees are available as public documents and the system has the additional interesting feature of providing for the active participation of workers and employers. In terms of size, continuity and time span, no other system of international supervision is comparable to that of the I.L.O.[2]

In addition to the system of automatic, regular supervision outlined above, the I.L.O. uses other techniques to promote its principles and objectives.[3] Aside from certain fact-finding and related techniques which will be referred to later in this study, there exists a formal representations and complaints procedure to secure compliance with ratified Conventions.

---

[1] In his article on international supervision, Professor Marcel Merle calls "the measurement of the effectiveness of supervision... an immense and highly delicate undertaking", adding that it cannot be "evaluated on a short-term basis or through fragmentary observations. It can only be grasped by those familiar with the practice and the development of international institutions" (*op. cit.*, pp. 430-431).

[2] To these factors might be added the seriousness with which the I.L.O. has always viewed its supervisory functions. In 1964, its Director-General reaffirmed this attitude before the annual Conference: "We must scrupulously safeguard the rigorous supervision over the application of I.L.O. standards. This is essential to the integrity of the Organization and to the self-respect of the member States which have through it undertaken international obligations" (48 R.P. 407).

[3] Professor Bowett considers that "supervision and enforcement procedures designed to ensure compliance with (international obligations) are seen, in the most 'sophisticated' form, in the I.L.O." (D. W. Bowett, *The Law of International Institutions* (London: Methuen, 1964), p. 129).

Although this procedure has been part of the I.L.O.'s Constitution from the outset, it has in fact been used on a very much more limited scale than the permanent system of routine supervision. It seems worthwhile, therefore, to explore in retrospect the interplay of these two distinctive systems, one incidental and judicial, the other systematic, technical and political. Why has this latter system, sometimes described as "quasi-judicial", evoked so much less interest among students of international supervision and of the I.L.O.?[1] Has this been due to a lack of data on the actual working and impact of a rather unspectacular method for promoting compliance with international obligations?

Opinions as to the prospects of achieving such compliance have always differed widely. In 1848, long before the I.L.O. came into being, citizen Morin discussed in the French National Assembly the possibility of making agreements between nations to regulate "the duration of labour uniformly". Asking whether such treaties could be negotiated and would be executed, he gave this categorical answer: "Without doubt such treaties could be written, but they would never be carried out".[2] More recently, an American observer closed his account of an annual session of the International Labour Conference by describing it as a forum "where it is reasonable to suppose that exposure of the facts and regard for the opinion of mankind will lead, at least in the long run, to corrective action".[3] Without going into the general question of the over-all influence of international treaties on the law and practice of States, the present study has set itself the much more limited and specific task of determining to what extent a permanent system of supervision such as the I.L.O.'s is actually able, through the "exposure of the facts", to promote compliance with international legislation. Stated more bluntly, what has been the impact of I.L.O. supervision on governments which have been found to infringe their treaty obligations?

In seeking some sort of useful and comprehensive answer to this question it is necessary, for each formal obligation under a ratified I.L.O. Convention, to ascertain whether the supervisory organs addressed critical comments to a government, whether such comments eventually led to fuller or full compliance and how much time elapsed before a government took the corrective action required. By tracing the comments of the supervisory Committees from year to year and by tabulating the results, it should be possible to compile precise statistical data indicating the extent to which I.L.O. supervision has failed or succeeded in its task, in individual cases and as a whole. If the concept of effectiveness is defined in such narrow

[1] This apparent lack of interest strongly contrasts with the thorough treatment given to the formal, more spectacular, methods. The article of Hugo J. Hahn, for instance, cited in footnote 1, p. 3 above, omits any reference to the I.L.O.'s three decades of systematic supervision. A standard work on international labour legislation devotes eight pages to a description and analysis of representations and complaints under the I.L.O. Constitution but takes just four lines to allude to the task of regular supervision: cf. Léon-Eli Troclet, *Législation Sociale Internationale* (Brussels: Cahiers de l'Institut de Sociologie Solvay, Editions de la Librairie Encyclopédique, 1952), pp. 600 and 603-610.

[2] As quoted in John W. Follows, *The Antecedents of the International Labour Organization* (Oxford: Clarendon Press, 1951), pp. 20-21.

[3] H. M. Douty, "The International Labor Conference of 1962", *Monthly Labor Review* (United States Department of Labor), Vol. 85, No. 9 (September 1962), p. 988.

and specific terms, this should also make it easier to identify a causal relationship between international advice and national action.[1]

In reading the findings and conclusions that emerge from the present study, it is essential to bear these very precise and limited terms of reference in mind. It does not deal with the general influence of I.L.O. standards on the law and practice of member countries.[2] Even less does it concern itself with the role of these standards, or of the I.L.O. as a whole, in promoting international integration—a subject of almost forbidding complexity.[3] Instead of attempting to assess the general impact of the I.L.O. from such a broad perspective, this study concentrates deliberately on one specific subject: to ascertain whether and to what extent supervision has promoted compliance with treaty obligations. Here again, the criteria used are narrow and precise: breaches of these obligations are not deemed to have been eliminated when a government has merely voiced its intention to initiate the necessary measures or when draft legislation has been introduced, but only when concrete action has been taken. Once a change has been made in the law, in administrative practice, etc. the question of day-to-day compliance remains, but this is primarily a matter for national supervision and enforcement and therefore also outside the scope of the present study.

The effectiveness of international supervision, as conceived here, thus covers only one phase and one facet of the activities of the I.L.O. But it is hoped that in circumscribing the terms of reference of the inquiry, more specific results will be obtained and that these findings will in turn provide a useful basis when other phases or facets of international organization come under scrutiny.[4]

In addition, the present inquiry may bring into focus certain broader issues of international supervision. Has the existence of such a system discouraged ratification of I.L.O. Conventions? What obstacles have prevented governments from responding to the comments of the supervisory committees? Have these organs functioned with a reasonable

---

[1] Such a relationship is usually difficult to corroborate because, as pointed out by Professor Siotis in connection with governmental decision-making, "national administrations are reluctant to recognize the 'international' origin or inspiration of decisions" (Jean Siotis, "The Secretariat of the United Nations Economic Commission for Europe: The First Ten Years", *International Organization*, Vol. XIX, No. 2 (Spring 1965), p. 194).

[2] A series of articles on the influence of international labour Conventions on the legislation of various States, published in the *International Labour Review* in recent years, deals with the problem from this broader point of view. The countries examined in this series are Greece (June 1955), India (June 1956), Switzerland (June 1958), Nigeria (July 1960), Italy (June 1961), Norway (September 1964), Tunisia (March 1965) and Poland (November 1965).

[3] Cf. in this connection Ernst B. Haas, *Beyond the Nation-State, Functionalism and International Organization* (Stanford: Stanford University Press, 1964) which includes a detailed study of the I.L.O., inquiring whether its structure, tasks and achievements meet the requirements posed by a general theory of international organization. As explained by Professor Haas in the Preface, his book "manipulates the experience of the International Labor Organization, on which it draws very heavily, in order to explore the nature of international integration" (*op. cit.*, p. VII).

[4] Thus Professor Haas quotes from the preliminary results of the present study when discussing the effectiveness of the I.L.O.'s systematic supervision procedure (*op. cit.*, pp. 257-258, 560).

degree of efficiency or has their mode of operation sometimes had a negative effect on implementing action? What remedies are available to overcome difficulties in the application or supervision of international obligations?

Since a purely numerical accumulation of data cannot by itself provide a clear picture of how a system of supervision works, or fails to work, in practice, it was essential to draw not only on statistical evidence but also on selected case histories in order to illustrate and discuss the main problems confronting the governments and the I.L.O. in the implementation of international standards. Under the plan adopted for this purpose, an initial survey of the institutional background of I.L.O. supervision attempts to show how procedures have gradually been devised to increase the effectiveness of the system. A second chapter deals with the criteria, the method and the results of the case-by-case inquiry. This is followed by a quantitative analysis of the statistical data so as to determine whether the character of the Conventions, the regional distribution of the results and the delays in implementation are subject to any discernible patterns. Chapters Four and Five attempt, on the basis of as wide a range of actual examples as possible, to review the principal reasons why States have not complied with their international obligations. Chapter Six catalogues the difficulties faced by supervisory systems such as the I.L.O.'s. In analyzing the problems of implementation and of supervision, some attention must also be given to possible measures to overcome difficulties in the application of international labour standards and to add to the effectiveness of international supervision.

Although the procedures evaluated in these pages rest on a solid constitutional foundation and are primarily concerned with the adjustment of national to international legislation, the present study does not concentrate primarily on the legal aspects of the subject but represents rather an attempt to describe the methods, difficulties and results in practical terms. As already noted, the I.L.O.'s quasi-judicial system of supervision combines technical and political phases. While its objectives are of direct interest to the practitioner of both international and labour law, the day-to-day problems of implementing and of supervising international standards go beyond the domain of the lawyer. They raise questions of public administration, of parliamentary action, of human relations and of diplomatic intercourse whose solution may depend on organizational, psychological, even political measures. Practical factors such as these often determine the success or failure of international action, not only within the particular technical sphere of the I.L.O. but elsewhere as well.

Thus, despite the specialized character of international labour standards, any lessons to be drawn from their supervision might conceivably prove useful beyond the immediate area of social and human rights. This question of the relevance of I.L.O. experience to other systems of treaty law will have to be explored when the findings and conclusions of the present inquiry are summed up at the end. For, as stressed at the outset, concrete progress in the establishment and operation of supervisory techniques has become a crucial issue of international organization.

# CHAPTER ONE

# THE I.L.O.'S. MACHINERY OF SUPERVISION

An attempt is made in this opening chapter to describe the framework and operation of the I.L.O. supervisory system. This requires first of all a review of the genesis of the network of treaty obligations developed by the Organization and of the emergence of systematic arrangements for assessing their implementation. The character, functions and procedures of the two committees set up for this purpose need to be analyzed, especially in their relationship to each other and to other features of the system. While this analysis will have to go into some detail, the main focus of interest is the quest for effective compliance and supervision insofar as it can be discerned throughout the various phases and aspects of I.L.O. supervision.

## I. The Institutional Background

It is unnecessary to relate here at length the origins, aims and history of the International Labour Organization or to review its efforts over several decades to formulate standards of labour and social policy.[1] Nor is there space to trace in detail the background of the machinery set up by the I.L.O. to supervise the implementation of its standards.[2] As stressed above, the purpose of the present study is less ambitious and more specific:

---

[1] The events which led up to, and resulted in, the establishment of the International Labour Organization are dealt with in John W. Follows, *Antecedents of the International Labour Organization, op. cit.*, and James T. Shotwell (editor), *The Origins of the International Labor Organization* (New York: Columbia University Press, 1934). For a review of the Organization's work see International Labour Office, *The International Labour Organization. The First Decade*. Preface by Albert Thomas (London: Allen & Unwin, 1931). Georges Scelle, *L'Organisation Internationale du Travail et le B.I.T.* (Paris: Marcel Rivière, 1930). Francis Graham Wilson, *Labor in the League System* (Stanford: Stanford University Press, 1934). Léon-Eli Troclet, *Législation Sociale Internationale, op. cit.*, International Labour Office, *Lasting Peace the I.L.O. Way. The Story of the International Labour Organization* (Geneva: 1953). Stuart Maclure, *"If you wish Peace, cultivate Justice"*. *The International Labour Organization after Forty Years* (Geneva: World Federation of United Nations Associations, 1960). Ernst B. Haas, *Beyond the Nation-State, op. cit.* L. Oppenheim, *International Law*, Eighth Edition (Edited by H. Lauterpacht) (London: Longmans, 1955), Vol. I, pp. 716-732.

[2] Two basic studies exist on this subject: Pierre-Arthur Visseur, *L'Evolution du Contrôle International sur l'Application de la Protection Ouvrière jusqu'à la Constitution de l'O.I.T. à Genève* (Bar-Le-Duc: Imprimerie du Barrois, 1950). Jean Zarras, *Le Contrôle de l'Application des Conventions Internationales du Travail* (Paris: Librairie Sirey, 1937). Chapters 9 and 11 of Haas, *Beyond the Nation-State, op. cit.*, also deal in detail with I.L.O. supervision.

to determine whether and to what extent these efforts at international supervision have led to action by governments. It is only in their relation to this concept of effectiveness that the history and working of I.L.O. standards and supervision can therefore be dealt with in the present context.

*Formulation of Standards*

A few paragraphs will thus have to suffice to sketch out rapidly the history and character of the I.L.O.'s efforts to originate labour standards of global validity. The events which led up to the establishment of the International Labour Organization illustrate clearly that the adoption and enforcement of international instruments for the protection of workers was the principal, if not the only, objective of those who before and after the turn of the century devised and propagated the idea of a "Permanent Organization for the Promotion of the International Regulation of Labour Conditions".[1] Regardless of whether their motives were primarily humanitarian or economic, they were in agreement that the aim could be effectively and durably secured only through the negotiation and implementation of international conventions.[2] Even at the present time, when the activities of the I.L.O. have expanded beyond the dreams of its founders, and when new changes of emphasis are clearly discernible, the Director-General concludes in his Report to the 1963 Session of the International Labour Conference that "standards have been and ... should remain in large measure the backbone of the I.L.O.'s work".[3] The treaty approach is thus generally accepted as an essential tool for achieving the Organization's objectives. In its present revised form, the I.L.O. Constitution devotes no less than 24 of its 40 articles to the preparation, adoption and implementation of international labour standards.[4]

In this process, the three principal organs of the I.L.O. each have certain well-defined functions assigned to them. The Governing Body, the I.L.O.'s executive council, (now composed of 24 government, 12 employers' and 12 workers' representatives), settles the agenda of the International Labour Conference, on the basis of suggestions made by governments, employers' and workers' organizations, or public international organizations.[5] The International Labour Office, the secretariat of the Organization, is responsible for examining the subjects proposed for submission to the Conference, the I.L.O.'s supreme, legislative organ. The consideration and adoption of the Conference agenda follows a closely regulated

---

[1] This is the title used in the first British draft of the Constitution of the Organization, prepared prior to the Paris Peace Conference. Cf. Shotwell, *op. cit.*, Vol. II, p. 138.

[2] The original Constitution mentions among the principal functions of the International Labour Office "the examination of subjects which it is proposed to bring before the Conference with a view to the conclusion of international Conventions" (article 10, paragraph 1).

[3] 47 D.R. 202.

[4] Articles 10, 14-35, 37.

[5] Article 14, paragraph 1, of the Constitution.

procedure so as to secure widespread agreement in the choice of subjects,[1] thorough technical preparation, adequate consultation,[2] and full discussion at one session, or at two successive sessions, of the Conference. Adoption of a decision in the form of a Convention or a Recommendation requires a majority of two-thirds of the votes cast by the delegates present.[3] Each member country has a delegation of four persons, two government delegates, one employers' and one workers' delegate. As a Recommendation is not subject to ratification, its acceptance by a member State does not create any binding obligations. In the absence of such obligations, and consequently of any enforcement measures, the implementation of Recommendations falls outside the purview of this study.

Over the past four and a half decades the International Labour Conference has adopted some 120 Conventions.[4] Appendix I contains a list of these Conventions, arranged in the chronological order of their adoption from 1919 to 1964.

*Consideration of Standards by Governments*

The Constitution of the I.L.O.[5] contains a series of requirements designed to ensure that the executive and legislative branches of member States give full consideration to the possibility of implementing and to the advisability of ratifying a Convention: the instrument must, within a period of 12 to 18 months after its adoption, be brought "before the authority or authorities within whose competence the matter lies, for the enactment of legislation or other action." In the case of a federal State it is up to the central government to determine whether it regards a Convention "as appropriate under its constitutional system for federal action" or for action "in whole or in part ... by the constituent states, provinces or cantons"; in the former case the obligation of the federal State to submit the Convention to the competent authorities does not differ from that of a unitary State; in the latter case the federal government must arrange for reference of the Convention to the appropriate federal, state, provincial or cantonal authorities and for periodical consultation with these authorities "with a view to promoting ... co-ordinated action and to give effect" to the instrument.

---

[1] Article 10, paragraphs 1-5, and article 18 of the Standing Orders of the Governing Body, also included as articles 34 and 35 in the Standing Orders of the Conference. See also article 16 of the Constitution and article 37 of the Standing Orders of the Conference, which deal with objections to the agenda.

[2] Article 10, paragraphs 6-9, of the Standing Orders of the Governing Body, included as article 36 in the Standing Orders of the Conference, and articles 38-39 *bis* of the Standing Orders of the Conference.

[3] Article 19, paragraph 2, of the Constitution.

[4] The text of these instruments is published in the *Official Bulletin* of the International Labour Office for the year of their adoption. A collection of the first 98 Conventions appears in *International Labour Conference, Conventions and Recommendations, 1919-1949* (Geneva: International Labour Office, 1949). *The International Labour Code, 1951* (Geneva: International Labour Office, 1952) contains in its Volume I the text of the first 100 Conventions, systematically arranged according to subject matter and fully annotated as to the history of their elaboration.

[5] Article 19, paragraphs 5 and 7.

I.L.O. constitutional practice holds that the competent authority should normally be the legislature,[1] that the Convention should be submitted to this body regardless of whether or not measures of implementation are contemplated and that in its message to the legislature the executive branch should indicate whether or not it proposes any action on the instrument.[2]

The underlying purpose of all these requirements is to make reasonably sure that the provisions of a Convention newly adopted by the Conference are given due consideration by a member State, even if it has voted against it or has not even participated in the Conference session which approved the instrument.[3] This effort to maintain a channel of communication between the International Labour Conference and national policy makers already–and perhaps especially–prior to ratification, has an important bearing on subsequent efforts to promote implementation of Conference decisions once they have been ratified.

If the competent authorities agree that a Convention should be ratified the member State will communicate a formal instrument of ratification to the International Labour Office and will "take such action as may be necessary to make effective the provisions of such Convention".[4] This terse phrase forms the basis for national measures to comply with the provisions of ratified Conventions. It is therefore the origin of the international arrangements designed to appraise the degree of such compliance.

## Conventions in Force

By 30 June 1964, a total of 2,919 ratifications had been communicated to the I.L.O., thus permitting the entry into force of over 100 Conventions.[5]

---

[1] The legal position was dealt with exhaustively in a memorandum appended to 26 Report I *Future Policy, Programme and Status of the International Labour Organization* 169-183, "The Nature of the Competent Authority Contemplated by Article 19 of the Constitution of the International Labour Organization". The memorandum reaches its findings on the basis of the text, the *ratio legis* and the preparatory work of article 19: a Convention should be brought before "an authority with power to implement nationally the provisions of the Convention"; the purpose of article 19 is "to prevent a Convention from being completely shelved without public opinion having an opportunity to assert itself upon the matter"; and even if effect can be given to Conventions by purely executive action, the framers of the I.L.O. Constitution intended such instruments to be made "an issue before public opinion by submission to a body of a parliamentary character".

[2] The Governing Body has adopted a *Memorandum concerning the Obligation to Submit Conventions and Recommendations to the Competent Authorities*, which sets out these various points in detail.

[3] Additional measures to this end include a general requirement to inform the International Labour Office of the steps taken to submit a Convention to the legislation and a requirement to report, at the request of the Governing Body, on "the extent to which effect has been, or is proposed to be, given" to an unratified Convention (article 19, paragraphs 5(e) and 7(b) (iv) of the Constitution).

[4] Article 19, paragraph 5(d), of the Constitution.

[5] The ratification total passed the 3,000 mark early in 1965. As a rule, ratification by at least two States is necessary to bring a Convention into force. Appendix I indicates the Conventions which have not yet received the number of ratifications required for entry into force.

They deal with the following subjects:[1] employment (four Conventions [2]), wages (five [3]), hours of work (eleven [4]), employment of children and young persons (ten [5]), employment of women (six [6]), industrial safety and health (six [7]), social security (seventeen [8]), freedom of association (four [9]), employment at sea (twenty-one [10]), forced labour (two [11]), discrimination (one [12]), migrant workers (two [13]) indigenous workers (six [14]), plantation workers (one [15]), social policy (two [16]), and labour administration (three [17]). It may be useful to follow this division by subject groups, during later attempts to analyze the results of the effectiveness survey.

Appendix I indicates the number of States which have ratified each Convention. It shows that 17 Conventions have been ratified by 50 or more countries. At the other end of the scale there are 21 Conventions in force which have so far secured less than ten ratifications. Wide variations also exist between the total numbers of Conventions ratified by individual States.[18] Twelve countries [19] have ratified 50 or more Conventions, while 14 countries [20] have ratified less than ten.

These ratification figures have given rise to much comment inside and outside the I.L.O. Like all statistics they are subject to cautious interpretation,[21] in the light of the numerous and often imponderable factors

---

[1] Any attempt at classification is bound to be somewhat arbitrary. Thus several seafarers and fishermen Conventions deal with the employment of young persons, a number of instruments relating to workers in agriculture (Nos. 10, 11, 12, 99, 101) are included under other headings, etc. It should also be noted that two Conventions (Nos. 80 and 116) do not deal with labour matters but with a purely procedural question, the revision of the final (formal) articles of other Conventions.

[2] Nos. 2, 34, 88, 96.

[3] Nos. 26, 94, 95, 99, 100.

[4] Nos. 1, 14, 20, 30, 43, 47, 49, 52, 67, 101, 106.

[5] Nos. 5, 6, 10, 33, 59, 60, 77, 78, 79, 90.

[6] Nos. 3, 4, 41, 45, 89, 103.

[7] Nos. 13, 27, 28, 32, 62, 115.

[8] Nos. 12, 17, 18, 19, 24, 25, 35, 36, 37, 38, 39, 40, 42, 44, 48, 102, 118.

[9] Nos. 11, 84, 87, 98.

[10] Nos. 7, 8, 9, 15, 16, 22, 23, 53, 55, 56, 58, 68, 69, 71, 73, 74, 92, 108, 112, 113, 114.

[11] Nos. 29, 105.

[12] No. 111.

[13] Nos. 21, 97.

[14] Nos. 50, 64, 65, 86, 104, 107.

[15] No. 110.

[16] Nos. 82, 117.

[17] Nos. 63, 81, 85.

[18] The International Labour Office publishes twice yearly a Chart of Ratifications, arranged by countries and Conventions.

[19] Argentina, Belgium, Bulgaria, Cuba, France, Italy, Netherlands, Norway, Peru, Poland, United Kingdom, Uruguay.

[20] Afghanistan, Bolivia, Ethiopia, Indonesia, Iran, Jordan, Kuwait, Laos, Lebanon, Paraguay, El Salvador, Sudan, Thailand, United States of America.

[21] C. Wilfred Jenks considers that there has been "a lot of loose talk at various times about the non-ratification of international labour Conventions." *The Common Law of Mankind* (London: Stevens & Sons, 1958), p. 185.

involved. These include, to mention only a few, the recent date at which certain Conventions have been adopted and at which certain States joined the Organization and the level of economic and social development of some countries which limits their ability to give effect to more advanced standards such as those on social security; the fact that Conventions on e.g. seafarers, on work in glass factories or on non-metropolitan labour conditions do not interest countries which have no merchant navy, no glass works or no colonies; the constitutional limitations preventing the central governments of certain federal States from legislating on matters within the jurisdiction of the constituent units of the federation. It would be neither pertinent nor wise in the present context to speculate on the relative importance of these and other factors or to attempt a judgment whether the actual ratification figures are satisfactory.

A few points need however be mentioned in connection with the progress and geographical distribution of ratifications because they have a direct bearing on the network of international obligations subject to I.L.O. supervision. There have been noticeable variations in the rate at which ratifications were received: the response to the Conventions adopted during the nineteenthirties, for instance, has been much below the average whereas progress has been especially marked during the past decade or so when the membership of the I.L.O., as of all other international organizations, practically doubled. Ever since about 1930 the proportion of ratifications by countries outside Europe to the total number of ratifications has been rising rapidly and now exceeds 50 per cent. Conventions adopted during the early years of the Organization continue to secure ratifications on a significant scale. Due to these various developments the number of ratifications now stands just below 25 per cent of the theoretical maximum, i.e. of the total obtained by multiplying the membership figure by the Conventions in force. As indicated above, much less than this maximum must reasonably be expected in an attempt to set binding standards for a widely varying array of countries and at a level which is above the lowest common denominator so that it cannot be attained immediately by all countries.[1]

*Application of Conventions in Non-Metropolitan Territories*

The number of obligations subject to I.L.O. supervision also covers the application of ratified Conventions in "non-metropolitan territories", i.e. in dependent countries for whose international relations an I.L.O. member is responsible. Under the Constitution such a member is bound to apply a ratified Convention to a territory except in three sets of circumstances: a) where the Convention is within the self-governing powers of the territory, the member brings the instrument to the notice of the territorial government in order to secure appropriate action; b) where local conditions are deemed to prevent the implementation of the Convention in full, it may be declared applicable subject to specified modifications; c) where the Convention is

---

[1] Cf. the discussion of flexibility in I.L.O. standards, pp. 122-124 below.

considered to be inapplicable owing to "local conditions", its implementation may be postponed or adjourned.[1]

A list of declarations, arranged by Conventions, is contained in the non-metropolitan territories section of the Summaries of Reports on Ratified Conventions.[2] Although new declarations continue to be received, their total has been gradually declining in recent years with the accession of numerous territories to full independence. The obligations previously in existence have not lapsed however but have remained in existence (in the form of ratifications) because the countries concerned recognized when they became I.L.O. members that they continue to be bound by the Conventions applicable to them in virtue of prior declarations.[3]

*Annual Reports*

The I.L.O. Constitution contains three distinct obligations which form the basis of its system of supervision. The first requires a member "to make an annual report to the International Labour Office on the measures it has taken to give effect to the provisions of Conventions to which it is a party. These reports shall be made in such form and shall contain such particulars as the Governing Body may request".[4] By communicating regularly a set of specified data on the manner in which they comply with the terms of a ratified Convention, governments make it possible for the I.L.O. to seek the kind of full and authoritative information which is an essential though not a sufficient precondition of any realistic attempt at supervision. Two subsidiary requirements further broaden the base of the system: the Director-General must lay before the next Conference session a Summary of the governments' reports; the governments must commu-

---

[1] Cf. article 35 of the Constitution, as revised in 1946. Under a further amendment adopted in 1964, article 35 is eliminated altogether and "members ratifying Conventions shall accept their provisions so far as practicable in respect of all territories for whose international relations they are responsible" (XLVII O.B. No. 3 Supplement I, pp. 5-7). This amendment has not yet entered into force.

[2] A chart of declarations last appeared in 1961 as Appendix II to Part Four ("Aspects of Social Evolution in Present and Former Non-Metropolitan Territories") of the Report of the Committee of Experts on the Application of Conventions and Recommendations.

[3] Cf. in this connection Francis Wolf, "Les Conventions internationales du Travail et la succession d'états", *Annuaire Français de Droit International*, Vol. VII (1961), pp. 742-751. As a result of the customary practice described above, 471 ratifications by 33 new members (Algeria, Burundi, Cameroon, Central African Republic, Chad, Congo (Brazzaville), Congo (Leopoldville), Cyprus, Dahomey, Gabon, Ghana, Republic of Guinea, Indonesia, Ivory Coast, Jamaica, Kenya, Malagasy Republic, Malaysia, Republic of Mali, Islamic Republic of Mauritania, Morocco, Niger, Nigeria, Rwanda, Senegal, Sierra Leone, Somali Republic, Tanzania, Togo, Trinidad and Tobago, Tunisia, Uganda, Upper Volta) had been recorded from 1950 until mid-1964. In the case of Conventions whose application is limited to non-metropolitan territories such as those on the right of association and on labour inspectorates in these territories (Nos. 84 and 85), ratification by an independent country is impossible, but new members often agree to continue to apply them, pending ratification of the corresponding instruments of general application, i.e. the Freedom of Association Conventions (Nos. 87 and 98) and the Labour Inspection Convention (No. 81). The interest of this practice on the part of new States, from the point of view both of international law and of international supervision, is obvious (cf. p. 61 below).

[4] Article 22 of the Constitution.

nicate copies of these reports to the organizations of employers and workers recognized as most representative for the purpose of selecting non-governmental representatives at the Conference.[1] There are thus additional and important opportunities for the implementing action taken by governments to be considered nationally, by those groups most directly concerned with labour questions, and internationally, by any Conference delegates who are particularly interested, for economic or social reasons, in promoting full application. The effectiveness of supervision mainly depends on the extent to which these opportunities have in fact been utilized and exploited. It is therefore necessary to describe what practical substance has been given to the constitutional requirements regarding reports on ratified Conventions.

*Need for Special Machinery*

Historically, the operation of the I.L.O.'s supervisory arrangements began with the adoption by the Governing Body, in 1921, of draft "questionnaires" prepared by the Office for the first two Conventions which had received a sufficient number of ratifications to bring them into force.[2]

The text of the early reports received from governments in reponse to the questionnaires figured *in extenso* in the Reports of the Director to the 1921, 1922 and 1923 sessions of the Conference and was submitted to the 1924 and 1925 sessions in summarized form. If it had been thought by the founders of the Organization that the availability of information from governments would suffice in itself to lead to its examination and discussion,[3] this expectation was soon to be disappointed. No one ever questioned the right of the Conference to undertake such an examination but in actual fact the voice of public opinion remained rather silent. During none of the sessions until 1925 did the steadily growing body of information on the application of Conventions give rise to more than passing references on the part of delegates. Discussions centred almost exclusively on the ratification, rather than on the application, of Conventions.

This was due, in the opinion of the special committee of the Conference which in 1926 considered what use should be made of annual reports, to

---

[1] Article 23, paragraphs 1 and 2, of the Constitution.

[2] These were Conventions Nos. 1 and 2 (7 G.B. 43, 91-92).

[3] The initial British proposals which led to the adoption by the Commission on International Labour Legislation at the 1919 Paris Peace Conference of the "Labour Convention" (i.e. the Constitution of the I.L.O.) already provided for annual reporting by governments and for the submission of a summary of the reports to the Conference. Unlike the suggestions for a representation and complaints procedure which gave rise to considerable debate in the Commission, the reporting system was adopted without discussion. It was clear from the start that main reliance in enforcing the whole labour standards scheme was to be placed on the power of public opinion, as witnessed by the admission which Mr. G. N. Barnes, vice-president of the Commission, made when he presented its report to the plenary session of the Peace Conference: "At one time I had a good deal more faith in penalties; but, Sir, closer inspection led me to the conclusion that penalties must be kept well in the background... It will be the duty of the organization which we propose, to collect and distribute information, to promote healthy public opinion and, generally speaking, to diffuse light in dark places, wherever such may be found" (I O.B. 288-289).

"the extent and technical complexity of the summary of annual reports".[1] Albert Thomas, the dynamic Frenchman, who, as the first Director, devoted until his death in 1932 all his energies to translating the administrative and legal structures created by the Peace Treaties into a living organism,[2] touched on this point already in 1923, in his reply to the discussion of his Report to the Conference.[3] In his Report to the 1925 Conference session this concern had become more specific: "Is it correct to affirm that many States which have ratified do not apply and do not strictly carry out their national laws?"[4] In his reply to the discussion he answered this question himself: "At the present time we cannot, perhaps by your fault, follow the details of application from day to day... Have you read the reports drawn up in accordance with article 408?[5] One speaker talked about them... It is a vital fact that the States, in sending their reports, submit to the mutual supervision which they can exercise on each other, and call to some extent for explanations".[6] And somewhat later in the same speech he said: "Shouldn't there be a debate, here in the Conference, on the reports submitted in pursuance of article 408?"[7]

The Summary of Reports had thus failed to provide an automatic stimulus for supervision through discussion. A more effective method had to be devised and it was at this same 1925 session that the first suggestion was made by the Irish government delegate, Professor O'Rahilly, to set up special supervisory committees at future sessions of the conference.[8] The idea received Albert Thomas' immediate support[9] and thus was

---

[1] 8 R.P. 404.

[2] Cf. in particular E. J. Phelan, *Yes and Albert Thomas* (New York: Columbia University Press, 1949).

[3] "As regards results, we can obtain them only to the extent to which you yourselves, members of the Conference, you yourselves, government representatives, you yourselves, representatives of the occupational organizations, develop your activity. Our life is made up of your life and of the efforts of all of you" (5 R.P. 108).

[4] 7 D.R. 1227 (The English version of the printed document does not render fully the meaning of the original French. The text quoted here, and in certain other citations below, is therefore a literal translation from the French version). The ensuing paragraphs even refer to the need for exercising supervision through the representations and complaints provided for by the Constitution.

[5] According to the numbering used in the Treaty of Versailles; now article 22 of the Constitution.

[6] 7 R.P. 191.

[7] 7 R.P. 200.

[8] "I wish to say one word about the reports which have been sent in under article 408. It is only now that these reports are beginning to be valuable and I think we do not yet sufficiently appreciate their value. The objection is often made, not only publicly but privately, that if such and such a country ratifies a Convention, it will not carry it out. But that is not a fair criticism; a country is not justified in not ratifying simply because it suspects that its neighbour will not carry out its obligations. For we have under that article an individual guarantee whereby we can supervise the application of every Convention, we have a complete system of reciprocal control... I venture to hope, we shall have in future Conferences a committee to examine such reports and see that they are properly presented in sufficient detail, so as to give a universal guarantee that the obligations undertaken by the different countries are carried out" (7 R.P. 156-157).

[9] 7 R.P. 200.

launched the most decisive move towards effective supervision, made by the I.L.O.

The new system was designed, in the minds of its authors, to serve two separate but closely related purposes: to remove suspicion, first of all, that ratified Conventions are not applied and therefore without any concrete effect;[1] to promote at the same time ratification of Conventions by dissipating doubts on the part of States which hesitate to assume obligations because they fear faulty application by other ratifying countries.[2] It could of course also be argued that the existence of strict supervisory arrangements might discourage rather than promote ratifications.[3] This aspect of the effectiveness of supervision is of more than theoretical interest and will be considered in more detail later in this study.[4]

It is unnecessary to describe here at length the discussions leading to the formulation by the 1926 session of the Conference of the procedure to be followed in examining reports on the application of Conventions.[5] In reading over the proposals and the debates on them, one is struck by the degree of imagination and foresight shown by the proponents of I.L.O. supervision at a time when much of their argumentation necessarily lacked the support of practical experience. On the other hand those who objected to the idea often did so, as will be seen shortly, out of an understandable

---

[1] This was emphasized in the British resolution placed before the Governing Body in January 1926 to follow up the Irish suggestion: "Careful examination of the information contained (in the annual reports) is calculated to throw light upon the practical value of the Conventions themselves" (30 G.B. 86). It was restated by the British delegate, Mr. Humbert Wolfe, when he proposed adoption of the scheme to the 1926 session of the Conference: "There is hope that we shall render application more solid and more frequent... Not only should we achieve a greater mutual self-confidence as a result of this procedure, but we should be able to prove to the world at large that the common taunt which is so often levelled at our work, namely, that our Conventions are purely paper Conventions, would be finally and completely dissipated and we should be able to prove to the world by the best possible means, by actual fact, that when we pass Conventions and when they are ratified a definite measure of social progress has followed" (8 R.P. 240).

[2] This was the point originally stressed by Professor O' Rahilly as quoted in footnote (8), p. 17. The British resolution of 1926 also stated that one of the aims was "to further... general ratification" of Conventions (30 G.B. 86).

[3] Such a suspicion was in fact voiced already at the 1926 session of the Conference by an Irish workers' representative who wondered "whether we have not here the beginnings of another excuse for non-ratification" (8 R.P. 108).

[4] Cf. pp. 203-204 below.

[5] The successive stages were, briefly, as follows: The original suggestion by the Irish government at the 1925 session of the Conference led to the adoption by the Governing Body, early in 1926, of a British-sponsored resolution calling for consideration by the next Conference session of specific proposals prepared by the Office (8 R.P. 393-402). The Report of the Conference "Committee on Article 408" set up for this purpose embodied the main points of the Office proposals; it recommended the setting up by the Conference, each year, of a committee "to examine the summaries of the reports" and the establishment by the Governing Body of a "committee of experts" entrusted with the advance examination of the reports (8 R.P. 402-408). The draft resolution submitted by the 1926 Conference Committee was adopted in its final form (8 R.P. 429) after some discussion (8 R.P. 238-244, 247-257) by a vote of 66 to 36 (8 R.P. 258). The Committee of Experts met for the first time in May 1927 and its Report (1927 R.C.E. 400-419) was considered at the Tenth Session of the Conference a few weeks later; the Conference Committee which discussed the Experts' findings reported (10 R.P. 555-559) to the plenary sitting.

hesitation to proceed too rapidly and too far into a largely unexplored sphere of international law and relations.

The two Committees which originated " as an experiment " have met since then on an annual basis [1] and have become integral features of the Organization. In the absence of tradition or precedents, these bodies have had to evolve their methods of work gradually, often by trial and error. The originality of the system, its emphasis on a technical and practical approach, the progressive emergence of an institutional consensus on the urgent need for effective implementation, the extension which I.L.O. supervision has taken in recent years,[2] all these are reasons why a full and methodical exploration of the functioning of the whole procedure seems called for at this stage.

Among the main points to be considered in relation, first to the Committee of Experts, then to the Conference Committee, figure their functions, their membership, their procedures (including any obstacles encountered and attempts to overcome them) and the formulation of their conclusions. It will be important to identify, step by step, any direct or indirect connections between procedural refinements and the search for effectiveness. The final stage in the reporting and examination process, discussion of the findings by the Conference itself, will also have to be analyzed.

## II.  The Committee of Experts

*Character and Functions*

As seen above, special machinery had to be created because the existing organs could not be expected, by themselves, to perform the essential, technical part of the supervision process. Neither the Office [3] which is the secretariat of the Organization, nor the Conference and its committees, which are essentially " deliberative and political bodies composed of the representatives of various interests, national or occupational" [4] could properly carry out a thorough and objective evaluation of the governments' reports. The task had therefore to be given to a special Committee of Experts which, although its name has changed with the passage of years,[5] has to this day remained the " technical committee " [6] contemplated at its

---

[1] Except during World War II. The Committee of Experts did not meet from 1941 to 1944, the Conference Committee from 1940 to 1943.

[2] The matter has not been treated in any detail since the publication of the Zarras study, *op. cit.*, over a quarter of a century ago. Since then the number of Conventions, and of I.L.O. members, has doubled, ratifications have quadrupled and the system has undergone the notable changes which are about to be described.

[3] A suggestion, in the 1926 "Committee on Article 408", that examination of the reports by the Office would suffice was turned down because "there might be a danger of the Director and the Office being accused of exceeding that function" (8 R.P. 406).

[4] 8 R.P. 396.

[5] It was renamed the "Committee of Experts on the Application of Conventions and Recommendations" in 1949 when it was also entrusted with the examination of information and reports on unratified Conventions and on Recommendations, supplied under article 19 of the Constitution.

[6] In the words of the 1926 Conference resolution approving its establishment (8 R.P. 429).

inception. Its purpose in relation to the reports on the application of ratified Conventions has remained equally unaltered, i.e. "making the best and fullest use of (the) information (in the reports) and ... securing such additional data as may be provided for in the forms approved by the Governing Body and found desirable to supplement that already available, and... reporting thereon to the Governing Body".[1] On the occasion of its thirtieth anniversary, the Committee of Experts has itself described the nature of its functions as "avoiding all political considerations in the technical and juridical examination of the matters entrusted to it".[2]

The novelty of the whole idea was such, however, that assurances as to the purely technical character of the Committee did not suffice, in the early days, to allay fears that it might exceed its functions. "You appoint innocuous experts" warned the Belgian government delegate, Professor Mahaim, in 1926, "and they easily become inspectors... I would consider it extremely dangerous to organize here an improvised tribunal, a council of war, as it has been called".[3] The Italian government went so far as to consider the Committee of Experts "unconstitutional" [4] and many of the employers were opposed to the idea at the start.[5] These doubts as to the authority and methods of the Committee of Experts and of the machinery as a whole dominated the discussions of the Conference Committee in 1927 [6] and 1928. The effect of such an attitude on the members of the Committee of Experts is easy to imagine.[7] But with the encouragement received from Albert

---

[1] 1926 resolution (8 R.P. 429). The relevant portion of its terms of reference, as revised in 1947, now reads as follows: "to examine... the annual reports under article 22 of the Constitution on the measures taken by members to give effect to the provisions of Conventions to which they are parties and the information furnished by members concerning the results of inspection" (103 G.B. 173).

[2] 1957 R.C.E. 3. In 1947 a United Kingdom employers' spokesman in the Governing Body called the work of the Committee "comparable to the service provided by auditors" (103 G.B. 58).

[3] 8 R.P. 249.

[4] 35 G.B. 69.

[5] As indicated above (footnote 5, p. 18), the Conference's decision, in 1926, to set up special machinery was taken by a majority of less than two to one with 16 of the 36 opposing votes coming from the employers' group; eight employers' delegates voted in favour.

[6] Its Report is very guarded on this point but the Minutes show the kind of objections raised. The Polish government member, for instance, remarked that it was "beyond the competence of the Committee of Experts" to call the standard of application "below the requirements of the Convention" in a given case (doc. C. 408/P.V./3 pp. 9-10 (roneoed)). During the discussion of its draft Report the Committee spent much time on deciding whether the annual reports should be defined as "a means of mutual verification" or "of mutual interchange of information", only to settle in the end on a bare statement that "the purpose of the annual reports... is to enable the States to take cognizance of the measures which each of them has taken" (doc. C. 408/P.V./6, pp. 3-5 and 10 R.P. 556).

[7] Writing of these difficulties in 1929 the Director related that they had led the Committee of Experts in 1928 "to consider very seriously whether it would serve any useful purpose for it to continue its work" (12 D.R. 122). "At first it seemed that this Committee would have difficulty in obtaining recognition for its authority. Some of its members, discouraged by the initial opposition, were tempted to resign their mandate" (12 D.R. 289).

Thomas [1] and from the Conference Committee itself,[2] which asked the Governing Body to maintain it in existence, the initial attitude of groping and overcautiousness [3] gradually gave way to a general realization that the machinery was soundly conceived and that it could not be expected to operate effectively without the help of technical experts.[4]

Other facets of these initial hesitations will have to be mentioned later as the means and methods of supervision are reviewed. But it is interesting to note now that since these early days there has been no further challenge to the existence of a body which, while not provided for in the I.L.O. Constitution, emerged organically and logically from a constructive reading of this Constitution. Even those who nowadays do not always agree with the Committee of Experts, readily recognize its stature.[5]

Inherent in the technical functions of the Committee of Experts is its most essential and distinctive feature, the independent character of its membership. If such a body is to evaluate objectively and to reach impartial conclusions, its members cannot represent any national or occupational interests and cannot therefore hold positions which would involve dependence on such interests. This basic point was recognized from the start,[6] and is illustrated by a review of the selection and composition of the Committee.

*Membership*

The Committee of Experts has 19 members, as compared with eight during its initial period of operation. The members are appointed by the Governing Body, on the proposal of the Director-General, for a period of three years. They may be, and often are, reappointed for successive periods

---

[1] A candid reference to this is contained in the Director's reply to the discussion of his Report in 1928 (11 R.P. 266).

[2] It concluded in its 1928 Report that "the work of the Committee of Experts has given useful results" (11 R.P. 619). Much of this change of heart seems to have been due to the strong stand taken by its reporter, Mr. Pfister, the Director of the Swiss Federal Labour Office, as revealed by the Minutes: the Conference should overcome its "rather hesitating and timid manner", its "attitude of reserve"; as to the Committee of Experts it "worked at a disadvantage due to its desire not to exceed the terms of reference which had been fixed for it" (doc. C. 408/P.V. 3, pp. 3-6 (roneoed)).

[3] Summing up this rather uncertain beginning, the Director noted with obvious relief in 1929 that "the discussions at the last Conference... not only approved the work of the Committee (of Experts) but encouraged it to continue and extend its task" (12 D.R. 289).

[4] During a discussion of the Report of the Committee of Experts in 1934, for instance, the Belgian government member, Professor Mahaim,a nd the employers' vice-chairman recognized the importance of the Experts Committee's work (66 G.B. 15-16). The Italian government member still voiced some reservations, but an Italian national had been sitting on the Committee since 1927, hardly without his government's tacit consent.

[5] A Czechoslovak government representative at the 1963 session of the Conference expressed the view that it had "become one of the most important organs of the Organization" (47 R.P. 428).

[6] In his original proposals on the selection of Experts, the Director suggested that they "should be chosen on the ground of their technical competence alone, that they should be completely impartial and that they should be in no sense considered as representatives of governments" (33 G.B. 106).

of service on the Committee.[1] A list of Committee members indicating their present and past functions appears in its Reports.[2] That the members of the Committee are all chosen for their personal independence is clear from a tabulation, based on its composition in 1964: four had in the past occupied key governmental positions, such as a premiership, ministerial or diplomatic appointments; four held or had held high judicial office; one was ambassador of her country; one had occupied many high posts in the field of labour relations and arbitration; and nine were or had been professors of international or labour law.

By analogy with the system which the original Constitution of the I.L.O. had instituted for the appointment of Commissions of Inquiry into complaints that a ratified Convention was not being observed [3] nominations were at first solicited from governments, employers and workers.[4] But when in 1929 the Conference Committee merely referred in its Report [5] to a suggestion that members of the Committee of Experts might be selected through employers' and workers' organizations, the ensuing discussion in the Governing Body so strongly reaffirmed the impartial and independent character of the Experts [6] that this character was henceforth deemed to constitute a fundamental principle. On the other hand, the possibility for employers and workers to provide the Committee of Experts with information on the application of Conventions emerged as another basic principle, as will shortly be seen below.

The size and composition of the Committee have naturally reflected the expansion in the membership of the Organization and in the network of obligations assumed by member countries. The first non-European members, a Uruguayan and an Indian, were appointed in 1934 and 1936. In 1964 the Committee included two members from Africa, three each from Eastern Europe, Asia and Latin America, one each from the Middle East, North America and the Caribbean region and five from Western Europe.[7]

There have been suggestions at times that membership might be limited to nationals of small States,[8] or of States which have ratified, and reported

---

[1] Cf. note submitted to the Governing Body when the Committee of Experts was reconstituted in 1945 (94 G.B. 213). Of the 46 persons who, by the end of 1964, had served or were serving on the Committee, 23 had been members for nine or more years.

[2] The list for 1964 will be found in 1964 R.C.E. 3-5.

[3] Under article 26 a panel was established through the nomination by each member State of three persons, two representing employers and workers respectively and one "a person of independent standing". The Secretary-General of the League of Nations was to appoint commissions of a tripartite character from this panel, on request by the I.L.O. Governing Body. No such commission was ever set up during the inter-war period and the relevant provisions were greatly simplified during the constitutional revision of 1946. Commissions of Inquiry are now appointed directly by the Governing Body (article 26, paragraph 3) and the practice has been to include in them only persons of independent standing.

[4] Cf. 33 G.B. 64-66, 106; 34 G.B. 59, 68; 35 G.B. 27-28, 69.

[5] 12 R.P. 816.

[6] Cf. 46 G.B. 128; 47 G.B. 71.

[7] An analysis of the composition of the Committee of Experts, by nationality and profession, appears in Haas, *Beyond the Nation-State, op. cit.*, p. 559.

[8] Director's original proposals in 1926 (33 G.B. 106).

on, a sizable number of Conventions.[1] But there was never any support for such restrictive criteria which might have implied a measure of doubt as to the members' independence of judgment. Instead, there has been a constant desire on the part of the Governing Body to do everything possible to assist the Experts in their task. This attitude has been in evidence, for instance, whenever the Experts considered that the effectiveness of supervision required the supply by governments of additional types of data on the application of ratified Conventions.

*Content of Government Reports*

It has already been noted that from 1921 onwards the Governing Body made use of its power to approve forms for the reports on Conventions, as they entered into force. These so-called "questionnaires" consisted of two parts, a first section which was the same for all Conventions and asked what legislation and administrative measures had been taken to give effect to them, and a second section, varying from instrument to instrument, which asked for information on the implementation of those articles leaving governments some discretion as to their application.[2]

In the Report on its first meeting, in 1927, the Committee of Experts had already pointed out that "verification"–a cautious synonym for "supervision"–is "an effective means of estimating the efforts made by each State with a view to application. It is therefore obviously desirable that the reports furnished by the States in accordance with article 408 should form a solid basis for this mutual verification".[3] But the Committee considered that the report forms had not proved adequate for this purpose: "The principal criticism to which the present forms give rise is that they do not secure a clear indication regarding the legislative and administrative measures corresponding to the several articles of each Convention".[4] The Committee therefore suggested to the Governing Body a number of detailed changes [5] in the existing forms of report. The Committee of Experts was thus fully aware from the very beginning that a key objective of supervision is to obtain full and accurate data. While the existence of a detailed, well-conceived questionnaire does not provide any guarantee by itself that the objective will be attained, it does constitute a solid basis for achieving it.

The Committee of Experts has always insisted that satisfactory compliance with a ratified Convention requires its enforcement both in law and in practice. It has also recognized that information on the legal position is much easier to obtain and to evaluate than evidence of the extent to

---

[1] Suggested by the Italian government in 1936 (75 G.B. 72-73).

[2] For instance article 1, paragraph 3 of the Hours of Work (Industry) Convention, 1919 (No. 1) leaves it to the "competent authority in each country" to "define the line of division which separates industry from commerce and agriculture". The form of report asked what decisions, if any, had been taken to this effect.

[3] 1927 R.C.E. 415.

[4] 1927 R.C.E. 418.

[5] They were designed to secure more information on a) the effect given to the individual articles of an instrument, b) the application of Conventions in colonial territories and c) their implementation in day-to-day practice. All the suggestions were approved by the Governing Body the same year (37 G.B. 46-48, 105-106).

which the legislation is given effect to in the day-to-day relationships which I.L.O. Conventions are designed to regulate. Many of its suggestions to the Governing Body have therefore had the purpose of coming as close to the realities of practical application at the national level as this is possible in an international system. The Governing Body, for its part, has welcomed this opportunity to have the views and suggestions of its technical experts when it adopts or revises forms of report [1] and has usually taken account of them.

Information on the position in law is elicited in the report forms through a general request for "a list of the legislation and administrative regulations, etc., which apply the provisions of the Convention" and through a further request for detailed indications how this legislation, etc., gives effect to *each* of the substantive articles of the instrument; individual questions under certain articles often ask for specific details.[2]

The Committee of Experts is generally able, on the basis of the information received, to check on the degree of legislative conformity; it is also able to ascertain on occasion whether laws and regulations have been "enacted or modified to permit of, or as a result of, ratification".[3] But in the case of countries where, in the words of the report forms, "ratification of the Convention gives the force of law to its terms", the Committee may find it difficult to gain a clear picture even of the position in law. The situation existing under such constitutional systems of the monistic type raises particular problems of application and supervision [4] and the supervisory organs have made repeated efforts to obtain the fullest possible information by means of a special question to the countries concerned.[5]

The principal changes introduced in the forms of report at the instigation of the Committee of Experts were aimed at obtaining pertinent data on the

---

[1] As indicated on p. 16 above, the Office prepares draft forms of report when Conventions enter into force. It also submits notes on suggested changes in the existing forms. At first these drafts were considered directly by the Governing Body; since 1937 they are placed before a Committee–now known as the "Committee on Standing Orders and the Application of Conventions and Recommendations"–which reports to the Governing Body as a whole.

[2] For instance, under article 3 of the Employment Service Convention, 1948 (No. 88), which requires a network of local and, where appropriate, regional offices to be maintained and to be kept under review, the following questions appear in the form of report:

"1. Please indicate the measures taken to establish and locate sufficient employment offices to serve the employers and workers in each of the geographical areas.

2. Please state what provision is made for review of the network of employment offices and revision, where necessary, to meet the changing requirements of the economy and the working population."

[3] A query on this point originally proposed at the suggestion of the Committee of Experts in 1954 (37 R.C.E. 10), was approved by the Governing Body only after some of its members had objected to the additional burden thus placed on the reporting governments (128 G.B. 22-25; 129 G.B. 44). This shows that the Governing Body sometimes approaches suggestions on report forms in a critical spirit.

[4] Cf. pp. 103-108 below.

[5] The question was first included in the report forms in 1930, at the suggestion of the Conference Committee (50 G.B. 57-60) and subsequently expanded in 1939 and 1951 at the suggestion of the Committee of Experts (Emergency Session, October 1939, G.B. 50-51; 115 G.B. 16, 92-93).

practical application of ratified Conventions. As noted above, their incorporation in internal law already falls to some extent under this heading. The main effort has however been concentrated on tapping three potential sources of information: judicial decisions, labour inspection services and the representative organizations of employers and workers. Questions were included for this purpose asking governments a) to report court decisions which have a significant bearing on the application of a Convention; [1] b) to supply information on "the organization and working of inspection" including "extracts from the reports of the inspection services and, if such statistics are available, information concerning the number of workers covered by the legislation, the number and nature of the contraventions reported, etc."; [2] c) to state whether they have "received from the organizations of employers and workers concerned any observations... regarding the practical fulfilment of the conditions prescribed by the Convention and the application of the national law implementing the Convention"; the report form also suggests that the government communicate a summary of such observations together with its comments on them.[3] The extent to which supervision has in fact been facilitated through the operation of these reporting provisions will be explored below when the role of labour inspection and of workers and employers [4] is discussed.

Two conclusions emerge from this rapid review of the type of data governments are called upon to supply to the I.L.O. First, that the amount and scope of the information requested are such that a considerable body of information should be available. Second, that the Committee of Experts has played a major part in shaping the content of the questionnaires and hence the potential content of the reports themselves. But supervision is impossible unless reports are in fact received and it is necessary therefore to consider whether governments comply in fact with the reporting obligation, i.e. how many reports are available for examination every year.

---

[1] Question included in accordance with a suggestion made by the Committee of Experts in 1930 (1930 R.C.E. 607).

[2] Questions rephrased and expanded in 1927 at the suggestion of the Committee of Experts (37 G.B. 46-48, 105-106). In 1929, the Committee made the further suggestion that labour inspection reports might "deal specially... with the application of international Conventions" (1929 R.C.E. 520) but the Governing Body failed to accept this rather more far-reaching proposal (47 G.B. 78-79).

[3] In its original proposal in 1931 the Committee of Experts went so far as to suggest the supply by governments, "if thought desirable, (of) the reports of employers' and workers' organizations" on "the practical results of the application of Conventions" (1931 R.C.E. 454). The Director cautiously endorsed the idea (53 G.B. 34), but it met with strong opposition in the Conference Committee (15 R.P. 617) and was not acted upon by the Governing Body (56 G.B. 81). Undaunted by such obvious reluctance, the Committee of Experts modified its proposal, in 1932, to cover only "observations" from the organizations (16 R.P. 602), and this secured endorsement by the Conference Committee (16 R.P. 675) and by the Governing Body (60 G.B. 79). With the entry into force of the constitutional amendments of 1946 the report forms also ask governments to indicate to which representative organizations of employers and workers copies of the reports have been communicated.

[4] Cf. pp. 156-157 and 180-193.

*Supply of Reports by Governments*

As the volume of reports requested depends on the total number of ratifications in force, the workload of supervision closely follows the progress of ratifications. At its first meeting in 1927 the Committee of Experts had 180 reports to examine; the figure had doubled by 1932, reached 600 by 1939, passed 1,000 in 1955 and jumped to 1,500 in 1959. These figures do not take account of the information received on the application of ratified Conventions in non-metropolitan territories; such information had originally been included, in a cursory form, in the metropolitan reports themselves but since 1948 is due in separate reports for each Convention and territory.[1]

The workload of examination had in fact become so heavy, by 1959, that the Committee of Experts considered it necessary to propose to the Governing Body to place detailed reporting on ratified Conventions on a two-yearly basis [2] except in those cases where the needs of close supervision call for examination without delay.[3] The institution of this system led to some drop in the number of reports to be examined by the Committee of Experts but by 1964 the total had again risen to over 1,300.

All these figures cover reports actually received in time for the annual session of the Committee of Experts. The Committee regularly includes in its Report a table showing, for each meeting from 1933 onward, the number and percentage of the reports due which were in fact available for examination. Leaving out of account the immediate post-war period (1945-1948) when administrative facilities were not yet back to normal in numerous countries, the proportion of reports received ranged from a minimum of 65.2 per cent in 1949 to a maximum of 95.2 per cent in 1959.

The average figure of 83.3 per cent, though falling short of a full response, is certainly impressive, especially in comparison with the results achieved by other reporting procedures.[4] The figures are higher yet if the reports

---

[1] Under the Governing Body's decision (105 G.B. 47, 94-96) the standard report forms are to be used in drawing up these reports and they are due regardless of whether a Convention has been declared applicable to a given territory. The Committee of Experts has therefore included in its statistics on the supply of reports all those on non-metropolitan territories. As the present study covers only those cases where a Convention has been declared applicable, the figures cited to illustrate the supply of reports will relate solely to those on metropolitan countries, for which fully comparable statistics are available since 1927.

[2] 1959 R.C.E. 4-5.

[3] These exceptions are the first reports due after ratification and cases of "important divergencies" noted by the supervisory organs. During the off-year a "general report" is due in which governments need only mention new developments of major importance. Despite some opposition in the government and workers' groups the system was approved by the Governing Body, first for an experimental two-year period (142 G.B. 33-35), then without any time limit (149 G.B. 27, 85).

[4] Comparable data, especially of the same order of magnitude, are difficult to obtain. In 1956 the Economic and Social Council of the United Nations initiated a system of triennial reports on developments and progress in the field of human rights (Resolution 624B (XXII)) to be supplied by all members; 41 of the then 80 members (51.2 per cent) reported in 1957, 67 of the then 101 members (66.5 per cent) in 1960 (United Nations, Report of the Commission on Human Rights, 18th Session, (doc. E/3616/Rev.1) p. 9).

received by the time the Conference meets are also taken into account.[1] On the other hand, the Committee of Experts and the Conference Committee regularly point out that the situation cannot be called satisfactory until every report requested has been communicated. They also complain that most reports arrive after the date for which they are requested (15 October) so that insufficient time is available for their examination.[2] To give governments more time for the preparation of reports, and the Committee of Experts more time for their evaluation, the reporting period, which had originally covered the calendar year, was moved back twice at the suggestion of the Committee of Experts [3] so as to end first on 30 September and now on 30 June. As a result, successive periods of about four months each are now available in principle at the national and international levels, first to compile and then to scrutinize the reports.

All these statistics and dates are of significance to the present study because the receipt of reports is the essential precondition of, and starting point for, any attempt at supervision. The supervisory organs have been acutely aware of the fact that a government's failure to comply with article 22 of the Constitution automatically prevents supervision from taking place. They therefore insist in the strongest terms that the government supply its reports.[4] States which have not done so are singled out for special mention and reiterated failure evokes increasingly strong language.[5]

The Committee of Experts has long been perturbed by the impossibility of examining the reports of certain countries. Not satisfied with verbal exhortations, and alarmed by the fact that a third of the reports were missing that year, as already noted above, the Committee pointed out in 1949 that governments represented on the Governing Body "should set an example of scrupulous observance of international obligations under the Constitution of the Organization". It therefore suggested that at the time of the triennial elections to the Governing Body the Government Electoral College be provided with the figures on the supply of reports for the preceding three-year period.[6] The proposal did not secure any definite support either in the Governing Body or in the Conference Com-

---

[1] The statistical table of reports also includes figures of reports received in time for the annual sessions of the Conference; these show percentages ranging from a minimum of 80.1 in 1951 to a maximum of 98.4 in 1936, the average being 89.4 per cent.

[2] Figures available since 1950 show that the proportion of reports received by the date due ranged from a minimum of 14.7 per cent in 1958 to a maximum of 31.7 per cent in 1952.

[3] In 1931 (1931 R.C.E. 453) and in 1948 (1948 R.C.E. 7).

[4] The Governing Body also expects the Office to remind governments by letter that their reports have not yet been supplied (cf. e.g., 66 G.B. 15-19).

[5] Referring to Nicaragua, the Committee of Experts observed in 1963 that such failure "effectively prevents the Committee and the Conference from performing their task of examination. Particular attention must therefore again be drawn to the seriousness of this case. The Committee urges the Government to supply its reports in future" (1963 R.C.E. 31).

[6] 109 G.B. 167-168. The Committee of Experts also mentioned in its Report to the Governing Body a more drastic proposal that non-reporting States be disqualified from voting (by analogy with article 13, paragraph 4, of the Constitution which provides for this when arrears in the payment of contributions exceed two years); it recognized however that this would involve amendment of the Constitution.

mittee.[1]   Improvements in the supply of reports in subsequent years reduced the urgency of the problem.   Certain measures have also been taken by the Conference Committee, as will be seen, to focus special attention on serious cases of non-compliance with the reporting obligation.[2]

In the great majority of cases supervision has thus been able to function because governments have duly communicated the reports requested by the I.L.O.   The next step is to explore how this body of information is subjected to the various supervision processes.


*Examination Procedure*

The task of the Committee of Experts, as noted above, is to secure from governments all the information required for effective supervision. Although the concept seemed to give offence at first,[3] this is an inherently critical function designed not only to clear up doubts and obscurities but, in the last analysis, to point out divergencies in national law and practice so that governments may eliminate them and bring about full conformity with ratified Conventions.   In 1952 the Committee itself clearly stated that its "essential function" is "that of criticism".[4]   Supervision would indeed be meaningless if it were limited to a mere verbal exercise from which any idea of corrective action was excluded.   Since it is not so limited, I.L.O. supervision represents a complicated and delicate kind of activity. It is complicated because intricate points of law and of fact must be assessed on the basis, usually, of written evidence.   It is delicate because sovereign States do not take easily to criticism, even when it is justified.   For all these reasons, success or failure often depends on the methods followed, first in examining the available information, then in commenting on the results of the examination.   The Committee of Experts carries the main burden of the two operations and has had to organize its work in consequence.

The Committee realized at a very early stage that, while its responsibility was a collective one, the actual task of examination had to be decentralized and started well ahead of its meetings by distributing to each member, for advance examination, the reports on a given group of Conventions.[5]

---

[1] 109 G.B. 59; 32 R.P. 439.

[2] Cf. p. 47 below.   The biennial system of detailed reporting acts moreover as an equalizing factor: whenever a report has not been supplied, it is simply requested for the following period so that no time is lost over the two-year cycle.

[3] In approving the Committee's Report, in 1928, the Governing Body ordered the word "critiques" in French changed to "observations" (45 G.B. 6).

[4] 1952 R.C.E. 4.

[5] This procedure was given its first trial in 1931 and the Committee reported that "the new system of dividing up the work has increased its effectiveness... It gives the Experts the certainty of having carried out their work more thoroughly.   It is their unanimous view that the method should be continued" (15 R.P. 452).   M. Jules Gautier, who was first reporter and then chairman of the Committee of Experts, explained in 1935 how the Committee had come to adopt this new procedure: "At our early meetings, we examined the Conventions in the course of our stay in Geneva.   We realized very quickly that this method was completely inadequate and that it did not permit us to go into the details of the reports which are often full of data and highly interesting... We decided therefore... that each member of the Committee would be entrusted with the examination

Each member thus acts as reporter to the Committee on a number of Conventions and is able through this division of labour to specialize in a given field, to become acquainted with the Conventions in it, and to follow from year to year the developments in the States which have ratified these Conventions. The Committee has insisted on retaining " its essential character of a working party in contrast to the more formal atmosphere which might prevail in a larger body".[1]

The Committee of Experts has also referred to the assistance it expects from the International Labour Office during the preliminary examination of reports.[2] Since 1949, when it introduced a new procedure of giving "special and searching attention to the reports submitted by governments on the first occasion after ratification by them of the Conventions in question", the Office prepares and submits to the Committee "particularly careful analyses" of such reports.[3] The officials of the technical services of the Office are moreover available for any information or explanations the Committee members may require during their preliminary examination and which the Committee as a whole may wish to have when it discusses the results of this examination.[4]

The accuracy of the Committee's examination depends to some degree on the choice of the materials used in the process. While the Committee has always considered that it "must base its work essentially on the particulars contained in the reports",[5] it emphasized as early as 1931 "the wideness of (the) terms (of article 22 of the Constitution) as regards means of obtaining information".[6] The Office's role in this connection was described to the Governing Body in 1936 by the Director as follows: "When the Office communicated the governments' replies (to the Experts) it also sent any additional information which it possessed or was able to obtain".[7] The materials primarily available in this connection consist of documents published by the governments themselves,[8] by the

---

of a certain number of reports on a certain number of Conventions and that these reports would be sent to us as and when they arrive in the International Labour Office, so that we could examine them at leisure... As we have been doing this for several years, we can carry out all the necessary cross-checking and comparisons, in order to see whether the application of Conventions in each State has remained stationary, whether there has been retrogression or whether there has been progress" (19 R.P. 681).

[1] 1947 R.C.E. 4.

[2] A "Supplementary Report" to the Governing Body, in 1948, indicated that the Office should be able to "analyze, supplement and interpret the material supplied by governments in the light of its detailed knowledge and past experience" (105 G.B. 102).

[3] 1949 R.C.E. 7-8.

[4] Cf. C. Wilfred Jenks, *The International Protection of Trade Union Freedom* (London: Stevens & Sons, 1957), p. 146.

[5] 1957 R.C.E. 3.

[6] 1931 R.C.E. 455.

[7] 74 G.B. 25.

[8] Two examples, drawn from the Committee's observations in 1962, illustrate cases where new legislation which had been omitted from the governments' reports had in fact eliminated previous divergencies in the application of Conventions by Czechoslovakia (1962 R.C.E. 66) and Spain (1962 R.C.E. 45). Official gazettes and similar publications offer useful sources of information.

I.L.O.,[1] or by the United Nations.[2] The Committee of Experts appeals moreover regularly to employers' and workers' organizations for their comments on the application of ratified Conventions in their countries. As already indicated, the forms of report contain a special question to this effect and the constitutional requirement for governments to communicate copies of the reports to the representative organizations provides a convenient starting point for channeling this type of data to the Committee.[3] The extent to which this potential source of information has in fact proved useful is discussed below, when problems of supervision are considered.[4]

It is on the basis of all this documentation, first provided by governments, employers and workers, then analyzed and supplemented by the Office, that the Committee of Experts can initiate "the second element in the scheme of international supervision (which) partakes in some measure of a judicial nature; it involves an assessment of the meaning and value of the materials placed before it".[5] This process comprises three consecutive phases: "preliminary examination... in advance of the session", followed by further examination and approval during the meeting.[6]

Despite the constant efforts, through this step-by-step procedure, to spread out the examination of reports over a maximum period so as to prepare as much of the work as possible in advance of its meeting, the Committee's mounting workload required a gradual lengthening of its annual sessions from as few as three days in some of the early years to two weeks.[7] It was hoped that sufficient time would thus be available "for comparing notes, examining files, etc., with the Office's (staff) and for holding subsequently a detailed general discussion".[8]

Due to the Committee's character of an informal working party, the only record of its deliberations is to be found in its Reports which, until

---

[1] In 1955, for instance, the Committee referred in an observation addressed to Pakistan to the Report of an I.L.O. Labour Survey Mission on Labour Problems in that country to illustrate the need for fuller implementation of the Fee-Charging Employment Agencies Convention (Revised), 1949 (No. 96) (1955 R.C.E. 75).

[2] In replying to an observation on the application of the Forced Labour Convention, 1930 (No 29), in Cameroon, the French government voiced the opinion in 1955 that "the observation was no doubt motivated by the statements which appeared in a report submitted by the French government to the United Nations" (1955 R.C.C. 619).

[3] The Committee is eager to have not only the observations of the occupational organizations but also the government's reaction to them. If the observations are sent directly to the Office, and no comment on them is available from the government, the Office is under instruction by the Committee to seek such comment so that "all the essential elements of the matter" are available for evaluation (1959 R.C.E. 6).

[4] Cf. pp. 180-193.

[5] 105 G.B. 102.

[6] Cf., e.g., 1963 R.C.E. 19.

[7] With the members of the Committee having to spend more and more time at its meetings, and with the need for examining more and more reports during the months preceding the meetings, the question of remuneration arose. After some consideration the Governing Body decided in 1964, "having regard to the exceptional character of the work involved", that a token honorarium should henceforth be paid to each member attending the yearly session (158 G.B. 44).

[8] 103 G.B. 170.

1961, were unanimous.[1] Since then, first one, then two, of its members registered a dissent, not from the observations on ratified Conventions as a whole but from those regarding "the application of the freedom of association Conventions in the socialist countries",[2] a matter to be considered further when certain application difficulties are discussed.[3]

## Results of Examination

Reference has already been made to the delicate nature of the task confronting any organ which has to gauge governmental compliance with international obligations. The term "observation"[4] has, from the beginning, been used to designate the findings which emerge. This rather neutral expression not only has the passive connotation of a finding of fact but can also be used in the more positive sense of suggesting the need for action. In the actual process of supervision the second purpose flows logically from the first: the Committee describes the situation as revealed by its examination and then indicates the steps required to bring about compliance with the provisions of the Convention.[5]

The matters raised in an observation range from minor points involving the implementation of a secondary provision to a finding that there has hardly been a start in application.[6] Of course there are also many cases

---

[1] In 1958, a veteran member of the Committee of Experts related in an article that it was only rarely necessary to vote in the Committee. Cf. Frederik M. van Asbeck, "Une Commission d'Experts", *Symbolae Verzijl* (The Hague: Martinus Nijhoff, 1958), p. 17.

[2] The members concerned were Messrs. Gubinski of Poland and Korovin of the U.S.S.R. (1963 R.C.E. 85). Mr. Korovin attended for the first time in 1963. Mr. Gubinski's dissents in 1961 and 1962 covered the same matter (1961 R.C.E. 60; 1962 R.C.E. 83).

[3] Cf. footnote 3, p. 95 below.

[4] According to the "Note on the Composition and Functions of the Proposed Committee of Experts" prepared by the Office for the 1926 Conference, the Committee was to "embody its observations... in its technical report" (8 R.P. 401). An amended formulation adopted by the "Committee on Article 408" at that session merely stated that the Committee of Experts "would present a technical report" (8 R.P. 406). The word "observations" was used again, however, the following year both in the historical outline of the genesis of the Committee which preceded the Summary of Reports (10 D.R. 261) and in the Committee of Experts' first Report (1927 R.C.E. 401).

[5] One example, among the many available, is the observation made to Austria, in 1961, regarding its application of the Minimum Age (Non-Industrial Employment) Convention, 1932 (No 33): "The Committee notes that, in its statements to the Conference Committee as well as in its report, the government declares that a new Bill has been prepared to give effect to the provisions of the Conventions, but that differences of opinion have so far prevented the Bill from being submitted to Parliament. Since children are at present excluded from the scope of the Act of 1 July 1948, the Committee must insist once more that measures prohibiting occasional work by children, or regulating such work in accordance with article 3 of the Convention, be adopted as soon as possible so as to ensure full application of the Convention, which was ratified 25 years ago" (1961 R.C.E. 49-50). The Committee noted in 1963 that the Act of 1948 had been duly amended (1963 R.C.E. 69).

[6] Some observations merely thank the government for information supplied or for action taken, when the Committee's previous comments have had the desired effect.

where the Committee does not have as yet in its possession all the evidence required to arrive at an appraisal and must therefore seek additional data.[1]

Requests for supplementary information used to appear in the Report itself, but faced with the increasing bulk of this printed document the Committee decided in 1958 to adopt a simplified procedure. Since these requests, as well as the observations on minor matters, concerned "points not of principle but of a technical and detailed nature and ... sometimes of considerable length", the Committee gave instructions that they be sent in future "by the International Labour Office direct to the governments concerned for reply in their next reports".[2] The Committee indicates in its Report, under the observations on a given Convention, to which States these so-called "direct requests" are being addressed. This novel device[3] has the advantage not only of reducing the size of the printed Report but also of focusing attention on cases where there is need for action rather than for information. The introduction of the two-yearly system of reporting in 1959 has made it possible to carry this process one step further since the special footnote asking the government "to report in detail" already for the next period or even "to supply full particulars to the Conference at its (forthcoming) session" implies additional degrees of urgency in securing governmental action with a minimum of delay.

The omission from the Experts' Report, since 1958, of most requests for information and minor observations, and the introduction in 1959 of the two-yearly reporting system, have helped somewhat to stabilize the number of printed observations in recent years.[4] On the other hand this figure no longer provides any indication of the Committee's total workload in supervising the application of ratified Conventions, as its findings may take the form either of observations or of direct requests.

Although the Experts' Report has included since 1950 the results of its work in relation not only to ratified Conventions but also to unratified Conventions and to Recommendations, the Committee still devotes the bulk of its time to the supervision of the application of ratified standards.[5]

The Committee has also attempted, over the past few years, to give added prominence to the over-all record of compliance of individual member States. For this purpose its "General Observations" concerning particular countries refer not only to cases of failure to supply reports but

[1] Professor van Asbeck states in his article that "the only weapon at the disposal of the Committee is... the question asked and the question repeated once more, suggestion, persuasion, incredulity..." ("Une Commission d'Experts", *op. cit.*, p. 21). He refers also to "the gamut of expressions (used by the Committee) to express its feelings" (p. 18).

[2] 1958 R.C.E. 2.

[3] The procedure was new in its application rather than in its conception. Among the Committee's functions, as defined in 1926, figured already the following: "It may suggest that the Office ask by correspondence for any further details which, within the limits of the questionnaires approved by the Governing Body, may be demanded" (8 R.P. 406).

[4] The figures for certain years during the past decade or so are as follows: 189 in 1953, 416 in 1956, 545 in 1958, 288 in 1960, 392 in 1962 and 497 in 1964.

[5] In 1950 the Committee emphasized that "it continues to regard the detailed examination of the annual reports... as constituting its main task" (1950 R.C.E. 5). In 1963, 139 pages of its 262-page Report dealt with the application of ratified Conventions.

also to delays in their communication, to insufficient information on practical application, to disregard of the Committee's previous comments, etc.[1] No doubt for the same reason, the Committee's Report has contained, since 1949, an "Index to Observations" classified by countries (individual observations are arranged Convention by Convention). This not only provides at a glance a key to the results of the Committee's yearly "audit", but also facilitates the discussions in the Conference Committee.[2]

The Committee of Experts has recently introduced another practical innovation in order to expedite its examination procedure. With the adoption of the system of direct requests and of the two-yearly reporting cycle, failure by a government to reply to an observation or a request is liable to lead to serious delays in the supervision process.[3] To avoid this the Committee decided in 1961 "to ask the International Labour Office in its capacity as the secretariat of the Committee to ascertain immediately upon receipt of a government's reports whether these reports take account of the comments of the Committee of Experts and of the Conference Committee." In the negative the Office would remind the government of the need for a reply, but its role would be limited to an attempt "to prevent material delays... and it would remain still for these two Committees to determine whether the contents of the government's reply were satisfactory".[4] This system operated with a moderate measure of success: about half of the governments concerned sent in their missing replies in response to the Office's letters of reminder.[5]

A brief reference must be made to another procedural device in which, at one point, the Committee of Experts placed high hopes but which in the end had little practical effect. This was the possibility of a "direct contact" between the Committee and governments.[6] Only on one occasion did a State take advantage of this opportunity [7] and renewed mention of the idea after the war, both in the Governing Body and in the Committee's

---

[1] E.g., in a general observation addressed to Rumania in 1962 "the Committee notes with regret that the reports did not arrive until late in February, i.e. over four months after the due date, and that in two cases no information is provided in response to a previous observation or request (Conventions Nos. 87, 89). The Committee urges the government to supply its future reports in time and to include all the information requested" (1963 R.C.E. 23).

[2] Cf. p. 44 below.

[3] In 1951 a new question had been inserted in the forms of report specifically asking governments to "supply the information asked for or indicate the action taken... to settle the points" previously raised by the Committee of Experts or the Conference Committee (114 G.B. 18, 99).

[4] 1961 R.C.E. 8.

[5] 12 out of 30 responded in 1962 (1962 R.C.E. 7), 11 out of 22 in 1963 (1963 R.C.E. 6). If no reply is received a report is automatically requested for the next period so as to avoid further loss of time.

[6] The proposal was made by the Committee in 1929 (1929 R.C.E. 520) and supported by the Director (46 G.B. 128) but ran into such opposition in the Governing Body that it secured approval only by a narrow margin (47 G.B. 68-75, 77-78).

[7] In 1937 the French government sent "a high official of the Ministry of Colonies to supply the Committee orally" with supplementary information on the social reforms undertaken in its colonial territories. The Committee appended a summary of the statement to its Report (1937 R.C.E. 5, 19-20).

Reports,[1] produced no further response. In actual fact there seems to be little need for such contacts because governments are able to provide supplementary information to the Committee of Experts through the Conference Committee and through their reports.

To sum up, the Committee of Experts has striven constantly over the years to improve and expand the information available, so as to place before the Conference the kind of findings which will permit the next phase of the procedure to operate effectively. However, before this crucial stage can be discussed, some mention must be made of the role the Governing Body and the Summary of Reports have come to play in the procedure.

### III. The Role of the Governing Body

The Governing Body intervenes in the supervision procedure in two important ways. Under article 22 of the Constitution it determines the form in which the governments' reports are to be drawn up and the particulars they are to supply. In pursuance of this provision the Governing Body has approved separate "questionnaires" for each of the Conventions in force and has thus been able to exercise an important influence on the content of reports. It has also fixed the time period to be covered by the reports and the date of their submission to the I.L.O. It was the Governing Body again which had to decide on appropriate measures when it was found necessary to place detailed reporting on a less frequent basis. Until 1936 all such matters were discussed in the Governing Body itself. Since then they are considered in the first instance by a tripartite committee which reports to the Governing Body.[2]

The second, potentially important, role played by the Governing Body as regards supervision is in connection with the Committee of Experts:[3] under its mandate this Committee "would make a Report which the Director-General would submit in due course to the Governing Body and to the Conference".[4] In actual practice consideration of the Committee of Experts' Report by the Governing Body has usually been rather perfunctory, because hardly more than two months are available from the time the Report is adopted until the opening of the Conference session which

---

[1] 103 G.B. 170, 1950 R.C.E. 4, etc. The Committee made no further reference to this matter after 1952.

[2] This was originally the "Committee on Periodical Reports". Since the war questions regarding supervision have been assigned first to the "Committee on the Application of Conventions and Recommendations", then to the "Committee on Standing Orders and the Application of Conventions and Recommendations".

[3] For whose appointment, terms of reference, times of meeting, etc., the Governing Body is also responsible.

[4] In the version adopted in 1947 (103 G.B. 173). When the Committee of Experts was established in 1926, there was some difference of opinion on how to deal with its Report; the Conference "Committee on Article 408" had proposed that the Report be submitted to the Director who would annex it to his Summary of Reports (8 R.P. 408); during the discussion in plenary, however, M. Fontaine, who was the French government delegate as well as the chairman of the Governing Body, moved an amendment under which the Committee of Experts would report to the Governing Body so that the latter would be consulted before the Report was submitted to the Conference (8 R.P. 255-256).

discusses it. During this short period it must be printed and sent to the governments which in turn have to prepare their comments and replies. Already in 1929 these exigencies of the supervision timetable had made it necessary to circulate to governments the passages of the Report concerning them, before the Governing Body had approved the document.[1] The Governing Body recognized the difficulty and agreed that only "so far as possible" should the Report be submitted to it before circulation to governments.[2] To maintain the principle of Governing Body control it was, however, arranged in 1932 that its members would receive copies of the Report so that their observations could be communicated to the Conference.[3] In 1934 the Japanese government member was told by the chairman that the Report of the Committee of Experts was "only communicated to the Governing Body for information" and that any modifications should therefore be proposed to the Conference; the Governing Body's right to examine the Report and express its views on it was, however, specifically reasserted on that occasion.[4]

The Governing Body thus has certain important responsibilities, especially in relation to the adoption of the report forms and the appointment of the Committee of Experts. As it is placed half-way between that Committee and the Conference [5] it can do little more than take formal note of the Committee's Report. On the other hand, as indicated above, the Governing Body has always been able to give adequate attention to the special suggestions occasionally received from the Committee of Experts in its regular or in supplementary reports.

## IV. The Summary of Reports

Special supervision machinery had to be established because the Summary of Reports, which the Director-General must lay before the Conference every year, under article 23, paragraph 1, of the Constitution, did not, as originally hoped, set off a supervisory process. Nonetheless, in devising the machinery, a key role was assigned to the Summary which was to be the basis of the Conference Committee's discussions.[6] Once again, however, the practical developments which followed de-emphasized this role.

In any case the Committee of Experts examines the reports and the Summary is published some time after its meeting. But even the Con-

---

[1] 45 G.B. 70. The process has been further speeded, since 1956, by sending governments the observations relating to them in typescript, before the Report is printed (39 R.P. 644).

[2] 47 G.B. 69.

[3] 56 G.B. 86.

[4] 66 G.B. 14-19. A more far-reaching proposal, made in 1936 by the employers' vice-chairman, that the Governing Body should in principle be represented on the Committee of Experts was defeated by 17 votes to 6 (74 G.B. 29). In 1950 the Governing Body again agreed that such representation was "neither necessary nor appropriate" (113 G.B. 120).

[5] An Office note once described this as "an intermediate stage in the supervision procedure" (103 G.B. 171).

[6] As clearly stated in the 1926 resolution (8 D.R. 429) and stressed in the title of the Conference Committee which, until 1930, was called "Committee Appointed to Examine the Summary of the Reports Submitted under Article 408".

ference Committee seldom refers to this document, because it has in the Report of the Committee of Experts a much more convenient basis for its discussions, providing not only a summing-up but also an appraisal of the information supplied by governments. The very size of the Summary may act as a discouragement, although steps have been taken to reduce it to more manageable and readable proportions [1] and in particular to include in it only the type of data (first reports, important changes in the subsequent application of a Convention, replies to observations and requests) which are of interest primarily from the point of view of supervision.[2]

While the constitutional obligation to publish it remains, the Summary of Reports is thus clearly of secondary importance, even to the Conference, and merely provides a convenient source of information on any major developments which may occur in the application of Conventions.

## V. The Conference Committee

*Character and Functions*

All the efforts just described–in order to obtain meaningful reports and to subject them to the independent judgment of technical experts–have one final goal: to provide as solid a basis as possible for the discussions at the annual sessions of the International Labour Conference. This, the focal point of the whole procedure, is of more general interest because it has added a new dimension to international supervision. The nature and operation of the Conference Committee on the Application of Conventions and Recommendations therefore warrant careful analysis.

If the establishment of the Committee of Experts had met with a number of objections in 1926, the need for a special Committee of the Conference to deal with the effect given to ratified Conventions was hardly questioned at all.[3] Experience had already shown that the Conference as a whole was unable to give any real attention to following up the implementation of its past decisions.[4] The basic function of the Application Committee is therefore to relieve the Conference of this task by drawing up an annual balance sheet of the state of application based on three separate but closely related sources: the Summary of Reports, the Report of the Committee of Experts and the additional information provided by governments. As just noted, the Committee of Experts' Report has proved far more useful than the Summary, for practical supervision purposes.

The main element in the Conference Committee proceedings is the opportunity for governments of "adding, through their representatives... any observations they may think desirable to make, or of clearing up any obscurities to which the Committee of Experts (has) drawn attention".[5]

---

[1] The Director first referred to this in 1937 in his Report (23 D.R. 53) and suggested simplifications to the Governing Body (81 G.B. 132).

[2] The Governing Body approved these new criteria in 1957 (134 G.B. 31, 97-98).

[3] The chairman of the 1926 Committee indicated to the Conference that "the one point which was unanimously adopted was ... the Committee of the Conference" (8 R.P. 240).

[4] Cf. pp. 16-18 above.

[5] As already defined in the note prepared by the Office in 1926 (8 R.P. 402).

The value of this element is greatly enhanced by the tripartite composition of the Conference Committee which gives its discussions their distinctive and dynamic character. The participation of non-governmental interests directly concerned with the questions at issue represents a vital factor because it enables the Committee, during its questioning of governments, to come more closely to grips with the problems of implementation than would be possible in a body composed exclusively of independent experts or of government representatives.[1]

The necessity for the Conference Committee to hear, to weigh and at times to disapprove led however, just as in the case of the Committee of Experts, to intimations that it was exceeding its role and its powers. Some Conference Committee members expressed their concern on this score repeatedly in 1927,[2] and only after the 1928 session was it possible to say that the "period of difficulty and uncertainty (had) been surmounted".[3] In subsequent years also the Conference Committee has been subject to occasional criticism, especially from those the Committee has found it necessary to criticize, i.e. governments.[4] The Committee has therefore attempted from time to time to explain the nature of its work and to define the extent of its powers. Committee members have done the same when the Report was discussed in plenary session. The phrases and images used on these occasions add up to a catalogue which delineates more vividly than any legal formulations the Committee's character and approach.

Significantly, the main emphasis has been on what the Committee is *not*: it is neither a "tribunal",[5] nor a "Court of Star Chamber", neither a "jury sitting in judgment" nor a "court of inquiry". Instead it is an "organ of international public opinion", an "adviser to the States which submit reports", the "keystone of the machinery of international supervision of the application of Conventions" and the "nerve centre towards which all the activities of the Organization converge".[6] Not unexpectedly, the main stress is often on the Committee's "moral influence" as "the conscience of the Conference" and "of the Organization", a "Court of Honour", or merely a "still small voice" which makes itself heard during an "examina-

---

[1] During the discussions in 1926 the Spanish government proposed, unsuccessfully, that this work be carried out by the Governing Body because it functions less intermittently than the Conference (8 R.P. 254-255). Only in the Conference do all the member States have an opportunity to make themselves heard.

[2] The Chilean government, for instance, considered that the Conference Committee was not the place in which to reply to the observations of the Committee of Experts (doc. C. 408/P.V./2, (roneoed) p. 11) and the Italian government argued that the Conference Committee had no right to ask for, or discuss, supplementary information from governments (C. 408/P.V. 3, p. 20).

[3] In the words of the Committee's reporter (11 R.P. 282).

[4] "Certain governments hold a grievance against the sub-reporters of the (Conference) Committee because of the care with which they study the reports submitted by the States. Some reproach them to act as 'censors' of their countries, to establish themselves as 'public prosecutors', and ask the reason why one is against their country. There exists here a series of misunderstandings; we only do our duty as workers' delegates and Conference members in pointing out the divergencies." Speech of Mr. Serrarens, Netherlands workers' adviser, in 1931 (15 R.P. 467).

[5] 12 R.P. 813; 23 R.P. 286; 24 R.P. 312; and on many other occasions.

[6] 37 R.P. 363; 38 R.P. 440; 16 R.P. 672; 43 R.P. 541; 34 R.P. 549 and 30 R.P. 291.

tion of conscience".[1] These and other phrases and images [2] reflect some of the feeling and atmosphere which pervade the Committee in its work. They show that faith in the value of its activities is mixed with apprehension that their purpose might be misinterpreted and their results neglected. Further evidence to this effect will come to light when the procedures of the Conference Committee are reviewed.

Two main points need be retained here: on the one hand, the Committee's mandate [3] is so general that it provides no more than the formal basis for its existence; on the other hand, the Committee has been able to crystallize a clear concept of its purposes and potentialities due to its institutional traditions and the cumulative experience of certain of its members.

*Membership*

In its periodic attempts "to review, to evaluate and to prepare the ground for future action" [4] the Committee could not hope to function effectively without a minimum of continuity. While this is ensured in part by the Committee of Experts which is a permanent body, and also by the existence of an established secretariat, much depends on the extent to which the membership itself includes persons familiar with the Committee's procedures and traditions. The Conference is free each year to determine the size and composition of its Committees,[5] depending on the degree of interest shown by delegates in the various agenda items. There is thus no formal guarantee that the Application Committee will include persons who were on it at previous sessions. In practice this has proved to be the case, from year to year. Former members are given some preference in the selection of officers because the Committee hopes to rely on their experience. Nonetheless the choice of a chairman also involves as a rule broader considerations: as in all international gatherings an effort is made to ensure a balanced distribution of key Conference posts to delegates representing as wide a cross-section of the membership as possible. Such factors weigh far less heavily in the selection of the employers' and workers' vice-chairmen and familiarity with the Committee's work also counts foremost in the choice of a reporter.

---

[1] 17 R.P. 411; 14 R.P. 508; 31 R.P. 382; 25 R.P. 414; 33 R.P. 376 and 34 R.P. 458.

[2] Delegates have sometimes given free rein to their imagination in their attempts to characterize the Committee. Its Report has been called the "Cinderella of the Conference which arrives at the stroke of midnight" (20 R.P. 509) and compared to "the Loch Ness monster (which) periodically puts in an appearance, creates a certain sensation, then disappears into oblivion, only to reappear the next year in the same form" (25 R.P. 287). The work of the Committee has been labelled "the X-ray department of the International Labour Organization" (29 R.P. 152) and even "a kind of social Interpol" (43 R.P. 543).

[3] "To consider . . . the measures taken by members to give effect to the provisions of Conventions to which they are parties and the information furnished by members concerning the results of inspections" and to "submit a report to the Conference" (article 7 of the Standing Orders of the Conference).

[4] 40 R.P. 653.

[5] On the proposal of its Selection Committee (article 4 of its Standing Orders). This method differs from that followed in the General Assembly of the United Nations where all governments are represented on each of the main committees.

All these elements are found to have played a noticeable role in practice. With the exception of one government delegate who was chairman on four separate occasions,[1] this post has been filled to an increasing extent, since the war, by persons who either hold important, often ministerial, posts in their own countries, or who are already well acquainted with the I.L.O., although not necessarily with the application of Conventions as such. The post of reporter is usually held by national officials whose work has brought them into close and steady contact with the I.L.O. and its system of standards. It is in the vice-chairmanships that there has been the most persistent tendency to ensure continuity, both on a national and a personal basis. The Swiss employers seemed for many years to be the most regular occupants.[2] Since then a United Kingdom employer held the post from 1953 to 1959, to be succeeded by a Danish employer during the following four years.[3] An even more consistent pattern has emerged in the case of the workers' vice-chairmen. During all but eight of the 37 sessions the post was held by a Belgian or Dutch labour leader.[4]

Because the two vice-chairmen act as the spokesmen for their groups, long-term participation and regularity of tenure are major assets when the application of Conventions is discussed with government representatives. No reading of the Reports or even of the Minutes of previous Committee sessions can replace familiarity with the terms of Conventions and especially with the more serious cases of non-compliance which inevitably require the Committee's greatest attention and therefore take up most of its time.

A review of the size of the Conference Committee's membership reveals certain interesting developments. Until the recent past there was obviously no great eagerness among Conference participants to sit on the Committee. In 1963, for the first time, the Committee's regular membership exceeded 100. The gradual rise in the number of Conventions and ratifications in force might have been thought to generate increased interest; on the other hand economic and political uncertainties might have acted in the opposite direction. Whatever the cause, this obvious reluctance to participate [5] could not have been due to the purely formal circumstance that the consideration of the application of Conventions did not constitute a separate item

---

[1] Mr. Mannio of Finland presided in 1930, 1936, 1938 and 1949 and took an active part in the Committee throughout its early years.

[2] During 11 of the 22 sessions before 1953.

[3] Mr. Bellingham-Smith and Mr. Poulsen.

[4] During nine sessions the post was occupied by Mr. Serrarens of the Netherlands and during 14 sessions (1951-1964) by Mr. Cool of Belgium. It is also interesting that Mr. Serrarens, by being elected reporter in 1951, demonstrated that the government group holds no monopoly on this important assignment.

[5] For instance, the Belgian workers' member recognized in the Governing Body in 1936 that "as chairman of the workers' group at the Conference he always had a difficulty in finding members for the Committee on the Application of Conventions. The discussions of that Committee were of limited interest and did not lead to important decisions" (74 G.B. 12). The Conference Committee urged in its Report in 1938 that "at least some of the States of great industrial importance should, as in the past, take a more active part in its proceedings" (24 R.P. 488).

on the Conference agenda until 1944.[1]   The real reason was to be found, perhaps, in the understandable reluctance of many governments to play an active role.[2]   The very technical and rather unspectacular character of the Committee's activities no doubt also discouraged many non-governmental representatives from taking any part.

There were even serious suggestions, during the early days, to narrow the membership of the Application Committee further by excluding persons from countries which had not ratified any Conventions.[3]   Recalling that the Constitution made it possible for any delegate at the Conference to lodge a formal complaint of non-application, the Director pointed out that it would therefore be difficult to impose limitations on a delegate's right merely to voice his criticism.[4]   No further suggestions to this effect were put forward in later years but the point is made from time to time that the participation of non-ratifying countries in supervision is basically inequitable.[5]   It must be recognized, however, that the argument steadily loses in weight as ratification becomes more and more general.

*Committee Procedure*

In the performance of its task, three things must be accomplished.   First, it must obtain the desired information from governments without exceeding its role as an organ lacking formal judicial powers.   Second, it must carry out its assignment expeditiously because it has scarcely two weeks to consider an ever-increasing number of cases.   Third, it must present its Report to the Conference in a form that will afford a succinct yet accurate picture of its deliberations.

The pattern of the Committee's work is still evolving, but certain basic features have by now crystallized.   Procedural refinements have been introduced, often on an experimental basis, because there is little precedent for the type of mutual supervision practised by the I.L.O.   An attempt was made, for instance, from 1929 to 1931, not to rely exclusively on the Committee of Experts' findings but to ask "sub-reporters" in the Conference Committee to carry out a separate examination of the reports.[6]

---

[1] Under article 1, paragraph 2, of the Standing Orders of the Conference, two advisers may accompany a delegate for *each* agenda item, so that there was ample opportunity even before the war to appoint advisers to sit on the Application Committee, as urged in the letters of convocation to the Conference (cf. 73 G.B. 143-145).

[2] It is only during the past ten years that half or more of the governments attending the Conference have chosen to be titular members of the Committee.   During some pre-war years this proportion dropped to 20 per cent.

[3] 11 R.P. 619.

[4] 14 D.R. 134.

[5] Cf. the remark of the French government member in the Governing Body in 1936 that States which had ratified no or few Conventions should not sit in judgment on States which "did their duty towards the International Labour Organization" (74 G.B. 21); and the statement of the Chilean government delegate in the 1963 Session: "It is astonishing that States members of the I.L.O. which have not ratified Convention No. 11 are represented (some by a government member) on the Committee on the Application of Conventions and Recommendations and consequently act as judges of countries like Chile, which are seeking to adopt the maximum number of Conventions" (47 R.P. 336).

[6] The sub-reporters were recruited from the three groups, with the employers refusing to take a part in this work in 1929 (cf. 12 R.P. 813; 14 R.P. 634;   15 R.P. 611).

However, this was soon found to be "an unnecessary duplication of work" [1] and the Committee of Experts' Report was henceforth recognized as the principal basis for the Conference Committee's discussions.

A similar development, though of more recent date, occurred in the examination of reports which arrive too late for consideration by the Experts. Starting in 1937, subcommittees were set up for this purpose [2] so that a full year would not be lost. By 1959 the subcommittee began to find it difficult to complete its work satisfactorily in the short time available, particularly in the case of first reports after ratification; [3] since 1962 late reports are regularly referred to the Committee of Experts for study at its next session. But the Conference Committee does so with reluctance because it recognizes that as a result "States which fail to supply their reports in time for examination by the Committee of Experts find themselves in an unduly privileged position in relation to the other States which fulfil their constitutional reporting obligation within the prescribed time limit". [4]

The Conference Committe was also concerned for many years with the material conditions under which it had to carry on its work. Its Reports, especially before the war, repeatedly referred to the delays which had occurred in getting its deliberations under way and in securing regular attendance by its members. [5] Lack of adequate interpretation facilities also slowed down the pace of work for a time but by 1955 the necessary arrangements had been made to overcome these practical difficulties. [6]

The shortage of time has forced the Conference Committee to introduce another procedural simplification: since 1955 it applies "a principle of selectivity", i.e. it asks its officers to retain for discussion only those observations of the Committee of Experts which appear to be of particular urgency and interest. [7] Committee members are able to ask that additional observations also be discussed. [8] This preliminary selection has helped the

---

[1] 16 R.P. 671.

[2] 23 R.P. 571. Subcommittees first consisted of the officers of the Conference Committee, to whom subsequently one member from each group was usually added.

[3] Since the introduction of the two-yearly system of detailed reporting this point has lost some of its validity because the Committee of Experts now simply examines late reports during the off-year, so that no over-all delay occurs; the matter is of course more serious if no reports at all are supplied for two or more years in succession, but this is exceptional.

[4] 43 R.P. 670.

[5] Cf., e.g., 19 R.P. 751 and the Swiss employers' delegate's statement in 1937 that "the Application Committee is more or less treated like a poor relation... (Its) sittings are only followed by a few of its members" (23 R.P. 287).

[6] Cf. 129 G.B. 89-91 and the speech of the Conference Committee reporter in 1955 (38 R.P. 431).

[7] 38 R.P. 582; 39 R.P. 645. In making their selection, the officers include as a matter of course all observations where the Committee of Experts has asked the government, in a special footnote, "to supply full particulars to the Conference" (cf. p. 32 above).

[8] The principle was even established, in 1963, that a discussion could be asked for in cases where the Committee of Experts had merely made a direct request (47 R.P. 513). In order to enable the Committee to consider these cases the text of certain direct requests was circulated at the request of the workers' group (47th Session, doc. C.App.C./PV. 8 (roneoed), pp. 1-3).

Committee to focus attention on the more essential cases and to complete its work on schedule despite the steady increase in the number of observations. At the same time action on observations which the Committee decides not to discuss is merely postponed since a government is required in any case to reply to all observations in its next report, regardless of whether they were considered by the Conference Committee.[1]

The Committee is now ready to embark on its main task, to review with the help of the governments concerned the matters raised by the Committee of Experts. This tripartite discussion constitutes the final and crucial instalment of the supervision procedure. It also represents its most delicate stage because there exists no formal obligation for a government which has made a report in accordance with article 22 of the Constitution to supply the Conference with additional information. During the first year of its operation some delegates went so far in fact as to deny the Conference Committee the right to ask for, or to discuss, such supplementary data.[2] Most of these fears and hesitations were dispelled early in the Committee's existence and the arrangements which crystallized little by little enabled it to perform its task.

Although there is no room here to trace developments in detail, it is interesting to recount rapidly how this practical problem of international supervision was overcome, so that States members came gradually to supply information and to discuss their problems with the Committee, almost as a matter of course. To do so it was necessary to make clear to governments that it was to their advantage to accept co-operation with the Application Committee rather than to refuse it. Delegates had to be convinced that the Committee's consideration of the observations regarding their countries would be more realistic and more balanced if they could state their case, i.e. provide such explanations and assurances as they felt able to give. The explanations permitted the Committee to perform its informational task. The assurances might lead directly to progress in implementation, and this promotional aspect of supervision came to be recognized as the key to its effectiveness.

A workable system was initiated in 1929 when the findings of the sub-reporters regarding any particular country were transmitted to the government delegations because "it was only right to give the States in regard to whom questions had arisen an opportunity of submitting explanations either orally or in writing if they desire to do so".[3] As a result oral or written statements were received from several governments and the foundation was laid for what has become the Conference Committee's most original and fruitful activity. In subsequent years the Committee insisted again on pointing out that "the government concerned is completely at liberty to decide whether it will appear before the Committee or not",[4]

---

[1] This is provided for in the forms of report. Cf. footnote 3, p. 33 above.

[2] Cf. footnote 2, p. 37 above. The Director had insisted at the time that the right to request supplementary information from a government was implicit in article 408 (10th Session, doc. C.408/P.V./3 (roneoed), p. 18).

[3] 12 R.P. 813-814. It was not necessary to follow this procedure when a government sat on the Committee but as the membership was small this was the exception rather than the rule.

[4] E.g. in 1930: 14 R.P. 634.

recorded its "appreciation of the courteous co-operation of the representatives of the governments concerned" [1] and emphasized that it "had no
doubt as to the propriety of this procedure".[2]

During the decade before the war there thus emerged a practice which
rapidly became part and parcel of the Conference's regular procedures:
"the representatives of governments were invited to appear, if they so
desired, before the Committee" [3] and their response constituted the key
element in "a system of mutual verification upon a basis of reciprocal
confidence and goodwill".[4]

The ready acceptance of this system was facilitated by two factors. On
the one hand its operation was recognized as a highly desirable alternative
to the representation and complaints machinery laid down in the Constitution.[5] This latent influence of an occasional procedure of supervision on
a permanent one will be further explored at a later stage.[6] On the other
hand, the Conference Committee was probably conscious of the fact, in
its early period, that it could not be unduly severe in its appraisals.[7]

Three decades of operation have permitted the discussions with government representatives to become a well-organized and businesslike part of
the Conference Committee's work. Governments are informed both by
individual letters from the chairman and by notices in the *Daily Bulletin* [8]
of the Conference that the Committee of Experts' observations concerning
their countries are up for discussion. Their response has been such in
recent years that almost all governments represented at the Conference

---

[1] In 1932: 16 R.P. 672.

[2] In 1937: 23 R.P. 571.

[3] Conference Committee Report, 1939 (25 R.P. 413). This was merely a description
of what actually took place. Yet two years previously Zarras maintained that "the
Committee simply draws the attention of governments to the points concerning them, but
in no case invites them to appear before it in order to supply explanations" (*op. cit.*, p. 182).
The difference may have been merely a verbal one, but in the end it was the result, i.e. the
government's response, which counted.

[4] 25 R.P. 414.

[5] Speaking in the Conference in 1931, the Netherlands workers' representative, Mr. Serrarens, explained that "the method followed in pursuance of article 408 permits to inves-
tigate divergencies without employing the more severe methods of the subsequent articles.
Thus, if article 408 could not be applied, it would be necessary to apply these other articles"
(15 R.P. 467). Mr. Kaufmann, the Swiss government representative, put the point even
more bluntly in 1933, when he was the Committee's reporter: "The more thoroughly the
Committee does its work, the less will be the need for having resort to articles 409, 411 and
423 of the Treaty" (17 R.P. 411).

[6] Cf. pp. 173-180.

[7] Thus a Belgian government representative expressed the wish in the Conference in
1935 that "the Committee would prove in future perhaps a little more difficult in accepting
the (governments') explanations ... which really were a little brief in certain cases"
(19 R.P. 683).

[8] A reference to the *Bulletin* appears in the Committee's 1948 Report (31 R.P. 382).
Since 1957 the notices sometimes mention the countries by name. Thus the *Bulletin*,
announcing the Committee's sitting of 18 June 1963, said that "The Committee is about
to conclude the consideration of the observations made by the Committee of Experts...
The Committee would be grateful if the government representatives of the following
countries would be good enough to attend the above sitting: *Argentina, Ecuador, Salvador,
Uruguay, Vietnam.*"

have agreed to supply additional information concerning the application of ratified Conventions in their countries.[1]

The Committee has learned, through experience, to organize its discussions in such a way so as to achieve "in the minimum of time... a maximum of results".[2] A government's written reply to the Committee of Experts' observations is circulated to the Conference Committee and its members have the right to ask that further clarifications be given orally. Discussions with governments are held country by country, using for this purpose the index which precedes the Experts' Report. As a matter of courtesy towards the representatives of governments which are not members of the Committee, they are customarily given priority so that their participation, in response to the Application Committee's invitation, will not unduly interfere with their other Conference duties.[3]

When the position concerning a given country is discussed, the government representative has an opportunity to make an introductory general statement and then to reply to each observation separately. Committee members are free, after each reply, to comment in the light both of the Experts' findings and of the government's supplementary information, and it is through these exchanges that the essence of the Committee's business is transacted.

The course of the discussion often depends on the seriousness of the case and on the nature of the government's reply. Generally, the labour and management representatives participate much more actively in this phase than do governments.[4] The vice-chairmen usually act as the spokesmen for their groups but other employer or worker members also intervene, asking questions, recalling the past history of the case, urging speedy action, etc. During such exchanges non-governmental representatives are able to make an especially useful contribution if it is their own country which is under discussion. During the pre-war period this opportunity was used regularly by the Indian workers' representatives who commented frequently, in critical terms, on the application of several of the Conventions which their government had ratified.[5] The Greek workers' member of the

---

[1] Since 1951, when the Committee began to inform the Conference which countries had not responded to its invitation, their number never exceeded two in any given year and in some years all the governments in question replied either in writing or orally. The Committee has also pointed out at times that it was unable to discuss the application of Conventions by States absent from the Conference.

[2] The phrase was used by the workers' vice-chairman in 1956 (39 R.P. 441).

[3] Committee members are informed of these customary arrangements in an explanatory note on the work of the Committee which is circulated early in the session. Cf., e.g. doc. C.App.C./D.1 (roneoed) at the 47th Session, 1963.

[4] During the 1963 session, e.g., there were only two occasions when government representatives intervened in the discussion of cases concerning other governments: one was a U.S.S.R. comment on the absence of replies from British Guiana; the other a British comment on the effect given to the Forced Labour Convention, 1930 (No. 29) in Bulgaria (47th Session, docs. C.App.C./PV.10 (roneoed), pp. 9-11 and C.App.C./PV.11, p. 3).

[5] In particular the Hours of Work (Industry) Convention, 1919 (No. 1), the Unemployment Convention, 1919 (No. 2) and certain of the maritime Conventions (Nos. 15, 16 and 22). Criticism was voiced both in the Application Committee and in the plenary sitting, and often without previous observations by the Committee of Experts. Madan Mohan Puri writes in his study *India in the International Labour Organization* (The Hague:

Committee intervened repeatedly during the nineteenfifties.[1] While non-European workers have also done so on occasion, e.g. those from Chile, Japan and Peru, it was the non-governmental members from such Western European countries as Austria, France, the Federal Republic of Germany, Italy, Switzerland, etc. who primarily participated in the discussions involving their own governments. It was mostly from the workers' side that such comments were heard, although employers' members, from Chile and Italy, for instance, have also at times taken an active part. As in the case of written comments on the application of Conventions by their governments, the representative organizations may feel reluctant to criticize their governments in an international forum;[2] nonetheless a sufficient number of such criticisms occurs every year to show that non-governmental intervention is far from being only a theoretical possibility.

When the discussion of a given case is completed, the chairman tends to sum it up by taking note of the governments' explanations and assurances, and by voicing the hope that compliance with the Convention will soon be brought about. This statement from the chair constitutes the Committee's formal conclusions and is inserted as such in its Report.[3] The Report

---

Institute of Social Studies, 1958) that "the non-governmental delegates from India not only used the... Conference as a platform for expressing their grievances of all kinds, they also urged the Organization to use its good offices and bring to bear upon the government of India some pressure so that the conditions in the country might improve" (*op. cit.*, p. 71). In 1928 the Indian workers' delegate admitted candidly, during his speech commenting on Convention No. 1: "We of course realize that the strength of our movement lies in us in India and not in the International Labour Conference, but we also realize the propaganda value of this Conference" (11 R.P. 184).

[1] Cf. the case history related on p. 122 below.

[2] Commenting on this aspect of non-governmental participation, the Netherlands workers' representative, Mr. Serrarens, expressed the hope, in 1933, that the workers' and employers' organizations "will not be too chauvinistic in their replies, but will tell us in all frankness the facts which the governments will perhaps have stated in veiled and diplomatic terms" (17 R.P. 412).

[3] An example of this type of exchange is the consideration by the Conference Committee in 1963 of the application in Spain of the Hours of Work (Industry) Convention, 1919 (No. 1). The Report of the Committee of Experts had urged the government to revise its legislation so as "to take full account of the observations and requests made by the Committee... and of the various comments made at the Conference Committee" (1963 R.C.E. 39-40). The government had sent in a written reply, but the workers' group had given notice that it would like to have supplementary information orally. During the ensuing discussion the Spanish government member of the Committee had supplied additional explanations, confirming that draft legislation, in the form "either of a code or a general labour ordinance", had already been prepared. The workers' vice-chairman then recalled that discrepancies with Convention No. 1 had had to be pointed out ever since Spain rejoined the I.L.O. in 1956. In reply to this and to questions asked by the workers' members from the Federal Republic of Germany and from Venezuela, the government representative insisted that internal law, though complying with the Convention, was being revised to obtain "a systematic and coherent compilation of provisions of general application". The chairman concluded that "the Committee took note of the explanations supplied and hoped that the bill mentioned would be adopted in the near future".

The Minutes which contain a record of the discussion (doc. C.App.C./PV.8 (roneoed) p. 11-12) form the basis, together with the government's written reply, for the record of the case included in Appendix IB of the Committee's Report, "Observations and Information concerning Certain Conventions" (47 R.P. 524-525). Since governments have the

contains a full record of the information submitted and the discussions held on those observations to which the Committee had decided to give immediate attention. The Committee considers that this "annual balance sheet should accurately reflect both the positive and negative aspects of the situation, leaving it to the Conference to gain an over-all picture from the extensive data which the Committee places at its disposal".[1]

The non-governmental members of the Committee insisted, however, that more than this detailed rendering of accounts was needed to stimulate interest in, and action on, observations. They contended that the very length of the Conference Committee's Report discouraged delegates from reading it and that this was responsible for the insufficient attention it received in the plenary.[2] They therefore proposed a special device to focus attention on those cases where "the discrepancies noted are of such a basic character or are of such long standing that the special attention of the Conference should be drawn to this unsatisfactory state of affairs".[3] A first step in this direction had already been taken during the pre-war period when States which had failed to carry out their reporting obligation were mentioned by name in the Committee's "General Report". By 1957 the Committee considered that non-compliance with the obligations under ratified Conventions was at least equally serious, in some cases, and it decided "to highlight certain of these cases" by including them in a special list in its "General Report".[4]

Although the idea was not entirely new,[5] it gave rise to considerable opposition, especially in 1957 and 1958, the first two years the list was included in the Conference Committee's Report. The main objections were the lack of clear criteria for including a case in the list, the method followed in inserting it in the Report and the possible false impression it might convey that all is well regarding cases not appearing on the list.[6]

---

right to make corrections in their declarations, as reproduced in the Committee's Minutes or in its draft Report, this record constitutes an authoritative statement of the position and of promises for future action.

[1] 46 R.P. 687.

[2] Cf. p. 50 below.

[3] In the words of the Committee's Report in 1957 (40 R.P. 657).

[4] 40 R.P. 657.

[5] The Conference Committee Report in 1932 had contained the following significant passage: "We consider that the time has come to draw up a special list of cases in regard to which the Committee on Article 408, and by implication the Conference itself, have for years past had to make the same observations again and again without result" (16 R.P. 673). During the consideration of this proposal in the Governing Body, the British workers' member "did not suggest that a black list should be drawn up but that there should be some intermediate step between the present ratification table and the application of sanctions under the Treaty". The Director considered, however, that the Conference Committee "had gone a little further than present circumstances warranted... If the publication of all the facts (regarding non-compliance with Conventions) gave no results, the proper procedure would be to have recourse to article 411", dealing with complaints. In the end the Governing Body decided not to alter existing practice (60 G.B. 79-80).

[6] In 1958 there was a strong move in the Committee to omit it from the Report (42 R.P. 490). During the discussion of the Report in plenary, government representatives of three States appearing in the list (Czechoslovakia, Guatemala and Italy) and a workers'

As a result the Committee took care in the following years to define the criteria used ("the persistent disregard of basic undertakings"); to give the governments concerned "every opportunity to place their views before the Committee" before taking "a specific decision in each individual case"; and to include in the list not only cases of non-application but also of failure to comply with other basic obligations, such as the supply of reports under articles 19 and 22 of the Constitution and the submission of Conventions and Recommendations to the competent national authorities.[1] The Committee has made sparing use of this device to stimulate progress in the application of ratified Conventions, so that between 1958 and 1964 the number of such cases listed never exceeded nine a year.

While criticism of the special list has not wholly subsided,[2] it seems to have become accepted as part of the Conference Committee's regular procedure and to have served its intended purpose to produce a sense of urgency by giving a fuller measure of publicity to the cases selected.[3]

*Committee Atmosphere*

A mere recital of the procedures followed by the Conference Committee when it considers the observations of the Committee of Experts and when it reports its findings to the Conference, fails to convey the rather special atmosphere which prevails. Yet it is on this somewhat intangible factor of atmosphere that the Committee's results largely depend. The active participation of non-governmental delegates on a basis of equality has always given a particular flavour to I.L.O. meetings, but in the case of the Conference's Application Committee, especially, tripartism can be either a cause of friction or a source of strength.

It is here that the traditions and postures which have developed over the years come to exercise their influence. Each participant must shape his conduct to fit his objectives. The employers' and workers' members must sense how far they can go in their questioning and criticism without losing the governments' collaboration which is so essential to the work of the Committee. The government representatives must prove by their attitude and response that their countries are open to persuasion and are striving in good faith to carry out international obligations. To do so successfully requires knowledge of the matters at issue and insight into the

representative of Bulgaria discussed it in their speeches and gave assurances that steps would be taken to move towards full compliance (42 R.P. 473, 476, 485, 489-490). The Committee's reporter pointed out, on the other hand, that sufficient progress had occurred during the past year to remove from the list seven of the 12 countries on it in 1957 (42 R.P. 472). In the end the paragraph in the Report containing the list was adopted by 104 votes to 33, with 49 abstentions, and the Report as a whole by 160 votes to 0, with 58 abstentions (42 R.P. 493). There was no voting on this issue in subsequent years.

[1] Cf. the Report of the 1960 Session (44 R.P. 604). Since 1962 the General Report includes a section entitled "Special Problems".

[2] A U.S.S.R. government representative pointed out in 1960 that "the listing of such countries is in itself rather a peculiar sanction against certain States–not only a moral sanction but also a juridical sanction. In effect it is a measure of reproof, a condemnation" (44 R.P. 433).

[3] The impact of the special list is discussed on pp. 170-171 below.

motives of the other parties–qualities needed in all types of negotiations, be they collective bargaining sessions or diplomatic meetings.

Throughout the Conference session the non-governmental groups in the Committee hold regular meetings where individual cases are reviewed and group strategy is planned, but the programme is so large and the pace of the Committee's work usually so rapid that it is much more difficult for the group spokesmen to prepare themselves in detail [1] than for government officials who are able to work with a full brief when they appear before the Committee. On the other hand the group spokesmen do have the advantage of being fully familiar with the Committee's atmosphere and potentialities.

The same is not always true of the government representatives who come to the Committee to reply to observations. If they are technicians who deal with the application of labour legislation at home they are able to make a real contribution to the discussion by clarifying doubtful points, explaining difficulties and giving an idea of the probable rate of progress.[2] If, on the other hand, they are unfamiliar with the national and international standards at issue, their contribution to the proceedings and hence to the cause of their country is likely to be slight.[3] There are, of course, cases where even skill of presentation will not alter the underlying difficulties of application, but the exchange of views will at least take place in an atmosphere of comprehension where the discussion can centre on technical rather than political or even personal considerations.[4]

All these factors exercise their influence on the Committee's "climate" which is consequently liable to vary from sitting to sitting and even from session to session. If at times individual reactions have been sharp,[5] the

---

[1] The employers' group has adopted a practice of asking several of its members to speak on its behalf in regard to a certain number of cases. The workers' vice-chairman is traditionally the spokesman for his group, but other members also intervene. In 1961 the Application Committee's reporter told the Conference that the governments' "replies and statements gave rise to many useful discussions in which the spokesmen of the workers' and employers' groups... took a particularly active and constructive part" (45 R.P. 486).

[2] These technicians who take an active part in the external relations of their countries have been accurately described as "paradiplomats". Cf. C. Labeyrie-Ménahem, *Des Institutions Spécialisées – Problèmes juridiques et diplomatiques de l'administration internationale* (Paris: Pédone, 1953), pp. 94-102.

[3] In 1956 the workers' vice-chairman urged governments to send representatives "who are competent in the subject and who are able to reply to the questions put to them" (39 R.P. 441).

[4] In 1960 the workers' vice-chairman, speaking of the discussion of the effect given to the Freedom of Association and Protection of the Right to Organize Convention, 1948 (No. 87) in the United Arab Republic, called the government representative "the most brilliant advocate I have ever heard in the Committee" (44 R.P. 443).

[5] In 1951, a Mexican government representative charged in the plenary that the atmosphere in the Application Committee was becoming "more rarefied and more difficult" as time went on. "We must get rid of the idea that those who are invited to appear before the Committee should be presumed guilty, treated like prisoners at the bar, subjected to an interrogation amounting to a cross-examination, during which an attempt is made to embarrass delegates who have no expert knowledge of the matter or are inadequately informed with regard to the matters under discussion in the Committee". To correct this state of affairs the representative suggested that the Conference Committee should be given "exact terms of reference" and that unless its Standing Orders were

general tone has been surprisingly good on the whole.[1]  The fact that in recent years all or almost all States have consented to respond to the Committee's invitations shows that it has been able to generate the kind of atmosphere which makes it possible for governments to come forward with explanations.  To this extent at least the subtle search for just enough psychological pressure to persuade governments that it is in their own interests to reply seems to have been successful.[2]

Viewed within the context of the supervision machinery as a whole, the Conference Committee thus brings to bear at the crucial stage of the process the special resources of a tripartite organization.  The presence and interplay of national and occupational interests add a certain dynamic impulse to the necessarily static results of the Committee of Experts' technical examination.  This persuasive element can, under favourable circumstances, generate a desire for action on the part of governments.  The procedures and atmosphere which have gradually given the Conference Committee its distinctive character emerge then as the mainsprings of effective mutual supervision.

## Discussion of Report in Plenary Conference

Although it is the final and culminating stage of the annual cycle of examination and discussion, the consideration of the Application Committee's Report by the Conference in plenary sitting constitutes something of an anticlimax.  In a sense the conclusions and appeals to be found in this document, although officially submitted to the Conference, are addressed over its head to the governments to which copies are communicated by the Office, shortly after the session.

---

revised "many of us will confine ourselves to submitting written reports to the Committee, so as to avoid being subjected to such completely unwarranted treatment" (34 R.P. 461). The background was that the Mexican government had failed in 1951 to supply its reports, even in time for the Conference, and had refused to give any information to the Conference Committee.  Speaking immediately after the Mexican representative, the French government delegate, M. Ramadier, urged that the Application Committee "should be severe in the interrogations which it addresses to certain countries" (34 R.P. 462).

[1] In 1952, the year after the incident mentioned in the preceding footnote, the Application Committee's chairman, M. Troclet of Belgium, reported to the Conference that there had been "an excellent atmosphere" in the Committee (35 R.P. 377).

[2] The unmistakable element of tension, sometimes created by the discussions, was described by one of the participants, the Austrian workers' representative.  Writing of the examination in 1960 of the effect given by Austria to the Labour Clauses (Public Contracts) Convention, 1949 (No. 94), he related: "The atmosphere was tense and rather unfavourable to our country, not only in the workers' group and on the part of most government representatives but also in the employers' group" (H. Leo Charak, "Auf absteigenden Pfaden. Vor Sanktionen der IAO gegen Österreich" ("On downward paths. Impending I.L.O. sanctions against Austria") Arbeit und Wirtschaft (Vienna), Vol. 14, No. 10 (October 1960), p. 270).  Cf. the fuller reference to this case on pp. 136-137 below. A similar picture is evoked in the Report of the Peruvian workers' delegation on the same 1960 session of the Conference: "There were difficult moments for the workers' delegate participating in the Conventions Committee, when confronted with criticism which, although addressed to the (Peruvian) government, affected us as trade union leaders" (Peru Ante el Mundo del Trabajo (Lima: Ediciones de Cultura Sindical, 1960), p. 37).

It is not surprising, therefore, that discussion of the Application Committee's Report was regarded for many years as little more than a formality, much to the dismay of those delegates who had had a part in its elaboration. There was a tendency to attribute this limited echo to the late stage at which the Report reached the Conference and steps were taken to get it adopted and circulated as rapidly as possible.[1] Experience proved, however, that delegates would not be deterred from intervening, regardless of the late date, if they really wished to take part in the discussion.

When the supervision machinery began to operate, its inherent novelty, and the hesitations some delegates felt towards it, were no doubt responsible for the interest evoked by its Report.[2] But during most of the pre-war period the lack of concern for the Application Committee's work was as evident during the consideration of its findings in the plenary as it was during its sittings. A number of interrelated circumstances led to a noticeable change during the nineteenfifties. Some of this increasing interest clearly arose from a feeling that the supervision procedure was gaining in strictness.[3] Moreover, the discussion of the application of Conventions provided an opportunity to raise burning political issues of the day, such as Algeria and Hungary.[4] Article 35 of the Constitution, the so-called "colonial clause", also figured frequently in the discussions in relation to the application of Conventions in non-metropolitan territories.

The main reason for the long and often sharp discussions of recent years is to be found in the prominence of the human rights Conventions whose implementation has given rise to considerable controversy. Freedom of association, prevention of discrimination and abolition of forced labour –all these are matters which transcend the I.L.O.'s primary concern with specifically social questions and open up political, racial and other issues. It is not surprising that the partisan points of view have influenced, if not dominated, the discussion of the Application Committee's Report in plenary.[5] As a result 20 or more speakers participated in 1961, 1962 and

---

[1] These measures, as approved by the Governing Body in 1955, included a quick start in getting the Application Committee under way, frequent sittings, full telephonic interpretation, etc. (129 G.B. 89-91). In recent years the Report has usually reached the Conference several days before the end of the session.

[2] In 1927 and 1928 six and nine delegates respectively participated in the discussion. The average for subsequent years was about four speakers.

[3] In 1951, when 12 speakers participated, repeated reference was made to the difficulties encountered by the Application Committee (cf. footnote 5, p. 48 above), and the Committee's reporter, in his summing up, welcomed the fact that "for the first time in many years, we have had a real discussion on the Report" (34 R.P. 463). In 1958, when 14 delegates spoke to the Report, it was the recently initiated special list which figured repeatedly in the discussion.

[4] Six of the eleven speakers in 1957 and three of the 14 in 1958 referred mainly to these two topics. Some plenary statements also served exclusively to reaffirm claims to disputed territories (British Honduras, Falkland Islands, etc.) but these are not counted in the figures.

[5] The United States government delegate, Mr. Weaver, appealed in 1962: "May I suggest that as we conclude the discussion on this Report ... we turn to the issues raised in it rather than to side issues which seek to divert attention from the lack of freedom" (46 R.P. 434).

1963, and the I.L.O.'s standard-implementing activities have certainly gained in prominence. Nor should the impression be conveyed that during these years the discussion centred exclusively on "Cold War" or related issues.[1]

The main value of discussion in the Conference from the point of view of supervision is the further airing, in the I.L.O.'s principal organ, of cases of non-application already examined in the Application Committee and therefore mentioned in its Report. This consideration in the broadest forum is more likely to stimulate public attention than any other means short of lodging a formal complaint or representation. The method has on occasion been used by workers' representatives, but never on a systematic basis. In the great majority of cases it is the governments themselves which come forward to repeat to the Conference what they had already explained to its Application Committee. In doing so they sometimes take issue with the Experts and Conference Committees' conclusions [2] or draw attention to recent events marking some progress in the application of a Convention.[3] Mostly they amplify their earlier statements in the Committee.

Despite the divergent views often expressed when the Application Committee's Report is discussed in the Conference, it is adopted without dissent as a rule. Only on rare occasions has a vote (by show of hands) had to be taken [4] and sometimes speakers simply indicated in the discussion that they would abstain.[5] Clearly, however, its consideration is no longer regarded as a mere formality but as an opportunity for airing issues. Even when these debates are focused not only on technical but also on political problems, they publicize the need for strict application of I.L.O. standards and further the purposes of supervision.

### VI. The Quest for Effectiveness

This chapter has attempted to chronicle the events which have shaped the I.L.O.'s supervision machinery and to portray the machinery in action. Due to the novelty of the system and to its steady expansion, a number of procedural, psychological and political problems have had to be faced.

---

[1] In 1961, for instance, half of the 22 speakers either ignored such issues or referred to them only in passing.

[2] For instance, the Liberian and United Arab Republic government representatives in 1960 (44 R.P. 444-445, 432-433) on the questions of forced labour and freedom of association respectively.

[3] In 1961, for example, a Chilean government representative informed the Conference that the Chamber of Deputies had just "approved the Bill to reintroduce freedom of association for agricultural workers' leaders" (45 R.P. 491) and a Belgian government representative took the floor to tell of the issuance, since the adoption of the Application Committee's Report, of an ordinance abrogating modifications in the application of the Forced Labour Convention, 1930 (No. 29), in Ruanda-Urundi (45 R.P. 502).

[4] For such a vote in 1958 cf. footnote 6, p. 46 above.

[5] In 1961, for instance, the Bulgarian, Czechoslovak, Polish, U.S.S.R. and Ukrainian government representatives, as well as the Czechoslovak workers' representative, stated that they could not vote for the Report.

These difficulties will be further explored in Chapters Four to Six below, but one preliminary conclusion is possible at this stage: the evolution of I.L.O. supervision has clearly been influenced by a concern to obtain tangible results.

The present chapter is therefore not merely historical and descriptive. It should also help to illustrate this underlying quest for effectiveness, as the whole procedure acquired a tradition and momentum of its own. Whether conscious and deliberate, or merely incidental and latent, this effort to maintain and increase the impact of supervision represents a significant new phenomenon of international organization.

If the I.L.O. has really been so intent, over the years, to strengthen and refine its standard-implementing procedures, then an inquiry into the actual record of performance may not only be of statistical interest but may even provide some indication whether it is realistic and rewarding to mobilize such a variety of resources for promoting compliance with treaty obligations.

# Chapter Two

# A CENSUS OF COMMITTEE OBSERVATIONS
# AND OF GOVERNMENTAL RESPONSE

Because I.L.O. supervision has operated on a continuous and repetitive basis it provides abundant documentation for measuring the extent of the response evoked by the comments of the Committee of Experts and the Conference Committee on the Application of Conventions and Recommendations. When these bodies have noted a divergency between the international and the pertinent national standards, they are able in subsequent years to ascertain whether progress has been made towards achieving conformity with the Convention concerned. A systematic survey of the Committee's findings should therefore provide evidence of the degree of effectiveness of past observations. To be valid, such a survey must be as comprehensive as possible. If the number of cases tabulated is sufficiently large, variations due to the time period, the Conventions or the countries covered by the inquiry are less likely to influence the overall results.

This requirement can be satisfied only through an attempt to include not just a limited proportion of the cases where international labour Conventions are currently in force but all the ratifications and declarations under which such binding obligations have been contracted for the metropolitan and non-metropolitan countries associated with the I.L.O. For the same reason, the survey should not be subject to any chronological limitations but should cover the whole period of operation of I.L.O. supervision. To guarantee moreover a maximum of clarity, the documentary evidence must be collected and presented in as systematic and uniform a manner as possible. It may be useful, therefore, to describe the method followed in compiling the results of the survey. Successive sections of this Chapter will deal with the documentation used, with the nature of Committee observations and of governmental response, with the continuity of supervision, and with the tabulation of the results.

## I. Documentation and Scope

The source material is based on the information supplied by governments in reply to the questions asked in the report forms and by the Experts and Conference Committees. Since these bodies initiate the supervisory process by drawing attention to the existence of shortcomings in the implementation of a Convention, evidence of any resulting action must also come from them and from the other authoritative source of information published by the I.L.O., the Summary of Reports placed before the International Labour Conference. Because I.L.O. supervision relies on publicity as the principal stimulus for action, the two Committees have to set forth their findings fully and clearly. These comments thus provide the most suitable basis of documentation for a study of this type. The fact that both the call for action and the evidence of any response to it come from the same source affords some guarantee of consistency in the approach and yardsticks used.

As the task of technical examination falls primarily and increasingly on the Committee of Experts, its Report constitutes the principal source of documentation. But when reports were received too late for examination by the Committee of Experts, lack of conformity or evidence of progress was sometimes discovered by the Conference Committee. Unfortunately neither Committee could be counted upon, especially in their earlier years, to take formal note without fail of all cases where they had found evidence of the elimination of discrepancies. In such cases the Summary of Reports may provide documentary confirmation of governmental action.

The terminal date of this study is the end of 1964. Between the establishment of the supervisory system and that year the Committee of Experts met on 34 occasions and the Conference Committee on 33. Due to the interruption of the procedure during World War II, the successive phases of technical and mutual examination did not function from 1939 until 1947, so that the documentation covers 31 years of full-scale supervision.[1] During this period the Committees examined reports on the application of the 100 odd Conventions which had entered into force before the end of 1963.

As indicated in the preceding chapter, the reports on the application of Conventions which have been declared applicable in a non-metropolitan country [2] are due in the same form and examined in the same way as reports covering a metropolitan country and so the present survey deals with both in exactly the same way. When the International Labour Conference concluded its 1964 session, a total of 2,919 ratifications and 1,297 declarations of application appeared on the I.L.O.'s registers.[3] Of these 4,216 formal undertakings, the Conventions included in the study account for 4,039. In some 600 cases, however, the ratification or declaration had not yet entered into force or the governments' first reports had not yet been examined by the terminal date of the survey. The total number of cases in respect of which I.L.O. supervision had actually functioned by then and which therefore form the basis of this study, stood at 3,420.[4] It should be possible to derive findings of more than limited validity from that large a number of international obligations which relate to practically all the metropolitan and non-metropolitan countries participating in the work of the International Labour Organization.[5]

---

[1] The Committee of Experts met in 1940 but its Report was not published since the Conference could not be convened that year. Both Committees met in 1945 and 1946 but did not make any individual comments on the application of Conventions.

[2] Without or with modifications.

[3] The figures, by Convention, are given in Appendix I.

[4] The total number of cases examined in respect of each Convention is indicated in Table 1.

[5] Cf. Appendix III.

By comparison, a survey of the effectiveness of observations, published by the Committee of Experts in 1954, covered 22 Conventions and 588 ratifications.[1] This pilot inquiry represented the first attempt to determine the results of observations on a systematic statistical basis and provided as such a methodological starting point for the present study. Although the Conference Committee voiced the hope, in commenting on the usefulness of the 1954 survey, that it would be "taken up again from time to time",[2] no further results have since become available.

## II. What Constitutes an Observation?

The first fact to be established is the existence of a statement by the supervisory bodies that all or some of the provisions of a ratified Convention are not complied with in a given country and that the government should, therefore, in the words of the I.L.O. Constitution, "take such action as may be necessary to make effective" these provisions. In many cases the terms of the Committee's remarks bring out unequivocally both the findings and the call for action.[3] In other cases however the position is not sufficiently clear from the start to enable the Committee to voice a definite opinion. Instead, it asks for additional information to determine whether there is conformity with the Convention.[4] If, on receipt of the requested data, it is found that conformity existed and no action had to be taken, the original comment must be classified as a mere demand for information. If, on the other hand, the additional data confirm that there is a divergency requiring removal, then the original comment constitutes an observation.

Although the Committee of Experts often acknowledges specifically that the reply to a request has removed doubts as to the degree of implementation,[5] it does not do so invariably, so that a mere request for information can only be distinguished from a genuine observation by ascertaining whether or not the matter was further pursued by the Committee in sub-

---

[1] 1954 R.C.E. 72-86.

[2] 37 R.P. 497.

[3] In 1955, for example, the Committee of Experts, in an observation regarding the Underground Work (Women) Convention, 1935 (No. 45), "notes from the report that there are no provisions in Hungarian legislation entirely prohibiting underground work in mines (for women) ... The Committee would be glad to learn what measures the government intends to take in order to ensure complete application of the Convention" (1955 R.C.E. 52).

[4] In 1948, for instance, an observation on the same Convention No. 45, addressed to Portugal, noted apparent inconsistencies in the information supplied and asked the government "to clarify the matter, and at the same time to indicate what steps have been taken to ensure the effective application of the Convention" (1948 R.C.E. 27).

[5] In 1954, for instance, an observation concerning the effect given to Convention No. 45 in Brazil "took note with satisfaction of the information supplied by the government which indicates that the national legislation strictly prohibits the employment of women for underground work in mines, regardless of whether the undertakings covered are private or public" (1954 R.C.E. 33). This followed comments made by the Committee on the matter in previous years.

sequent years.[1]   In the absence of any such follow-up it must be assumed that the Committee considered that no governmental action was necessary. As indicated in the preceding chapter, the Committee of Experts decided, as from 1958, not to include requests for information in its Report but to communicate them directly to the governments and to indicate simply in the Report that such a "direct request" had been made. The procedure to be followed in this survey is not affected by this change as it is still possible, by tracing the Committee's comments from one session to another, to ascertain whether the request for information has settled the matter[2] or whether it needs to be pursued further.   If, in the latter case, the request eventually leads to an observation, it is necessary, in recording the sequence of events chronologically, to indicate as the original date of the observation the year when the request for information set the supervisory process in motion.   Only in this way can due weight be given to the fact that the government had knowledge since that date of the Committee's doubts regarding compliance.

Unless and until an observation has appeared in print, no evidence of a divergency exists, because the contents of a direct request are not made public as a rule.   On the other hand matters originally raised in the form of an observation have not been disposed of, for the purposes of this survey, until any mention of them–explicit in an observation or implicitly in a direct request–has disappeared from the Committee's Report for a minimum of two years.

It may also happen that an observation has been initiated and then abandoned by the supervisory bodies.   One reason for such a reversal may be that the information on which the observation was originally based turned out to be inaccurate.[3]   Another possible reason why an observation was expressly or tacitly dropped is a reassessment of the position by the Committee of Experts following a lengthy interruption in the process of reporting and examination.[4]

---

[1] Thus the Committee of Experts did not make any further comment regarding the effect given to Convention No. 45 in Portugal, following the observation quoted above.

[2] The existence of a direct request does not permit any conclusions to be drawn one way or the other.   The Committee of Experts emphasized in 1960 that such requests "do not necessarily in all cases imply any doubt on the part of the Committee in regard to the extent of conformity with the ratified Convention.   Some of these communications to governments consist, for example, ... of acknowledgments of information previously requested by the Committee and now supplied by the governments concerned" (1960 R.C.E. 6).

[3] For instance in 1937 the Committee of Experts, noting from Bulgaria's first report that a bill to give effect to the Marking of Weights (Packages Transported by Vessels) Convention, 1929 (No. 27) had been submitted to the competent authorities, expressed the hope that "the government will lose no more time in taking steps for its full application" (1937 R.C.E. 15).   As the government's next report confirmed however that the necessary legislation had already been adopted in 1935 (1938 S.R. 210), the Committee of Experts made no further reference to the matter.

[4] This set of circumstances is especially likely to arise after the eight-year break in the continuity of supervision, caused by World War II, or when a country resumes participation in the I.L.O. following a prolonged period of absence (Spain and Rumania, for instance, withdrew in 1941 and 1942 respectively and did not return until 1956).

Since the supervisory bodies do not hesitate to raise the same matter again and again until the action they call for has been taken, observations which have disappeared under circumstances like those just described have no place in the present survey. The criterion for including an observation thus resides in the fact that it involves points of substance which have either been settled or which, in the absence of such action, continued to be actively pursued by the Committee until the year 1964. For want of a better term, both these categories will be referred to as "operative observations".

Any definition of what constitutes an observation, for the purpose of this survey, must also take into account the fact that the primary emphasis in the work of supervision has been on the achievement of legislative conformity. While the Committee of Experts has often stressed that it must concern itself with the implementation of I.L.O. standards not only in law but also in every-day practice, efforts to supervise and promote the "practical application" of ratified Conventions differ basically from those aiming at compliance in law.[1] In particular, the evidence available on actual breaches of national laws and regulations is neither clear-cut nor copious, so that an attempt to take account of all observations dealing with practical application could not be based on the kind of precise criteria essential to the present study.[2] Only in the case of Conventions dealing with administrative machinery, such as labour inspection or the employment service, will observations on compliance both in law and in practice form a useful basis for assessing the effectiveness of I.L.O. supervision.

In deciding on the observations to be included in the survey, it must also be remembered that the two Committees do not limit their comments to obvious and serious infringements of ratified standards but raise and pursue every point of non-compliance which comes to their attention until the necessary action has been noted. This inherent strictness of I.L.O. supervision [3] makes it all the more important to follow a similarly consistent and consequential approach in tabulating its results.

### III. Governmental Action in Response to an Observation

Once the existence of an operative observation has been established, the next step is to determine whether and what action has been taken in response to it by the government concerned. Evidence should be available in the comments made by the Committees in subsequent years. If no measures have been adopted to bring about conformity, these comments will consist

---

[1] Cf. pp. 155-159 below.

[2] For instance, in 1957 the Committee of Experts referred to allegations by the Greek General Confederation of Labour concerning violations of Convention No. 45 (1957 R.C.E. 63). The following year the Committee noted "with interest that ... measures have been taken to confirm that the Convention is strictly applied and that reports so far received (by the government) from local inspection offices indicate that no contraventions of the relevant legislation have been discovered" (1958 R.C.E. 43). This observation has not been included in the survey.

[3] Professor Haas emphasizes that the Committee of Experts' "criteria are admittedly very stringent" (*Beyond the Nation-State, op. cit.*, p. 372).

of a call on the government to fulfil its international obligations. With the passage of time such an appeal is likely to become increasingly urgent. If action has been taken, the Committee of Experts usually expresses its appreciation of the progress achieved. However, a mere statement of this kind does not warrant a finding that the supervision procedure has met with success. Such a finding should be based on a clear link of cause and effect, i.e. the Committees must previously have mentioned the divergency and asked for its removal.[1] The absence of such a sequence of events prevents inclusion of the case in the survey.[2]

Although the Committee of Experts usually welcomes "with satisfaction" action in response to an observation, it cannot be relied upon to do so in all cases. In the early years, in particular, the Expert or the Conference Committees' Report did not always take express notice of such a development. But there should be other indices for determining whether a breach has in fact disappeared. Most useful among these is a reference by the government to measures it has taken in accordance with the Convention, as reproduced in the Summary of Reports. While such a unilateral affirmation would not, by itself, suffice to prove that progress has in fact occurred, a reasonably conclusive finding is warranted if the Committee of Experts fails to raise the point again in subsequent years. The sequence of observation, governmental action reported in the Summary and absence of further observations, should afford circumstantial evidence in the relatively rare cases of this kind that the desired result has been obtained even if the supervisory organs have not expressly acknowledged this fact.[3]

The absence of further supervisory comment can also provide a clue whether the measures taken in response to a previous observation were deemed by the Committees to have led to full compliance or whether additional action is needed. The distinction is an important one: if an observa-

---

[1] Referring, for example, to the observation to Hungary quoted in footnote 3, p. 55 above, the Committee of Experts noted, in 1963, "with satisfaction that Decree No. 4 of 5 April 1962 of the Minister of Labour, regarding the protection of life and health of women and young persons, prohibits underground work of women in mines, as laid down in article 2 of the Convention" (1963 R.C.E. 75).

[2] Such cases may arise when it is the government rather than the Committee of Experts which discovers the divergency and acts on it. The effect of supervision is therefore a latent one at best. Examples of this type of situation include the removal of a penal clause in Mauritius (1955 R.C.E. 95) and of exceptions to the prohibition on night work by women in Gabon (1963 R.C.E. 72).

[3] A case in point is the application by Belgium of the Workmen's Compensation (Accidents) Convention, 1925 (No. 17). In 1929 and 1930 the Committee of Experts had urged the government to bring its legislation into conformity with this instrument (1929 R.C.E. 523 and 1930 R.C.E. 614). The government reported in 1931 that "Belgian legislation concerning workmen's compensation for accidents has been brought completely into agreement with the Convention by the Acts of 15 May 1929, and 18 June 1930" (1932 S.R. 258). There were no further comments by the supervisory bodies concerning the legislation and the survey indicates that due action had been taken. Similarly, in 1930, the Conference Committee observed that "Cuba has not yet fulfilled the obligations involved in its ratification" of a number of Conventions (14 R.P. 641). After reiterated appeals to the government, legislation was adopted, as reported in the Summary in 1935. The Committee of Experts continued to comment on the application of several of these Conventions. In those cases where no such observations were made before and shortly after the war, the survey classifies the observation of 1930 as acted upon.

tion noting progress indicates that there remain other divergencies requiring removal, this is classified in the survey as "action in part" and it must be ascertained whether "action in full" was observed at a later stage. In all such cases the survey must differentiate clearly between the concepts of full and partial action.

It can be considered that full action has been taken only if, as indicated above, acknowledgment of the progress made is not combined with a statement that further measures are required to eliminate all remaining divergencies. The call for additional progress may be contained in the observation itself.[1] But even when the observation is silent on this point, the existence of a simultaneous direct request gives reason to believe that the Committee of Experts is not yet entirely convinced of the existence of full conformity. Whenever the Committee combines an observation with a direct request, the survey therefore classifies a case of this kind as partial compliance.[2] A similarly cautious policy of classification is followed when full action has been reported by a government to the Conference Committee without the Committee of Experts having as yet had an opportunity to review the position. Here also the matter will presumably be further evaluated on receipt of the government's next report.

### IV. Continuity of Observations

In tracing the effect of an observation through the years, it is important not to lose the thread of the supervisory process even if interruptions occur. Such breaks may have been due to the war, to the withdrawal of a member State from the I.L.O. or to the achievement of independence by a non-metropolitan country. How does the survey take account of developments of this kind?

The suspension of the regular supervision procedure from 1939 until 1947 may have led to the discontinuation of certain observations. The upheavals which occurred during this period in the legal and constitutional structures of many countries help to explain why some previous comments no longer had any relevance to post-war conditions. At the same time, changed circumstances often gave rise to observations on entirely new points. Although there was never any doubt that hostilities did not interrupt the validity in law of ratified Conventions,[3] the fabric of the corresponding national standards had often been seriously disrupted, govern-

---

[1] In 1950, for instance, the Committee of Experts welcomed the adoption by Switzerland of provisions on hoisting appliances which resulted in fuller compliance with the Safety Provisions (Building) Convention, 1937 (No. 62). It observed at the same time that additional regulations on the matter were envisaged (1950 R.C.E. 33). This was classified as action in part and full action was noted two years later.

[2] This was done, for instance, in the case of the observation to Hungary on Convention No. 45 when the observation noting the adoption of a new decree was coupled with a direct request (1963 R.C.E. 76).

[3] The Committee of Experts stressed at its first post-war meeting that there could be no question as to "the continuance and survival after the end of a war of the legal obligations of the contracting parties arising from the ratification of Conventions" (1945 R.C.E. 5). Difficulties encountered in the application of Conventions in time of war will be discussed in a later chapter (cf. pp. 148-149).

mental archives destroyed and administrative services disorganized. Nonetheless, in a surprising number of cases, observations made before the war could be taken up again, not only for the countries of the American continent but even for European States. The survey has attempted, therefore, to pursue the thread of supervision whenever the Committees' comments provide sufficient evidence for bridging the gap.[1]

The continuity of supervision is jeopardized most seriously when a country withdraws from the Organization. While the obligations of ratified Conventions are deemed to continue unimpaired,[2] the absence of reports for a prolonged period effectively nullifies the process of supervision. Germany, Japan, Spain and Rumania remained outside the I.L.O. for some ten to fifteen years; when these countries rejoined the Organization, recognized that they remained bound by Conventions previously ratified and resumed reporting, the Committee of Experts felt it necessary to examine their reports with special care.[3] Although, in the case of Nicaragua, the period of absence was even longer (1938-1957), the interruption proved to be less absolute because the government not only recognized formally at the time of its withdrawal that it remained bound by the Conventions it had ratified in 1934[4] but it also resumed reporting on their application several years before it rejoined.[5]

When, in the circumstances just mentioned, the supervisory organs have been unable to scrutinize a given country's reports for a considerable period, the Committee attempts first of all to ascertain whether some pattern of continuity can be discerned. If this is not the case, the resumed cycles of reporting and examination may bring to light divergencies entirely different from those pending or eliminated during the previous membership period.[6] It is thus possible that two totally unrelated observations

---

[1] In 1947, of the six observations made by the Committee of Experts on the Seamen's Articles of Agreement Convention, 1926 (No. 22), for instance, four (Canada, India, Mexico, New Zealand) refer back to observations made in 1939 (1947 R.C.E. 19).

[2] The pre-war doctrine that withdrawal affects neither the obligations of a ratified Convention nor the constitutional obligation to report on its application (cf. 82 G.B. (Private) 19-22) was subsequently spelled out in article 1, paragraph 5, of the Constitution as revised in 1945, which provides that withdrawal does not "affect the continued validity for the period provided for in the Convention of all the obligations arising thereunder or relating thereto". Cf. also *The International Labour Code, 1951, op. cit.*, pp. XCVII-XCVIII.

[3] When the Federal Republic of Germany became an I.L.O. member in 1951 it declared itself formally bound by the 17 Conventions originally ratified by the German Reich (XXXIV O.B. 168). The Committee of Experts set up a special subcommittee in 1953 to examine the first post-war reports received from the Federal Republic and from Japan which had also returned in 1951 (1953 R.C.E. 5, 44-45).

[4] Cf. XXIII O.B. 126.

[5] The reports supplied by Nicaragua in 1955 and subsequently, indicated in fact a measure of progress over the position existing before 1938 (1955 R.C.E. 19).

[6] In 1934, for instance, an observation to Rumania had welcomed the fact that "the new unified social insurance legislation (Act of 8 April 1933) has put an end to the divergencies noted in previous years with regard to the benefits" prescribed by the Maternity Protection Convention, 1919 (No. 3) (1934 R.C E. 225). In 1956, on the other hand, after Rumania rejoined the I.L.O., the Committee of Experts drew attention to divergencies between the same Convention and the Labour Code adopted in 1950 (1956 R.C.E. 25).

have to be recorded in the survey in regard to the same formal undertaking. If there is no apparent link between the two series of observations, they will be listed and followed up separately. A similar situation arises even when there has been no break in the continuity of supervision but when newly adopted legislation is found, on examination, to be incompatible with a ratified Convention.[1] In such an eventuality also, two separate series of observations are tabulated in relation to the same ratification.

## V. Continuation of Observations Concerning a Non-Metropolitan Country, after its Independence

Fortunately, the problems of continuity just described seldom arise when a non-metropolitan territory achieves independence and becomes an I.L.O. member in its own right. Whenever such a country confirms the obligations under ratified Conventions previously declared applicable, the process of reporting and supervision can continue without interruption.[2] The governmental authorities to which observations had hitherto been addressed will have changed, but the Committee of Experts is able to follow up on points previously raised, as well as to ascertain that the change of sovereignty does not involve any modification in the degree of compliance with binding obligations.

The survey is designed to reflect these various contingencies in as clear and logical a manner as possible, and the absence of any differentiation in the method of supervision used for metropolitan and non-metropolitan countries facilitates this task. Depending on whether action on an observation took place before or after the change of international status, the survey lists it in the non-metropolitan or metropolitan sections provided for under the various Conventions.[3]

---

[1] In 1952, for instance, the Committee of Experts had noted that a divergency raised in 1939, and again from 1947 onward, regarding the implementation by New Zealand of the Workmen's Compensation (Accidents) Convention, 1925 (No. 17), had been eliminated (1952 R.C.E. 22). But in 1958 the Committee observed that an act adopted in 1956 gave rise to entirely different divergencies (1958 R.C.E. 26).

[2] Cf. p. 15 above. In a few cases formal obligations have lapsed because the terms of the Conventions concerned are limited to non-metropolitan territories, so that they cannot be ratified by independent States (e.g. Nos. 84 and 85).

[3] In 1954, for instance, the Committee of Experts noted that an Act of December 1952 had led to the more satisfactory application of the Forced Labour Convention, 1930 (No. 29) in the French Overseas Territories (1954 R.C.E. 51). The survey carries this observation under *France*–non-metropolitan countries. In 1962, on the other hand, the Committee of Experts noted the elimination by the Congo (Leopoldville) of certain compulsory porterage provisions (1962 R.C.E. 54), to which it had taken exception for a number of years when the relevant Convention, No. 29, was in force in the Belgian Congo. The observation is therefore listed in the metropolitan section of the survey of Convention No. 29.

In two instances, non-metropolitan countries where action was taken in response to observations subsequently changed their status, but did not become members of the I.L.O.: Western Samoa achieved independence and Western New Guinea passed under Indonesian administration. In these cases, as in those mentioned earlier, a chronological criterion is applied and the survey carries the observations under the countries responsible at the time for the international relations of the territories concerned.

## VI. Observations Leading to Denunciations

When governments despair of eliminating breaches of binding international standards, they sometimes decide that the only solution is to denounce a Convention. Cases of this kind, though rare, require inclusion in the survey because they are the direct consequence of supervisory pressure. As denunciation terminates the relevant international obligations, there no longer exists any formal violation of the obligations. Even such an essentially negative development must therefore be taken into account when tracing the effect of supervision on governmental action.

Two types of denunciations can be distinguished, depending on whether obligations under a revised Convention have been assumed to replace those which have lapsed. If in the former case the revised Convention is applied in full this represents in fact over-all progress because conformity has been achieved.[1] If on the other hand no corresponding new obligations are assumed, this represents a net loss which both the governments and the Committee of Experts envisage with obvious reluctance.[2] Cases may also occur where the government has taken partial action only to consider, in the end, that it is unable to achieve full compliance.[3] Although references to such partial action are included here, these cases must be classified as "denunciations" since there is no hope of action in part being eventually followed by full conformity.

## VII. Tabulation of Findings

The observations made by the two Committees during their three decades of full operation have been examined and tabulated according to the method and criteria described above. Appendix II contains the findings of this survey for each Convention, arranged under six consecutive headings. The first two columns indicate the country and the year in which the Convention entered into force there. The list of metropolitan countries is followed by that of the non-metropolitan territories, grouped in turn under the country responsible for their international relations.

The next two columns indicate the initial observations and, as appropriate, direct requests in which the Committees first drew the governments' attention to the existence of divergencies and the need for eliminating them. If a second series of observations has been initiated it is listed after the first. The last two columns indicate whether any measures have been taken on these operative observations, in order to bring about fuller con-

---

[1] Yugoslavia's ratification of Convention No. 90 in 1956, concurrent with its denunciation of No. 6, is an example of this contingency.

[2] Cf. pp. 97-98 below. When New Zealand denounced Convention No. 60 in 1961, e.g., the government stated that "it will consider the question of becoming a party to the Convention at a later date, if it is able at that stage to bring its legislation to the appropriate standard" (1962 R.C.E. 71).

[3] The same New Zealand denunciation of Convention No. 60 provides a case in point. Two years earlier the Committee of Experts had been able to note some progress (1959 R.C.E. 40). There are similar cases, involving Conventions Nos. 3 (Brazil, Uruguay), 6 (Uruguay, Yugoslavia) and 41 (Greece).

formity. Observations noting action in part are arranged in consecutive chronological order, one below the other. Observations noting action in full appear in the final column on the same line as the last corresponding observation or request. This last column is also used to indicate cases where an observation has led to the Convention's being denounced.

It was necessary to eliminate from the final tabulation such double counting between Conventions or countries as might have tended to lead to inflated totals.[1] Similarly, a proliferation of cases must be avoided when certain large colonial territories are subsequently divided into separate, independent units [2] or where the legislation and observations for a group of territories are identical.[3]

## VIII. Summary of Results

Table 1 contains the findings for each Convention covered and for the survey as a whole. The results are arranged so that the first five columns indicate the number of formal undertakings (ratifications and declarations) on whose application reports have been received and the extent to which the supervisory organs have found it necessary to make operative comments on these reports. Cases where, as explained above, two series of observations have been made, are listed in a separate column. The last five columns indicate the effect which these observations have had on the application of the Conventions. This effect is tabulated under successive headings denoting the degree of impact, which can range from full action to total inaction. Cases where full conformity was achieved in one or in several steps are listed in separate columns. Because the results achieved by a second series of observations are tabulated separately, the total of observations surveyed exceeds the number of ratifications and declarations on which operative comments have been made.

Table 1 shows that in 1964, after some three decades of I.L.O. supervision, the Committee of Experts and the Conference Committee on the Application of Conventions and Recommendations had examined the effect given to formal international undertakings arising out of a total of

---

[1] For instance, countries bound by both the original Workmen's Compensation (Occupational Diseases) Convention, 1925 (No. 18) and the revised Convention of 1934 (No. 42) may have received identical observations for one and the other instrument because in respect of certain diseases the obligations are identical for both. In such cases the tabulation simply disregards the earlier Convention.

[2] Thus the former colony of French West Africa (A.O.F.) has now evolved into eight independent States and French Equatorial Africa (A.E.F.) into four. When dealing with observations in respect of these territories, the determining factor is the date at which the resulting action was taken. If the original colony was still in existence at that time, a single case is counted; if the measures were adopted subsequently by one of the successor States, acting on its own, this also counts as a separate case. The Explanatory Note to Appendix II below indicates the cases where the achievement of independence has involved the emergence of separate new States, the combination of former territories or a change in the name of a country.

[3] This is the case for the four Overseas Departments of France (French Guiana, Guadaloupe, Martinique and Reunion) where the metropolitan legislation is usually applicable but separate declarations of application have been communicated for each territory.

*Table 1*

OBSERVATIONS MADE AND ACTION TAKEN IN RESPONSE,
TABULATED BY CONVENTIONS

(as at 30 June 1964)

| Convention No. | Formal Undertakings Covered | No Operative Observations | First Series of Observations | Second Series of Observations | Action Taken | | | Denunciations | No Action Taken |
|---|---|---|---|---|---|---|---|---|---|
| | | | | | in Full | in Part, then in Full | in Part | | |
| 1 | 27 | 10 | 17 | 3 | 4 | 1 | 11 | — | 4 |
| 2 | 45 | 30 | 15 | 1 | 4 | 2 | 5 | 2 | 3 |
| 3 | 25 | 5 | 20 | 6 | 3 | — | 14 | 2 | 7 |
| 4 | 60 | 35 | 25 | 1 | 10 | 1 | 1 | 7 | 7 |
| 5 | 81 | 60 | 21 | 1 | 10 | 1 | 3 | 1 | 7 |
| 6 | 61 | 29 | 32 | 5 | 17 | 3 | 7 | 3 | 7 |
| 7 | 57 | 46 | 11 | — | 6 | — | 1 | 1 | 3 |
| 8 | 51 | 35 | 16 | 3 | 12 | 1 | 1 | — | 5 |
| 9 | 28 | 19 | 9 | 1 | 3 | — | 4 | — | 3 |
| 10 | 41 | 38 | 3 | — | 2 | — | 1 | — | — |
| 11 | 112 | 97 | 15 | — | 2 | — | 1 | — | 12 |
| 12 | 88 | 85 | 3 | 1 | 1 | — | 1 | — | 2 |
| 13 | 52 | 23 | 29 | 2 | 13 | 3 | 6 | — | 9 |
| 14 | 75 | 59 | 16 | 1 | 5 | 1 | 4 | — | 7 |
| 15 | 54 | 37 | 17 | 1 | 9 | 3 | 1 | — | 5 |
| 16 | 56 | 41 | 15 | 1 | 10 | — | 2 | — | 4 |
| 17 | 52 | 33 | 19 | 2 | 7 | 2 | 8 | — | 4 |
| 18 | 55 | 41 | 14 | 1 | 4 | — | 7 | — | 4 |
| 19 | 84 | 65 | 19 | 3 | 14 | 1 | 3 | — | 4 |
| 20 | 13 | 3 | 10 | 1 | 5 | — | 2 | 1 | 3 |
| 21 | 31 | 30 | 1 | — | — | — | — | — | 1 |
| 22 | 42 | 26 | 16 | — | 5 | — | 6 | — | 5 |
| 23 | 22 | 13 | 9 | — | 5 | — | 1 | — | 3 |
| 24 | 23 | 10 | 13 | 1 | 3 | — | 7 | — | 4 |
| 25 | 19 | 9 | 10 | — | 2 | — | 6 | — | 2 |
| 26 | 88 | 75 | 13 | 2 | 4 | 1 | 4 | — | 6 |
| 27 | 49 | 35 | 14 | 3 | 10 | — | 4 | — | 3 |
| 28 | 4 | 2 | 2 | — | 1 | — | — | — | 1 |
| 29 | 147 | 101 | 46 | 2 | 6 | 4 | 22 | — | 16 |
| 30 | 18 | 11 | 7 | 1 | 2 | — | 3 | — | 3 |
| 32 | 25 | 10 | 15 | 1 | 4 | — | 7 | — | 5 |
| 33 | 29 | 17 | 12 | — | 6 | 1 | 3 | 1 | 1 |
| 34 | 10 | 7 | 3 | — | 1 | — | 1 | — | 1 |
| 35 | 12 | 8 | 4 | — | — | — | 2 | — | 2 |
| 36 | 11 | 8 | 3 | — | — | — | 1 | — | 2 |
| 37 | 11 | 8 | 3 | — | — | — | 2 | — | 1 |
| 38 | 10 | 9 | 1 | — | — | — | 1 | — | — |
| 39 | 9 | 7 | 2 | — | — | — | 2 | — | — |
| 40 | 8 | 7 | 1 | — | — | — | 1 | — | — |
| 41 | 43 | 33 | 10 | — | 3 | 1 | — | 1 | 5 |
| 42 | 48 | 24 | 24 | 1 | 3 | 3 | 9 | — | 10 |
| 43 | 9 | 3 | 6 | — | 1 | — | — | 1 | 4 |
| 44 | 13 | 11 | 2 | — | — | — | 1 | — | 1 |
| 45 | 84 | 73 | 11 | — | 4 | — | 3 | — | 4 |
| 47 | 4 | 4 | — | — | — | — | — | — | — |
| 48 | 7 | 3 | 4 | — | — | — | 2 | — | 2 |
| 49 | 7 | 3 | 4 | — | 1 | — | — | — | 3 |
| 50 | 55 | 45 | 10 | — | 4 | — | 2 | — | 4 |

| Convention No. | Formal Undertakings Covered | No Operative Observations | First Series of Observations | Second Series of Observations | Action Taken | | | Denunciations | No Action Taken |
|---|---|---|---|---|---|---|---|---|---|
| | | | | | in Full | in Part, then in Full | in Part | | |
| 52 | 35 | 15 | 20 | — | 3 | 2 | 8 | — | 7 |
| 53 | 24 | 22 | 2 | — | — | 1 | — | — | 1 |
| 55 | 13 | 11 | 2 | — | 1 | — | 1 | — | — |
| 56 | 12 | 12 | — | — | — | — | — | — | — |
| 58 | 36 | 31 | 5 | — | 3 | — | — | — | 2 |
| 59 | 16 | 8 | 8 | — | 2 | 1 | 2 | — | 3 |
| 60 | 9 | 3 | 6 | — | — | 1 | 3 | 1 | 1 |
| 62 | 19 | 9 | 10 | — | 1 | 1 | 5 | — | 3 |
| 63 | 29 | 16 | 13 | 1 | — | 5 | 7 | — | 2 |
| 64 | 50 | 41 | 9 | — | 1 | 1 | 3 | — | 4 |
| 65 | 50 | 33 | 17 | — | 9 | 2 | 6 | — | — |
| 67 | 2 | — | 2 | — | — | — | — | — | 2 |
| 68 | 14 | 12 | 2 | — | — | — | 1 | — | 1 |
| 69 | 18 | 12 | 6 | — | 1 | 4 | — | — | 1 |
| 71 | 10 | 10 | — | — | — | — | — | — | — |
| 73 | 16 | 7 | 9 | — | 6 | 1 | — | — | 2 |
| 74 | 21 | 18 | 3 | — | — | 1 | 2 | — | — |
| 77 | 19 | 9 | 10 | — | 1 | — | 2 | — | 7 |
| 78 | 18 | 7 | 11 | — | — | — | 5 | — | 6 |
| 79 | 13 | 6 | 7 | — | — | — | 4 | — | 3 |
| 81 | 69 | 36 | 33 | — | 4 | 1 | 11 | — | 17 |
| 82 | 43 | 30 | 13 | — | 2 | — | 5 | — | 6 |
| 84 | 41 | 36 | 5 | — | 1 | — | 2 | — | 2 |
| 85 | 36 | 24 | 12 | — | 1 | 1 | 2 | — | 8 |
| 86 | 42 | 36 | 6 | — | 3 | — | — | — | 3 |
| 87 | 85 | 57 | 28 | — | 2 | — | 6 | — | 20 |
| 88 | 49 | 34 | 15 | — | 1 | — | 5 | 1 | 8 |
| 89 | 35 | 18 | 17 | — | 5 | — | 4 | — | 8 |
| 90 | 25 | 9 | 16 | — | 1 | 1 | 4 | — | 10 |
| 92 | 16 | 12 | 4 | — | — | — | 2 | — | 2 |
| 94 | 61 | 40 | 21 | — | 4 | — | 9 | — | 8 |
| 95 | 83 | 68 | 15 | — | — | — | 5 | — | 10 |
| 96 | 26 | 17 | 9 | — | 2 | — | 1 | — | 6 |
| 97 | 37 | 35 | 2 | — | — | — | — | — | 2 |
| 98 | 79 | 62 | 17 | — | 1 | — | 5 | — | 11 |
| 99 | 26 | 26 | — | — | — | — | — | — | — |
| 100 | 36 | 32 | 4 | — | — | — | 2 | — | 2 |
| 101 | 35 | 28 | 7 | — | 3 | — | 1 | — | 3 |
| 102 | 12 | 7 | 5 | — | — | — | 3 | — | 2 |
| 103 | 7 | 5 | 2 | — | — | — | 2 | — | — |
| 104 | 9 | 9 | — | — | — | — | — | — | — |
| 105 | 100 | 90 | 10 | — | — | — | 6 | — | 4 |
| 106 | 19 | 18 | 1 | — | — | — | — | — | 1 |
| 107 | 12 | 12 | — | — | — | — | — | — | — |
| 108 | 4 | 4 | — | — | — | — | — | — | — |
| 110 | 3 | 3 | — | — | — | — | — | — | — |
| 111 | 34 | 33 | 1 | — | — | — | — | — | 1 |
| 112 | 8 | 8 | — | — | — | — | — | — | — |
| 113 | 5 | 5 | — | — | — | — | — | — | — |
| 114 | 3 | 3 | — | — | — | — | — | — | — |
| 115 | 3 | 3 | — | — | — | — | — | — | — |
| Total | 3,422 | 2,465 | 957 | 46 | 264 | 54 | 294 | 22 | 369 |

3,422 ratifications and declarations. In 2,465 or 72 per cent of these cases no operative observations have been made by the Committees regarding compliance with these obligations.

In the remaining 957 cases operative observations have been made, including 46 cases where a second, separate series of comments was initiated. The survey thus covers a total of 1,003 observations which have had the following results:

|  | Cases | Per cent |
|---|---|---|
| Full action taken in one step . . . . . . . . . . | 264 | 26.3 |
| Full action taken in several steps . . . . . . . | 54 | 5.4 |
| Partial action taken . . . . . . . . . . . . . | 294 | 29.3 |
| Ratification denounced . . . . . . . . . . . . | 22 | 2.2 |
| No action taken as yet . . . . . . . . . . . | 369 | 36.8 |

To sum up these findings, 32 per cent of the observations have led to full action, either directly or by stages, 29 per cent have been followed by partial action, 2 per cent have merely led to denunciations, while in the remaining 37 per cent the observations have not yet had any effect apparent at this time. An analysis of these findings will be attempted in the next chapter.

CHAPTER THREE

# ANALYSIS OF THE RESULTS

If the results of the survey are only set out by Conventions, as in the preceding chapter, this does not give a full picture of the impact of I.L.O. supervision. A further examination of the findings is possible on the basis of Appendix II, which indicates the countries involved as well as the successive phases of the supervisory process in each of the 1,000 cases. When a sample of this size is subjected to additional analysis, such tabulations can be carried to considerable lengths. Yet the resulting figures, however detailed and revealing, would not in themselves provide a sufficiently clear idea of the working and impact of supervision. An attempt is therefore made in the Chapters Four and Five to supplement quantitative with qualitative analysis by illustrating the types of difficulties which may prevent governments from eliminating the breaches discovered by the supervisory organs of the I.L.O.

The primary purpose of the present chapter is to assess to what extent the results so far recorded tend to vary according to the types of Conventions concerned and according to the countries and regions involved. It may also be interesting to discover in a general way how much time was required before governments took action or, in the absence of any response, for how long the various observations have remained without effect. Finally, some reference must be made to the relative seriousness of the cases examined.

## I. Results by Groups of Conventions

A glance at Table 1 indicates how considerably the results vary between Conventions and how the observations on certain instruments have been more successful than those on others. As this may be due in some cases to differences in the period of time over which the application of a given Convention has been the subject of international supervision, the tabulation of results by groups of Conventions is likely to yield more useful results. This classification is facilitated by the natural categories into which the various instruments fall when arranged according to their subject-matter.[1]

The results of this tabulation will be found in Table 2. Aside from the Conventions concerning non-discrimination, migrant workers and social policy, the total number of cases examined in each group (from 130 to 510) and the number of observations made (from 42 to 136) appear sufficiently large to permit reasonably general conclusions, especially when expressed in the form of percentages, as is done in Table 3.

---

[1] Cf. the groups enumerated on p. 13 above.

The degree of effectiveness of international supervision may also be brought more sharply into focus if it can be ascertained to what extent there was in fact a need for such supervision. It might be of interest, in other words, to discover in what proportion of the cases examined no breaches had been noted by the supervisory organs. This proportion can be calculated for each group of Conventions by using a scale ranging from a maximum of 1.00 (if no observation was ever made) to a minimum of .00 (if there was lack of compliance for all the cases examined). The resulting figure is called the "conformity score" because it permits comparisons based on the extent to which conformity has obviated the need for supervisory criticism.

*Table 2*

TOTAL RESULTS, TABULATED BY GROUPS OF CONVENTIONS

(as at 30 June 1964)

| Groups | Formal Undertakings Covered | No Operative Observations | First Series of Observations | Second Series of Observations | Action in Full | Action in Part | Denunciations | No Action Taken |
|---|---|---|---|---|---|---|---|---|
| Employment Service (Nos. 2, 34, 88, 96) . . . . . . . . . . | 130 | 88 | 42 | 1 | 10 | 12 | 3 | 18 |
| Wages (Nos. 26, 94, 95, 99) . . . | 258 | 209 | 49 | 2 | 9 | 18 | — | 24 |
| Hours of Work (Nos. 1, 14, 20, 30, 43, 47, 49, 52, 67, 101, 106) | 244 | 154 | 90 | 6 | 28 | 29 | 2 | 37 |
| Children and Young Persons (Nos. 5, 6, 10, 33, 59, 60, 77, 78, 79, 90) . . . . . . . . . . . | 312 | 186 | 126 | 6 | 47 | 34 | 6 | 45 |
| Women Workers (Nos. 3, 4, 41, 45, 89, 103) . . . . . . . . | 254 | 169 | 85 | 7 | 27 | 24 | 10 | 31 |
| Occupational Safety & Hygiene (Nos. 13, 27, 28, 32, 62, 115) . | 152 | 82 | 70 | 6 | 33 | 22 | — | 21 |
| Social Security (Nos. 12, 17, 18, 19, 24, 25, 35, 36, 37, 38, 39, 40, 42, 44, 48, 102) . . . . . . . | 462 | 335 | 127 | 9 | 42 | 54 | — | 40 |
| Freedom of Association (Nos. 11, 84, 87, 98) . . . . . . . . . | 317 | 252 | 65 | — | 6 | 14 | — | 45 |
| Employment at Sea (Nos. 7, 8, 9, 15, 16, 22, 23, 53, 55, 56, 58, 68, 69, 71, 73, 74, 92, 108, 112, 113, 114) . . . . . . . . . . . . | 510 | 384 | 126 | 6 | 72 | 22 | 1 | 37 |
| Abolition of Forced Labour (Nos. 29, 105) . . . . . . . . . . | 247 | 191 | 56 | 2 | 10 | 27 | — | 21 |
| Non-Discrimination (Nos. 100, 111) . . . . . . . . . . . . | 70 | 65 | 5 | — | — | 2 | — | 3 |
| Migrant Workers (Nos. 21, 97) . | 68 | 65 | 3 | — | — | — | — | 3 |
| Indigenous and Plantation Workers (Nos. 50, 64, 65, 86, 104, 107, 110) . . . . . . . . . . | 221 | 179 | 42 | — | 20 | 11 | — | 11 |
| Labour Administration (Nos. 63, 81, 85) . . . . . . . . . . . | 134 | 76 | 58 | 1 | 12 | 20 | — | 27 |
| Social Policy (No. 82) . . . . . | 43 | 30 | 13 | — | 2 | 5 | — | 6 |
| All Groups . . . . . . . . . . | 3,422 | 2,465 | 957 | 46 | 318 | 294 | 22 | 369 |

*Table 3*

COMPARATIVE TABLE, ARRANGED BY GROUPS OF CONVENTIONS

(as at 30 June 1964)

|  | *Need for Observations* | | | *Results of Observations* | | | |
| Groups | Formal Undertakings Covered | No Operative Observations | Conformity Score | Action in Full | Action in Part | Denuncia- tions | No Action Taken |
|  |  |  |  | (in percentages) | | | |
| All Groups . . . . . . . . . . . . | 3,422 | 2,465 | .72 | 32 | 29 | 2 | 37 |
| Indigenous & Plantation Workers . . | 221 | 179 | .81 | 48 | 26 | — | 26 |
| Employment at Sea . . . . . . . . | 510 | 384 | .71 | 54 | 17 | 1 | 28 |
| Occupational Safety and Hygiene . . | 152 | 82 | .54 | 43 | 29 | — | 28 |
| Social Security . . . . . . . . . . | 462 | 334 | .72 | 31 | 40 | — | 29 |
| Children & Young Persons . . . . . | 312 | 186 | .60 | 36 | 26 | 4 | 34 |
| Women Workers . . . . . . . . | 254 | 169 | .67 | 29 | 26 | 11 | 34 |
| Abolition of Forced Labour . . . . | 247 | 191 | .77 | 17 | 47 | — | 36 |
| Hours of Work . . . . . . . . . . | 244 | 154 | .63 | 29 | 30 | 2 | 39 |
| Employment Service . . . . . . . . | 130 | 88 | .68 | 23 | 28 | 7 | 42 |
| Labour Administration . . . . . . | 134 | 76 | .57 | 20 | 34 | — | 46 |
| Wages . . . . . . . . . . . . . . | 258 | 209 | .81 | 18 | 35 | — | 47 |
| Freedom of Association . . . . . . | 317 | 252 | .79 | 9 | 22 | — | 69 |
| Non-Discrimination . . . . . . . . | 70 | 65 | .93 | — | 40 | — | 60 |
| Migrant Workers . . . . . . . . . | 68 | 65 | .95 | — | — | — | 100 |
| Social Policy . . . . . . . . . . . | 43 | 30 | .67 | 15 | 39 | — | 46 |

Table 3 shows that, among the 12 groups which are sufficiently representative in size, the conformity score varies from .81 for the standards
on indigenous and plantations workers and on wages to .54 for those on
occupational safety and hygiene.  At the lower end of the scale, the Conventions on labour administration, on young workers and on hours of
work have all given rise to application difficulties in more than a third of
the cases examined.  At the upper end the instruments dealing with freedom of association and with the abolition of forced labour have so far
led to observations in only about a fifth of the cases.  The more technical
types of instruments seem thus to have given rise to observations more
frequently than those dealing with human rights questions, but no clear-
cut pattern can be discerned between the various groups.

The principal purpose of Table 3 is to provide comparable data on the
results of the critical comments by the supervisory organs.  To facilitate
this comparison the various groups are arranged according to the extent
of governmental response to observations.  Here also the results show a
considerable degree of dispersion.  The indigenous and plantation workers
Conventions again head the list, with some response recorded in almost
three-quarters of the cases,[1] whereas the corresponding figure is less than

---

[1] These percentages take account of all cases where some kind of action has been taken
to comply with an observation.  The relatively small number of cases where full conformity was achieved in two successive stages is no longer tabulated separately, as in Tables 1
and 2.

one-third of the cases for the freedom of association standards which are at the bottom of the table. This low level of response may not only be due to the delicate political aspects of the right to organize but also to the relatively recent date of the Conventions in question, all but one of which have been adopted since 1947. On the other hand, supervisory comment on the abolition of forced labour instruments has met with a greater measure of success, since almost two-thirds of the observations have had some result.

If attention is focused on those cases where the supervisory comments have led to full action, three rather specialized groups of Conventions, those dealing with indigenous and tribal workers, with seafarers and with occupational safety and hygiene, stand out, as about half the infringements could be eliminated, a notably higher proportion than for the remaining groups. Many of these Conventions date back to the I.L.O.'s early period, so that there has been ample time to take the necessary measures of implementation.

The figures on denunciations show that most of these are to be found in the groups involving women and young workers. Because many of the pertinent Conventions were subsequently revised, governments have been able to terminate their obligations under the original instruments and to ratify new, often more flexible standards. Only nine of the 22 denunciations have therefore not been offset by such new ratifications.

If the left and right hand columns of Table 3 are read in conjunction this might reveal a possible connection between the conformity score and the degree of responsiveness to criticism. In other words, has there been any noticeable link between the need for observations on the one hand and the results of such observations on the other? The findings do not seem to show any significant correlation between the two.[1] Even a possible hypothesis that the relative frequency of observations has some direct bearing on their chances of success is thus not borne out by experience.

Without attempting any general conclusion at this stage, it is noteworthy that for three groups (seafarers, social security and young workers) where more than 100 observations were made, the results have so far been clearly above average. It would be interesting to review these figures in the future so as to see whether the period of operation constitutes a major element in the system's impact. A partial answer to this question is however attempted later in this chapter, when the time factor is briefly analyzed.

## II. Tabulation by Countries

The counterpart to Table 1 where the results are classified Convention by Convention is Appendix III where they appear country by country. To facilitate further analysis, countries are grouped by regions. As in Appendix II, non-metropolitan territories are listed separately, according to the States responsible for their international relations.

In evaluating the results for a given country, a number of factors have to be kept in mind. The figures in Appendix III depend, first of all, on

---

[1] The coefficient of linear correlation for this admittedly small number of percentages works out to only − 0.24.

the extent to which obligations under I.L.O. Conventions are binding on a country. Any comparison of the impact of supervision is therefore unrealistic unless the total number of formal undertakings is also kept in mind. Obviously, countries which have ratified few Conventions [1] are less likely to be criticized for faulty compliance than those which have extensive obligations. Another factor is the period over which obligations have been in force. It must also be remembered that since the introduction of the two-yearly system of reporting in 1959 the supervisory procedure operates somewhat less quickly.

The transition of a country from colonial to independent status may equally have some bearing on the rate at which supervision is able to operate. As noted earlier, there is usually no interruption in the continuity of supervision, but the transfer of the reporting obligation from the colonial to the local government often involves administrative and even legislative changes which in turn make it necessary for the Committee of Experts to ascertain whether the observations or requests made to the former government continue to be justified. This sequence of events has delayed the appraisal of the application of Conventions by some of the new African States.

The second series of observations already tabulated in Table 1 and again in Appendix III was often due to profound changes in the political and hence the legislative conditions of a country. More than half the cases (24 out of 46) concern only six countries–Bulgaria, Greece, India, Spain, Rumania and Yugoslavia.

Some of the factors just mentioned have no doubt contributed to the wide disparities in the number of observations made to individual countries. A rough yardstick for measuring the extent of these variations may be provided by using the "conformity score", introduced above to compare different groups of Conventions.

If one takes, for example, the countries which have had 20 or more observations (Argentina, Bulgaria, Chile, Colombia, Cuba, France, Greece, Italy, Nicaragua, Spain, Uruguay and Yugoslavia), one finds that their combined conformity score of .42 is very considerably below the score of .78 for all remaining countries. Even among the 12 States enumerated above, the individual scores range from .03 for Nicaragua to .64 for Italy. These figures show how widely the need for supervision varies from country to country. They also prove that a relatively small number of ratifications have accounted for a relatively large proportion of the observations made. Do these pronounced differences persist when the findings are analyzed by regions?

### III. Results on a Regional Basis

Regional groupings are sufficiently large and homogeneous, as a rule, to provide a more meaningful basis for comparison than individual countries where the number of Conventions in force, the length of supervision, etc.

---

[1] Cf. footnote 20, p. 13, which lists the States with less than 10 ratifications. The United States is the only industrialized country to figure in this list.

are liable, as noted, to have a determining influence on the results. Table 4 aims at discounting this influence. In addition to the customary lines of division, by continents, Europe and the Americas have each been subdivided into separate regions and the countries of the Middle East have been listed together. A slightly different approach had to be followed in the case of the non-metropolitan countries. While local conditions are the principal consideration in determining the applicability and application of Conventions, the final decision often still rests with the metropolitan government.[1] The non-metropolitan territories are therefore tabulated separately, without regard to their location.

Table 4 shows that 70 per cent of the undertakings examined are ratifications and that most of the rest are declarations for the application of Conventions in United Kingdom territories. The balance is made up of the present or past territories of eight other States.

*Table 4*

TOTAL RESULTS, TABULATED BY REGIONS

(as at 30 June 1964)

| Regions | Formal Undertakings Covered | No Operative Observations | First Series of Observations | Second Serie | Action in Full | Action in Part | Denunciations | No Action Taken |
|---|---|---|---|---|---|---|---|---|
| Africa . . . . . . . . . . . | 518 | 465 | 53 | — | 14 | 18 | — | 21 |
| America – South, Central & Caribbean . . . . . . . . | 472 | 208 | 264 | 8 | 56 | 81 | 10 | 125 |
| America – North . . . . . . | 22 | 19 | 3 | — | — | 3 | — | — |
| Asia & Far East . . . . . . | 178 | 108 | 70 | 4 | 18 | 16 | 2 | 38 |
| Europe – West . . . . . . . | 709 | 504 | 205 | 15 | 106 | 61 | 3 | 50 |
| Europe – East . . . . . . . | 330 | 179 | 151 | 15 | 59 | 41 | 6 | 60 |
| Middle East . . . . . . . . | 134 | 100 | 34 | 1 | 11 | 13 | — | 11 |
| Oceania . . . . . . . . . . | 63 | 54 | 9 | 1 | 5 | 2 | 1 | 2 |
| Total . . . . . . | 2,426 | 1,637 | 789 | 44 | 269 | 235 | 22 | 307 |
| *Non-Metropolitan Territories* | | | | | | | | |
| Australia . . . . . . . . . . | 35 | 34 | 1 | — | 1 | — | — | — |
| Belgium . . . . . . . . . . | 4 | — | 4 | — | 1 | 3 | — | — |
| Denmark . . . . . . . . . . | 33 | 28 | 5 | — | — | 1 | — | 4 |
| France . . . . . . . . . . . | 122 | 101 | 21 | — | 10 | 4 | — | 7 |
| Netherlands. . . . . . . . . | 45 | 22 | 23 | — | 4 | 4 | — | 15 |
| New Zealand . . . . . . . . | 15 | 14 | 1 | — | 1 | — | — | — |
| Republic of South Africa . . . | 4 | 2 | 2 | — | — | 1 | — | 1 |
| United Kingdom . . . . . . | 721 | 610 | 111 | 2 | 32 | 47 | — | 34 |
| United States . . . . . . . . | 17 | 17 | — | — | — | — | — | — |
| Total . . . . . . | 996 | 828 | 168 | 2 | 49 | 60 | — | 61 |

---

[1] The two Netherlands territories, as well as British Guiana and Southern Rhodesia are, however, notable examples of self-government in labour and other matters.

With the exception of North America and Oceania, the number of cases in each region seems sufficiently large to permit comparisons and conclusions. As might be expected, the over-all figures reflect the historical developments in the I.L.O.'s membership and in the acceptance of its standards. Europe accounts for over 40 per cent of the ratifications examined and the American and African continents for some 20 per cent each.

Taken as a group, the declarations of application to non-metropolitan territories exceed in number the ratifications for any single region. But individually, only the French and United Kingdom declarations are sufficiently numerous to permit significant findings. The total figures for all territories are therefore counted as a group which can be compared with the regional groupings as well as with the metropolitan countries taken together.

Table 5 is designed to provide comparable results, for all regions. As in Table 3, the conformity scores are indicated. Among the regions where the number of cases examined is sufficiently representative, the most striking feature is the low proportion of observations made to African countries in comparison with other regions. As explained above, the attainment of independence by most of these States has been so recent that the supervisory comments frequently take the form of direct requests to the new governments. The 1964 figures for Africa must therefore be regarded as rather tentative and some time will probably have to elapse

*Table 5*

COMPARATIVE TABLE, ARRANGED BY REGIONS
(as at 30 June 1964)

| Regions | *Need for Observations* | | | *Results of Observations* | | | |
|---|---|---|---|---|---|---|---|
| | Formal Undertakings Covered | No Operative Observations | Conformity Score | Action in Full | Action in Part | Denunciations | No Action Taken |
| | | | | (in percentages) | | | |
| All Regions | 3,422 | 2,463 | .72 | 32 | 29 | 2 | 37 |
| All Metropolitan Countries | 2,426 | 1,637 | .67 | 32 | 27 | 4 | 37 |
| All Non-Metropolitan Territories | 996 | 828 | .82 | 29 | 35 | — | 36 |
| Europe – West | 709 | 504 | .71 | 48 | 28 | 1 | 23 |
| Middle East | 134 | 100 | .75 | 32 | 36 | — | 32 |
| Europe – East | 330 | 179 | .54 | 35 | 25 | 4 | 36 |
| Africa | 518 | 465 | .90 | 28 | 32 | — | 40 |
| America – South, Central & Caribbean | 472 | 208 | .44 | 20 | 30 | 4 | 46 |
| Asia & Far East | 178 | 108 | .61 | 24 | 22 | 3 | 51 |
| America – North | 22 | 19 | .86 | — | 100 | — | — |
| Oceania | 63 | 54 | .86 | 50 | 20 | 10 | 20 |

before the data for this region become fully comparable with those for the rest of the world.[1]

For the remaining regions the conformity score ranges from .44 for South and Central America to .75 for the Middle East. The need for observations seems thus to have varied to a considerable extent, not only between States but between groupings of States as well. It is also significant that the conformity score of .82 for non-metropolitan countries is considerably in excess of the corresponding figure for metropolitan States. This difference seems to suggest that a greater degree of precaution was exercised before declarations of application were communicated to Geneva than in the case of some ratifications.[2]

The most interesting figures in Table 5 are those in the right-hand columns, where the results of the observations are expressed in percentages. As in Table 3, the criterion for classification is whether any action has been taken on the observations. Western Europe emerges here as by far the most responsive of the various regions. The countries of Eastern Europe and the Middle East also appear to have acted more fully on the comments of the supervisory Committees than those elsewhere. The results for Africa approximate the world-wide percentages. In the case of South and Central America, and of Asia and the Far East, the degree of response has been well below average.

These regional disparities reappear when attention is focused on the full action cases only: Europe–West and East–has a record of compliance which is definitely above average. In the South and Central America countries, on the other hand, breaches have been fully eliminated in only one-fifth of the cases examined. The corresponding proportion for Asia and the Far East is one-quarter of the cases.

The percentages for all metropolitan States and for all non-metropolitan territories differ little from the global figures. This is a significant achievement in the case of the non-metropolitan territories, where the conformity score is, as noted, definitely above the world-wide average. Not only were fewer observations required on the application of Conventions in dependent territories, but the record of response is as good as in independent countries taken as a whole.

The question of a possible correlation between the conformity scores and the effectiveness figures thus arises once again. A clear-cut pattern is however even less discernible here than in Table 3. Despite relatively

---

[1] The 1959 study "Influence of Article 35 of the Constitution of the I.L.O. in the Application of Conventions in Non-Metropolitan Territories" (International Labour Office, Geneva, 1959, roneoed) contains a table indicating the situation of member States and non-metropolitan territories as regards international labour Conventions, grouped by continents (p. 29). The study points out, on the basis of this table, that "the majority of the more important non-metropolitan territories are on par with or better than a large number of non-European States members ... as far as the application of Conventions is concerned" (p. 30). Population figures indicate that practically all the "more important" territories in question are African countries, most of which have now joined the I.L.O.

[2] Another factor may have been the limited size and population of many of the territories so that it was less difficult to ensure satisfactory application there than in the case of most member States.

similar conformity scores for Western Europe and for the Middle East, e.g., the results for these two regions are in marked contrast. The only generalization which the figures appear to warrant is that the two regions ranking lowest in their responsiveness to supervision are also among those where the need for critical comment was clearly above average. That I.L.O. supervision should have been relatively least successful in those areas where the need for its intervention was most urgent is hardly surprising: the economic and working conditions prevailing in many parts of the world not only render the need for labour protection and social measures particularly acute; as illustrated in the subsequent chapters, these conditions also constitute the most serious obstacles to the implementation of I.L.O. Conventions. The findings thus tend to confirm in statistical terms the size and character of the challenge confronting national and international efforts in the crucial sphere of social development.

## IV. The Time Factor

The difficulties which delay implementation are further pinpointed when the statistics are analyzed to determine the periods over which the process of supervision has operated. This time factor is potentially significant regardless of whether a government has taken implementing action or not. If it has, the figures should indicate the period which elapsed before the necessary measures were adopted. If it has not, the results should show whether the government has had sufficient time to respond to the original observation; a lengthening period of inaction tends therefore to add to the seriousness of a given case.

It would be possible to show in tabular form the exact number of years since supervisory comments were initiated, but such a wide dispersion of figures would not only be cumbersome statistically but would also lead to difficulties of presentation. To simplify both calculation and interpretation, it appeared preferable to divide the results into three time periods, depending on whether the governmental response has been almost immediate (one to three years), somewhat delayed (four to nine years) or very tardy (ten years or longer).[1]

Table 6 shows the proportion of cases falling within each of the above time periods. With Table 4 as the frame of reference, this scheme of presentation provides a separate set of percentages for the four types of action taken on observations. Thus the global figures at the top of Table 6 reveal that full or partial measures of implementation occurred primarily during the early or intermediate periods. In close to half of these cases the response was almost immediate, occurring no more than three years after the original comment. This suggests a high degree of initial impact, when the impression of I.L.O. criticism is still relatively fresh. Repetition,

---

[1]The time periods are calculated from the year of the initial comment to the year when progress was noted by the Committees, or to the year 1964 in the absence of any action. When a country has taken several steps towards compliance, only the first has been counted. Interruptions in the process of supervision either during the 1939-1947 period or due to a country's absence from the I.L.O. have been excluded.

though an inevitable element of the supervisory process, is bound to have a blunting effect over the long run.

This conclusion is confirmed by an analysis of the "no action" cases, some 80 per cent of which have been pending without success for ten years or more. Individual instances show that there is hope for progress even in such "hard core" cases, but the odds are not very favourable. These difficult and therefore important cases usually require special efforts for their solution. Once these efforts succeed,[1] they also provide international supervision with its most useful results.

*Table 6*

TIME ELAPSED SINCE INITIAL OBSERVATIONS
(Percentages)

| Regions | Action in Full | | | Action in Part | | | Denunciations | | | No Action | | |
|---|---|---|---|---|---|---|---|---|---|---|---|---|
| | 1-3 | 4-9 years | 10+ | 1-3 | 4-9 years | 10+ | 1-3 | 4-9 years | 10+ | 1-3 | 4-9 years | 10+ |
| All Regions . . | 50 | 46 | 4 | 43 | 51 | 6 | 14 | 38 | 48 | 19 | 65 | 16 |
| Africa . . . . | 62 | 38 | — | 55 | 36 | 9 | — | — | — | 100 | — | — |
| America–South, Central & Caribbean . . | 33 | 60 | 7 | 38 | 60 | 12 | 10 | 20 | 70 | 24 | 46 | 30 |
| Asia & Far East | 41 | 53 | 6 | 31 | 69 | — | 50 | — | 50 | 10 | 70 | 20 |
| Europe – West . | 54 | 43 | 3 | 39 | 58 | 3 | 33 | 67 | — | 11 | 81 | 8 |
| Europe – East . | 46 | 48 | 6 | 55 | 37 | 8 | — | 80 | 20 | 23 | 68 | 9 |
| Middle East . . | 60 | 40 | — | 50 | 50 | — | — | — | — | 18 | 73 | 9 |
| Non-Metropolitan Territories. | 65 | 33 | 2 | 59 | 37 | 4 | — | — | — | 5 | 93 | 2 |

Though based on a small sample, the figures for denunciations are also of some interest. They indicate that, even when criticism has continued for some time, governments seem reluctant to denounce a Convention and do so only as a last resort: ten years or more were allowed to elapse in half of the cases and over four years in most of the others.

Regional comparisons supplement the findings which emerge from Table 5. In those regions [2] where the degree of response has been better than average, action has also been speedier on the whole. The case of Africa is again somewhat special because of the relatively recent date of many of the observations made. The same is true of the countries of the Middle East, the vast majority of which joined the I.L.O. only after World

---

[1] Cf., e.g., the discussion of the "special cases", pp. 170-173 below.

[2] As the figures for North America and Oceania are too limited to yield meaningful percentages, they have been omitted from Table 6.

War II. These factors may help to explain why the immediacy of response by African and Middle Eastern countries is well above average.

Among the remaining regions, Western and Eastern Europe again head the list, but with one significant distinction. The percentage of immediate but partial response is particularly high for Eastern Europe and below average for Western Europe. While this may be accounted for to some extent by the speed with which a number of Western European countries responded to comment, it also seems to indicate that there has been a persistent effort in Eastern Europe to take early action toward compliance, even if only on a partial basis.

In the South and Central American countries and in those of Asia, action occurred preponderantly during the intermediate four-to-nine year period, confirming once again the special obstacles encountered by those States. The proportion of hard-core cases where no action has occurred is well above average, especially in Latin America.

The figures for the non-metropolitan territories show that implementing action has on the whole been more speedy than in the case of member States but that, on the other hand, the delays in disposing of "no action" cases have been considerably above average. Delays of this kind are especially noticeable among the territories which are self-governing in labour matters, such as the Netherlands territories, British Guiana and Southern Rhodesia, to which reference was made earlier.

## V. Relative Seriousness of Observations

In examining the results of I.L.O. supervision, it might have been tempting to differentiate between observations according to their degree of seriousness. As emphasized, the individual comments vary considerably in their relative importance [1] and so do the steps which governments take in response. Might the findings not have gained in validity if they had also been tabulated with reference to the intrinsic gravity of the breaches analyzed?

The attraction of such an approach would be undeniable if a reliable yardstick could be found to assess and classify observations on a quasi-automatic basis. It is true, of course, that the supervisory Committees themselves occasionally single out some cases as particularly serious: the Committee of Experts adds a footnote to certain observations and the Conference Committee has adopted the habit of listing "special cases" in its Reports. But aside from such major and patent cases, the classification of observations by degree of seriousness would be a rather hazardous undertaking and open to constant challenge as to its objectivity.

The various tabulations already carried out above may however contain certain indications on the weight to be attributed to the results. Thus, the substance and complexity of a given Convention or group of Conventions are bound to affect the degree of importance of the observations made and the impact secured in relation to these standards. The analysis of Table 3, for instance, shows how the results secured for purely technical Conventions such as those on occupational safety and hygiene differ from

---

[1] Cf. the reference to the strictness of supervision on p. 57 above.

those for the more delicate standards on human rights. Again, the seriousness of an observation presumably increases with the time required to achieve compliance and Appendix II therefore constitutes a useful source of information on this score.

But the great variety of the cases examined by I.L.O. supervision made it preferable to let the reader draw his own conclusions from case to case, rather than attempt the task of classification on a largely intangible basis. Such an attempt can always be made at a later stage, if satisfactory criteria and adequate safeguards can be devised for the purpose.

# CHAPTER FOUR

## SOME REASONS FOR THE NON-OBSERVANCE
## OF RATIFIED CONVENTIONS : LEGAL PROBLEMS

The effectiveness of I.L.O. supervision is bound up closely with the difficulties which governments encounter in implementing the Conventions they have ratified.  If systematic supervisory arrangements had not been established, shortcomings in implementation might not have been discovered in the first place.  Once breaches are brought to light, the success of supervision depends on whether the obstacles to compliance can be surmounted.  A survey of the results of international supervision must therefore also concern itself with the root-causes of non-application and with the remedies available for their elimination.

Such an attempt to catalogue and classify the difficulties preventing or delaying the discharge of treaty obligations is bound to be incomplete and artificial.  But reference to a series of concrete examples, drawn from actual I.L.O. experience, should help to illustrate some at least of the principal obstacles.  This qualitative approach constitutes in fact an essential counterpart to the quantitative method followed in the preceding chapters.  Taken by themselves, the statistical findings merely provide an over-all picture of the results but do not explain why supervisory comment has failed or succeeded in certain cases.  Further clues should emerge if certain typical case histories can be examined so as to bring the working and effectiveness of supervision more fully into perspective.

For purposes of presentation two broad types of problems can be distinguished, depending on whether the root-causes of non-observance are of a legal or practical nature.  The present chapter attempts to review the former type, i.e. the problems connected with the character of international labour standards, with the timing of their ratification and with their effective incorporation in municipal law.  Successive sections of this chapter will therefore deal with such questions as overly rigid Conventions, premature ratifications, the special situation of federal States and implementation through collective agreements.

No attempt is made in this or in the next chapter to be exhaustive or systematic.  If every aspect of these problems were to be covered, many more illustrations would have to be given than can be included here.


### I.  Detailed and Rigid Conventions

The requirements of a Convention may be difficult to satisfy because they cannot be fitted, in every detail, into the legislation of the ratifying country.  This type of problem is mentioned first, not because it constitutes a major or frequent obstacle to implementation, but because it finds its origin in the terms of the instrument itself so that, in contrast to other obstacles, remedial measures can be sought internationally during the drafting of an instrument.

It is important to spell out the dimensions of this problem with clarity. The terms of a Convention may be difficult to implement because the level of social protection it sets exceeds the economic capabilities of a country. This type of practical difficulty which is primarily encountered by the less industrialized countries will be dealt with in the next chapter.[1] The problem under consideration now is liable to arise in all countries, regardless of their level of development, since it concerns the need to comply with detailed international requirements, regarding such matters as scope, exceptions, enforcement, etc. If insufficient latitude is left to governments in settling matters of this kind, such rigid provisions may render exact compliance very difficult.

*Sources of Rigidity*

It is not necessary to trace the reasons why the Conference chose to frame certain provisions in great detail, although something will have to be said about its motives when possible remedies are discussed. The fact remains that when such Conventions were negotiated, it was thought desirable to include precise clauses as to scope, exceptions permitted, day-to-day enforcement, etc. To quote a few examples, the definition of the term "industrial undertaking", as used in the Conventions of 1919, includes a long enumeration of mining, manufacturing, construction and transport establishments;[2] the Minimum Age (Industry) Convention (Revised), 1937 (No. 59), permits children under 15 years to work in family workshops on condition that "only members of the employer's family are employed" there; the Medical Examination of Young Persons (Non-Industrial Occupations) Convention, 1946 (No. 78), requires special measures of identification to ensure application of the instrument to young persons engaged in "itinerant trading or in any other occupation carried on in the streets or in places to which the public have access". In each case the relevant provision has caused difficulties in its implementation.[3]

---

[1] Cf. pp. 119-133.

[2] Article 1 of Conventions Nos. 1, 4, 5, 6. It is true that the same article leaves it to each country to "define the line of division which separates industry from commerce and agriculture", but this gives no latitude to exclude any of the types of undertakings enumerated.

[3] Examples of observations on the definition of industrial undertakings are those concerning the application of Convention No. 1 to handicraft undertakings (such as the pre-war comments to Luxembourg (16 R.P. 605 and 1933 R.C.E. 7)) and the application of Conventions Nos. 6 and 89 to "small-scale food industries " (observations made to France since 1956 (1957 R.C.E. 25 and 86-87)).

In its comprehensive survey of the effect given, *inter alia*, to Convention No. 59 the Committee of Experts noted, in 1960, that there were "several cases where the relevant exceptions contained in the protective legislation do not fully comply with the (Convention) because the definition of family undertaking is broader" (1960 R.C.E. 91).

The identification of young persons engaged in itinerant trading has formed the subject of observations to Bulgaria (1955 R.C.E. 62), Cuba (1957 R.C.E. 77), France (1954 R.C.E. 37), Italy (1955 R.C.E. 62-63) and Poland (1952 R.C.E. 32).

In other cases, highly complex and technical subjects such as compensation for workers incapacitated by occupational diseases (Conventions Nos. 18 and 42), the protection of dockers against accidents (Nos. 28 and 32) or safety provisions for workers in the building industry (No. 62) were dealt with by the Conference in rather detailed instruments.[1] Because of the obstacles which undue rigidity places in the way of ratification, the choice between general and detailed standards has been debated throughout the I.L.O.'s history.

## The Search for Flexibility

Stated in its simplest terms, the alternative is between Conventions of broad principle and the kind of very specific instruments just described. There exist serious arguments in support of each. The general Convention will avoid the type of difficulties referred to above and will therefore secure more widespread acceptance. The detailed Convention, by spelling out in precise terms the bearing of its requirements, will more adequately guarantee equality of obligations among ratifying States. Generally speaking it has been the employers' group and the governments of industrially advanced countries which have favoured the former, although for different reasons. The employers may have felt that standards phrased in general terms will be easier to comply with.[2] Certain highly developed countries, especially in Scandinavia, have contended that excessive detail has prevented them from ratifying Conventions already applied in all their essentials, thus giving a misleading impression of the countries' social advancement.[3]

---

[1] Convention No. 42 contains a schedule listing ten diseases and toxic substances together with the 26 trades, industries or processes where the diseases may be contracted. If the relevant national legislation excludes any of these diseases or trades from its terms, the full application of the Convention is jeopardized. Convention No. 32 enumerates the precautions to be taken to keep approaches to docks, wharfs, etc., means of access to ships, holds of vessels, hoisting gear and so on in safe condition; for this purpose the minimum height of fences and the minimum width of gangways are specified in inches and centimetres, the time intervals for periodic inspection of chains and wire ropes of hoisting gear are laid down, etc. Convention No. 62, while going into somewhat less detail, contains rules for scaffolds, hoisting machines and safety equipment on building sites.

[2] In 1927 the Danish employers' delegate suggested in the Conference: "We must try in future to arrive at Conventions containing a limited number of provisions, yet sufficiently precise and clear to ensure uniformity of application in all countries" (10 R.P. 117). In 1963 the Ceylon employers' delegate complained about "the continued adoption of rigid instruments overburdened with detail and unrealistic in approach" (47 R.P. 106).

[3] In her speech to the Conference in 1963 the Finnish Minister of Social Affairs referred to a letter the governments of the Northern countries (Denmark, Iceland, Norway and Sweden, in addition to her own) had sent to the Director-General in 1961, "in which it was suggested that future draft Conventions be prepared with maximum regard to the desirability of avoiding provisions of so narrow or detailed a nature as to impede ratification of the Conventions by member States with a high standard in the field concerned" (47 R.P. 48). A Canadian government delegate at the same session made a similar plea: "Very often an instrument may contain a few points, perhaps minor, which do not take adequate account of the needs and requirements of delegates from some countries" (47 R.P. 238).

The very fact that the dilemma seems as real today as it was four decades ago points to the conclusion that there is no general solution to it.[1] If avoidance of the difficulties of application were the sole objective, an instrument drawn up in very flexible terms would doubtless be the answer, but neither the need for meaningful international obligations nor the task of effective supervision would be served in this way.[2] Writing in 1963, the Director-General called the question "primarily one of good judgment applied to the facts of a particular case".[3] He recalled that a number of devices had been developed in recent years to render Conventions more flexible and he advocated recourse to these in a long-term programme for the revision of a whole series of existing Conventions.[4]

Flexibility clauses may thus provide a remedy for difficulties encountered in giving effect to excessively rigid and detailed Conventions. Because the discussion, adoption and ratification of a new Convention are however time-consuming procedures, they should be initiated only after governments have made a genuine attempt to cope with standards in their present form. If this has proved unsuccessful and if revision seems the only solution, the I.L.O. has acquired experience in making a Convention less rigid without emptying it of its social content. Two successive operations of this kind were performed, for instance, in the case of the Night Work (Women) Convention of 1919, which was first revised in 1934 to exempt managerial personnel from its scope, and again in 1948 to permit women to work on the second day shift until as late as midnight. In another case, that of the Fee-Charging Employment Agencies Convention of 1933, the revision in 1949 introduced two elements of flexibility: enforce-

---

[1] Writing in 1933, Professor Joseph P. Chamberlain stated the problem but refrained from providing an easy answer: "A general principle may be widely applicable, but the details that would answer the need in one continent or country may be inadequate or improper in another. Therefore, in laying down the provisions of labor conventions the Conference must use a wise discretion in eliminating requirements which are not of universal application, and in escaping the Scylla of generality as well as the Charybdis of inflexible detail" ("Legislation in a Changing Economic World", *Annals of the American Academy of Political and Social Science* Vol. 166 (March 1933), p. 34). A similar note was sounded, the same year, by the Director in the reply to the Conference discussion of his Report: "I think one is driven back to the conclusion that there is perhaps no general rule which one can lay down; each Convention must be taken by itself. On the whole, however, it would seem that what should be aimed at is a mean, a middle way between something very detailed and just a broad principle which creates no international obligation" (17 R.P. 319).

[2] The New Zealand government suggested in 1946 that a method be devised for "enabling a member to ratify a Convention where the general principles are already embodied in existing legislation but such legislation does not conform with the Convention in minor or technical details" (29 Report II (1), p. 165). The idea is tempting but its realization would probably raise more problems than it would solve.

[3] "A Convention should deal with essentials; it should not contain rigid requirements in regard to matters in respect of which national practice may reasonably vary widely; it should not enter into too much administrative detail; where specific difficulties are known to exist in particular countries or groups of countries when the Convention is under consideration, appropriate exceptions or discretionary powers should be included in the Convention unless a substantial question of principle is involved" (47 D.R. 169).

[4] 47 D.R. 160-163. The minimum age and medical examination Conventions were among those mentioned.

ment is not mandatory in sparsely populated areas and a ratifying country has the choice between two alternatives, the progressive abolition of the agencies or their regulation. In addition to this "excluded area" clause [1] and this choice of alternatives, other devices have been developed such as ratification by parts [2] or by branches of social security,[3] optional annexes [4] and the possibility of applying the Convention to a specified percentage of workers only.[5] In some cases governments are required to consult the representative organizations of employers and workers.

Recourse to these devices, separately or in combination, and the introduction of other appropriate expedients, should go a long way toward facilitating the application of Conventions found to be overly detailed. The devices should prove equally useful when, as mentioned, it is not only the rigidity but also the level of the standards which is impeding application. It should be re-emphasized however, in conclusion, that flexibility is not an end in itself and that it loses its justification and value when the basic I.L.O. purpose of raising and equalizing social standards is no longer served by it.

## II. Premature Ratifications

The greatest source of difficulty in the early days of the I.L.O. was undoubtedly the tendency of some countries to accept standards for which there was little or no basis in national law and practice. To these countries, ratifications merely represented "a declaration of sympathy with the principles embodied in a Convention" [6] coupled at best with a desire to give effect to it in due course. Regardless of whether the government believed that it was acting in good faith or whether it merely ratified as "a means of propaganda",[7] the fact remained that the Convention was not applied, even after it entered into force for the country concerned. The situation was further aggravated when, as will be seen, it involved not just one but a group of Conventions. Such ratifications were also open to special objection because, in addition to the good name of one country, it was the reputation of the whole system of I.L.O. standards which was called into question.[8]

---

[1] Also found in Conventions Nos. 24, 25, 62, 63, 77, 78, 81, 88, 94 and 95.

[2] Conventions Nos. 63, 81, 109 and 110.

[3] Conventions Nos. 102 and 118.

[4] Convention No. 97.

[5] Convention No. 102.

[6] In the words used by the Conference Committee in 1930 (14 R.P. 637). The expression "ratification of principle" is that generally used by the Committee of Experts (e.g. 1930 R.C.E. 453). The Conference Committee expressed the idea in the more incisive terms of "window-dressing ratifications" (in French "de façade") and "platonic ratifications" (15 R.P. 615). Professor Scelle called them "bare" (*L'Organisation Internationale du Travail et le B.I.T.*, *op. cit.*, p. 177) and Zarras "empty ratifications" (*Le contrôle de l'application des conventions internationales du travail, op. cit.*, p. 73).

[7] In the words of a Swiss government spokesman in 1936 (20 R.P. 504).

[8] In 1928, a British government delegate warned the Conference that ratifications of principle "were used as an argument by reactionary associations in the world to resist Conventions, ratification and application" (11 R.P. 294).

## The Origin of Empty Ratifications

The practice originated during the formative years of the Organization, and much attention had to be given to the resulting difficulties during the pre-war period. The countries concerned often had only limited contacts with Geneva and they conceived their ratifications as tangible tokens of their desire to take a more active part in the work of the I.L.O. As members they were bound, in any case, to bring all Conventions before their competent national authorities "for the enactment of legislation or other action".[1] The Governing Body had moreover issued specific instructions to the Director "to continue his efforts to obtain in all countries the ratification of the various Conventions adopted by the International Labour Organization".[2] Albert Thomas always considered the promotion of ratifications as one of his most important tasks and as the means of giving the work of the Organization a broad and lasting basis.[3] The resulting response of governments was not always realistic, however, either in its scale or in its pace. Instead of adopting a gradual approach by ratifying a few instruments at a time, in line with their real capabilities, some countries least ready for such sudden leaps forward decided to ratify a whole group of Conventions at once. These so-called "block ratifications" only served to compound the difficulties.

## Block Ratifications

It is by multiple ratifications, therefore, that the problem can best be illustrated. Among the major cases of this kind, those of Cuba and Luxembourg in 1928 may be cited for this purpose.[4] Cuba and Luxembourg ratified 16 and 25 Conventions respectively that year. Although

---

[1] Article 19 of the Constitution. Cf. p. 11 above.

[2] A resolution to this effect was adopted with one abstention in 1924, following a discussion on the slow progress of ratification of the 48-hour week Convention of 1919 (21 G.B. 41). Resolutions calling on States to ratify international labour Conventions have been adopted during the post-war period by the Governing Body, regional meetings of the I.L.O., the Economic and Social Council of the United Nations and the Consultative Assembly of the Council of Europe.

[3] In an address in Warsaw in 1924 he explained: "I do not know whether you have any very clear idea of what the life of a Director of the International Labour Office is like. He hurries through all the capital cities of Europe, and indeed of the world. He calls on all the Ministers of Labour and on all the governments. He tries to make them see the necessity of ratifying the international labour Conventions adopted by the Conference" (Albert Thomas, *International Social Policy* (Geneva: I.L.O., 1948), p. 15. Speaking a year later, in his native Champigny-sur-Marne, he used this picturesque image: "Like a Wandering Jew of social progress, I go all over the world ... only too happy ... if I can carry back in my big despatch-case the ratification of some international Convention or the draft of some national bill which means a small step forward towards the just and peaceful organization of the world" (*Ibid*, p. 14).

[4] Among the other countries which, during that period, also communicated *en bloc* their first ratifications were Colombia (24 Conventions in 1933), Nicaragua (30 in 1934) and Uruguay (30 in 1933). It should be emphasized however that not all block ratifications were necessarily premature. In many cases the basic obstacle to implementation was economic under-development but in others (e.g. Luxembourg and Uruguay) the reasons were more complex.

the first reports on the application of these instruments were due for examination in 1930, each government merely sent a letter. The Cuban government indicated that no legislation existed as yet but that a draft had been submitted to Congress which would pass it "as speedily as possible".[1] The letter from Luxembourg stated that at the time of ratification the legislation either already was or had been brought into conformity with the Conventions, except for one, Sickness Insurance (Agriculture), 1926 (No. 25), for which a bill was under consideration.[2] Without relating all the subsequent developments in detail, they serve to show the nature of ratifications of principle and the efforts often necessary to give effect to them.

In the case of Cuba, the two supervisory Committees urged the government in increasingly strong language to adopt the legislation required. The Conference Committee went so far in 1932 as to suggest the initiation of the complaints procedure. After finding some progress the following year, the Committee of Experts noted in 1934 that "a period of severe political and civil disturbance" had caused new delays.[3] In 1935, the annual reports which were finally supplied showed that legislation had been enacted.[4] This episode illustrates two interesting points. On the one hand the government clearly was not in a position to ratify when it decided to do so, as a demonstration of goodwill.[5] On the other hand steady pressure over four to five years did lead to legislative action, even during a period of economic depression and political upheaval.

The case of Luxembourg is also instructive, but for different reasons. Eight of its 25 ratifications related to maritime Conventions[6] which, in the government's own words, had "no practical application in the Grand Duchy".[7] They were therefore purely platonic unless this land-locked country was to acquire a merchant navy.[8] Despite the government's assurances, the supervisory organs found it necessary to make observations

---

[1] 1930 R.C.E. 626.

[2] 1930 R.C.E. 602.

[3] 1934 R.C.E. 221.

[4] In the ensuing period further observations were made in respect of two maritime Conventions, Nos. 8 and 15.

[5] In 1930 the Swiss employers' delegate referred to this case during the discussion of the Conference Committee's Report: "With a large gesture, one of the States members ratified, in 1928, 16 Conventions as a welcoming gift for the Director, on the occasion of his visit. But today, two years after the ratifications, nothing has yet been done to give effect to them" (14 R.P. 510).

[6] Nos. 7, 8, 9, 15, 16, 22, 23 and No. 21 which deals with the inspection of emigrants on board ship.

[7] 15 D.R. 208.

[8] Such a possibility is not so far-fetched as might appear. Hungary, which also ratified three maritime Conventions in 1928, subsequently acquired some vessels flying its flag and issued a decree in 1933 to give effect to the Convention. Switzerland adopted a more realistic course when it was forced to form a merchant marine of its own to keep the country supplied during World War II; an Order of 1941 declared six I.L.O. Conventions concerning seafarers "applicable" to the crews of these ships (cf. A. Berenstein, "The Influence of International Labour Conventions on Swiss Legislation", *International Labour Review*, Vol. LXXVII, No. 6 (June 1958) pp. 513-515) and four of these instruments were eventually ratified in 1960.

on six of the remaining instruments, and action was taken on four of these [1] with little delay. However, the two Sickness Insurance Conventions (Nos. 24 and 25) gave rise to financial difficulties, due to the "economic crisis",[2] and conformity could be observed only after the war.

The absence of effective implementation prompted the Conference Committee in 1930–the year when the position in Cuba and Luxembourg first came up for international scrutiny–to express the opinion that "no ratification at all is better than a ratification which remains ineffective".[3] This statement sums up the reaction of the supervisory bodies to such ratifications. Already at its first meeting the Committee of Experts alluded to them in guarded terms, pointing out that "non-observance... is sometimes prolonged".[4] Four years later, in 1931, it used much stronger language: "Although ratifications of principle might have been explicable at a time when the International Labour Organization had only just begun to work, they can no longer be contemplated at the present time... An adhesion which is not followed by concrete application is an ineffectual gesture, the only result of which is to perpetuate an illusion".[5] There can thus be little doubt as to the Committees' attitude on this subject.[6] Quite aside from the legal implications, the troubles that such ratifications have caused, both to the States concerned and to the I.L.O., explain this attitude. But a word need be said about the stand taken by the supervisory Committees on two related problems, the timing of a ratification and the need for legislative action when the conditions contemplated in a Convention do not exist in a country.

## When to Ratify?

No difference of opinion can arise on legal grounds that national legislation should fully conform to a Convention when it enters into force in a given country. In the case of the early Conventions (Nos. 1-23) this coincides with the date of registration of the ratification and the government is therefore left no transitional period for taking such measures of implementation as might still be necessary.[7] When the government has 12 months for this purpose, as is the rule for most Conventions, this simplifies the

---

[1] Conventions Nos. 1, 3, 13, 20.

[2] Cf. the government statement to the Conference Committee in 1934 (18 R.P. 539).

[3] 14 R.P. 637.

[4] 1927 R.C.E. 415.

[5] 1931 R.C.E. 453.

[6] Professor Scelle made the point in characteristically terse and imaginative terms: "The policy of the I.L.O. is to track down ("pourchasser") bare ratifications" (*L'Organisation Internationale du Travail et le B.I.T., op. cit.*, p. 178).

In the face of this clear-cut and general condemnation, it is difficult to accept Professor Haas' contention that "a certain number of States maintain that ratification constitutes merely an endorsement of the standards *in principle*, without creating any immediate obligation to revise national law or enact new law" (*Beyond the Nation-State, op. cit.*, p. 246).

[7] It was no doubt for this reason that the Director expressed the view in 1921 that it was "logical to reform the legislation first, this being the essential thing, and to proceed later to the communication of the formal ratification" (3 D.R. 930).

position but also introduces a danger that hopes for speedy adjustment will fail to materialize. It is on this issue that opinions have been divided, with the employers insisting that national law and practice should, as a precautionary measure, be brought into harmony with a Convention before its ratification is communicated.[1] A similar point of view was expressed in a resolution adopted in 1949 by the Fourth Conference of the American States members of the I.L.O.[2] After a full discussion of the problem of timing, in 1960, the Conference Committee laid down the some-what more flexible rule that "Conventions should be fully applied as soon as their terms have become binding".[3] The question thus turns primarily on whether a government which ratifies in advance of full compliance is reasonably certain that conformity can be achieved before the Convention enters into force.

## The Need for Implementing Legislation

The second question sometimes raised by a ratification of principle is the need for implementing legislation in cases where the conditions dealt with in the Convention do not exist in a country. The application of mari-time Conventions by countries without a seaboard, as just discussed above, shows that even in such an apparently simple contingency no cut and dried rule can be established. The need for legislation could arise not only when merchant ships are acquired but also when shipping penetrates as far as the ratifying country's territory.[4] A variety of other similarly unpredictable situations can be imagined. They may arise because of purely physical factors, such as the absence of mines to which the Under-ground Work (Women) Convention, 1935 (No. 45) could be applied; because of factual circumstances, e.g. when the harmful materials dealt with in the White Lead (Painting) Convention, 1921 (No. 13) are said not to be used in a country.[5] Sociological conditions, such as the absence of women from industry, or economic conditions, such as the non-existence

---

[1] Sir John Forbes Watson, a British employer, went so far as to suggest, in 1945, that "a country's ratification ... should not be accepted and registered until its law has been put into accordance with the Convention" (27 R.P. 282). Clearly, there would be no foundation in law for such a refusal to register a ratification.

[2] The "Resolution concerning the Application of International Labour Conventions and Recommendations in American Countries" suggested that "before ratification takes place, a government should ascertain whether its laws, regulations and practice (including necessary sanctions) ensure the application of the provisions of the Conventions in ques-tion" (XXXII O.B. 80-82) (the words in brackets appear as such in the text).

[3] 44 R.P. 603. In practice governments have an additional "period of grace" because the first annual report is not due for another nine months at least after a Convention enters into force.

[4] In the case of Luxembourg, e.g., the canalization of the Moselle river now renders necessary the application of the Protection against Accidents (Dockers) Convention, 1929 (No. 28) which applies to inland as well as maritime navigation. The Convention was ratified in 1931 and the Committee of Experts noted this possibility in 1958 (1958 R.C.E. 34).

[5] The Committee of Experts did not agree with the Mexican government's contention that no special regulations were needed in such a case, to give effect to the Convention (1960 R.C.E. 26).

of unemployment in a country, may also be a factor. While aware of the preventive purpose of I.L.O. Conventions, the Committee of Experts has hesitated to take an unduly dogmatic attitude: "It would be going too far to ask a State to take regulatory measures in cases where it has been established without question that such measures would find no application because there exists no subject matter for regulation and there is no prospect of the subject matter arising in the near future".[1] This statement must be read in the light of the Committee's constant endeavour to keep changing national circumstances under review and of the evolution which may occur in the purview attributed to a Convention by the Committee itself. This latter possibility is illustrated by the application of Conventions in non-metropolitan territories. If the terms of the instrument make it applicable only to such territories,[2] its ratification by a non-colonial country would be devoid of practical meaning and no such ratifications have in fact ever been received. It had also been thought, originally, that application of the Forced Labour Convention, 1930 (No. 29) was limited to colonial possessions because at the time of its adoption the practices with which it deals were inconceivable except in such territories. When forced labour subsequently became a problem elsewhere, the 1930 Convention was used as a means of combatting new evils to which its terms did not precisely apply and the Committee of Experts came to consider it an instrument "of general concern".[3] This broad construction was accepted by the non-colonial countries, such as Ecuador, Greece, India and Sweden, to which the Committee proceeded to address observations in subsequent years. Ratifications conceived originally as mere manifestations of international solidarity [4] can thus, in certain circumstances, have more immediate results, especially if the countries concerned take new measures of implementation. Paradoxical as it may seem at first sight, it is the very difficulties inherent in ratifications of principle which may thus give them their potential value. This paradox is closely bound up with the effectiveness of I.L.O. supervision and therefore merits some elaboration.

*The Potential Value of Premature Ratifications*

The impact of a ratification depends, in the last analysis, on whether it leads to an improvement in the labour and social conditions of the country concerned. If the standards laid down in a Convention were attained long before it was ratified, the value of ratification must be looked for

---

[1] 1951 R.C.E. 10.

[2] Conventions Nos. 82-85 fall in this category.

[3] 1950 R.C.E. 27. Article 2, paragraph 1, of Convention No. 29 defines "forced or compulsory labour" as "all work or service which is exacted from any person under the menace of any penalty and for which the said person has not offered himself voluntarily"; paragraph 2 specifies the types of work excluded from the definition (compulsory military service involving "work of a purely military character", service exacted "as a consequence of a conviction in a court of law", "minor communal services" etc.).

[4] In its first report on the Convention, the Swiss government stated that its ratification was inspired by the same principles which led it to adhere to the Slavery Convention, i.e. to give its moral support to work in the humanitarian field (1949 R.C.E. 26).

elsewhere–i.e. on the political level, in particular internationally.[1]  If, on the other hand, internal law and practice fall short of the requirements of a Convention, the act of ratification implies acceptance of a commitment to effect improvements.  The argument, though not acceptable in law, is tempting in its practical implications.[2]  To the extent to which the difficulties raised by a ratification of principle have eventually been overcome, its validity and value have been confirmed.  It is true that the issue seldom arises in such absolute terms because violations do not usually encompass all or even the major requirements of a Convention.  Nonetheless the supervisory organs have never left any doubt as to the dangers inherent in any tendency to ratify in the absence of application.[3]  But must there be an inevitable link between the achievement of progress and the objectionable features of premature ratifications?

*Possible Remedies*

The remedies are both national and international.  They imply a readiness on the part of governments to take the necessary corrective measures before rather than after a Convention becomes binding.  The key lies thus in the element of timing to which reference was made above.  Because it is for a government alone to decide what and when to ratify, the I.L.O.'s role must be educational and advisory.  It is unable to refuse registration of a ratification communicated in due form, but it can and does discourage ratifications which clearly would give rise to difficulties.  The educational task falls primarily on the supervisory Committees which by their very existence, by the character of their past observations and by the clear stand they have always taken on ratifications of principle, should impart a sense of caution and responsibility to governments contemplating ratification.[4]  This role has been further enlarged and facilitated since 1950

---

[1] The Report of the Director to the 1928 session of the Conference stressed the "international significance of ratification... If ratification loses some of its interest from the national point of view where it is not calculated to result in legislative progress, it nevertheless continues to be of considerable importance from the international point of view" (11 D.R. 113).

[2] After having condemned what he calls "paper ratifications" because they raise false hopes and lower the juridical value of Conventions, Professor Berenstein concedes: "But one must also see the other side of the coin.  Even ratifications on paper can represent a positive element.  For these ratifications lead in the long run, in many cases, to the adoption of the implementing legislation they call for." ("L'Activité de l'Organisation internationale du Travail et ses Résultats", *Rivista di diritto internazionale e comparato del lavoro* (Bologna), Vol. II, No. III, pp. 379-395).

[3] In 1937, for instance, the Committee of Experts referred to "the disadvantages for the International Labour Organization, and for international life as a whole, that arise from the infringement of the principle of scrupulous respect for the mutual international undertakings implied by the ratification of a Convention, that takes place when ratification is not immediately followed by application" (1937 R.C.E. 4).

[4] An example of caution traceable to supervision is the explanation given in 1953 to the Lower House ("Bundestag") of the Federal German Parliament by the Minister of Labour, in reply to an opposition query concerning the ratification of I.L.O. Conventions: "A number of additional Conventions which appeared originally to be appropriate for immediate ratification, had to be subjected to further examination in view of the fact that the International Labour Organization has begun recently to use stricter crititeria as

when the two Committees began to examine the reports on certain unratified Conventions requested by the Governing Body under article 19 of the Constitution. The Committee of Experts adopts "General Conclusions" covering both these reports, and the corresponding ones from ratifying States. These Conclusions, and their subsequent discussion by the Conference Committee, are designed to clarify the terms and bearing of the instruments examined and thus to help governments in deciding whether to ratify.[1]

The International Labour Office's advice, though somewhat less formal, can also assist governments in reaching a decision. Under the I.L.O. Constitution the International Court of Justice alone may give an authoritative interpretation of a Convention,[2] but the Office's advice is always available, and regularly sought, when governments contemplating ratification require clarification of the meaning of a Convention.[3] Member States are of course also able to contact I.L.O. Field Offices, Branch Offices or national correspondents, as well as the technical services of the Office directly.[4] When officials avail themselves of these opportunities for informal consultation and discussion, they are able to learn of the experience of other countries. This experience, as reflected in the findings of the supervisory Committees, should go a long way towards discouraging premature and unrealistic ratifications.

### III. Ratifications Which Raise Unforeseen Difficulties

In certain cases it is not the timing of the ratification which causes difficulties but the fact that divergencies had not been anticipated. The

---

regards absolute conformity between the provisions of the national legislation and the terms of a given Convention. As soon as it appears from this examination that these Conventions can be ratified, even according to the stricter Geneva criteria, they will forthwith be submitted to the legislative authorities" (*German Bundestag, First Legislature*, No. 4497, Bonn, 12 June 1953).

[1] Thus the Indian government had originally decided not to ratify the Equal Remuneration Convention, 1951 (No. 100). Subsequently however the Labour Ministry's tripartite Committee on Conventions re-examined the question because the "General Conclusions" on the effect given to this instrument, published by the Committee of Experts in 1956, had explained "the instrument in such a way as to limit the area of the government's responsibility in the matter of enforcement" (*Indian Labour Gazette*, Vol. XV, No. 10, April 1958). India's ratification of Convention No. 100 was registered in September 1958.

[2] Article 37, paragraph 1. This provision was only invoked on one occasion, in 1932, when the Governing Body asked the Court to give an interpretation of the Night Work (Women) Convention, 1919 (No. 4).

[3] An average of four to five such interpretations are supplied each year and published in the *Official Bulletin*; the explanations are therefore available not only to the governments which asked for them but to other member countries as well. Cf. in this connection C. Wilfred Jenks, "The Interpretation of International Labour Conventions by the International Labour Office", *British Year Book of International Law, 1939*, pp. 132-141. Cf. also, by the same author, *Law, Freedom and Welfare* (London: Stevens & Sons, 1963), pp. 121-124.

[4] The secretariat of every general session of the International Labour Conference includes a "Conventions Information Unit" whose services are, according to the *Daily Bulletin*, available to "members of delegations wishing to discuss questions concerning the ratification of Conventions and related matters". Regular use is made of these facilities, particularly by delegates from the newly independent countries.

government may have been convinced, when it ratified, that it was giving full effect to the instrument, only to discover that it had not fully foreseen the bearing of the obligations assumed. International supervision has an especially useful role to perform in such cases. Without it, such misunderstandings might not be discovered at all. Once the true bearing of the obligations has been clarified, the process of supervision can help governments to remove the difficulties they had not anticipated.

The misconceptions may merely relate to technical points or they may touch the very basis of a Convention.

*Unforeseen Technical Difficulties*

Leaving aside purely material errors which are easily rectified,[1] governments sometimes consider that existing provisions are sufficient to ensure implementation. The Mexican government, for instance, has maintained that two pieces of legislation suffice to prevent any infringement of the Unemployment Indemnity (Shipwreck) Convention, 1920 (No. 8), under which a seaman who is jobless due to the loss or foundering of his vessel is entitled to payment by his employer of an indemnity totalling at least two months' wages.[2] Except for one passing reference to the possible amendment of the Federal Labour Act,[3] the government has steadfastly taken the view that no real discrepancies exist, so that the Committee of Experts has had to explain in increasingly strong terms why it cannot agree.[4] While the problem is essentially technical and doubtless of limited importance, no solution appears in sight until the government abandons its loose construction of the standard of compliance required by the Convention.

Often it is not the application of the Convention as a whole which causes difficulty but only certain of its provisions. This circumscribes the problem without altering its basic character, i.e. the elimination of a divergency of whose existence the government was not aware at the time of ratification. The supervisory organs themselves may not have realized its existence at first, until their attention was drawn to it by a national organization of workers or employers. This happened in connection with the implementa-

---

[1] In 1954, for instance, the Belgian government informed the Conference Committee, in reply to an observation, that "a typographical error had unfortunately occurred" in the text of a decree designed to give effect to the Workmen's Compensation (Occupational Diseases) Convention (Revised), 1934 (No. 42) (37 R.P. 514). A further decree of 1956 introduced the necessary correction (1957 R.C.E. 60).

[2] Cf. in particular the Committee of Experts' review of this case, first mentioned in 1938, in its 1958 Report (1958 R.C.E. 20). The Federal Labour Act of Mexico (section 126) only requires unemployment compensation if the shipowner is insured and has himself received payment from his insurance company. The General Communications Act (section 221) empowers harbour masters to prohibit the departure of a vessel unless its crew is insured for certain types of contingencies, unemployment not being specifically mentioned.

[3] Cf. 1961 R.C.E. 35.

[4] Cf. 1963 R.C.E. 47-48. In the absence of any change of attitude by the government, the Conference Committee decided, in 1963, to place this case on its special list (47 R.P. 515, 527).

tion of the Maternity Protection Convention, 1919 (No. 3) in France. Although the government's initial report was examined in 1952 it was in 1956 that the Committee of Experts first commented on the effect given to article 4 of this instrument which prohibits the dismissal of a woman worker absent on maternity leave. The French Confederation of Christian Workers had pointed out that the Labour Code forbids dismissal for reasons of pregnancy or confinement but not for any other reason. Without going into all the intricacies of this case one basic point emerged. Agreeing with the Confederation's contention that it may be impossible for the woman to prove that she has been dismissed because of pregnancy, the Committee of Experts stressed that the Convention "makes no distinction as regards the possible reasons" for dismissal and called on the government to amend the Labour Code accordingly.[1] The government contended in the Conference Committee that this was unnecessary because the necessary safeguards were laid down in other legislation.[2] In 1959 however the Committee of Experts reiterated its request because it had discovered certain court decisions based exclusively on the Labour Code.[3] In its reply the government insisted that it had "always considered that the (national) provisions gave protection at least equal to that called for by article 4 of the Convention, as interpreted by it"; it would take a final decision when the interpretation of the Committee of Experts had been further clarified.[4] Regardless of the solution which will be reached in due course it is clear that the root of the problem can again be traced to the fact that the implications of the Convention were not fully appreciated at the time of ratification.

A different requirement of the same Convention gave rise to difficulties of such far-reaching importance in Brazil that they led in the end to its denunciation, although other major divergencies pointed out by the supervisory bodies had already been eliminated.[5] This requirement, to which the supervisory Committees had referred from 1947 onward, specifies the method of payment of maternity benefits. Under the Brazilian legislation existing already prior to ratification, in 1934, it is the employer who must continue to pay a woman's wages during her maternity leave. Under the Convention wages and other benefits must be "provided either out of public funds or by means of a system of insurance" (article 3 (c)) so that employers will not be inclined to discharge married or pregnant women before the period of leave because of the added financial burden their employment entails. While maintaining that its system was more favourable to the persons concerned,[6] the government submitted draft legislation to

---

[1] 1956 R.C.E. 23.

[2] The Maternity Protection Act of 1941 (39 R.P. 659).

[3] 1959 R.C.E. 19. The Committee quoted in particular from a 1953 decision of the "Cour de Cassation" which ignored the Act of 1941.

[4] 45 R.P. 745.

[5] Action in 1943 and 1953 respectively ensured compliance as regards the length of maternity leave (30 R.P. 554) and the scope of application of the Convention (1954 R.C.E. 15).

[6] Because the benefits women received, not only from their employers but also from Welfare Funds, exceeded those prescribed by the Convention. The government consequently invoked article 19, paragraph 8, of the I.L.O. Constitution under which the rati-

the Congress making the social insurance institutions solely responsible for the payment of maternity benefits.[1] The Chamber of Deputies eliminated this provision from the Act[2] and, despite a special appeal by the President to the Senate "to revert to the original text, in order that we may observe the terms of the ratified Convention along the lines given by the I.L.O.",[3] the Social Welfare Act as adopted in 1960 made no change in the method of payment of maternity allowances.[4] Discouraged by the failure of its efforts to secure conformity, the government denounced the Convention in July 1961.

This decision, though regrettable in itself,[5] had the merit of putting a formal end to the violation of a ratified Convention, not through national action to comply with the Convention, but at the price of terminating the international obligations. The success of supervision was thus merely juridical and negative, since fuller application could not be secured.[6]

Sometimes a country ratifies a Convention it considers to be so fully applied that no special implementing measures are necessary. In its first report on the Fee-Charging Employment Agencies Convention (Revised), 1949 (No. 96), the government of Pakistan indicated that no such agencies existed in the country, but the Committee of Experts pointed out that the instrument covered not only companies, institutions and organizations but also "persons" acting as intermediaries "for the purpose of procuring employment for a worker or supplying a worker for an employer".[7] The government replied that "it had only recently come to (its) notice that labour contractors were acting as intermediaries"[8] and that "in the initial stages it had not been considered necessary to introduce legislation with a view to giving effect to Convention No. 96".[9] Draft legislation was eventually prepared in 1962, but has not yet been adopted.[10] The government would perhaps have deferred the ratification of this instrument if it had realized its full implications in time.

---

fication of a Convention shall not be "deemed to affect any law, award, custom or agreement which ensures more favourable conditions to the workers concerned than those provided for in the Convention" (33 R.P. 465). The Committee of Experts did not accept this argument (1954 R.C.E. 15).

[1] 1956 R.C.E. 22.

[2] 42 R.P. 661-662.

[3] 43 R.P. 678-679.

[4] 1961 R.C.E. 31.

[5] The Committee of Experts expressed the hope, to the last, that "the government will find a way of bringing the national legislation into full conformity ... rather than denouncing the Convention" (1961 R.C.E.31).

[6] A more positive result was achieved later when the Brazilian government secured the adoption of new social security legislation (49 R.C.E. 232, 258) which enabled it to ratify the Maternity Protection Convention (Revised), 1952 (No. 103), in June 1965.

[7] 1955 R.C.E. 75.

[8] 40 R.P. 680.

[9] 43 R.P. 692.

[10] The Conference Committee considered the delays so serious that it decided in 1963 to place this case on its special list (47 R.P. 515, 539).

*Unforeseen Basic Difficulties*

The situation becomes especially delicate if the divergencies noted after ratification go to the core both of a Convention and of a country's social and political system. Instead of technical standards, it is the human rights of workers which are at issue. Such divergencies take on a different dimension because they require measures transcending the limits of labour protection in its traditional sense.

If the I.L.O. was able to reach a consensus on a small but important group of human rights Conventions this was due to a workable combination of two techniques: the selection of those civil liberties which are within its sphere of responsibility and their expression in broad yet enforceable terms. This "I.L.O. method of breaking down general aspirations into a series of definable problems and tackling each on its merits" [1] was applied with considerable success to the rights of association, of organization and of collective bargaining which are central to the Organization's composition, objectives and mode of operation. The two Conventions adopted for this purpose in 1948 and 1949,[2] at the request of the United Nations, are among the most widely ratified, but they have also given rise to persistent difficulties of implementation because of a reluctance on the part of some governments to face all the implications of their requirements. As has been seen, the Committee of Experts has made observations to countries in all parts of the world regarding the application, in particular, of the 1948 Convention (No. 87), but it is in relation to the Eastern European member States that the most serious problems have been encountered. After the U.S.S.R. ratified the Convention in 1956, all the countries of the region followed suit. While the points raised by the supervisory organs have of course varied according to the relevant national legislation, there has been a basic similarity between all these cases. A review of the observations and discussions regarding the Soviet Union will therefore illustrate this type of difficulty.

In its comments, queries and criticisms the Committee of Experts has concentrated on the application of Convention No. 87, with cross references to related problems arising under Conventions Nos. 11 and 98. Since its examination of the government's first report, in 1959, the Committee has made extensive observations centring on compliance with three basic requirements of Convention No. 87: that workers and employers "shall have the right to establish and ... join organizations of their own choosing without any previous authorization" (article 2); that the organizations so established "shall have the right to draw up their constitutions and rules, to elect their representatives in full freedom, to organize their administra-

---

[1] Cf. C. Wilfred Jenks, *Law, Freedom and Welfare, op. cit.*, p. 58.

[2] Freedom of Association and Protection of the Right to Organize Convention, 1948 (No. 87) and Right to Organize and Collective Bargaining Convention, 1949 (No. 98). The Right of Association (Agriculture) Convention, 1921 (No. 11) lays down no substantive rights but guarantees to agricultural workers "the same rights of association and combination as to industrial workers". The Right of Association (Non-Metropolitan Territories) Convention, 1947 (No. 84) also belongs in this group of instruments.

tion and activities and to formulate their programmes" (article 3, paragraph 1); and that the organizations "shall have the right to establish and join federations and confederations" (article 5). In support of its findings that full effect is not given to these requirements in the U.S.S.R. the Committee has referred to the national Constitution, to the legislation on the right of meeting, to the Labour Code of the Russian Soviet Federative Socialist Republic [1] and to the Rules of the All-Union Central Council of Trade Unions. It has explained repeatedly and in great detail why these national provisions are not compatible with the above-quoted requirements.[2]

The government has used several lines of argument in reply. It has claimed, first of all, that the Committee of Experts has misunderstood the terms and bearing of Soviet law and conditions.[3] At the same time it has indicated, since 1960, that draft "principles of labour legislation" are under discussion with a view to revising the Labour Codes of the Union Republics.[4] Application of the Convention should moreover be assessed,

---

[1] The Committee has pointed out that although separate Labour Codes exist for each of the fifteen constituent Republics of the Union, the text of most of these has not been communicated by the government (cf. 1963 R.C.E. 33). It has therefore has to found its observations to the U.S.S.R. on the text of the Labour Code of the R.S.F.S.R. which has appeared in the I.L.O. *Legislative Series* (1936–Russ.1; 1958–U.S.S.R. 1). The observations to Byelorussia and to the Ukraine refer to the Labour Codes of these Republics which are very similar to that of the R.S.F.S.R.

[2] In 1962, for instance, the Committee's observation covered seven pages (1962 R.C.E. 104-111). The major points made in relation to the national provisions referred to above were the following: article 126 of the Constitution of the U.S.S.R. which declares "the Communist Party ... the leading core of all organizations of the working people, both public and state" seems to make it legally impossible to set up a workers' organization independent of the Party (paragraphs 26-28 of the observation); the Order of 15 May 1935 which requires an authorization from the competent authorities for any meeting and conference makes it possible for these authorities to prevent the holding of the constituent assembly of a new organization, federation, etc. (paragraph 22); sections 152, 153, 156, 157 and 158 of the Labour Code of the R.S.F.S.R., under which trade unions must be registered with the All-Union Central Council of Trade Unions and only one union can exist in an undertaking, interfere with the free choice of the workers in founding their organizations (paragraphs 2, 3, 8-17); under the Decrees of 23 June 1933 and 21 August 1934 empowering the Central Council of Trade Unions to issue Rules, for instance for the registration of trade unions, the Central Council is able to interfere in the formation of such unions (paragraphs 4-7).

[3] This was the initial reaction, in 1959, when the government representative in the Conference Committee called on the Committee of Experts to "correct the inaccurate conclusions at which they had arrived in their observations" (43 R.P. 690), and has been largely maintained since. In 1962, the representative remarked that "the majority of the Committee of Experts had made the same comments as last year ..." and "not a single one of the explanations given by (the government) had been accepted" (46 R.P. 708). The reference to the majority is due to the dissent registered by Mr. Gubinski, the Expert from Poland, who stated in 1961 and 1962 that he "could not associate himself with the Committee's observations" on the application of Convention No. 87 in the Eastern European countries "since, in his opinion, account should be taken of the economic and social system existing in these countries" (1961 R.C.E. 60; 1962 R.C.E. 83). Apparently Mr. Gubinski did not call into question the Committee's legal findings. The Committee indicated, in reply, that its task is "simply to examine, from a purely legal point of view, to what extent the countries which have ratified Conventions give effect in their legislation and practice to the obligations which derive therefrom" (1962 R.C.E. 83).

[4] 1960 R.C.E. 46. The U.S.S.R. workers' member informed the Conference Committee in 1961 that "the legislation which had given rise to the observation of the Committee of

the government said, "in the light of social and economic conditions" because "conditions in the socialist and the capitalist countries were radically different".[1]   In addition to rebutting the arguments of the Committee of Experts,[2] the government has finally called into question its attitudes and motives, thus raising broader issues to which reference is made in a later chapter when the problems of supervision are analyzed.[3]

*Possible Remedies*

There remains the more limited question what courses of action are available when the implementation of a Convention has brought to light unexpected obstacles of a fundamental, perhaps even political, character. Here, as in the case of premature ratifications, prevention constitutes the best remedy.   The educational task of the supervisory Committees is of essential importance because a government can gauge in advance the full implications of a ratification it is considering.   The fact that in recent years the Governing Body has repeatedly selected human rights instruments for reporting under article 19 of the Constitution, should prove especially helpful.[4]   Regular recourse to the interpretation and advisory facilities of

---

Experts dated from the early years of the Soviet State.  This legislation did not completely take into account the evolution of the factual situation.  Measures were being taken at the present time to adapt this legislation to the evolution" (45 R.P. 756).  The government representative assured the Committee in 1961 and 1962 that the new legislation would not contain any provisions on the registration of trade unions (45 R.P. 754); he promised that it would be sent to the I.L.O. but cautioned at the same time that "on account of the vast programme of legislative revision, some delay might still occur" (46 R.P. 710-711).

[1] Statement in the Conference Committee in 1962 (46 R.P. 708).  Already three years earlier the government representative had stressed that "there existed a new form of democracy in the U.S.S.R.  The position of trade unions should be considered in this context" (43 R.P. 690).  In 1963, Professor Korovin, the newly appointed Expert from the U.S.S.R., and Mr. Gubinski said in their joint dissent that the Committee's conclusions were "influenced by the mechanical transfer to the socialist system of concepts tied to the capitalist system.  In their view this transfer distorts the aspects of social reality and may lead to erroneous conclusions".  Reiterating its previous opinion the Committee added that "States which have ratified Convention No. 87 must grant to workers and employers the rights and guarantees laid down in the Convention" (1963 R.C.E. 85). The workers' vice-chairman of the Conference Committee also referred to this issue when he concluded in 1961 that "there were two opposing conceptions of freedom of association...  The trade union movement as it was envisaged in the Freedom of Association Conventions did not fit with conditions in countries such as the U.S.S.R." (45 R.P. 754-755).

[2] Reference should also be made here to the detailed statement of the government's case in the Report of the I.L.O. survey mission on freedom of association which paid a two months' visit to the U.S.S.R. in 1959.  While corroborating the legal findings of the Committee of Experts, the Report emphasized the "considerable power and influence which the Soviet trade unions enjoy...  They are firmly established as part of the (Soviet) system but ... their situation has been evolving".  Cf. International Labour Office, *The Trade Union Situation in the U.S.S.R.* (Geneva: 1960), p. 136.

[3] Cf. pp. 193-196 below.

[4] From 1959 to 1963 the comprehensive surveys of the Committee of Experts dealt with the three major topics in this field:  freedom of association in 1959, forced labour in 1962, discrimination in 1963.  Its 1959 conclusions, for instance, caution that "in the field of freedom of association and protection of the right to organize ... actual practice

the I.L.O. should also aid governments to clarify doubtful points before any binding obligations are entered into.

Recourse to a more formal interpretation procedure may represent a possible avenue when the Convention has already been ratified. In addition to providing for reference of "any question or dispute relating to the interpretation ... of any Convention" to the International Court of Justice, article 37 of the I.L.O. Constitution also contemplates in its paragraph 2 "the appointment of a tribunal for the expeditious determination" of such a question or dispute. Although this latter possibility has not been resorted to, it could undoubtedly prove of value in determining the merits of a specific case for which the regular supervisory procedures have failed to turn up a solution.[1]

There exists another, more radical, answer to a problem of this kind: denunciation. Admittedly it is a solution of despair and one which, from the point of view of world organization and the development of international obligations, is greatly to be regretted. Yet it may be precisely in the interest of the rule of law to put an end to obligations when efforts to observe them encounter fundamental obstacles and when there apparently exists no ultimate hope for gradual compliance. As indicated in Chapter Two, governments have been most hesitant to take this extreme step, and it is especially significant in the present context that there has never been a denunciation of a human rights Convention of the I.L.O.[2] The motives for this reluctance can only be surmised. In addition to the rather recent adoption of most of the instruments, the reasons are probably psychological. Governments may shrink from conveying the impression, however erroneous, that they are taking a step backward in cancelling an international

---

is of exceptional importance, inasmuch as such practice necessarily reflects the more general background of the civil and political liberties enjoyed by the inhabitants of a country" (1959 R.C.E. 128).

[1] The Conference Committee was concerned with this type of difficulty in its early years in connection with the scope of application of certain Conventions. In 1933, for instance, it drew attention to the problem in the following terms: "A Convention can be properly applied only on condition that the provisions which have to be applied are properly interpreted. If the meaning of these provisions is interpreted differently by the States which have ratified, then the application of the Convention will not be uniform but will be to some extent contrary to the real intention of its provisions" (17 R.P. 520). The Committee's request that interpretations be obtained from the Permanent Court of International Justice was not granted by the Governing Body which agreed with the Director that "the parties concerned, and particularly the governments, should avail themselves in the first place of the existing facilities for obtaining either an unofficial interpretation from the Office, or an authentic interpretation from the Permanent Court" (64 G.B. 25-26, 138-139). As indicated in footnote 2, p. 90 above, advantage was taken of the second of these possibilities only in 1932, when the Governing Body adopted a proposal of the British government to obtain an advisory opinion from the Court as to whether "women who hold positions of supervision or management and are not ordinarily engaged in manual work" fall within the scope of the Night Work (Women) Convention, 1919 (No. 4); the Court replied in the affirmative (XVII O.B. 179-197).

[2] Only 12 denunciations not followed by the subsequent ratification of a revising Convention had been received by the end of 1964. In nine such cases the denunciation had been preceded by observations.

undertaking.[1] The workers' spokesmen have always viewed denunciations with suspicion and distaste.[2] The employers, on the other hand, have maintained that there is "nothing dishonourable about the act of denunciation".[3]

In the relatively rare instances when an impasse seems to have been reached on a fundamental issue,[4] the wisest course might be to rely on the effects of time. Such a course would not merely constitute a resigned effort to temporize: as in the case of certain political controversies, the avoidance of acute and reiterated confrontations might help to soften rigid attitudes and might, in the long run, do more to advance both the principles involved and the purposes of international organization in general.

## IV. Retrogression in the Application of a Convention

The essential aim of ratification is to promote higher labour standards or, at least, to prevent the lowering of standards. Cases where satisfactory application at the time of ratification is followed by infringement at a later stage are therefore deemed by the supervisory organs to be especially serious. It is an indication of the preventive value of supervision that few such cases of backsliding are discovered, and this only serves to give greater prominence to those which occur.

### Cases Where Conformity Was Restored

Sometimes the adoption of legislation contrary to a ratified Convention may have been due to an oversight, corrective action being taken as soon as the matter is drawn to the government's attention.[5] The Committee

---

[1] In a lecture given at the Free University at Bruxelles, the possible denunciation of Convention No. 87 was described as "causing great international difficulties for Belgium" (Michel Magrez, "Le Statut des organisations syndicales des travailleurs salariés en droit positif", Université Libre de Bruxelles, Faculté de Droit, *Travaux et Conférences*, 1962, Vol. X, pp. 12-13). Cf. also footnote 1, p. 101 below.

[2] In 1961 they asked the Director-General to indicate the reasons given by governments for denouncing Conventions (150 G.B. 56). When the Governing Body was consequently told in 1964 of the lengthy explanations given by Albania for denouncing Convention No. 4, the workers' members voiced their regret (160 G.B. 50, 142).

[3] As put by a United Kingdom employers' representative in 1953, when discussing cases of persistent non-compliance (36 R. P. 257). In 1961 the employers' members of the Conference Committee on Application suggested, in relation to Convention No. 87, that "it would better for the U.S.S.R. to denounce the Convention or for the government to request its revision" (45 R.P. 755).

[4] A stalemate on the issue of freedom of association was formally recognized in the Report of the Conference Committee in 1963: "As the various members of the Committee who had opinions different from those of the representatives of the countries in question maintained their position, the workers' group proposed that the discussion should not be renewed, that additional information concerning the Conventions should not be requested, and that it be indicated in the Report that the Committee noted the absence of any new elements in this regard in the Report of the Committee of Experts and in the position of the governments concerned" (47 R.P. 516). A similar passage appears in the Conference Committee Reports in 1964 and 1965 (48 R.P. 650 and 49 P.R. No. 33, p. II).

[5] For instance in 1962 the Committee of Experts, calling on the Cuban government to repeal a resolution of 1959 which had authorized the employment of young persons at

of Experts is liable to give special prominence to such *ex post facto* violations, if they seem to have been glossed over.[1]  However, cases of this
kind usually relate to matters of limited importance, and it is the principles
rather than the points involved which explain the Committee's strong
reaction.

The situation is somewhat different if the divergency goes to the heart
of a Convention and if the government fails to eliminate it as soon as an
observation has been made.  The government may ascribe such action to
economic or political difficulties.  The former possibility is illustrated by
the application in Hungary of the Underground Work (Women) Convention, 1935 (No. 45), which prohibits the employment of women on manual
work underground in mines.  The government's first report indicated that
no such employment occurred in Hungary before the adoption of the
Convention and that no legislation was required.[2]  After an interruption
of several years in the supply of reports the Committee of Experts, finding
that the new Labour Code authorized women to do underground work
not considered harmful to their health, called for complete application of
the Convention.[3]  During the discussion in the Conference Committee
the government referred to "difficulties caused by manpower shortage"[4]
and eventually promised that the Labour Code would be suitably amended.[5]
The necessary action was taken in 1962 in the form of a special decree
regarding the protection of the life and health of women and young persons.[6]

The government never denied that the Convention was being infringed
but stressed that the percentage of women miners was small[7] and promised
that full compliance would be restored when the labour shortage had been
overcome.  There is no way of telling therefore whether it was the disappearance of this shortage or the steady supervisory pressure which was the
determining factor.

*A Case Where Conformity Has not yet Been Restored*

It may be expected that retrogression in the application of a human
rights Convention would be likely to have political implications and give

---

night, expressed the hope that "the legislation will again be brought into full conformity"
with Convention No. 60 (1962 R.C.E. 77).  The government announced at the Conference
that the Resolution of 22 May 1962 had repealed this violation (46 R.P. 703).

[1] In 1958 it referred to an order issued in the Dominican Republic and published in the
*I.L.O. Legislative Series* (1956–Dom. 2) but not mentioned in the government's report.
The Committee stated that it could "only place on record its deep regret" because this
order, covering hours of work of workers in urban transport, was contrary not only to
Convention No. 1 but also to assurances given by the government in a previous report
(1958 R.C.E. 11).  In this case as well, corrective action occurred rapidly, on 30 April
1958 (1959 R.C.E. 16).

[2] 30 S.R. 119-120.  The Convention came into force in 1939 and the first report was
received in 1947.

[3] 1955 R.C.E. 52.  The Labour Code had been adopted in 1951.

[4] 38 R.P. 603.

[5] 1958 R.C.E. 43.  The case appeared on the Conference Committee's special list in
1957 but was omitted subsequently as a result of the government's assurances.

[6] 46 R.P. 701.  The government had indicated that if the new Labour Code could not
be promulgated shortly, separate legislation would be adopted (1962 R.C.E. 64).

[7] The proportion reported in 1955 was 2.5 per cent of the total (39 S.R. 91).

rise to even greater difficulties. The classical example is the prolonged infringement of the Right of Association (Agriculture) Convention, 1921 (No. 11), in Chile. As mentioned, this instrument does not contain any substantive provisions but requires those working in agriculture to enjoy "the same rights of association and combination" as workers in industry.

When Chile ratified the Convention in 1925 such equal rights applied and this situation remained unchanged until 1947, when an act on the establishment of unions of agricultural workers modified the Labour Code in such a way as to restrict severely the setting up and the functioning of such unions. The Committee of Experts analyzed and criticized these restrictions in a series of increasingly detailed and severe observations.[1] The Conference Committee was equally severe and completely unanimous in its appraisal and laid stress repeatedly on the past history of the case.[2] The government's response has varied over the years: guarded admission that some legislative changes were under way was followed by emphasis on the parliamentary, political and economic difficulties preventing return to full compliance; in recent years, when the adoption of amendments by the Congress seemed within sight, the government has been less reticent in agreeing with the findings of the supervisory organs.

Certain interesting features have marked the decade and a half of efforts to secure renewed application of Convention No. 11 in Chile. Workers' and employers' representatives from that country have participated on several occasions in the Conference discussions on this case. It was a Chilean workers' adviser who drew the attention of the Conference Committee in 1947 to the impending adoption of the act[3] and similar critical statements were made by Chilean workers at three subsequent sessions. Employers' representatives from Chile also intervened repeatedly in the Application Committee or the plenary session to explain the serious dangers to food production which uncontrolled labour agitation in the farming areas might cause.[4] As to the government spokesmen, their task has

---

[1] The main divergencies were: prohibition to set up a union covering more than one undertaking and consequently to federate; prohibition to present claims during the sowing and harvesting periods; implicit prohibition for seasonal or occasional workers to unionize (cf. e.g. 1957 R.C.E. 30).

[2] Its observation in 1951 termed it "a case of regression on a very important aspect of freedom of association" and "addressed an earnest appeal to the government to continue its efforts ... so that the Convention would again be fully implemented" (34 R.P. 564).

[3] He charged that the government's report "did not give a full picture of the truth in stating the reasons why Chile had nothing of importance to report concerning the association of agricultural trade unions because it should have mentioned the step backwards which had occurred in his country in the matter" (statement of Mr. Orjikh of the Chilean Confederation of Labour in doc. XXX/C.App.C./P.V.3 (roneoed), p. 3).

[4] A Chilean employers' representative, Mr. Feliú Segovia, took an especially active part in the discussion in 1961. His motion that this case be removed from the special list was rejected by the Committee (doc. C.App.C./PV. 18 (45th Session of the Conference) (roneoed), p. 2). The employers' group in the Conference Committee has been as vocal in its reproval as the workers' group and this case is in fact the only one which has figured on the special list uninterruptedly from 1957 till 1964.

The application of Convention No. 11 has also been examined by the Governing Body Committee on Freedom of Association. Complaints were filed in 1956 by two Chilean trade union federations, alleging infringement of the right of association of rural workers.

not been an easy one. Aside from certain variations from year to year in the degree of acceptance of supervisory criticism, as noted above, there have been significant differences in tone when the delegate was a member of parliament rather than a government official, the attitude of the former being much more resilient.[1] Chile has a long and democratic tradition and elective office does not necessarily imply commitment to a fixed policy. Congressional opinion, moreover, has been long concerned with the 1947 Act and bills designed to revise it were repeatedly submitted in Congress.[2]

The history of this case both in the I.L.O. and within the country itself shows that the difficulties encountered were in fact merely the reflection, at the international level, of a fundamental domestic problem. It is because Chile happened to include Convention No. 11 among the first Conventions it ratified that measures to inhibit freedom of association and collective bargaining in agriculture had an echo beyond its borders.[3] These measures were maintained over a prolonged period despite a combination of internal and external pressures, but recent developments provide

---

As noted by the Conference Committee in 1957 (40 R.P. 667), the Governing Body at its 135th Session formally endorsed the conclusions of the Committee of Experts and the Conference Committee in regard to this case, drew "the urgent attention of the government of Chile to these conclusions" and emphasized "the importance of its taking steps without further delay to bring its national legislation into harmony with the obligations solemnly undertaken by the ratification of the Convention" (XL O.B. 148, 167-168, 182).

[1] Senator Torres Cereceda has played a rather remarkable role in this connection. When confronted with the Chilean worker's charges in 1947 he candidly agreed that he had himself spoken against the new Rural Trade Union Act in the Senate (doc. XXX/ C.App.C./PV. 9 (roneoed), p. 1). Five years later, when he was again a government delegate he conceded that "he shared the point of view expressed by the Committee of Experts" and that "when he returned to his country, and in the light of the discussion which had just taken place (in the Conference Committee), he would do his utmost to have his point of view adopted" (doc. C.App.C./PV.8 (35th Session of the Conference) (roneoed), p. 4). In 1963 he was much more definite in explaining the difficulties faced by his government in giving effect to Convention No. 11; he replied not only in the Application Committee but also in the plenary, where he warned of "disturbances which demagogic elements have recently sought to introduce in Latin America in order to disturb the whole democratic structure. We believe that in this ideological struggle, it would not make for stability of our institutions to leave the peasant class exposed to foreign elements who preach hatred and violence." He also stressed: "We have not denounced Convention No. 11. What we do believe in is its gradual application" (47 R.P. 335).

[2] In June 1961, the Chamber of Deputies, after a long and sometimes bitter debate– during which speakers stressed the need for giving effect to Convention No. 11– adopted an amendment bill by 54 votes to 19 (La Nación (Santiago de Chile), 16 June 1961, pp. 6-8). After discussion in the Senate, this bill was sent back to the Chamber of Deputies. The government's report commented as follows: "Though the bill in question does not altogether eliminate differences existing between the trade union situation in agriculture and that in other sectors, it is a step forward in trade union legislation . The labour services will continue to press for the complete harmonization of legislation with the Convention by the competent authorities" (47 S.R. 31).

[3] A competent observer, Professor Francisco Walker Linares of the University of Chile at Santiago, concluded in 1953 that "Chilean legislation upon agricultural trade unions suffers from very serious defects. It offends against the most elementary principles of trade unionism and in practice, so far from achieving any positive results it has completely stifled trade unionism among agricultural workers." Cf. "Trade Unionism among Agricultural Workers in Chile", International Labour Review, Vol. LXVIII, No. 6 (December 1953), pp. 509-523.

concrete hope that compliance with the Convention may be restored as the more comprehensive efforts at social reform now initiated in Chile are translated into reality.[1]

Another example of possible retrogression in the effect given to human rights standards is of more recent date. The Committee of Experts observed in 1962 that a number of newly independent countries which, at the time of their admission to the I.L.O., had accepted the obligations of the Forced Labour Convention, 1930 (No. 29), had subsequently originated certain types of labour services "which may be used for economic development." Noting that the Convention had been declared applicable without modification by the former metropolitan power, France, and formally ratified by the countries concerned, the Committee emphasized that these States "are therefore bound not to institute new forms of forced labour and not to reintroduce those already abolished".[2] The governments' initial response was to point to the need to develop their economies,[3] an argument more fully considered when economic obstacles to compliance are reviewed below.[4]

## Possible Remedies

How can cases of backsliding be prevented, or dealt with once they have occurred? The realization that supervisory comment is inevitable may dissuade some governments from taking a retrograde measure deliberately. If it is a case of inadvertence, reminders by the Committee of Experts should suffice. If, on the other hand, a government is aware of its obligations yet regards them as being outweighed by considerations of a political or

---

[1] The government informed the Conference Committee in 1964 that "the most important political groups participating in the coming elections had included in their programme the adjustment of the legislation regarding agricultural trade unions, so as to bring it into conformity with the Convention" (48 R.P. 661). After the election of Mr. Eduardo Frei Montalva as President of the Republic in September 1964, the necessary amendments have in fact been drafted. During the 1965 session of the Conference the Chilean Minister of Labour and Social Welfare indicated that the new legislation which had been prepared with the help of an I.L.O. expert "involves strict and complete application" of Convention No. 11 (49 P.R. No. 13, p. 114) and the workers' members of the Application Committee "congratulated the government on the measures it was taking" (49 P.R. No. 33, p. XVI).

[2] The Committee made these comments in its General Conclusions concerning Forced Labour and mentioned in this connection legislation adopted in 1960 and 1961 in Chad, Congo (Brazzaville), Gabon, Ivory Coast, the Malagasy Republic, Mali and Senegal (1962 R.C.E. 214-215). It also addressed a detailed observation on the same subject to Congo (Brazzaville) (1962 R.C.E. 53-54).

[3] "In their opinion, the Experts had treated the problem in an excessively abstract and legal manner and ... account should be taken of actual economic and social conditions... After having attained political independence, such countries also wished to gain economic independence" (46 R.P. 686). The government representative of Congo (Brazzaville) considered that "one could not draw a parallel between the situation of the newly independent States and that of the other countries. The measures ... were justified by prevailing circumstances. They were, however, never applied. The government was determined to comply with its obligations under the Convention, but certain transitional situations would have to be borne in mind" (46 R.P. 698-699).

[4] Cf. pp. 119-133.

an economic character, or both,[1] then the supervisory organs have no choice but to face the situation squarely.

## V. Effective Incorporation of a Convention in Municipal Law

The implementation of a Convention becomes more difficult if its terms are not clearly incorporated in national law, thus leaving those concerned in doubt as to their precise rights and obligations. This problem arises especially, but not exclusively, in countries where ratification is deemed to give force of law to a treaty. The question is a complex one both in legal and in practical terms, and the supervisory Committees have had to face it since their early days. Their objective is, briefly, to remove any ambiguity as to what legislative provisions are applicable so as to ensure the every-day observance of a ratified Convention.

*Monistic and Dualistic Concepts*

Without attempting to discuss the doctrinal problems raised by the incorporation of international Conventions in municipal law,[2] it is necessary to refer to the setting within which application difficulties of this kind are liable to arise. From a theoretical point of view, the distinction between the monistic and dualistic concepts is well known. Under the former, no special incorporation clause is required to make a duly ratified and promulgated treaty "the supreme law of the land".[3] Under the latter, such a clause is often used to transform a ratified treaty expressly into domestic law. In certain countries following the monistic concept, such as France and the Netherlands, a ratified treaty is deemed, furthermore, to override all legislation inconsistent with its provisions, whereas other countries using this concept, such as the United States, consider subsequent laws to supersede a prior treaty if its terms are incompatible with the more recent legislation.[4] Among the practical questions which may arise, it must be ascertained, first, whether the introduction of a ratified I.L.O. Convention can, by itself, guarantee its application.

---

[1] War or other cases of *force majeure* are considered justified reasons (when authorized in a Convention) for suspending the application of certain Conventions, as will be seen below (pp. 147-150). In all other circumstances the clause *rebus sic stantibus* cannot be invoked and any attempt to do so would clearly have the gravest consequences for the network of obligations under I.L.O. Conventions. Cf. in this connection Gerhard Schnorr, *Das Arbeitsrecht als Gegenstand internationaler Rechtsetzung* (Munich and Berlin: C.H. Beck, 1960) pp. 150-161.

[2] For a full treatment of the question in connection with international labour Conventions, cf. Nicolas Valticos, "Conventions internationales du travail et droit interne", *Revue Critique de droit international privé*, 1955, No. 2, pp. 251-288.

[3] Article VI, paragraph 2, of the Constitution of the United States.

[4] The matter is discussed in some detail in *Report of the Commission Appointed under Article 26 of the Constitution of the International Labour Organization to Examine the Complaint Filed by the Government of Portugal concerning the Observance by the Government of Liberia of the Forced Labour Convention, 1930 (No. 29)* (XLVI O.B. No. 2 Supplement II), pp. 158-161. This document is subsequently referred to as *Commission of Inquiry Report (Portugal-Liberia)*.

*Non-Self-Executing Provisions*

As just noted, incorporation may be automatic or may have to be specifically provided for in the ratification act. In both cases the need for additional measures of implementation depends essentially on the text of the instrument itself, i.e. on whether all its provisions are "self-implementing".[1] Mere ratification of the Shipowners' Liability (Sick and Injured Seamen) Convention, 1936 (No. 55) would not be enough to make it fully effective because, under its article 9, "national laws or regulations shall make provision for securing the rapid and inexpensive settlement of disputes concerning the liability of the shipowner under this Convention." Many international labour Conventions contain similar provisions requiring special action to define their scope, to authorize exceptions, to secure the participation of employers' and workers' organizations in their implementation, to lay down measures for their enforcement, etc.

It was to ensure the full application of provisions of this type under the circumstances described above that the Governing Body, at the suggestion of the Committee of Experts, included in the forms of report–first in 1930, then on two subsequent occasions [2]–an increasingly precise question on the "action... taken to make effective those provisions of the Convention which require a national authority to take certain specific steps for its implementation".[3] The information received in response to this question sheds light on the cases where non-self-executing provisions have been a source of delay or uncertainty.

The first prerequisite of implementation is the existence of appropriate measures to make the Convention effective. Such measures do not necessarily consist of statute law [4] and may even involve collective agreements [5] or action of a practical character.

Paradoxically, the very fact that a Convention has force of national law may be a cause of delay if it is thought, incorrectly, that no special measures are needed. This seems to have been the case when Brazil ratified the

---

[1] The following definition, formulated in terms of United States practice but valid generally, may serve for the present purpose: "A self-executing treaty is one which furnishes by its own terms (or by reason of the existence of previously enacted statutes which can implement it) a rule of law for the executive branch of the government, the courts, the states, or for private individuals" (Alona E. Evans, "Some Aspects of the Problem of Self-Executing Treaties", *Proceedings, American Society of International Law, 1951*, p. 68).

[2] Cf. footnote 5, p. 24 above. In 1963 the Committee of Experts reviewed in some detail how it can follow up the extent of practical application of ratified Conventions; within the framework of this review it also explored the problem of the incorporation of Conventions in domestic law (1963 R.C.E. 8-12).

[3] Part II, paragraph 2, of the forms of report.

[4] When the International Labour Office was asked by the United States government in 1950 whether the term "national laws or regulations" as used in Convention No. 55, refers solely to statutes or covers also the principles of general maritime law enunciated and enforced by the courts, it replied that the term "includes not merely legislation in the narrowest technical sense, but other forms of legal prescription including decrees, ordinances of various types and, where applicable, principles of customary law" (XXXIII O.B. 305-306).

[5] Cf. pp. 114-118 below.

Accommodation of Crews Convention (Revised), 1949 (No. 92) in 1954. In its first report the government stressed that the instrument had force of law but added that regulations were to be issued to give effect to its provisions.[1] The Committee of Experts noted in 1960 that such regulations had been adopted.[2]

The position is much more difficult if the government considers that there is no need for special measures of implementation. In Mexico, for instance, article 133 of the national Constitution provides for the incorporation of a ratified Convention in the national law and the repeal of any contrary legislation. Because the government's reports insisted repeatedly that the existence of this article guaranteed full application, the supervisory Committees pointed out that some positive steps were called for to give effect to the non-self-executing provisions of ratified Conventions.[3] The government eventually ceased to question the need for special action to implement such provisions and took concrete measures in certain cases.[4]

*Self-Executing Provisions*

The problems encountered in giving effect to self-executing provisions are sometimes even more complex than those just reviewed, because of the doubts and uncertainties which may arise when different standards exist side by side. To quote again an example involving Mexico: under the above-mentioned article 133 of its Constitution, the Night Work of Young Persons (Industry) Convention (Revised), 1948 (No. 90), acquired force of law following ratification in 1956. The government pointed out in particular that the period of night rest which the Federal Labour Act had previously fixed at ten consecutive hours had automatically been increased to 12 hours because article 2 of the Convention providing for this longer period operated as a self-executing treaty provision. The Committee of Experts drew attention to this ambiguous situation: in the absence of any formal amendment of the previous legislation, "reference by employers and workers to the Federal Labour Act would not in any way enable

---

[1] 1956 R.C.E. 78. In a statement to the Conference Committee in 1957 the government explained the legal position as follows: "The ratification of this Convention... has automatically incorporated the provisions of the Convention in the national legislation. According to section 2(2) of the Act instituting the Brazilian Civil Code, a Convention duly ratified and promulgated and in force on the international plane repeals or amends all pre-existing legal provisions incompatible with its terms. However, where an international standard merely lays down a programme or where domestic law lays down no express sanction for contraventions, or where no competent body exists to supervise and enforce the Convention, it becomes necessary to enact legislation or issue regulations to ensure the effective application of the international instrument" (40 R.P. 679-680).

[2] 1960 R.C.E. 50.

[3] Cf. in particular the general observations made by the Committee of Experts in 1952 (1952 R.C.E. 14-15) and by the Conference Committee in 1953 (36 R.P. 372-373). There ensued a series of detailed observations on the Conventions concerned.

[4] In 1957 the Committee of Experts noted that joint bodies of shipowners and seafarers had been established in accordance with the Placing of Seamen Convention, 1920 (No. 9), and that modifications in the Labour Code had led to fuller compliance with the Holidays with Pay Convention, 1936 (No. 52) (1957 R.C.E. 29, 67).

them to ascertain their rights and obligations" under the Convention.[1] The Committee insisted in this and similar cases that, to clarify the position, legislation implicitly repealed or amended by self-executing provisions should be reissued in its revised form. When the Italian government contended, for instance, that effect had been given to the Holidays with Pay Convention, 1936 (No. 52), by virtue of its ratification, as well as through the national Constitution, the Civil Code and many collective agreements, the Committee of Experts called for the adoption of specific legislation.[2]

*Interim Solutions*

When the necessary legislative revisions could not be carried out immediately, interim solutions were devised in certain countries to reduce to a minimum the risks of ignoring or infringing a ratified Convention. In Guatemala, the government decided to print its Labour Code with special footnotes referring to the I.L.O. Conventions which had automatically amended certain provisions of the Code.[3]

Interim measures were also taken in France to ensure compliance with the Safety Provisions (Building) Convention, 1937 (No. 62), which was ratified in 1950. The detailed character of this instrument necessitated a number of legislative changes. Pending their completion, the government sent a circular to the labour inspection services in 1959 asking them to convince employers in the building industry that "the safety of their personnel" made it desirable "to observe scrupulously the provisions of Convention No. 62".[4]

In Uruguay a legal system of penalties for violations of ratified Conventions, instituted in 1954, was apparently envisaged as a temporary measure, pending revision or enactment of the necessary legislation.[5]

---

[1] 1962 R.C.E. 118-119.

[2] 1962 R.C.E. 66-67. The following sentence in the observation is especially significant: "It seems unlikely that all persons interested (magistrates, workers, employers, inspectors, etc.) are fully informed of the provisions of the Convention and that the latter can be effectively applied solely through the principle of incorporation" of ratified Conventions in the national legislation.

One case where the judiciary did take account of a ratified treaty was noted by the Committee of Experts in connection with the Maternity Protection Convention, 1919 (No. 3). In 1962, the French "Cour de Cassation" decided that the provisions of this instrument regarding the duration of maternity benefits should be applied, "notwithstanding provisions of the Social Security Code to the contrary". The Committee expressed the hope that the measures of implementation which the government intended to take would "be based on the above judgment" (1963 R.C.E. 42).

[3] 46 R.P. 690. The Conference Committee suggested that "this practice, which goes some way towards preventing confusion, might usefully be followed elsewhere in similar cases" (46 R.P. 679).

[4] 1960 R.C.E. 39. The circular, which was also published in the review *Travail et Sécurité* (No. 7, July 1959), contained in an appendix the text of those provisions of the Convention to which, in the words of the circular, "the Committee of Experts of the I.L.O. had drawn special attention".

[5] Cf. 1955 R.C.E. 20, and p. 135 below.

*Difficulties Caused by Subsequent Legislation*

Interim or simplified measures may not be sufficient, however, in countries where legislation contrary to previously ratified standards is not deemed to supersede a ratified treaty. Such cases not only constitute particularly serious examples of retrogression in the application of a Convention, they also give rise to intricate conflicts between the most recent national provisions and the country's international obligations. While difficulties of this kind are not insuperable,[1] their elimination has taken so long in the two major cases of this kind that neither of the countries concerned has as yet been able to overcome them.

In the case of Nicaragua the Committee of Experts noted in 1956, when the government resumed supplying reports,[2] that its first Labour Code, adopted in 1945, contained provisions contrary to the Conventions ratified in 1934 which, according to the government, had automatically become part of national law.[3] The government promised to introduce amending legislation but as it has not done so thus far the problem remains unresolved.

In a similar situation in Colombia a solution is beginning to emerge. This country ratified a number of Conventions in 1933 but adopted its Labour Code only in 1950. In reply to a series of observations by the Committee of Experts,[4] the government recognized in the Conference Committee in 1956 that, while in theory ratified treaties took precedence over internal legislation and "occupational organizations were entitled to appeal to the Supreme Court of Justice in any case where there was a contradiction" between the two, in practice "the provisions now applied were those of the Labour Code although they were contrary" to certain Conventions.[5] To eliminate this ambiguous situation as well as to give effect to certain Conventions not covered so far by any legislation, the government submitted to Congress a "Bill to Adapt Labour Legislation to the International Labour Conventions Ratified by Colombia".[6] Unless a clear judicial ruling can be secured, such a revision would seem to represent the only acceptable

---

[1] The only insuperable situation so far encountered was a conflict between a provision of the Night Work (Young Persons) Convention, 1919 (No. 6), and article 123 of the Mexican Constitution. The former prohibits the night work of young persons up to 18 years, whereas the latter fixes the corresponding age at 16 years (1947 R.C.E. 14). Since the Constitution takes precedence over a ratified treaty, the government denounced the Convention rather than envisage a change in its Constitution. Mexico ratified the revised Convention (No. 90) in 1956.

[2] Cf. p. 60 above.

[3] 1956 R.C.E. 16-17. The Committee of Experts inquired whether it would be the international or the more recent national provisions which would apply "if the matter is brought before a court of law"; it also asked the government to "take steps in order to clarify the position in all cases where conflicts may arise between the Conventions ratified in 1934 and the Labour Code promulgated 11 years later."

[4] Cf. in particular 1956 R.C.E. 15-16.

[5] 39 R.P. 655-656.

[6] 1959 R.C.E. 15. This bill was subsequently replaced by a "comprehensive revision of the Labour Code" (1961 R.C.E. 21-22), prepared with I.L.O. assistance (45 R.P. 742), which is still pending before Congress. Cf. also footnote 4, p. 171 below.

remedy in cases of this kind, because the existence side by side of two incompatible sets of provisions not only prevents compliance with international obligations but is also liable to impede the rule of law within a country.

## The Crucial Role of Supervision

Through all the various situations and sets of circumstances reviewed above there runs like a thread the role which the supervisory committees play when the incorporation of I.L.O. standards in internal law appears in jeopardy.[1] International supervision is thus able to provoke remedial action in a particularly sensitive area where the overlapping of two legal orders may be the source, first of considerable confusion and later of real progress: "By their appraisal of the international legality of internal measures in the field covered by ratified Conventions, (the supervisory) organs attempt to induce the national legislator to bring the internal order into conformity with the international one. In this way they help, through a variety of national techniques, to ensure closer unity between these two orders".[2]

## VI. Difficulties Encountered by Federal States

A federal State, in the sense in which it is used here, is not only a country composed of units (states, provinces, cantons, republics, etc.) enjoying a degree of self-government, but one where the power to give effect to I.L.O. Conventions lies to some extent at least with these constituent units rather than with the central government. The distinction is necessary because in the majority of federal countries the central government's powers in labour matters now differ little from those of a government of a unitary State.[3] The obstacles to implementation are however sufficiently real in some federal States to have required the Organization's attention ever since its inception.

## Submission to the Competent Authorities

The federal government must first of all decide what effect, if any, is to be given to a newly adopted Convention. If the government is unable to

---

[1] Professor Virally stresses this need for machinery to co-ordinate the rules of internal and international law: "The conformity of inferior norms with superior norms is never achieved automatically and, so to speak, necessarily. It needs to be ensured by a suitable technical mechanism, which may in fact be lacking" (*La Pensée Juridique* (Paris: Librairie Générale de Droit et de Jurisprudence, 1960), p. 207).

[2] N. Valticos, "Conventions internationales du travail et droit interne", *op. cit.*, p. 288.

[3] Tables appended to the 1963 Report of the Conference Committee listed the following 16 member countries as federal States: Argentina, Australia, Austria, Brazil, Canada, Federal Republic of Germany, India, Libya, Federation of Malaya, Mexico, Nigeria, Pakistan, Switzerland, U.S.S.R., United States, Yugoslavia. As regards the special position of two other States, Cameroon and Somalia, cf. footnote 4, p. 113 below.

assume international obligations or to carry them out, or both,[1] it cannot be expected to bring a Convention before the "authorities within whose competence the latter lies, for the enactment of legislation or other action"[2] in exactly the same manner as a government which is not subject to such limitations. In recognition of this difference the Constitution of the I.L.O. contains special provisions concerning Conventions which "the federal government regards as appropriate under its constitutional system, in whole or in part, for action by the constituent" units: such Conventions must be referred to the local authorities and "periodical consultations" must be arranged with these authorities so that separate or "co-ordinated" action can be taken on the instruments in question (article 19, paragraph 7).[3]

It is necessary to stress from the outset that the Conference has made an effort, especially during the post-war years, to facilitate the acceptance and implementation of I.L.O. Conventions by federal States. This effort, which represents but another facet of the search for flexibility, has resulted in the adoption of a number of Conventions envisaging compliance on the basis of action by the "federal",[4] "national"[5] or "central"[6] authorities. Once ratification has taken place, a series of questions may arise in connection with the division of powers in a federation.

*The Division of Enforcement Powers*

One source of difficulty which, without being fundamental, can nonetheless have widespread repercussions, is a decentralized system of super-

---

[1] For a full treatment of both aspects of the question cf. Robert B. Looper, " 'Federal State' Clauses in Multilateral Instruments", *British Yearbook of International Law, 1956-6*, pp. 162-203.

[2] Article 19, paragraph 5, of the I.L.O. Constitution.

[3] If a Convention is deemed appropriate for federal action, the obligations as regards submission to the competent authorities are the same as those of unitary States. The problem of the implementation of Conventions by federal States gave rise to much controversy during the framing of the I.L.O.'s Constitution in 1919. The United States members of the Commission, which was responsible for this task, insisted that the obligations of federal States would have to reflect the limitations on their treaty-implementing powers. As a result article 19, as adopted in 1919, authorized federal States to treat a Convention as a Recommendation, an instrument which, though subject to submission to the competent legislative authorities, is not subject to ratification. The revised version of article 19, as quoted above, was adopted in 1946 in an effort to achieve greater equality of obligations as between States of a federal and a unitary character. An account of the 1919 negotiations is given in Shotwell, *The Origins of the International Labor Organization, op. cit.*, Vol. I, pp. 127-198. The reasons underlying the 1946 amendment are set out in 29 Report II (1) pp. 173-186. Cf. also *The International Labour Code, op. cit.*, Preface, pp. LXXIX-LXXXI and a series of studies, published in the *International Labour Review* between 1940 and 1947, which dealt with the implementation of I.L.O. standards in Canada (Vol. XLII, pp. 347-376), the United States (Vol. XLIV, pp. 123-193), India (Vol. XLIX, pp. 415-445), Australia (Vol. LIV, pp. 285-308) and Switzerland (Vol. LVI, pp. 1-21).

[4] Labour Inspection Convention, 1947 (No. 81), and Migration for Employment Convention (Revised), 1949 (No. 97).

[5] Employment Service Convention, 1948 (No. 88), and Discrimination (Employment and Occupation) Convention, 1958 (No. 111).

[6] Labour Clauses (Public Contracts) Convention, 1949 (No. 94).

vision of the application of labour legislation. In certain countries legislation adopted by the federal authorities may thus be enforced by the inspection services of the constituent units. This decentralization exists of course in unitary States as well,[1] but its effects in a federal country may impede compliance with a ratified Convention not only in practice but even in law. While the former contingency falls outside the scope of the present study,[2] the latter is especially relevant to the application of the Labour Inspection Convention, 1947 (No. 81), which the supervisory Committees regard as one of the foremost instruments in the International Labour Code.

If the central authorities of the federation are not exclusively or even primarily responsible for giving effect to this Convention, action by the federated units constitutes the only acceptable alternative. It is essential in this case that the local labour inspection services should possess all the powers and perform all the functions prescribed by the Convention. Failure to satisfy these requirements has caused difficulties, for instance, in the application of Convention No. 81 in Argentina. In 1962, the Committee of Experts divided its observation to this country into two parts, dealing respectively with application in the Federal Capital and in the provinces.[3] It noted certain shortcomings in regard to Buenos Aires, but placed the main emphasis on the absence of sufficient information in regard to the rest of the country [4] and on the need for applying the Convention fully in all parts of the federation. Clearly, the local authorities must be aware of their responsibilities under the Convention which requires co-operation between the central and the local inspection services. It is significant that these minimum conditions are important even in the case of a Convention permitting a high degree of administrative decentralization, such as No. 81.

When an instrument is less flexible and deals in some detail with a highly technical subject such as industrial safety, its implementation in a federal

---

[1] The Labour Inspection Convention, 1947 (No. 81) leaves a considerable amount of latitude in this respect: labour inspection need be centrally controlled only to the extent "compatible with the administrative practice of the member"; in the case of a federal State, decentralization is specifically provided for (article 4, paragraphs 1 and 2).

[2] Cf. p. 57 above. A case of this kind which, for the reasons mentioned, was not included in the survey may nonetheless serve to illustrate this type of problem. Although the Swiss Confederation has, over the years, acquired "almost unlimited" competence to legislate on labour matters (cf. A. Berenstein," The Influence of International Labour Conventions on Swiss Legislation", *op. cit.*, pp. 496-497), supervisory functions continue to be entrusted primarily to the cantons. When the federal government encountered certain difficulties in securing compliance with the Night Work of Young Persons (Industry) Convention, 1919 (No. 6), in the case of bakers' apprentices, it attempted by means of correspondence and meetings with the competent cantonal authorities to draw their attention to the need for strict enforcement of the relevant federal legislation throughout the Confederation (cf. in particular the references to these difficulties in the Conference Committee in 1951, 1952 and 1958: 34 R.P. 563; 35 R.P. 496; 42 R.P. 664).

[3] 1962 R.C.E. 78. Argentina exemplifies the type of federal country, particularly prevalent in Latin America, where labour legislation is largely federal in character.

[4] A government representative had assured the Conference Committee in 1960 that "the labour inspectorate was established throughout the national territory. However, due to long distances, the federal authorities had difficulty in obtaining the necessary information from the provincial authorities" (44 R.P. 621).

country is impossible unless legislation exists throughout the whole of the territory. In Mexico, where the regulation of safety and hygiene is left to the constituent states, the implementation of the Safety Provisions (Building) Convention, 1937 (No. 62), outside the Federal District has, for this reason, met with special difficulties. Acknowledging that some 70 per cent of the country's building workers are without the minimum protection laid down in the Convention, the government has recommended that the regulations which have been in force in Mexico City since 1951 be extended to the various states. But this requires the consent of the local authorities.[1]

## Problems Due to Greater Decentralization

If, as will be seen shortly, the normal trend toward a greater degree of federal responsibility in the labour field tends to facilitate the implementation of I.L.O. Conventions, developments in the opposite direction have occasionally interfered with the performance of international obligations. The possibility is rather remote, but a development of this kind was invoked as the principal reason for India's denouncing the Unemployment Convention, 1919 (No. 2), in 1938. Although the real difficulty was undoubtedly the government's inability to set up the necessary employment agencies,[2] the government's explanations referred mainly to the new Constitution of 1935 which removed the subject of "unemployment" from federal jurisdiction.[3]

## The Division of Legislative Powers

A somewhat analogous problem arises when a federal government ratifies in the belief that implementation is possible by means of federal law, only to discover that the necessary legislative powers are in fact reserved to the federated units. Such a situation emerged following the ratification of the Hours of Work (Industry) Convention, 1919 (No. 1), the Weekly

---

[1] Cf. 1963 R.C.E. 79-80. A government representative explained to the Conference Committee in 1963 that "the procedure for this extension fell within the competence of the federal units, but the government had requested them to adopt the necessary measures" (47 R.P. 533).

[2] The supervisory Committees had been concerned with this matter since their inception and a representation was also made to the Governing Body in 1936 by the Madras Labour Union of Textile Workers. Cf. XXII O.B. 61-66.

[3] The government stated in a letter to the Director of the International Labour Office that, as regards this subject, "the power both of legislation and administration has passed entirely from the hands of the central government" (XXIII O.B. 66). Writing in 1944, one of the veterans of labour policy in pre-independence India made a strong plea for the reversal of this trend: Sir Atul C. Chatterjee "Federalism and Labour Legislation in India", *International Labour Review*, Vol. XLIX, Nos. 4-5 (April-May 1944), pp. 441-444. The Indian Constitution of 1950 gives the central government overriding jurisdiction on labour legislation: cf. V.K.R. Menon "The Influence of International Labour Conventions on Indian Labour Legislation", *International Labour Review*, Vol. LXXIII, No. 6 (June 1956), pp. 552-554. In 1959 India ratified the Employment Service Convention, 1948 (No. 88), in the implementation of which responsibility is shared by the central and the state governments (46 S.R. 173-176).

Rest (Industry) Convention, 1921 (No. 14), and the Minimum Wage-Fixing Machinery Convention, 1928 (No. 26), by Canada in 1935. Three acts adopted by the Dominion Parliament later the same year were declared *ultra vires* of the Parliament by the Judicial Committee of the Privy Council in 1937.[1] As a result the main burden for implementing the Conventions was thrown on the provincial legislatures and governments.[2] At the same time the decision did not affect the international validity of the three ratifications nor did the Dominion government attempt to shirk its responsibilities in this respect. Two courses of action were open to it. One was to admit its inability to ensure compliance through federal action and to denounce the Conventions.[3] The other was to work toward gradual application through co-operation with the provincial authorities. The government never seems to have hesitated in following the second course. In its replies to the Committee of Experts it referred to the contacts established and maintained with the provinces and paid tribute to their "increasing degree of co-operation".[4] As this is inevitably a slow process, supervisory comment has alternated over the years between satisfaction at the progress made [5] and emphasis on the need for further action.[6] In a situation of this kind the role of the central government in relation to its federated

---

[1] *Attorney-General for Canada v. Attorney-General for Ontario* (1937), A.C. 326. In 1940 a Royal Commission recommended reversal of this decision and suggested that "the best method would be for the provinces to give the Parliament of Canada power to implement such international labour Conventions as the government has ratified" (*Report of the Canadian Royal Commission on Dominion Provincial Relations* (Rowell-Sirois Commission), Book II, p. 48). Since 1949 it is the Supreme Court of Canada which has the final word on constitutional interpretation, but no occasion has apparently arisen for reopening the 1937 judgment.

[2] The Dominion government is able to legislate for the Yukon and North West Territories.

[3] In 1948, the Committee of Experts alluded to this alternative, suggesting that if compliance with one or all of the Conventions proved impossible even by provincial legislation "the question inevitably arises whether the Dominion government should not give serious consideration to the desirability of taking the necessary steps to liberate itself from the obligations" of the Conventions (1948 R.C.E. 14-15).

[4] As related to the Conference Committee in 1949, these contacts took the form of correspondence and of meetings of senior officials. The government also asked the International Labour Office to compile "a table indicating the precise points in respect of which provincial legislation appeared to fall short of full compliance with Convention No. 26. This table had been communicated to the various provinces in the hope that it would prove useful in an eventual revision of their legislation" (32 R.P. 444).

The Federal Minister of Labour of Canada informed the International Labour Conference in 1964 that a meeting of Labour Ministers from the federal and provincial governments had recently decided to devise "a procedure for ratifying I.L.O. Conventions that fall within both federal and provincial jurisdiction. Such a procedure, we believe, would ... help toward the harmonization of our labour standards" (48 R.P. 429). There also exists in Canada an association of Labour Department administrators which meets regularly each year, as well as other methods for federal-provincial consultation on I.L.O. matters. Cf. 48 Report III (Part III), p. 7.

[5] In 1954, for instance, the Committee of Experts noted "the gradual extension of the eight-hour day to new categories of workers and the continual lowering of working hours in several provinces" (1954 R.C.E. 14).

[6] In 1957 the Committee of Experts asked for information on "all new developments" and "all steps taken to co-ordinate the measures envisaged by the provincial legislatures in regard to hours of work" (1957 R.C.E. 13).

units resembles somewhat that of the I.L.O. toward its member countries. In both cases the task is one of promotion and persuasion, but the important financial powers wielded by federal authorities can provide an added stimulus.

It is also significant that in another federation which is not so very different from Canada either in number of units or in distribution of powers, the possibilities of Commonwealth-state co-operation in the ratification and implementation of I.L.O. standards have been successfully demonstrated: the government of Australia has examined together with the authorities of the six states whether effect can be given jointly to international labour Conventions which are appropriate primarily for state action. Although the process is inevitably slow because the concurrence of all the state governments must be secured,[1] among the 24 Conventions ratified by Australia, nine deal with matters for which the states are principally responsible. It is especially notable from the point of view of the present study that the application of these Conventions does not appear to have caused any difficulties.

*The Evolution of Federal Systems*

The problems facing federal States must be viewed in the perspective of their size, their constitutional practice and their possible evolution towards a greater degree of central influence.[2] If the limitations placed on federal action in the labour field gradually disappear, so will the difficulties. In the absence of a general trend, however, no universal solution exists, especially because labour questions are not among the main factors which determine the character and development of federalism. While some traditional and some new federations have opted for primacy of central control in labour matters,[3] the decision of other, formerly separate, countries to unite has led to the emergence of new structures whose precise forms are often slow to crystallize and difficult to categorize.[4]

---

[1] A committee appointed to review the powers of the Commonwealth Parliament described the process as follows: "Where state law is involved, Commonwealth policy has been to ensure that the law and practice in each of the states are in accord with Convention requirements and that each state is agreeable to ratification". The committee also referred to "the insurmountable difficulties sometimes experienced in obtaining approval of six independent states to a single course of action" (*The Parliament of the Commonwealth of Australia. Report from the Joint Committee on Constitutional Review, 1959*, paragraph 777).

[2] Cf. in this connection C. Wilfred Jenks, *Human Rights and International Labour Standards*, (London: Stevens & Sons, 1960), pp. 143-152.

[3] India, Nigeria and Switzerland, for example. In one case, Libya, the country changed its federal structure to a unitary one.

[4] Cameroon (composed of an Eastern and a Western part which were previously under French and British administration repectively), the Somali Republic (composed of the former Trust Territory and British Somaliland) and Malaysia (composed of Malaya, North Borneo and Sarawak) are cases in point. Under the practice consistently followed in such cases the obligations under I.L.O. Conventions which existed in the constituent units prior to federation continue in force within their previous territorial limits, pending their eventual extension to the whole of the federation; in the case of Cameroon, for example, nine Conventions are applicable throughout the country, six only in Eastern Cameroon and eight others only in Western Cameroon.

*Possible Remedies*

The most promising line of approach lies in the direction of preventive rather than remedial action. As already noted, the Conference is conscious of the need to render the acceptance and implementation of certain Conventions easier for federal States and this policy has begun to bear fruit, e.g. when Australia and Canada decided to ratify the Employment Service Convention.

The Committee of Experts stressed this flexible policy when it reviewed the effect given to the Discrimination Convention: "By providing specially for action by methods appropriate to national conditions and practice, the Convention takes into account, *inter alia*, the special problems which may stem from the federal structure of a State".[1]

Attempts to pave the way for acceptance of I.L.O. standards by federal countries, which have so far centred on the fields of employment policy and labour administration, might be extended to other spheres. Nonetheless, the most positive area of initiative involves joint and co-ordinated action by the central and the local authorities of a federal State. If such joint action is found to be impossible, a system might be devised whereby a federal State would be able to ratify a Convention in respect of some rather than all the units composing it.[2] Such a system, though based on considerations similar to those underlying the federal clause in article 19, would represent an entirely new departure in the implementation of ratified Conventions by federal countries.

## VII. Implementation Through Collective Agreements

To the possible ways of helping certain federal States to give effect to I.L.O. Conventions on a wider scale, another could be added: implementation on the basis of collective agreements. By obviating or reducing the need for legislation, this method might enable the countries concerned and in fact any other countries facing similar difficulties to base their international obligations entirely or partially on the contractual arrangements existing between employers and workers. Resort has been had to this method, but only on a limited scale and with a great deal of caution, so as not to impair the validity of the resulting obligations or to endanger their supervision. Although it is not possible to go into all the complex problems

---

[1] 1963 R.C.E. 199-200. The Committee noted that eight federal States had ratified the Convention; since then Canada has followed suit. The Equal Remuneration Convention, 1951 (No. 100), also provides for implementation "by means appropriate to the methods in operation" for wage determination.

[2] A suggestion to this effect was placed before the Governing Body by the Director-General in 1963, in connection with the amendment of article 35 of the Constitution. The proposed text considered "universality of application as an objective rather than as an unvarying obligation of the ratifying member, and recognized that this objective can be achieved only as far as is practicable without prejudice to the self-governing powers of autonomous territories" (doc. G.B. 154/24/19 (roneoed)). The amendment adopted in 1964 does not incorporate the Director-General's suggestion.

involved,[1] the subject is relevant to the present study because of the obstacles sometimes encountered in trying to give effect to a ratified Convention through collective agreements.

### Conventions Which Refer to Collective Agreements

Article 19, paragraph 5 (d), of the Constitution merely requires a ratifying State to "take such action as may be necessary" to ensure full application. But many Conventions specifically call for the adoption of legislation and the supervisory organs have been reluctant to accept the substitution of less permanent measures to implement such instruments.[2] There are on the other hand a number of Conventions which envisage their implementation by means of collective agreements. The extent to which this is permitted varies from instrument to instrument:[3] in some cases practical issues, such as the distribution of working hours,[4] the payment of wages or overtime compensation,[5] or the organization of inspection,[6] may be so determined; in other cases collective agreements constitute one of several "appropriate" methods for giving effect to a Convention;[7] finally three maritime Conventions envisage partial or full implementation by means of agreements between shipowners and seafarers and provide, in this case, for special supervisory arrangements.[8]

The main risk is of course the cancellation or revision of a collective agreement which previously ensured compliance. If such a contingency should arise, the government would have the obligation to remedy the situation by taking alternative action. But in view of the latitude afforded

---

[1] The Conference Delegation on Constitutional Questions considered the matter in 1946 but did not feel able to make any definite recommendations, beyond a suggestion for further study (cf. 29 Report II (1), pp. 48-50). Developments since then have done little to clarify the issue.

[2] The Conference Committee insisted, during its early years, that legislation is normally required. When the question of application through agreements was raised in 1952, it emphasized the fact that "the parties to collective agreements are normally free to amend or rescind them" (35 R.P. 486). The Committee of Experts has adopted a similar attitude. During its first post-war meeting, for instance, it pointed out that "the legal basis and scope of ... collective agreements should be examined to ascertain whether they rest merely upon the voluntary agreement of the parties thereto or ... become part of the law of the countries and legally enforceable ... and whether they cover all the persons affected by the Conventions or are limited to those who happen to be members of the ... organizations which are parties" (1945 R.C.E. 5).

[3] For a detailed classification of the various types of provisions, cf. C. Wilfred Jenks, "The Application of International Labour Conventions by Means of Collective Agreements", *Zeitschrift für Ausländisches Öffentliches Recht und Völkerrecht*, Vol. 19, Nos. 1-3 (August 1958), pp. 197-224.

[4] Conventions Nos. 1, 30, 67, for instance.

[5] Conventions Nos. 43, 49, 95.

[6] Convention No. 68.

[7] Nos. 100, 101, 106, 111.

[8] Cf. article 10 of the Social Security (Seafarers) Convention, 1946 (No. 70); identical provisions were included in Conventions Nos. 72 and 76, adopted at the same time, but none of these instruments have so far secured enough ratifications to enter into force in either their original or revised versions (Nos. 91, 93 and 109).

by all the Conventions concerned, this would only rarely have to take the form of legislation and a more gradual approach is usually followed instead.[1]

## The Promotion of Implementing Action

For instance the Equal Remuneration Convention, 1951 (No. 100), provides that "the principle of equal remuneration for men and women workers for work of equal value" can be promoted by means of collective agreements whenever wages are not determined by laws, regulations or officially recognized wage-fixing machinery (article 2). When the Austrian government indicated in 1957 that a few collective agreements fixed differential rates according to sex,[2] the Committee of Experts asked for particulars of such agreements so that it could make "an assessment of the extent to which the equal pay principle ... is implemented in the private sector".[3] Simultaneously the government called on the Austrian Trade Union Federation to carry out a parallel inquiry and drew "the attention of a group of trade unions ... to the need to modify the wage rates in conformity with the requirements of the Convention".[4]

In Italy the same Convention has given rise to difficulties of a somewhat different order: the employers' and workers' organizations disagreed on the correct application of the equal pay principle and on the extent to which certain existing practices were compatible with it. In 1960 the Committee of Experts examined the organizations' detailed comments and formulated a series of suggestions designed to assist them in implementing the principle through collective agreements.[5] An "interconfederal agreement" adopted the same year has since found its way into 70 collective contracts and has also been incorporated in a legislative decree.[6]

These examples illustrate the problems to be expected when collective agreements represent a major element in ensuring implementation. While

---

[1] Commenting on the implementation of the Discrimination (Employment and Occupation) Convention, 1958 (No. 111), the Committee of Experts explained in 1963 that this instrument "in no way requires members to abandon such principles of free collective bargaining as prevail in national practice... National authorities can use various means... such as persuasion and consultation, or they can bring their influence to bear through the procedures for the approval, enforcement, or extension of collective or wage agreements, etc." (1963 R.C.E. 207).

[2] 40 R.P. 681.

[3] 1961 R.C.E. 99-100.

[4] 47 R.P. 540. This survey, completed in 1963, also "recognized that the salaries of women must be brought into line with those of men in the cases where different scales still subsisted in collective agreements. In practice this has led to the conclusion of new agreements respecting wage rates in certain branches of industry."

[5] 1960 R.C.E. 52-54. The Italian employers' and workers' members of the Conference Committee had taken an active part when this case was first discussed in 1959 and the government had suggested at that time that they submit written statements to the Committee of Experts (43 R.P. 693).

[6] 1963 R.C.E. 114. In this observation, the Committee of Experts also drew attention to the measures which the government itself can take, by virtue of existing constitutional and legislative provisions, to ensure application of Convention No. 100.

governments must rely primarily on advice and persuasion, their role is by no means passive. They must keep in touch with the course and results of collective bargaining, stimulate co-operative action and help, where appropriate, in setting up machinery for promoting compliance with the Convention. When the application of Convention No. 100 in Italy was discussed in the Conference Committee in 1960, a Norwegian government representative pointed out that it had been found necessary in his country "to establish a permanent tripartite organism to study and promote the principle of equal remuneration."[1] The existence of such machinery, though not obligatory under any of the Conventions concerned, clearly affords the best chance of avoiding or overcoming difficulties in their implementation.

### Collective Agreements as a Substitute for Legislation

A gradual and flexible method is not possible when a Convention requires immediate application to all persons falling within its scope. In such cases reliance on collective agreements is unlikely to provide a sufficient guarantee. Italy's attempts to give effect to the Holidays with Pay Convention, 1936 (No. 52) in this way demonstrate the problems involved. This instrument provides for an annual vacation of at least one working week,[2] but its scope is comprehensive (industry and commerce) and it implies the adoption of laws and regulations, and the intervention of the competent authorities, when dealing with exceptions and effective enforcement. It is not surprising therefore that efforts to give effect to its terms in the absence of legislation have been considered inadequate by the supervisory organs of the I.L.O. Since 1955, when the matter was first raised by the Committee of Experts,[3] the government has relied principally on the existence of a wide-spread network of collective agreements, whereas the Committee has stressed "the necessity of adopting legislation ensuring the application of the minimum requirements of the Convention, insofar as they may not be already clearly implemented by existing provisions of the legislation or collective agreements, it being understood that higher standards could be fixed by collective agreements".[4] Even the adoption in 1959 of legislation authorizing the extension of existing collective agreements to all the workers in a given industry or occupation did not fulfil this basic requirement that all categories of workers should enjoy the one week vacation as well as the other minimum standards (concerning, e.g., vacation pay, exclusion of sick leave and public holidays, etc.) provided for by the Convention. Nor has the contention that ratification of the Conven-

---

[1] 44 R.P. 632. Norway had ratified the Convention the previous year.

[2] A Recommendation (No. 98) adopted in 1954 calls for a minimum vacation of two working weeks per year and a resolution adopted by the Conference in 1961 suggests that a new Convention providing for the same minimum be adopted at an early date (XLIV O.B. No. 1, pp. 18-19).

[3] 1955 R.C.E. 56. The Committee noted that the principle of annual holidays is laid down in the Italian Constitution and the Civil Code.

[4] 1957 R.C.E. 66-67.

tion gives automatic effect to its terms been found acceptable by the Committee of Experts,[1] so that the difficulties have remained unresolved so far.

It thus appears that, while the supervisory Committees do not, as a matter of principle, exclude the alternative of implementation through collective agreements, they do insist that all the terms of a Convention be fully guaranteed in this way. When an instrument calls explicit or implicitly for legislative action, this alternative method is liable to cause, rather than resolve, difficulties of application and resort should be had to it only when insurmountable obstacles prevent the adoption of laws or regulations.[2]

---

[1] 1962 R.C.E. 66-67.

[2] In 1957, the Committee of Experts noted as regards the Sheet-Glass Works Convention, 1934 (No. 43), that in Mexico "the glass industry is not within the competence of the federal authorities" (1957 R.C.E. 62-63). On the apparent assumption that legislative action by the constituent states is unlikely, the Committee has attempted to ascertain whether in all existing factories of this kind hours of work are at least regulated by collective agreements (cf. 1963 R.C.E. 75).

CHAPTER FIVE

# SOME REASONS FOR THE NON-OBSERVANCE
# OF RATIFIED CONVENTIONS : PRACTICAL DIFFICULTIES

Whereas the problems discussed in the preceding chapter were mainly of a legal character, such as the adjustment of international and internal standards to each other, the national constitutional setting and so forth, the present chapter is concerned with certain practical obstacles to implementation. Successive sections will deal with economic, administrative and political factors which may delay compliance and thus necessitate supervisory comment; the final section will discuss the possibility of a national emergency interfering with the discharge of treaty obligations.

## I. Economic Difficulties

In a speech to the International Labour Conference in 1959, the Indian Minister for Labour and Employment commended the I.L.O. for concerning itself increasingly with "the processes of economic and social change and the basic causes of the present incapacity of certain countries to keep pace with the rest in respect of the observance of the standards which have been laid down".[1] In his Report to the 1963 session of the Conference, the Director-General listed as the foremost issue confronting the Organization "the division between North and South, between the industrialized countries enjoying relatively high levels of income and those countries, many of them only now emerging to independence from colonial status, in which incomes are very low and economies underdeveloped".[2]

These two statements reflect the main task of the I.L.O., and emphasize the principal barrier to the implementation of its standards. They show that, although there was an awareness of this barrier in the early days,[3] it looms even larger today, first because the gap between the industrialized and the less developed countries has widened rather than narrowed during the past half-century and second because the countries of the "South" now play a much more active role in international life. In a sense, the very purpose of international labour standards is at stake, since Conventions aim at leveling social disparities not only inside a State but between States.

---

[1] 43 R.P. 26.

[2] 47 D.R. 3.

[3] Cf. in particular the second and third paragraphs of the Preamble to the Constitution (which continue unchanged since 1919) and the second paragraph of the "General Principles", figuring in an appendix to the original Constitution (this so-called "Labour Charter" was replaced in 1946 by the "Declaration of Philadelphia"), which recognized that "differences of climate, habits and customs, of economic opportunity and industrial tradition, make strict uniformity in the conditions of labour difficult of immediate attainment" (I O.B. 345).

It is unnecessary to discuss here whether the motives underlying this effort are primarily economic or humanitarian.[1]

## Economic Development and International Obligations

In many of the cases where Conventions were ratified prematurely, the countries were not in a position, economically, to implement them. Capacity to comply may be impaired either because the level of protection prescribed by a Convention is too high or because the machinery required proves too costly for the private and public interests involved. While nothing short of full compliance is acceptable in law, account must be taken in practice of the rate of progress a given country can realistically be expected to maintain in pursuit of this goal. A gradual approach is justified in the case of social and technical standards which may be costly in their application. In the case of human rights Conventions, however, their violation on ostensibly economic grounds can hardly be countenanced either by the workers themselves,[2] or by the supervisory organs of the I.L.O.[3]

The extent to which social charges tend to retard industrial development is a highly controversial subject both among economists [4] and among those who have a direct personal stake in the matter. Translated into I.L.O. terms, it involves a choice by the Conference between higher and lower, specific and flexible standards,[5] and a decision by each country

---

[1] For an interesting discussion of this issue, cf. Francis Graham Wilson, "*Labor in the League System*", *op. cit.*, pp. 272-297. The author concludes that the main springs of I.L.O. action are humanitarian but that economic factors are not ignored. Albert Thomas recognized this as early as 1927: "The aim is not merely to create a balance between different countries, but also to give just treatment to individuals. Even if the first objective has lost some of its force, the second is as important as ever" (10 D.R. 243).

[2] The Uganda workers' delegate observed in 1963 that the freedom of association standards "may sometimes seem slow and cumbrous to those who think they know best what the workers want and lack the patience to await the slow but sure process of self maturity. But we... want improvements made in freedom, and not by dictatorship-even benevolent dictatorship claimed to be necessary for the national interest" (47 R.P. 114).

[3] In 1962, the Committee of Experts considered it "inconceivable that the solution for accelerating economic development should consist of the imposition of forced labour in more or less clear or disguised forms" (1962 R.C.E. 244).

[4] Thus *Labor and Economic Development*, a collection of regional studies edited by Walter Galenson (New York: John Wiley & Sons, 1959), fails to provide a clear-cut answer. In the Introduction, real wage gains in French West Africa are called "a danger to development": "The more democratic a government is, the easier it will be to force it to translate legislative codes into real services, and *pari passu*, the greater the diversion of resources from investment to consumption" (p. 17). The chapter on Egypt concludes, on the other hand, that "the protective labor legislation enacted thus far in Egypt has not had any perceptible effect in retarding the country's industrial development... We do not agree with those who argue that Egypt's labor legislation is a factor which will impede either foreign or domestic investment in Egyptian business enterprises" (p. 183).

[5] During the 1963 Conference discussion of the Director-General's Report–which dealt with the I.L.O.'s "Programme and Structure" and contained a chapter on "International Labour Standards and the Passage of Years" (47 D.R. 152-171)–nine government and eight employers' spokesmen, mostly from the developing countries, pleaded in favour of more flexible Conventions. Only two workers' representatives expressed a similar opinion.

whether a given instrument is capable of implementation. A government's unduly optimistic evaluation of the country's capacity to support the burden full application represents, will lead to the type of difficulties which are classified here as basically economic.

## Governmental Reluctance to Admit Economic Difficulties

A survey of the observations of the supervisory Committees and of the governments' replies to them reveals two interesting points. In the first place governments often seem to be reluctant, once they have ratified, to admit outright that delays in application are due to economic factors. This is particularly so in the case of some of the block ratifications which were clearly premature in relation to the level of industrial development; yet the explanations given in reply refer as a rule to political or administrative difficulties, i.e., to the symptoms rather than to the cause. The motive underlying such an attitude is understandable: if Conventions are ratified mainly in order to demonstrate active participation in the work of the I.L.O. and if their implementation proves difficult, to avow this openly would be tantamount to admitting that the demonstration has failed.

Another notable point is that the government's reaction often depends on whether the cost of implementation must be borne mainly by the private or the public sector of the economy. The burden falls mainly on private business when the standards call for protective measures (such as minimum wage-fixing, safety and hygiene, working hours, etc.). When they deal with the establishment of labour administration machinery (inspection services, employment agencies, etc.) the government itself feels the financial implications and hence refers to them more readily.

## The Cost of Implementation

This cost factor is illustrated, for instance, by the social security Conventions which may call for financial contributions not only by the workers and employers but also by the public authorities. The latter must in addition assume responsibility for setting up the necessary institutional structures throughout the country. Thus the Peruvian government indicated in 1951 that application of the Sickness Insurance (Industry) Convention, 1927 (No. 24), to all manual workers and domestic servants had met with "considerable financial difficulties" which it hoped to surmount over a period of years.[1] The Committee of Experts welcomed therefore "the gradual application of the compulsory sickness insurance system to new regions"[2] and has followed closely the subsequent progress made in this way.[3]

When the Brazilian government mentioned similar difficulties in giving effect to the Employment Service Convention, 1948 (No. 88), the Committee expressed the hope that "with the help of technical assistance if

---

[1] 34 R.P. 567-568.

[2] 1954 R.C.E. 24.

[3] Cf. e.g. 1962 R.C.E. 50-51.

necessary, or by other means, it will be possible gradually" to move towards conformity.[1] An especially difficult situation arises when budgetary restrictions lead to the type of "back-sliding" to which reference has already been made in the preceding chapter. This happened in the Philippines where nine out of ten employment offices were closed for economy reasons in 1956, although Convention No. 88 had been ratified three years earlier.[2] The government asked Congress subsequently to authorize increased expenditures[3] but the effect of these proposals is not as yet clear.

The necessity to comply with a ratified Convention may thus be an element in determining the allocation of public funds. Considerations of this kind certainly had a bearing on the extension of the eight-hour day to some 6,000 workers on the Greek railways which are publicly-owned. The government pleaded at first "insurmountable financial difficulties"[4] and asked for additional time to work out the complex problems of rail modernization. Measures to extend the provisions of the Hours of Work (Industry) Convention, 1919 (No. 1), to all railway workers were finally adopted in 1963.[5] A problem of much broader practical importance arose after Italy's ratification of the Minimum Age (Industry and Non-Industrial Employment) Conventions (Revised), 1937 (Nos. 59 and 60) in 1952. In order to bridge the gap between the school-leaving age of 14 years and the 15 years minimum laid down by the above Conventions, it was found necessary to institute vocational training courses the financing of which seemed to prove difficult at first.[6] A law raising the minimum age was passed by the Italian Parliament in 1961.

*The Search for Preventive Action During the Drafting of Standards*

Because economic difficulties such as those illustrated interfere with the implementation of I.L.O. standards, much thought has gone into the search for practical solutions. What are the remedies available internationally and nationally to promote the applicability and application of Conventions under widely varying circumstances? Obviously this is an especially challenging aspect of the more general problem of flexibility which was already discussed above. In addition to the various devices mentioned earlier,[7] the I.L.O. has attempted to take account of the particular problems confronting the many countries "in which climatic condi-

---

[1] 1960 R.C.E. 47.

[2] 1957 R.C.E. 85-86.

[3] 46 R.P. 712.

[4] Cf. e.g. 40 R.P. 663-664. The Greek workers' member of the Conference Committee said however that "the reasons given by the government were not convincing" and that the operating deficit was due to "faulty organization of the railways".

[5] Cf. 47 R.P. 524.

[6] Cf. 40 R.P. 675; 42 R.P. 676. The government candidly admitted that "some of these obstacles (had not) been foreseen at the time of ratification", another example of unexpected difficulties of application.

[7] Cf. pp. 82-83.

tions, the imperfect development of industrial organization or other special circumstances make the industrial conditions substantially different".[1]

In practice, the Conference has made sparing use of this constitutionally sanctioned opportunity to lay down special provisions for certain countries. Of the 122 Conventions adopted by 1964, only 13 contain clauses relating to specified countries and the States in question are concentrated in Asia.[2] Successful attempts to this effect have, in fact, become more and more rare.[3] Nor has the initiation of a simplified amendment procedure had concrete results so far: Conventions Nos. 59, 89 and 90 provide for the extension of their special provisions to additional countries but this has never been done as yet.[4]

Other devices, also inspired by article 19, paragraph 3, of the Constitution, are available for more general use. Among these are "transitional clauses" which permit a country to substitute a lower age limit, if prior to ratification it had no legislation on the matter [5] or had protective standards for lower age groups only.[6] There are also exceptions, in the night work Conventions for instance, for "tropical countries" or "countries where the climate renders work by day particularly trying to the health". The "excluded area clause" and the other flexibility provisions mentioned earlier, in Chapter Four, may also facilitate implementation by the less industrialized countries. The Social Security (Minimum Standards) Convention, 1952 (No. 102), in particular, contains temporary exceptions for States "whose economy and medical facilities are insufficiently developed" as well as a number of other clauses (lower percentages of coverage, linking of the benefit level to the national standards of living, etc.) applicable to such States.

---

[1] Article 19, paragraph 3, of the Constitution. It is significant that this language, which was used originally in 1919, has been retained without change. In proposing the addition of this clause to the Peace Conference, Mr. Barnes pointed out that it was designed to avoid any misunderstanding as to the possibility "of imposing upon an Eastern country for instance what was altogether out of the question for our day and generation" (I O.B. 291). India and Japan had both insisted on this addition. Cf. also the other relevant passages in the original Constitution, mentioned in footnote 3, p. 119 above.

[2] Special standards for India are contained in all the instruments in question (Conventions Nos. 1, 4, 5, 6, 14, 33, 41, 59, 60, 77, 79, 89, 90), special standards for Japan in five (Nos. 1, 5, 6, 14, 59), for Pakistan in two (Nos. 89, 90), for Thailand in two (Nos. 4 and 41) and for China in one (No. 59). Ratification ensued in 12 of these 23 cases, i.e. at a rate definitely above the general average.

[3] The last Conventions in this group date back to 1948. The Preface to *The International Labour Code 1951*, *op. cit.*, observes that "changes in political and economic conditions have made it increasingly difficult to secure general approval for differing standards for different parts of the world" (p. LXXIX).

[4] In 1951 the government of Vietnam asked that such a provision be inserted for its benefit in the Minimum Age (Industry) Convention (Revised), 1937 (No. 59). A proposal by the workers' group in the Governing Body to reject this was defeated by such a narrow margin (14 votes to 13) that the matter was never placed on the agenda of the Conference. Noting that Vietnam had only recently joined the Organization, one workers' member stated that "to refuse to grant exceptions would be to render a service to such a country" (115 G.B. 16-17, 93).

[5] Medical Examination of Young Persons (Industry and Non-Industrial Occupations) Conventions, 1946 (Nos. 77 and 78).

[6] Night Work of Young Persons (Industry) Convention (Revised), 1948 (No. 90).

*The Practical Impact of Flexibility Devices*

In theory, the need to adjust the level of protection and the pace of implementation of Conventions to the special requirements of the less developed areas has been recognized [1] and considerable thought and ingenuity have gone into the various devices designed to give practical meaning to the theory. Yet the impression is strong that these efforts have on balance had a rather limited effect. Attempts to set lower standards for specified countries have met with less and less success. Only a few countries have used the "excluded area" or the "transitional" clauses or have availed themselves of the opportunities inherent in instruments which deliberately set "minimum standards".[2] Despite the constant emphasis on the need for flexibility when standards are framed, the available evidence tends to show that only in exceptional cases the Conference's efforts to meet these demands have convinced the governments concerned that the latitude left them in the process of implementation militates in favour of accepting the instruments.

The determination of the objectives and priorities which have a bearing on ratification and application naturally raises questions of over-all national policy. But from the international point of view there has never been the slightest doubt that the basic objective of I.L.O. standards is to enable countries to strike a proper balance between their economic circumstances and their need for social progress. And experience has proved that this aim can best be served through the negotiation of practical, even pragmatic, standards from case to case, rather than through any preconceived and doctrinal solutions.[3]

---

[1] Writing in 1927, an American economist explained this theory in the following terms: "In the existence of economic obstacles, in fact, is to be found a great part of the explanation of some of the agreements formulated by the International Labour Organization up to the present. The States members, even if their action is not made cautious by the caution of the employers, even if the will exists to participate in international action dealing with labour conditions, must feel their way slowly about the economic difficulties they may face" (Herbert Feis, "International Labour Legislation in the Light of Economic Theory", *International Labour Review*, Vol. XV, No. 4 (April 1927), pp. 508-509).

Professor Haas speaks of "ambiguity" rather than "flexibility" in standard-setting and considers that economic "reasons advanced for non-ratification... tend to undermine the I.L.O. ideology with respect to the equalization of labor standards among developed and underdeveloped countries" (*Beyond the Nation-State, op. cit.*, pp. 246 and 260). This line of reasoning is open to question. If equalization of social charges is really one of the purposes of I.L.O. standards, then it is only fair that lower labour productivity in the developing countries should be offset by a greater degree of latitude in their level of social protection. Otherwise the competitive position of these countries would become untenable.

[2] Referring to Convention No. 90, the Committee of Experts termed it "surprising that only one country has thus far ratified in making use" of the clause which authorizes application to be restricted to lower age groups" (1960 R.C.E. 121). Only four of the 16 countries which had ratified Convention No. 102 by the end of 1964 are non-European (Israel, Mexico, Peru and Senegal).

[3] The Director-General's Report to the 1963 session of the Conference contains a strong appeal for the negotiation of instruments in a spirit of accommodation and compromise: "A Convention is not an opportunity to secure a victory for the winning team but a contribution to the common law of the world the value of which depends on the measure of general assent which it commands" (47 D.R. 170). Summing up the arguments for

*The Special Case of Non-Metropolitan Territories*

It is interesting that in the case of a special group of countries a more radical method was adopted to take account of economic difficulties in application. Whereas the flexibility devices authorize partial compliance with a ratified Convention only to the extent specifically laid down, article 35 of the Constitution which deals with non-metropolitan territories permits a ratified Convention either not be applied there or to be applied "subject to such modification as may be necessary to adapt the Convention to local conditions". Within the limits set by the supervisory Committees in evaluating the nature of these conditions, a very considerable degree of latitude is thus available in regard to the degree and pace of implementation. As the present study deals only with cases where a Convention has already been declared applicable to a territory and as the practical importance of the question is diminishing rapidly with the accession of most of the major territories to independence, article 35 is referred to here mainly as another possible approach to the problem of applying standards in less developed countries.

There has been considerable controversy in the I.L.O. in recent years over the admissibility and value of such a special regime. Without entering into the larger issue of "decolonization", with all its political overtones, the main difference of opinion has turned on whether article 35 has delayed or advanced social progress in non-metropolitan territories.[1] Those opposing this "colonial clause" maintained that there was no reason to give unequal treatment to certain countries merely because of their dependent status. The main argument put forward in reply stressed the value of applying a ratified Convention gradually while a territory developed its economy; the metropolitan government would be unable, otherwise, to ratify, until a Convention can be applied in full to all its territories.

On the whole, the degree of latitude inherent in article 35 has proved, in the long run, to be a dynamic element, as recognized by the Committee of Experts which concluded from its 1961 review of "Social Evolution in Present and Former Non-Metropolitan Territories" that considerable progress had been made "both as regards the acceptance of new international obligations and as regards the adoption of legislative and practical measures".[2] Although the "winds of change" have greatly reduced the area of operation of article 35 and its elimination has now been approved, this provision has had a positive influence on the application of ratified standards in economically less advanced countries. Its potential value on

---

and against more flexible standards, put forward during the discussion in the Conference, the Director-General concluded that "these are arguments about issues which cannot be decided in terms of general propositions. We should deal with them, I believe, as considerations to be taken into account in fixing specific Conference agendas and in bringing forward proposals for the revision of specific Conventions" (47 R.P. 439).

[1] Cf., e.g., the arguments summarized in the 1959 and 1961 Reports of the Conference Committee (43 R.P. 671-672; 45 R.P. 735-736).

[2] 1961 R.C.E. 323. This review, while focused on the years 1955-1960, covered the whole period of existence of the I.L.O.

a broader basis might therefore be considerable, on condition that the element of co-ordinated economic and social progress is made subject to supervisory follow-up. Unless this factor is present, modified application provisions might hinder instead of promote the implementation of I.L.O. standards.

## Regional Standards as a Solution

Another possible solution, proposed on occasion, is the framing of Conventions on a regional rather than a global basis. By limiting instruments to a given area with similar economic conditions and problems, it is said, their application might be rendered more uniform and less difficult.[1] Though attractive at first glance, the idea seems neither theoretically acceptable nor desirable in practice. Since international labour standards lay down minimum conditions, the crystallization of a series of regional levels would accentuate rather than reconcile differences.[2] In addition the supervision of such instruments, whether attempted on a global or a more limited basis, might give rise to controversy.[3] It is not surprising, therefore, that, despite the expansion in the I.L.O.'s regional activities (through regional conferences, technical assistance field offices in the various continents, etc.), no concrete attempt has been made to deal in this way with the difficulties raised by uneven economic development.[4]

However, an interesting attempt was made by the I.L.O.'s first Asian Regional Conference, which met in New Delhi in 1947, to give a regional imprint to the application of universal standards: the meeting called for the formulation by each country of "a national programme of action" which would involve the "progressive implementation" of 15 Conventions singled out for this purpose.[5] The selection of instruments especially suited to local conditions and the utilization of a step-by-step procedure suggest that a global and a regional approach can be realistically combined. It has been proposed that a similar combination might be possible in drafting standards, i.e., by consulting regional meetings on the provisions to be included in new or revised Conventions.[6] While regional methods

---

[1] For an examination of the regionalist doctrine, cf. Léon-Eli Troclet, *Législation Sociale Internationale, op. cit.*, pp. 425-441.

[2] This objection falls when purely regional subjects, such as the conditions of work of Rhine boatmen, are being regulated; or when higher standards are the aim, as in the case of the European Social Charter. Cf. in this connection the passage on regional instruments in the Director-General's Report to the 1963 Conference (47 D.R. 188-189).

[3] The Canadian workers' delegate stressed this point in the 1964 Conference: "We should be flexible in the formulation of... standards; once adopted by the Organization as a whole, we should remain inflexible in their application" (48 R.P. 54).

[4] Article 21 of the Constitution, which authorizes member States "to agree... among themselves" to any Conventions not adopted by the Conference, contains the germ of regional agreements. No use has been made of this possibility either.

[5] Resolution concerning Programmes of Action (XXX O.B. 195-200).

[6] The idea was put forward in 1946 by the Conference Delegation on Constitutional Questions (29 Report II(1), 72) and also mentioned by the Director-General in the Conference in 1963: "I am personally attracted to the suggestion that the problems in application of, perhaps, certain groups of Conventions be explored through regional conferences... They could carry out a thorough review (which) would give valuable guidance to the Governing Body and the General Conference as to whether or not certain instruments needed to be revised in any important respect" (47 R.P. 440).

are unlikely to exert any direct influence on implementation, they could add a further guarantee that in formulating standards account is taken of the special difficulties of less developed countries.[1]

*National Remedies*

To sum up, flexibility in the drafting of I.L.O. Conventions and in the pace set for their application should go some way towards enabling countries to accept and implement such instruments as are of interest to them at a given stage of development. In addition to these international elements, there exists an even more crucial aspect of the problem, national action. Two phases can again be distinguished, ratification and application.

As regards the first phase, reference must be made once more to the dangers implicit in premature ratification. As emphasized earlier, the risks involved, both for the State in question and for the I.L.O., clearly outweigh any potential advantages. Nothing of what is said here should therefore be interpreted as suggesting that obligations under international labour Conventions might be accepted before the law, the practice and the economic circumstances of a country provide reasonable assurance that these obligations can be discharged as soon as they enter into force. In the case of the less developed countries, especially, it is the timing of a ratification which is important. In other words, application difficulties are less likely to arise if the act of ratification is viewed as a deliberate step to synchronize social and economic progress.

*Balanced Economic and Social Development*

The problem of timing is thus part of the more general question of development planning and of the balance which must be struck between economic and social progress. This concept of balanced development can be made more concrete in terms of the labour policies it implies.

No better illustration could be found for this purpose than the programme for international economic co-operation which the General Assembly proclaimed in 1961 under the name of "United Nations Development Decade". The objective of this programme is "to accelerate progress towards self-sustaining growth of the economy of the individual nations and their social advancement" [2] and the measures to be taken to this end include planning, the mobilization of available resources, improvements in administration, the use of science and technology, action in the fields of trade and finance, etc. The size and variety of these tasks tend to obscure their specifically social aspects [3] and the economic obstacles are

---

[1] A resolution adopted by the Conference in 1964 requests the Governing Body to consider "the problems associated with the implementation of international labour Conventions... in African and other developing countries, and the review by regional conferences of such implementation" (XLVII O.B. No. 3 Supplement I, p. 72).

[2] Resolution 1710 (XVI).

[3] This point was stressed in the proposals which the Secretary-General placed before the Economic and Social Council in 1962: "Although there has been increasing recognition that the ultimate objective of economic development is social progress, and that social reform is a necessary condition of economic improvement, these principles have not yet

often such that they seem to exclude concern for other matters. It is at this point that the special role of I.L.O. standards emerges most clearly. The objectives they set in the field of labour and social policy logically supplement those in the other fields, so that economic progress will be accompanied by advances in the social sphere. As it makes headway in the economic field, a government must consider periodically whether a point has been reached where the implementation of a Convention has become a practical possibility. This simultaneous promotion of "economic and social advancement of the less developed regions of the world" is mentioned in the I.L.O. Constitution as one of the Organization's main objectives.[1]

Such a decision inevitably implies a broad view of the development process, i.e., an awareness that economic and social change are complementary and that glaring inequalities should be removed. Just as economic growth is the key to social progress, so the redistribution of income can not only promote political stability but economic growth itself.[2] In a very real sense, the availability of I.L.O. Conventions tests a government's willingness to pay more than lip service to balanced development. Naturally this willingness can find expression in a variety of other measures both inside and outside the purview of the I.L.O. But when a government deliberately assumes new obligations under a Convention, it not only demonstrates its belief that the additional cost is socially desirable but also signifies that the progress involved is to be more than temporary. If the economic implications of such a step have been accurately weighed, the gain in the standard of living of the workers should be real and lasting. In the case of the protective Conventions, labour legislation can keep pace with economic change without inhibiting it. In the case of the machinery Conventions, administrative improvements can follow time-tested patterns. In the case of the human rights Conventions, finally, the existence of fundamental guarantees can prevent economic development from relying on predatory and coercive practices.[3]

---

come to guide practical policies everywhere. Continued neglect of the social aspects of economic development might result either in stagnation in economic progress or violent reversal of the existing order" (United Nations, Department of Economic and Social Affairs: *The United Nations Development Decade, Proposals for Action* (doc. E/3613), p. 6).

The "Charter of Punta del Este", adopted by the Inter-American Economic and Social Council in 1961, also stipulates as one of the basic requirements (Title II, Chapter One) that the necessary social reforms should be effected to permit a fair distribution of the fruits of economic and social progress.

[1] Annex, Part IV. The Social Policy (Basic Aims and Standards) Convention, 1962, states in its article 2 that "the improvement of standards of living shall be regarded as the principal objective in the planning of economic development".

[2] A full statement of this philosophy appears in the section entitled "Making Social Policy", in the Director-General's Report to the 1963 Conference (47 D.R. 18-31).

[3] In 1963, the Economic and Social Council submitted to the General Assembly a draft Resolution urging all governments to make special efforts during the United Nations Development Decade to promote respect for and observance of human rights and fundamental freedoms and particularly inviting the governments of developing countries to include measures to this effect in their plans for economic and social development (Resolution 958 (XXXVI)).

There is no doubt that the full potentialities of such an integrative approach have not yet been fully realized at either the international or the national level. To tackle economic difficulties and social evils together involves a multitude of political, financial and other decisions. To enforce these decisions requires a degree of structural stability which many developing countries have not yet reached. But real progress hardly seems possible if priorities cannot be fixed and choices made in consequence. As governments are confronted with the necessity of planning ahead, of allocating resources and of catering to opposing interests, the problems and possible solutions may come more sharply in focus. The emphasis on economic development could thus create a more favourable climate for the acceptance of international social standards.

Three factors will affect this process of implementation: advances must be gradual, as envisaged for instance in the Programme of Action Resolution of 1947;[1] the crucial decisions concerning the extent and speed of action are for the individual governments to take; international assistance is available to facilitate implementation. It is this last point which now requires some elaboration.

## Technical Aid to Overcome Difficulties

Since World War II, "technical co-operation", the term most commonly used for the technical aid given to the developing countries on a bilateral or a multilateral basis, has become one of the salient features of international life. Although the I.L.O. and other bodies carried on activities of this type on a limited scale during the inter-war period, the United Nations Expanded Programme of Technical Assistance and the Development Decade mark a milestone in the history of international organization. It was to be expected that the bearing of these operational activities on the implementation of I.L.O. standards should quickly become a subject of practical interest and experimentation, in the hope that these activities would help countries to comply with Conventions.[2]

---

[1] An article in a Pakistani publication concluded that the International Labour Organization "is helping within its sphere of responsibility to shape and guide the social policy of the countries of the region. Much which has been achieved in Asian countries shows that the I.L.O. standards have served and will continue to serve as an essential guide in the formulation and implementation of measures for labour protection and social welfare" ("The Influence of I.L.O. Standards", *Eastern Worker* (Karachi), Vol. III, No. 1 (January 1963), p. 25).

[2] Obversely, the existence of standards should prove helpful in carrying out certain types of technical assistance projects. Cf., for instance, the observation in the Director-General's Report to the 1963 Conference that "in all the fields in which technical co-operation, promotional work, and educational and practical activities are closely related to policy it is the existence of the authoritative consensus of responsible opinion expressed in international standards which gives the programmes of the International Labour Organization their distinctive character and a large part of their value" (47 D.R. 163).

Not unnaturally, there has been a temptation in some quarters to view the operational and the pre-legislative work as being in conflict with each other. In 1958 the Conference Committee disagreed with this point of view in the following terms: "It has at times been intimated that there exists a certain antithesis between the Organization's standard-setting and practical activities and that the emphasis in the I.L.O.'s programme of work

Under the I.L.O. Constitution the International Labour Office must "accord to governments at their request all appropriate assistance within its power in connection with the framing of laws and regulations on the basis of the decisions of the Conference and the improvement of administrative practices and systems of inspection" (article 10, paragraph 2 (b)). Advisory missions to this effect are mentioned from time to time in the Reports of the supervisory Committees. As indicated in the constitutional mandate, they may involve the drafting of legislation,[1] or help in setting up the basic machinery provided for in the Conventions on the employment service,[2] to enable governments to dispense with private placement activities.[3] Practical aid is also given in the fields of labour statistics, inspection, wage-fixing machinery and social security. Other spheres of application are the I.L.O.'s programmes to promote workers' education and to combat discrimination in employment and occupation.

The supervisory Committees have become increasingly conscious of the potential value of technical assistance in surmounting difficulties of application. The Conference Committee made special mention of this possibility for the first time in 1953, noting that several governments had asked for the advisory services of the I.L.O.[4] The Committee of Experts occasionally includes references in its observations to governments and follows up the results from year to year. In 1959, for instance, Guatemala stated, in reply to an observation, that it was asking for assistance to set up a public employment service in conformity with Employment Service Convention.[5] After the Committee observed tersely, the following year, that "no request

---

must necessarily be either on its traditional approach or on its activities in the field. The Committee's deliberations made it clear that these two concepts are in fact closely interrelated and supplement each other at every stage" (42 R.P. 651). The same point was stressed by the United States workers' member of the Governing Body, speaking before a meeting of the Industrial Relations Research Association in 1962: "I would be the last to deprecate the significance of the I.L.O.'s technical assistance activities... But in no sense do they replace the I.L.O.'s standard-setting job. Instead, these two phases of the I.L.O.'s work should be regarded as mutually reinforcing. Generally, when an I.L.O. expert goes into a country to provide assistance, it is the standard set forth in the appropriate Conventions and Recommendations of the I.L.O. which guides him in his work. The other side of the coin is that technical co-operation can lay the foundation for the kind of improvements which will permit the developing countries to obtain the kind of standards contemplated in I.L.O. instruments" (Rudolph Faupl, "International Labor Organization", *Labor Law Journal*, Vol. 13, No. 7 (July 1962), p. 518.

[1] Cf. for instance the assistance to Colombia referred to in footnote 6, p. 107, above. A similar project in China (Taiwan) was mentioned by a government spokesman in the Conference Committee in 1963 (47 R.P. 529).

[2] Missions for this purpose were sent, e.g., to Iraq (1962 R.C.E. 114-115) and to Venezuela (37 R.P. 503).

[3] The governments of Chile and Mexico reported in 1958 on I.L.O. assistance to enable them to comply with the Fee-Charging Employment Agencies Convention, 1933 (No. 34) (1958 R.C.E. 37).

[4] "While the Committee does not suggest that all problems of securing conformity... either could or should be treated in this way, it ventures to draw the attention of the Conference to the possibilities presented by this practical and positive approach and hopes that, in appropriate cases, governments will take advantage of them" (36 R.P. 365).

[5] 1959 R.C.E. 51.

for technical assistance in this field has since been made"[1] the government confirmed in its next report that this had been done subsequently.[2]

In certain cases the Committee of Experts does not hesitate to suggest that assistance on the spot may be the best means of working toward compliance with a ratified Convention. This was illustrated above in connection with the difficulties experienced by Brazil in giving effect to the same Employment Service Convention.[3] Governments are free of course to accept or decline such suggestions. Thus, reminders to Pakistan in 1959 and 1960 that technical assistance might help to eliminate infringements of the Labour Inspection Convention, 1947 (No. 81),[4] merely evoked replies that the Committee's observations "have been noted for consideration"[6] and that such assistance "would be requested as and when needed".[5]

Even if assistance is made available, there is no guarantee that it will have the desired results. Although an expert went to Uruguay, for example, to help the government establish a sickness insurance system, in conformity with the 1927 Conventions on this subject (Nos. 24 and 25),[7] it is clear from later observations that serious divergencies continue to exist. In addition to basic economic factors, administrative or political difficulties may inhibit implementation both of the international obligations and of the practical measures required. When there are basic difficulties to overcome, it would be unrealistic to expect rapid and automatic progress. Experience has already shown, however, that technical assistance can, in favourable circumstances, exert a definite influence, particularly in developing administrative structures, e.g., in the vital area of manpower utilization.[8] A special study would be necessary to gauge the extent of this influence with any degree of accuracy.[9]

## Some Preconditions for Remedial Action

It is possible, nonetheless, to formulate some general conclusions regarding the role and effectiveness of operational activities in helping the less developed countries to comply with international labour Conventions. There is a need first of all for maximum co-ordination which is implicit in the complementary nature of standard-setting and field operations, as

---

[1] 1960 R.C.E. 47-48.

[2] 1962 R.C.E. 114.

[3] Cf. pp. 121-122.

[4] 1959 R.C.E. 45; 1960 R.C.E. 43.

[5] 43 R.P. 686.

[6] 44 R.P. 622.

[7] 1956 R.C.E. 46.

[8] Thus, in the cases of Chile and Iraq, the Conference Committee learned of measures taken as a result of technical assistance (44 R.P. 618 and 46 R.P. 712).

[9] The Economic and Social Council seems aware of this need for fuller data. In 1962 it called for the "systematic and objective evaluation of the impact and effectiveness of programmes undertaken by the United Nations as well as the specialized agencies... directed toward the advancement of economic and social development of the developing countries" (Resolution 908 (XXXIV)).

mentioned above. Otherwise their mutually beneficial action may be minimal and the two may even operate at cross-purposes.[1] Another point to be noted is the potential value of practical assistance in furthering the implementation of the human rights standards of the I.L.O. It is natural that requests for help should have been concentrated in the technical fields of legislation, administration, safety and hygiene, etc., where the need for specialized knowledge and experience is most urgent. There is no reason, however, why outside expertise should not also be utilized to promote freedom of association, freedom from compulsion and the elimination of discrimination. The importance of the relevant Conventions is generally recognized, as witnessed by the wide scale on which they have been ratified. The difficulties in their application noted by the supervisory organs of the I.L.O. might well be dealt with in certain cases by methods which have already proved their value. The possible resort to technical assistance in the field of human rights has been stressed for some time both in the United Nations [2] and in the International Labour Organization. It has been written into the Draft Covenant on Economic, Social and Cultural Rights [3] and referred to repeatedly in General Assembly Resolutions.[4] Within the I.L.O., the Committee of Experts concluded its survey on forced labour in 1962 by suggesting that technical co-operation and educational programmes might help governments to use "methods which, without involving recourse to compulsion, enabled maximum use to be made of available labour".[5] Governments feel perhaps that to accept such assistance is to concede that they fail to give effect to standards of

---

[1] The Administrative Committee on Co-ordination which consists of the Secretary General of the United Nations and the executive heads of the specialized agencies stressed in 1961 that "the general objective of policy should be to ensure that each of the various types of international action reinforces the others and that an appropriate balance and synthesis is secured in which research, standards, education and operations are accepted as equally vital elements in a comprehensive programme" (Twenty-Fifth Report, doc. E/3495, p. 10).

[2] Cf. Rosalyn Higgins, "Technical Assistance for Human Rights–A New Approach to an Old Problem", *The World Today* (Chatham House), Vol. 19, Nos. 3 and 5 (April and May 1963) pp. 174-180, 219-224.

[3] Under article 23, the Economic and Social Council may "bring to the attention of the international organs concerned with technical assistance... any matters arising out of the (governments') reports... which may assist such organs in deciding... on the advisability of international measures likely to contribute to the progressive implementation" of the Covenant.

[4] In 1953 a Resolution authorized the Secretary-General "to render technical advice and other services" to assist governments "in the eradication of discrimination or in the protection of minorities or both" (Resolution 730 (VIII)). A draft Resolution submitted to the General Assembly by the Economic and Social Council in 1963 called on the technical assistance authorities of the United Nations family to provide help, within the framework of their programmes during the Development Decade, with a view to the achievement of progress in the field of human rights (Resolution 958 (XXXVI)).

[5] 1962 R.C.E. 244. Referring to this suggestion in the reply to the discussion of his Report, the Director-General admitted: "We have not put sufficient effort and thought into this.... We are confronted... with an opportunity to help shape the evolution of new societies in free and democratic paths" (46 R.P. 450-451). He re-emphasized this point in his reply to the 1964 Conference: "(T)he I.L.O.'s primary concern is not to condemn but to help... countries resolve their development problems and their unemployment problems in a manner which is consistent with I.L.O. principles" (48 R.P. 407).

a particularly sensitive character.[1] But without their request, assistance cannot be given.

This leads to the third and perhaps the most important point to be made. Among all the obstacles to application, those due to economic factors are no doubt the most difficult to overcome. At best, only gradual improvements can usually be hoped for and these long-term changes demand action in many related fields. In such circumstances all types of assistance, whether financial or technical, are essential in order to reach the goals set. If these goals include the achievement of social and human rights laid down in ratified Conventions and if technical aid is needed and available for the purpose, everything would seem to militate in favour of its use: economic necessity, national self-interest and the duty to give effect to freely assumed international obligations. Yet the fact remains that assistance offered in this way is not always accepted or utilized to best advantage. This is a problem which confronts the I.L.O. in many different ways,[2] but it far transcends the scope of I.L.O. action. The solution will depend to a large extent on the willingness of the governments of the developing countries to subscribe to the basic purposes of multilateral technical aid and to carry through the measures its acceptance implies.[3]

---

[1] Referring to governmental reluctance to request assistance in the field of discrimination, Professor Sørensen of Denmark wrote in 1956: "In the great majority of cases... discrimination is practiced by the groups in power, and there is little likelihood that they will ask for assistance from outside to bring about changes to their own disadvantage. What is needed is not mere technical knowledge but a willingness on the part of governments and influential national groups to take action" (Max Sørensen, "The Quest for Equality", *International Conciliation*, No. 507 (March 1956), p. 330).

[2] Speaking of the specific question of trade union development and industrial relations, for instance, the Director-General noted that governments "often assign low priority to technical assistance connected with labour relations." He suggested that "it should become a consistent objective in the programming of technical co-operation through the I.L.O. to encourage more requests in this field... It may also be desirable for the I.L.O. to take greater initiative in discussing projects with governments, trade unions and employers' organizations so as to attempt to have set in motion, in countries where action seems propitious, a number of long-term projects involving comprehensive and co-ordinated action" (47 D.R. 76-77).

[3] A former Minister of Labour of Iran concludes his study of "International Aspects of the Problem of Economic and Social Development" with an urgent plea for a massive increase in the scope of international assistance and suggests that "in all the under-developed, economically and socially weak countries, where two-thirds of the world's population live and die in misery, an International Committee should be set up, presided over by a resident representative of the United Nations and composed of the representatives of the various specialized agencies. The aim of this permanent Committee would be to study, separately as well as together with the governments, all questions regarding 'social justice', i.e. relating to the economic and social development of these countries" (Ahmad-Ali Bahramy, *La Législation Internationale du Travail et son Influence sur le Droit Iranien – Aspects Internationaux du Problème du Développement Economique et Social* (Geneva: Librairie Droz, 1963), p. 283).

The suggestion is an interesting one but the question inevitably arises to what use the studies and conclusions of such an "international committee" would be put in practice. If its suggestions for the utilization of international aid were to conflict with the views and desires of the government, who would have the final say? In other words, could the provision of greatly increased outside aid on a multilateral basis be made dependent on the acceptance and implementation by the government of the internal measures (such as tax reform, land reform, trade union rights, etc.) which the "international committee"

## II. Administrative Difficulties

In giving effect to a Convention, the first question to be faced is whether its provisions have been fully taken into account in the national legislation. One aspect of this question, the incorporation of a Convention in municipal law, was discussed earlier. But, aside from complex legal issues, administrative difficulties may also arise. The divergencies noted by the supervisory Committees fail to receive prompt attention, for instance, if there exist no adequate arrangements for maintaining contact between a government and the International Labour Office.

If the Ministry of Foreign Affairs is the channel of communication, it must bring the observations of the Committee of Experts to the attention of the Ministry of Labour which usually prepares instructions for Conference delegates and, as appropriate, addresses a preliminary written reply to Geneva. As time is short and the questions involved may be highly technical, any delays between ministries,[1] or even within the ministry responsible for labour matters, will not only render discussion at the Conference more difficult, but may even prevent the early adoption of the necessary measures of compliance.[2] This need for maximum co-ordination is especially acute in the case of governments whose contacts with Geneva are tenuous and irregular outside Conference sessions. Geographic remoteness was a complicating factor during the first two decades and even the shrinking of distances through modern communications has not removed this difficulty altogether, especially when it is combined with others.

*Administrative Delays*

The main point at issue here is not so much failure to supply reports [3] as delays in taking the necessary measures of implementation. This may

---

may deem to constitute an essential part of development? Unless this issue is faced in concrete terms, a mere expansion in the scope of the aid available is not likely to solve by itself the problems of under-development.

Under the technical assistance procedures currently in operation, governments have full freedom to heed or disregard the advice they receive: "The resident representative knows that in whatever direction he looks... he can order no one. For the essence of the post is that the person holding it achieves results not by commanding and ordering, but by persuasion and giving good counsel". Cf. C. Hart Schaaf, "The Role of Resident Representatives of the U.N. Technical Assistance Board", *International Organization*, Vol. 14, No. 4 (Autumn 1960), p. 556.

[1] Article 11 of the I.L.O. Constitution provides that "the government departments... which deal with questions of industry and employment may communicate directly with the Director-General". Although this provision was inserted already in 1919, when it represented a major innovation, there still remain cases where the Ministry of Foreign Affairs insists on maintaining control. In some instances the I.L.O. sends copies of its communications to the government departments most directly concerned.

[2] The Conference Committee expressed regret in 1932 that "in some cases there appears to be a lack of co-ordination between the government delegates at the Conference and the administrators responsible for preparing the annual reports, so that the comments made on the previous annual reports and the promises made by the delegates at the preceding Conference are ignored" (16 R.P. 673).

[3] As an obstacle to regular supervision, this problem is discussed on pp. 151-154 below.

of course be due to basic economic circumstances, as noted above. There are nonetheless cases where the principal difficulties seem to be administrative and Uruguay's prolonged attempts to secure full application of a number of Conventions illustrates such a situation.

This small country which counts among the most advanced of the American continent[1] ratified in 1933 and 1954 a total of 57 Conventions. Already before the war and especially since 1947 the supervisory Committees made observations regarding the application of a large number of these instruments but with so little effect that the Conference Committee decided on several occasions to include Uruguay in the special list.[2] How could such a situation have continued for so long? A review of the record points to the conclusion that, aside from an initial period when appeals for action were largely ignored, the government's periodic efforts to bring about conformity with I.L.O. standards relied mainly on administrative studies and measures. Thus in 1954 a "legal system of penalties" for the violation of ratified Conventions was established[3] which proved ineffective in the absence of more specific action. In the following year "several committees" were set up "in order to examine measures which would give effect" to the international standards.[4] When the Committee of Experts noted in 1959 that no further reference was being made to such measures,[5] the government explained in the Conference Committee that there had been "a total change of administration" and that a new committee had been set up to prepare the necessary steps of implementation.[6] In 1961 and 1962 reference was made to yet another body described as an "inter-ministerial committee"[7] and a "working group"[8] which was mentioned again in 1963.[9]

The government has thus been aware of its international obligations but the administrative steps for their implementation have clearly been insufficient to secure results and this purely procedural approach may actually have delayed rather than promoted compliance. The fact that Uruguay is widely regarded among Latin American countries[10] as advanced econo-

---

[1] In 1952 the Conference Committee described Uruguay as "a highly developed and democratic country" (35 R.P. 493).

[2] In 1957, in 1960-1962 and in 1964. During recent years this took the form of a blanket reference to the effect, e.g., that "the Committee particularly regrets the government's repeated failure... to eliminate long-standing discrepancies between the national legislation and many ratified Conventions" (46 R.P. 680).

[3] 1955 R.C.E. 20.

[4] 39 R.P. 657. These bodies included a tripartite committee which was to draft labour legislation.

[5] 1959 R.C.E. 16.

[6] 43 R.P. 677.

[7] 45 R.P. 744.

[8] 46 R.P. 691.

[9] 47 R.P. 523.

[10] American Regional Conferences of the I.L.O. have long been concerned with this problem of efficient administration. The first such Conference, meeting in Santiago (Chile) in 1936, discussed the implementation of international labour Conventions and adopted a Resolution which called on member States "to establish in each country the administrative, technical and research bodies especially necessary for the proper application of the Conventions approved and of labour law in general" (XXI O.B. 62).

mically and socially adds further likelihood to such a possibility.[1] Some continuity and persistence in the work of the various administrative bodies, coupled with a greater degree of interest in their work at the top levels of the government, might materially increase the chances of success. It is clear, moreover, that the mere existence of a considerable governmental apparatus does not suffice, by itself, to make national and international labour legislation effective and that excessive reliance on bureaucratic procedures may risk, in fact, to have quite the opposite result.

*Disagreements Between Government Departments*

Administrative delays in the implementation of Conventions may also occur when government departments fail to agree on the steps to be taken. Such disagreements are as a rule resolved internally, especially if they arise inside a ministry. If two or more ministries are involved the problem is apt to assume sufficiently large proportions, so that mention of it appears in the government's reports and replies to the I.L.O. This happened when Austria was called upon to formulate labour clauses for insertion in public contracts, as required by Convention No. 94 of 1949. Following a first observation in 1954, the Council of Ministers decided in 1955 that appropriate regulations were to be drafted by the Federal Ministry of Commerce and Reconstruction.[2] The text so prepared was however taken exception to, first by the Austrian Assembly of Chambers of Labour, a semi-official entity,[3] then by the Ministry of Social Affairs itself.[4] A deadlock seemed thus to have developed by 1960 which the I.L.O. was asked to help to resolve.[5] When the information made available in reply failed to lead to agreement[6] the Committee of Experts observed that it could not "any longer accept the government's repeated explanation that the very long delay involved is due to differences of opinion between the governmental departments and other organizations concerned".[7] The government now promised that it was seeking a solution "through personal negotiation between the two Federal Ministers" and if necessary through

---

[1] Speaking in the plenary Conference in 1965, a Uruguayan government delegate gave the following significant explanation for his country's failure to comply with certain of its obligations as an I.L.O. member: "The paradox can be explained by the fact that Uruguay, while deeply concerned with social legislation, has no satisfactory labour administration" (49 P.R. No. 44, p. 459).

[2] 1956 R.C.E. 79-80.

[3] 1957 R.C.E. 89.

[4] 43 R.P. 691.

[5] The government placed before the Conference Committee a detailed statement of the divergent points of view as regards the various steps required to give effect to the Convention and added that "negotiations between the competent ministries could be continued successfully only if the I.L.O. would give a clarification concerning the points in dispute... This request was made in the name of both ministries concerned". The Conference Committee referred the request to the Office and the Committee of Experts (44 R.P. 628-629).

[6] In 1961 the government informed the Conference Committee that "new difficulties have arisen... the employers' representatives have raised objection" (45 R.P. 757-758).

[7] 1962 R.C.E. 121.

a decision by the Cabinet.[1] Agreement was finally achieved and a text approved by the Cabinet in 1963.[2]

Although divergent views could eventually be reconciled, the time needed in this case shows what serious delays may be caused by such differences, even in the application of a relatively non-controversial instrument. Perhaps the fact that a coalition government is in power in Austria had some bearing on the difficulties. Nonetheless the main issues were technical ones and final solution through administrative channels might well have been speeded up if a greater sense of urgency had prevailed. In particular the timing of the discussions, usually in the wake of a new session of the International Labour Conference, tends to confirm that it was external rather than domestic pressures which brought about progress. This is not to imply that the government's attitude was essentially negative,[3] but that it needed to be crystallized and that an administrative consensus is sometimes slow in emerging.

*Inadequate Administrative Machinery*

In the two examples cited so far the formulation of policies was impeded although well-developed administrative machinery was available for the purpose. There was even a suspicion that the key to the problem was an excess rather than a lack of bureaucracy. It is obvious however that insufficient development of governmental administration, as a symptom of under-development in general, represents a far more serious obstacle to satisfactory implementation. As indicated earlier in this section, it inhibits both national and international supervision due to a lack of trained personnel,[4] to language difficulties,[5] etc. It renders relations with the governments concerned more uncertain [6] and thereby prevents that "uniformity in administration" which is an essential objective of world standards.[7]

---

[1] 46 R.P. 713. Despite these formal assurances, the Conference Committee placed the case on its special list for the first time in 1962. An article in a Viennese labour law journal described this action as "most humiliating... The general respect which Austria has always enjoyed hitherto within (the I.L.O.) was seriously impaired by this measure" (Dr. Otto Scheer, " Die Internationale Arbeitskonferenz 1962 ", *Das Recht der Arbeit* (Vienna) Vol. 12, No. 4 (Sept. 1962) p. 207). In previous years the Austrian workers' member of the Committee had taken an active part in the discussions and had also attempted, through articles published in 1959, 1960 and 1961, to draw domestic attention to the problem (cf., e.g., footnote 2, p. 49 above).

[2] 47 R.P. 538-539.

[3] Gunnar Myrdal's opinion that "national administrations have... a tradition of negativism in all international matters" seems rather sweeping (cf. *Realities and Illusions in Regard to Inter-Governmental Organizations* (L.T. Hobhouse Memorial Trust Lecture No. 24, Bedford College, London, 1954) (Oxford University Press, 1955), p. 11).

[4] The governments of Gabon, Mali and Togo, e.g., mentioned "administrative and personnel difficulties" to explain delays in reporting in 1962 (46 R.P. 690-691).

[5] Repeatedly cited by the Indonesian government, for instance (39 R.P. 656; 43 R.P. 677).

[6] E.J. Phelan tells of Albert Thomas that "he had an experience, or an instinctive sense, of more imperfect national administrations... and there is no doubt that in numbers such administrations far exceed the more perfect ones" (*Yes and Albert Thomas, op. cit.*, p. 113).

[7] Joseph P. Chamberlain, "Legislation in a Changing Economic World", *op. cit.*, p. 42.

In their more general effects, the administrative difficulties of the less developed countries engender delays in eliminating divergencies. Thus, even the government of Pakistan, whose civil service has a long tradition, has mentioned such difficulties to explain why it had not yet introduced the relatively minor amendments needed to ensure application of the Night Work of Young Persons (Industry) Convention (Revised), 1948 (No. 90), to apprentices and to young persons employed in mines. The government gave this explanation already in its first report [1] and it assured the Conference Committee in subsequent years that the necessary amendments had "reached an advanced stage" (1954), had "been speeded up" (1955), were "being expeditiously pursued" (1959), would be "enacted before the end of the year" (1962) and "would be promulgated shortly" (1963). Although Pakistan's federal reorganization may have been partly responsible, administrative delays and a low priority assigned to the question of full application by the responsible officials may well be the main reasons for continued non-compliance.

Administrative difficulties become especially complex when uncertainty and confusion render compliance with a ratified Convention doubtful and tenuous. The problem may originally have legal implications in connection with the introduction of international standards into internal law. When the position is such, however, that important pieces of legislation, though obsolete, continue to be in force and when most of the population in unable to understand its rights, there is a real danger that a binding Convention will simply remain a dead letter.

Serious situations of the kind just mentioned are exceptional and are due to a combination of factors–involving representative government, freedom of association, illiteracy, etc.–which far transcend a mere deficiency in the techniques of public administration. The most striking example of such a situation is provided by the I.L.O.'s protracted efforts to secure compliance by Liberia with the Forced Labour Convention, 1930 (No. 29). The history of this case is particularly well documented because, in the end, it led to a complaint under article 26 of the I.L.O. Constitution.

The Forced Labour Convention constituted the Organization's first effort to frame a comprehensive instrument for the protection of a fundamental human right; the Convention has binding force in a larger number of countries than any other international labour Convention. Liberia ratified Convention No. 29 in 1931, at the suggestion of the Council of the League of Nations, as a demonstration of its earnest to do away with slavery and other compulsory labour practices.[2] As the first observation dates back to 1933, this represents in fact the most protracted case of non-compliance dealt with by the supervisory Committees and it would be impossible to review here in detail all the comments they have made on this case.

The process of supervision over that period met with two major obstacles: the difficulty of obtaining information and the government's insistence

---

[1] 1954 R.C.E. 41.

[2] For a summary of the background of the ratification, cf. *Commission of Inquiry Report (Portugal-Liberia), op. cit.,* pp. 53-55.

that forced labour did not exist, that any legislation authorizing it was obsolete and that no further measures were therefore required. In these circumstances the Committee of Experts used increasingly strong language [1] and the Conference Committee maintained the case on the special list ever since 1957. In 1961 a subcommittee of the Conference Committee had "a long interview with a tripartite delegation from Liberia" which maintained the position previously taken by the government but promised that "no effort would be spared to eliminate the remaining discrepancies before the next session of the Conference".[2] Shortly afterwards, in August 1961, a formal complaint of non-observance was lodged by the government of Portugal.

The problem to be explored in the present context is not so much the character of the violations of the Convention,[3] nor the intricate legal points involved, but why no progress was made for so long. Whereas the Liberian government representatives in the Conference Committee merely reiterated again and again in their replies that the legislation to which objection was taken was in fact obsolete,[4] a much fuller picture of the administrative difficulties emerged from the hearings of the Commission of Inquiry in 1962, as reported to the Governing Body early in 1963. To buttress their contention that any legislation contrary to the Forced Labour Convention was obsolete, the high Liberian government officials who testified before the Commission gave two explanations which illustrated the degree of uncertainty surrounding the administration of labour law in their country. They pleaded ignorance as to the reasons why certain laws and regulations had been adopted and insisted that such legislation had not been enforced by the responsible authorities.[5]

---

[1] In 1957 and subsequently it characterized the situation as a "clear violation of the Convention" (1957 R.C.E. 53).

[2] 45 R.P. 748. The Conference Committee's Report described the exchange of views with the delegation as "extensive, completely frank and extremely useful". It noted in conclusion that "the competent services of the International Labour Office are at the disposal of the delegation to provide any documentation which it may desire." There is no evidence that any use was made of this offer.

[3] Following a series of very detailed observations in the preceding years, the Committee of Experts summed up the position in 1960 by singling out three types of forced labour still authorized by the national legislation (for the benefit of private individuals, for public works and for porterage of officials and private travellers) as particularly serious breaches of the Convention (1960 R.C.E. 31).

[4] In 1959, for instance, the representative prefaced his explanations by stating that "a distinction should be drawn between those countries which had ratified Conventions and did not apply them in practice and other countries which, although applying provisions of Conventions..., did not amend their legislation specifically. Liberia fell in the second category" (43 R.P. 682).

[5] "The Under-Secretary of the Department of the Interior stated that he did not know why the regulations on compulsory porterage had been continued, since they had not been enforced during his 11 years of service in the Department" (*Commission of Inquiry Report (Portugal-Liberia) op. cit.*, p. 121). "The Attorney-General, the Under-Secretary of the Department of the Interior, and the Secretary of Agriculture and Commerce stated that they did not know why these provisions (concerning the supply of labour by chiefs to persons engaged in prospecting, mining and farming) had been adopted in 1949. The last-mentioned witness also stated that no such regulations had ever been enforced by his Department" (*ibid.*, p. 125).

They conceded at the same time that no clear instructions as to the applicable provisions had been sent to these authorities.[1] In the circumstances, two conclusions appear unavoidable: the enactment of such legislation "constituted a failure to discharge the obligations accepted by Liberia"[2] and the state of confusion was such that law enforcement became a practical impossibility. Both conclusions point to serious administrative shortcomings.

It is significant therefore that, in addition to the repeal of most of the discrepancies by three acts adopted a few months after the filing of the complaint,[3] an "administrative reorganization of the responsible agencies of the government" was initiated[4] and the Commission stressed in its final recommendations that any request by the government for help in connection with "the improvement of administrative practices and systems of inspection" (under article 10, paragraph 2 (b) of the I.L.O. Constitution) "should be regarded as of the highest priority".[5] This technical assistance aspect, as well as other implications of the case, will be further explored below.

Another difficulty involving labour administration, although not specifically raised in the case of Liberia, was stressed in general terms: all persons in employment should know the legislation concerning them. This essential guarantee of due process and of effective administration is absent when the legislation remains unpublished and confidential. The Committee of Experts referred to this practice in its 1962 conclusions on forced labour.[6] The Commission of Inquiry which dealt with another complaint under article 26–filed by Ghana regarding the observance by Portugal of the Abolition of Forced Labour Convention, 1957 (No. 105)–took specific exception to such a procedure[7] and recommended that regulations on the recruitment of labour or bearing on the application of Conven-

---

[1] "The Under-Secretary of the Department of the Interior which had drawn up the Hinterland Regulations of 1936 and 1949 and had been responsible for the application of these Regulations and of the Aborigines Law, stated that the Secretary of the Interior had not sent any orders to district commissioners or other officials not to enforce certain of these provisions, and the Attorney-General stated that no such orders had been sent by the Department of Justice or any other government department" (*ibid.*, p. 112).

[2] This was one of the findings of the Commission, as given on p. 162 of its Report.

[3] *Ibid.*, p. 96.

[4] *Ibid.*, p. 26. The reason given for doing so was to facilitate reporting on the application of the Convention.

[5] *Ibid.*, p. 175.

[6] "Legislative provisions currently in force have not all been published, or are never published, and sometimes are communicated only to the authorities responsible for enforcing them" (1962 R.C.E. 196). The Committee merely stated that this was a "difficulty, peculiar to certain countries" without naming any countries.

[7] "The Commission has noted that on a number of occasions regulations concerning or affecting labour matters, such as the obligation to work, recruitment procedures (including recruitment for the public services and the Diamond Company of Angola), and the cultivation of certain crops have taken the form of confidential, unpublished circulars" (XLV O.B. No. 2, April 1962, Supplement II: *Report of the Commission Appointed under Article 26 of the Constitution of the International Labour Organization to Examine the Complaint Filed by the Government of Ghana concerning the Observance by the Government of Portugal of the Abolition of Forced Labour Convention, 1957 (No. 105)*, p. 237).

tion No. 105 "should be published and made available to all interested parties". No more serious obstacle to the implementation of a Convention could in fact be imagined than to prevent those subject to its provisions from knowing the national standards applicable to them. In such a case the guarantees laid down in the instrument are emptied of their practical content by administrative fiat.[1]

*Possible Remedies*

It would be unrealistic to imagine that the remedy for the difficulties discussed above is to be found solely in an attempt to improve administrative structures and procedures. In most cases other fundamental difficulties will also have to be overcome. But good administration does constitute an indispensable condition for ensuring observance of ratified Conventions.[2] International assistance in the field of labour administration represents an available remedy which has in fact been used on an increasing scale. Such assistance can help in developing national machinery in the fields of social security, employment information, minimum wages, statistics, inspection, etc., thus promoting the implementation of the Conventions in these fields. Alternatively, aid can be provided in the field of labour administration in general and concentrate on the training of personnel. In this case it is the over-all question of public administration which is involved and the programmes initiated for this purpose by the United Nations and the specialized agencies can have a direct or indirect effect on the application of Conventions[3].

---

[1] In a Resolution concerning Publication of Labour Laws, adopted in 1958, the Conference urged member States to "publish promptly laws, decrees and regulations which affect the terms and conditions of employment of workers" so as "to apprise the people concerned of their rights and obligations" (XLI O.B. No. 2, p. 80). Such publicity is especially important when the bulk of the labour force is illiterate and thus even more in need of protection.

[2] In his Report to the 1958 Session of the Conference the Director-General emphasized that "good labour administration is the heart of social policy" (42 D.R. 66). In its 1961 review of social evolution in non-metropolitan territories the Committee of Experts pointed to the "especially significant task (of labour administration) in developing countries where changing economic and social conditions necessitate the adoption sometimes of new and often complex legislative and other measures designed to cope with labour problems as they emerge. Efficient labour administration services also fill a vital need in these countries because the general level of education and trade union development often makes it difficult for the workers themselves to play a major role in ensuring the adoption and implementation of protective measures" (1961 R.C.E. 306).

[3] The Secretary-General referred to this aspect in 1962 in his Report to the Economic and Social Council on the programmes of the United Nations family in the field of public administration: "There comes a time in the implementation of international instruments when the attainment of the main objectives laid down entails the installation or modification of national structures, mostly in the public sector; the adoption of provisions and procedures; and the training of personnel who, while essentially technicians, must also possess some knowledge of administration... The existence of an efficient administration is the indispensable mainstay of any international action, whether undertaken pursuant to a convention or recommendation, through the giving of advice, or in any other way." ("General Review of the Development, Co-ordination and Concentration of the Economic, Social and Human Rights Programmes and Activities of the United Nations and the Specialized Agencies as a Whole", 34th Session of the Economic and Social Council, doc. E/3630, paragraphs 83 and 84.)

From the point of view of the I.L.O., the role of the labour ministry and the other departments working in conjunction with it naturally looms largest. There is no need to describe in detail the different types of assistance available. They range from the services of experts on the spot,[1] to fellowships awarded to government officials for training in other countries or in the International Labour Office, and to the organization of seminars, often on a regional basis.[2] A country's capacity to develop its administrative machinery is of course dependent on its financial resources and on the general level of education.[3] But assistance in this direction can, if successful, act as a multiplier: it can play a crucial role in all the many fields of labour policy which depend on administrative planning and action; it can also, as a consequence, buttress the I.L.O.'s network of international obligations. For all these reasons top priority should be given to practical help in the field of administration and the amount of effort and expenditure so far allocated[4] hardly seems adequate for this purpose. The I.L.O. by virtue of the formulation of standards, and the governments, by virtue of their ratification, have a common interest and duty to raise the level of administrative competence on which the execution of social policies so closely depends.

---

[1] Missions of this kind were, for instance, carried out in Afghanistan in 1957-1958 and 1960-1961 to advise on "a) the improvement and strengthening of the existing machinery of labour administration; b) the enforcement of the existing labour and social legislation, with special reference to its application in the larger industrial undertakings" (International Labour Office, Regular Programme of Technical Assistance, *Report to the Government of Afghanistan on Labour Administration and Legislation*, I.L.O. Geneva, 1962 (doc. OIT/OTA/Afghanistan/R.6 (roneoed), p. 1).

[2] A meeting of this kind was held, for example, in Sierra Leone in 1962. Cf. International Labour Office, Expanded Programme of Technical Assistance, *Report of the Labour Administration Seminar for English-Speaking Participants from African Countries, Freetown, 2-15 November 1962, Practical Problems of Labour Inspection"*, I.L.O. Geneva, 1963 (doc. ILO/TAP/AFR/R.2, (roneoed)). Training facilities can also be provided on a more permanent basis. Thus the I.L.O. proposed to the Inter-American Economic and Social Council the setting up of a Labour Administration Training Centre for Latin America (Press Release ILO 12D of 4 October 1963).

[3] The above-mentioned Report to the Afghan government refers to the difficulties encountered by the Labour Department in recruiting and training administrative and secretarial staff, due to the vast demand for such personnel in commerce, industry and teaching: "The number of persons leaving the University and the secondary schools is not fully adequate to satisfy the demand and Public Administration is at a disadvantage in meeting competition because the salaries it offers are generally less high" (*Report to the Government of Afghanistan on Labour Administration and Legislation, op. cit.*, p. 27).

[4] During the years 1952-1963 the percentage of total I.L.O. expenditure from Expanded Programme of Technical Assistance funds on the sector "Labour Conditions and Administration" fluctuated between a maximum of 27.7 per cent (in 1956) and a minimum of 17.6 per cent (in 1963) (doc. G.B.150/O.P./D.1/2 (roneoed), p. 19 and doc. G.B./O.P./D.1/3 (roneoed), p. 37). No definite conclusions can be drawn from these figures because no separate breakdown for labour administration alone is available. It is unlikely however that more than one-third of the total was expended for this purpose. On the other hand, technical assistance funds have also become available in recent years from the I.L.O.'s own budget. Although rather limited (they rarely exceeded 10 per cent of the sums available through E.P.T.A.) they provide, in proportion, a much larger amount for labour conditions and administration, i.e. about 50 per cent in 1961 and 1962 (doc. G.B.154/O.P./D.1/4 (roneoed), p. 30).

### III. Political Difficulties

Political factors which sometimes stand in the way of full compliance are of particular interest because of the broader issues they raise in relation to the principle that ratification is an act binding the State and that its validity, for the period provided for in the instrument, cannot be influenced by changes of government or internal difficulties standing in the way of due performance of freely assumed international obligations.[1] Fortunately, no government has ever denied the legality of a ratification which its predecessor had communicated to the I.L.O. On more than one occasion, however, governments have pleaded inability to apply a Convention in full due to a division of powers, or similar sweeping reasons.

#### Serious Political Upheavals

When the circumstances invoked represent profound political upheavals they involve an element of *force majeure* which cannot be disregarded, even if a Convention contains no specific provisions to cover the situation.[2] Despite the high degree of instability which has characterized the period since World War II, governments only rarely refer to events of this type to explain why observations of the supervisory Committees have not been acted upon.[3] Nor would it be possible to give such an explanation for several years in succession unless, as during the Spanish Civil War, an internal struggle deteriorates into a protracted conflict of major proportions.

#### Parliamentary Difficulties

Another type of political obstacle to compliance, which is much more frequently mentioned, is a government's alleged inability to secure action by the legislative authorities to remove divergencies between national laws or regulations and the terms of a Convention. Although, as noted, there can be no doubt regarding the position under international law, the practical implications are complex. Much depends, in such circumstances, on the degree of influence the executive branch can exert on its parliament. This, in turn, hinges on the constitutional relationship between the two branches. Although one would expect real difficulties to arise in countries with a truly independent parliament, experience seems to show that long legislative delays are cited mostly by States which do not fit this description.

The time required to secure compliance by Cuba with the Unemployment Indemnity (Shipwreck) Convention, 1920 (No. 8), illustrates the point. Although neither the instrument nor the divergencies noted raised

---

[1] Cf. Lord McNair, *The Law of Treaties, op. cit.*, pp. 668-672.

[2] Cf. pp. 147-150 below.

[3] One such explanation was given by the Guatemalan government in the Conference Committee in 1958: "The reasons for which there was lack of conformity between the ratified Conventions and the national legislation in practice were as follows: there had been a fundamental military, political and constitutional crisis following which several provisional governments were in power" (42 R.P. 658). The government representative of Haiti also referred, the same year, to "the political events which had occurred" and "the repeated changes in the administration" (42 R.P. 658).

any basic problems, the government assured the Conference Committee in 1949 that the necessary amendments could only be introduced with the approval of the Congress, at the request of the Executive.[1]  A bill to this effect failed, according to the government, to secure adoption because "by reason of the principle of the separation of powers, it was not possible to compel the legislative power to adopt the proposed text.  The only action which could be taken by the President of the Republic was to send a new message to Congress requesting that the consideration of the bill should be speeded up".[2]  The Committee of Experts considered the case sufficiently important to refer to it in its General Report in 1952, pointing out that "the independence of the legislative powers does not exempt a State member from the obligation of bringing national law into conformity with Conventions which have been ratified by it".[3]  In the end a new government which took power by force the same year issued a legislative decree, apparently after Congress had been dissolved.[4]  Although the problem was thus settled because of a suspension of constitutional processes, it is to be wondered whether the same result could not have been attained through congressional action if the government had made full use of its influence.

Any such speculations are of little value.  Even if it should prove possible to gauge accurately the interplay of political forces at a given moment –in itself a hazardous undertaking–there remains the question of the exact motives for which a government does or does not stake its prestige on a social issue.  The more recent example of Colombia is particularly pertinent.  In 1960 the government submitted to Congress a comprehensive bill to amend the Labour Code.  Eighteen of the 25 Conventions then ratified were to be applied more fully in this way [5] and I.L.O. technical assistance had been provided for this purpose.[6]  Since then the amendment bill has been considered and revised by the Colombian Senate and Chamber of Deputies, but the government seems to have had little success in promoting early action or ensuring strict adherence to ratified standards.  The Minister of Labour himself told the Conference Committee in 1963 that while "the bill submitted by the government took the Conventions into account... Congress was sovereign and could modify the bill.  The government had no power to compel Congress to speed up the adoption of the bill".[7]  Without wishing to question the Minister's statement, the problem of the government's commitment to its declared aims and to its international obligations remains.  This is in fact a concrete case where the determination of the national authorities to follow a policy based on treaty obligations and on the related technical advice, is being tested.  Legally, a plea of *non possumus* is unacceptable in such a case.  In practical

---

[1] 32 R.P. 454.

[2] 34 R.P. 563-564.

[3] 1952 R.C.E. 5.

[4] 35 R.P. 496; 36 R.P. 377-378.

[5] 1961 R.C.E. 21-22.

[6] 45 R.P. 742.

[7] 47 R.P. 521.

terms much depends on the efforts actually made to persuade parliament to take the necessary action. As already noted, this type of political manœuvring is usually carried on behind the scenes, so that evidence of it remains undocumented. The rare occasions when the veil is lifted are therefore of special interest.

One such instance which has attracted widespread attention, both inside and outside the country concerned, is the application by Japan of the two basic Conventions of 1948 and 1949 on freedom of association and the right to organize (Nos. 87 and 98). The case had two separate but connected aspects which must be clearly distinguished. One aspect which has received much more publicity than the other involved the intended ratification of Convention No. 87, as announced to the Governing Body Committee on Freedom of Association in 1960.[1] The other element involved the application of Convention No. 98 which Japan had ratified in 1953, two years after rejoining the International Labour Organization. The link connecting the two issues is the amendment of certain legislative provisions concerning trade union officials.[2]

A bill to this effect, as submitted to the Japanese Diet in 1960 and resubmitted to subsequent sessions, has been the subject of intensive negotiations between the government party, the Liberal-Democrats, and the opposition Socialist Party and has been debated repeatedly in parliament. Within the I.L.O. the case has been discussed at successive sessions of the Governing Body and has continued to figure in the Reports of the Committee of Experts and the Conference Committee. In 1961, for instance, a detailed discussion in the latter Committee provided an opportunity for the Japanese government and workers' representatives to state their case. Their disagreement was in contrast with the identity of views of the employers' and workers' groups of the Committee that national law and practice were contrary to Convention No. 98.[3]

In 1964 the government consented that the case be referred to the I.L.O. Fact-Finding and Conciliation Commission on Freedom of Association and a panel of the Commission visited Japan early in 1965. The

---

[1] XLIII O.B. No. 3, pp. 253-261. The announcement was made in connection with complaints against the government, presented by the General Council of Trade Unions of Japan, the International Confederation of Free Trade Unions, the International Transport Workers' Federation, the Postal, Telegraph and Telephone International and the All-Japan Postal Workers' Union. These complaints were examined under the procedure set up by the I.L.O. to deal with alleged infringements of the right of association; cf. pp. 176-177 below.

[2] Section 4(3) of the Public Corporation and National Enterprise Labour Relations Law and section 5(3) of the Local Public Enterprise Labour Relations Law required union officials to be employed in the undertaking in which the union operates. The Committee of Experts considered that these provisions were contrary to Convention No. 98 because they "may facilitate acts of interference on the part of the managements" (1959 R.C.E. 56).

[3] When the government contended that "employees have never been dismissed by the managements for the purpose of interfering in the election of union officers" the employers' members commented candidly that "if an employer wanted to find an excuse for dismissal, he would very often be able to do so without difficulty. The very fact that there was no case in which it had been held that a worker in a public enterprise had been dismissed for trade union activities might be an indication of a worker's difficulty in proving the true cause of dismissal" (45 R.P. 758-760).

proposals made by the Commission at the end of this visit led to the ratification of Convention No. 87, the revision of the legislation so as to comply with Convention No. 98 [1] and the initiation of periodic high-level meetings between the government and the General Council of Trade Unions (Sohyo). While the Report of the Commission [2] describes very fully the background and intricacies of this case and bears witness to the political factors and negotiations involved, the interest which the issue aroused in the Japanese Diet and throughout the country for many months can best be gauged from parliamentary and press reports. [3]  Three main conclusions seem to emerge from this revealing case-history.  Firstly, there can be little doubt that concern with I.L.O. standards is especially intense in Japan and that supervisory comments are given thorough consideration by the government. [4]  Secondly, the lengthy period over which this case held the spotlight of public opinion did not suffice by itself to secure action and the political difficulties may well have delayed a solution.  Thirdly, when results were finally achieved, this implied "far-reaching changes of attitude on the part of both government and labour". [5]

*Possible Remedies*

It is obvious that internal political problems of application can only be resolved at the national level.  A government can strengthen its own hand in its parliamentary negotiations, however, if it succeeds in demonstrating to the members of the legislative branch that compliance with international obligations is a real necessity.  This task of information and education can be performed mainly in two ways.  In the first place, it is indispensable to direct the attention of the law-makers to the decisions of the

---

[1] The Government so informed the Conference Committee in June 1965 (49 P.R. No. 33, p. XXVI).

[2] *Report of the Fact-Finding and Conciliation Commission on Freedom of Association concerning Persons Employed in the Public Sector in Japan*, submitted to the November 1965 session of the Governing Body (doc. G.B.163/5/5 (roneoed)).

[3] For instance, in 1963 detailed front-page articles appeared in the press, such as a story that talks had been held between the political parties and Sohyo to speed up passage of the amendment bills and that these negotiations were to continue during the Diet recess (*The Japan Times*, 5 July 1963).  A report in *The Times* of London of 25 May 1964, describing the sequence of events which led to the referral of the case to the Fact-Finding and Conciliation Commission, bore the title "Japan's Race to Save Honour on Unions". And an editorial in *The Mainichei Daily News* (Tokyo) of 22 April 1965, headed "The Diet Gets Back on its Feet" included the following comments: "After a stupefying five-day vacuum caused by the controversy over the I.L.O. bills the National Diet has finally been brought back to normal... It is gratifying to note the spirit of concession shown by the opposing political parties".

[4] Professor Robert A. Scalapino indicates that this is not a new development: "After the First World War, the I.L.O. served as an external pressure group, causing some attention to be focused upon the health and working conditions of the Japanese worker" (*Labor and Economic Development, op. cit.*, p. 114).

[5] As apparent from the Commission's findings and recommendations (*op. cit.*, paragraph 2089).  The Commission also considered that the future depends, *inter alia*, on "whether the trade unions give the government on a non-political basis the measure of co-operation necessary to enable it to make a reality of the new (labour relations) policy" (paragraph 2098).

International Labour Conference. A constitutional obligation to do so exists in relation to newly adopted Conventions. It would seem to be of at least equal importance to bring to the notice of the legislative branch any criticism made as regards a ratified Convention. The reports some governments regularly submit to their parliaments on the sessions of the International Labour Conference could provide a convenient vehicle for this purpose.

There exists moreover a second, more personal, method for stimulating interest in, and knowledge of, the country's international obligations among those who must vote the laws and the funds to implement them. Certain countries include members of parliament in their government delegation to the I.L.O.'s conferences.[1] Reference was made earlier to the prominent role played by a Chilean Senator in the discussions of the Conference Committee on Application.[2] Despite the risks which such a practice may involve,[3] it has the great advantage of acquainting influential members of the legislature with the realities and decisions of an international meeting. This occasional association in the country's external relations may well strengthen the legislators' awareness that participation in the I.L.O. and acceptance of its standards impose continuing obligations which should not be disregarded.

## IV. Suspension of Application During a National Emergency

Interruptions in the implementation of treaty obligations during a time of serious emergency are admitted by the general principles of international law and specifically provided for in certain international labour Conventions. What has been the attitude of governments and of the supervisory organs in the face of such difficulties? It is interesting to note that, apart from suspensions of application in times of war, this contingency–which is tantamount to a case of retrogression–seems to have arisen on a limited scale only.

### Suspension Clauses in Certain Conventions

It is mainly the Conventions dealing with hours of work[4] and with night work[5] which provide for the suspension of their application in what is variously described as "emergency" conditions endangering "national

---

[1] During the decade 1954-1963 the United States government delegation repeatedly included members of the House of Representatives: e.g., two in 1956 and 1957, three in 1961, four in 1963. Senators have also on occasion attended the Conference.

[2] Cf. footnote 1, p. 101.

[3] Madame C. Labeyrie-Menahem wonders "to what extent the Executive which issues instructions to (the) delegation can impose its views on the representatives of the legislative branch" (*Des Institutions Spécialisées - Problèmes juridiques et diplomatiques de l'administration internationale, op. cit.,* p. 104).

[4] Nos. 1, 30, 43, 49, 67.

[5] Nos. 6, 20, 89, 90.

safety". Although no detailed definition of these terms is given,[1] they clearly allude to circumstances where the public interest is at stake on more than a localized or limited scale. Reference to *force majeure* in some of the Conventions would seem to indicate moreover that it is sudden and unexpected occurrences which are envisaged there.

## War-Time Interruptions

Of all major emergencies, direct or indirect involvement in an armed conflict is of course the most serious. Many States which were parties to international labour Conventions had to face this contingency during World War II and the experience gained during this period has enabled the I.L.O., and especially its supervisory organs, to determine the effect of war on the obligations under its Conventions.[2] The two principal conclusions which emerged were mentioned by the Committee of Experts when it resumed its annual sessions in 1945: on the one hand it was clear that governments pleading *force majeure* had suspended the application not only of Conventions which contained a special clause to this effect but also of those which did not; on the other hand there was never any doubt as to "the continuance and survival after the end of a war of the legal obligations of the contracting parties arising from the ratification of Conventions".[3] When the Conference Committee discussed these findings the same year it drew attention to the need to consult "the responsible employers' and workers' organizations concerned before the suspensions, etc. are put into effect".[4] The two Committees also noted, in 1946, that suspensions or derogations had been abrogated in a number of countries [5] and that some governments had expressly confirmed the "survival and

---

[1] Except in the rather special case of the Forced Labour Convention which defines cases of emergency as "war... calamity or threatened calamity, such as fire, flood, famine, earthquake, violent epidemic or epizootic diseases, invasion by animal, insect or vegetable pests, and in general any circumstance that would endanger the existence or the well-being of the whole or part of the population" (article 2, paragraph 2(d)).

[2] A memorandum on this subject which the Director submitted to the Governing Body in 1945 (94 G.B. 238-240) suggested that a fuller study of this problem was desirable within the I.L.O. and on a more general international scale. Although this suggestion was not followed up, the conclusions subsequently reached by the supervisory Committees coincided with those in the above memorandum.

[3] 1945 R.C.E. 5. The principle that multilateral law-making treaties are not abrogated even as between opposing belligerents was confirmed by a French tribunal in 1951. The Civil Court of Aix-en-Provence found that an Italian working in France who was a victim of an industrial accident was entitled to the benefits provided for in the Equality of Treatment (Accident Compensation) Convention, 1925 (No. 19), even when a state of war existed between the two countries. The court held that the Convention was not a bilateral treaty between France and Italy and that the "special obligations... with an international body" created by its ratification had therefore not lapsed as a result of hostilities (36 S.R. 60). For a fuller discussion of this decision, cf. I.L.O., *Industry and Labour*, Vol. IX (1953), pp. 306-307.

[4] 27 R.P. 439-440. A requirement to carry out such consultations in the circumstances mentioned has since been included in some Conventions, e.g. Nos. 89 and 94.

[5] Belgium, Czechoslovakia, India and the Netherlands were singled out for mention by the Committee of Experts (1946 R.C.E. 5).

continuance" of their obligations "in their entirety".[1] One case of war-time suspension which gave rise to some discussion in the Conference was the partial lifting, in India, of the ban on underground work by women (Convention No. 45). The government indicated that it had been com-pelled to do so by "an urgent war necessity",[2] in order to maintain the output of coal. The Indian workers' representatives who had criticized this decision welcomed the return to full application, early in 1946.[3]

*Internal Emergencies*

Cases of internal emergencies have seldom been referred to by govern-ments and the supervisory Committees have been reluctant to admit a plea of exceptional circumstances. Thus the Committee of Experts indi-cated in 1955 that manpower and electricity shortages in Czechoslovakia could not be invoked to have recourse to the suspension clause in the Night Work (Women) Convention (Revised), 1948 (No. 89).[4] In 1951, a request by the Swiss government that an identical clause in the Night Work of Young Persons (Industry) Convention, 1919 (No. 6), be used to permit "the general training of apprentices" during the night in "a trade such as the bakery trade which was of vital importance to the whole popu-lation" was not granted by the Conference Committee.[5]

In the case of the Forced Labour Convention, 1930, the Committee of Experts has been at pains to clarify the bearing of the emergency clause,[6] so that it should be invoked only in cases of genuine necessity. It has also asked governments to supply the fullest possible information on any cases of this kind.[7] When it noted for instance that under emergency regulations issued in Kenya, adults of either sex could be obliged to carry out unpaid work or services for up to 90 days a year, the Committee followed the matter closely, insisting that the regulations not be applied to women, that the duration of unpaid work and services be reduced and that these excep-tional measures be repealed as soon as the emergency conditions had disappeared.[8] In one of its replies, the British government assured the Conference Committee, in 1958, that the maximum duration of work had been cut to 40 days, that the "regulations now applied in a very limited number of districts and that the government was anxious to abolish this form of communal labour altogether as soon as local conditions permitted".[9]

---

[1] As stated by the French, Italian and Polish governments in the Conference Committee (29 R.P. 506).

[2] 27 R.P. 204.

[3] An Indian worker claimed at the Conference session in 1946 that "due to the pressure of public opinion, the wrong has been righted" (29 R.P. 153).

[4] 1955 R.C.E. 69. Article 5, paragraph 1, of the Convention authorizes the night work prohibition to be suspended "when in case of serious emergency the national interest demands it". The government repealed the derogation in 1959 (1960 R.C.E. 48).

[5] 34 R.P. 563. Cf. also footnote 2, p. 110 above.

[6] Cf. footnote 1, p. 148.

[7] Cf. the Committee's general conclusions on forced labour (1962 R.C.E. 210-211, 217).

[8] 1956 R.C.E. 103-104. 1957 R.C.E. 112-113.

[9] 42 R.P. 691. The government reported subsequently that the emergency regulations had been repealed in January 1960 (46 S.R. 289).

As the termination of a genuine emergency is, by definition, beyond a government's control, the decisive points are the character of the circumstances invoked and the date of their disappearance. The existence of international supervision should go some way towards guaranteeing that the suspension clauses in I.L.O. Conventions and the general principles governing *force majeure* are not departed from in such cases.

# Chapter Six

# PROBLEMS AND PROSPECTS OF I.L.O. SUPERVISION

An inquiry into the long-range effectiveness of a system of international supervision inevitably raises a number of broader questions regarding the operation of such a procedure. A general understanding of the root-causes of non-application often does not suffice to explain why the supervisory comments have failed to promote governmental action. It is necessary, therefore, in looking for explanations, to analyse the supervisory procedures themselves, i.e. the difficulties and delays met with in their operation. The present chapter attempts to size up the nature of the problems inherent in the system and the methods adopted or available to solve them.

Two objectives can be discerned in the process of supervision: first, full information must be obtained on the degree of application; then governments must be persuaded to adopt the measures required to achieve compliance. These two successive phases are examined in sections I and II below. A further section deals with the bearing of non-governmental participation, the most distinctive element of the I.L.O. system, on the operation and results of supervision. Finally, the emergence of certain political problems is briefly discussed.

## I. The Problem of Securing Information

As seen in Chapter One, the basis of the system of examination and follow-up is article 22 of the I.L.O. Constitution which requires a ratifying State to report regularly to the International Labour Office " on the measures which it has taken to give effect to the provisions of Conventions to which it is a party". The working and success of the whole procedure depend on satisfactory compliance with this basic requirement.

### Failure to Supply Reports

Generally speaking supervision has never been impeded by any failure on the part of ratifying countries to send in their reports. The two-yearly system of detailed reporting, instituted in 1959 to relieve the pressure both on the national administrations, which have to compile the information, and on the international bodies which have to examine it, has further improved the situation: in those cases where a report is not supplied the first year, it may still become available the second so that the proportion of the reports due which is received over a period of two years, is higher than that for any one year.[1] Cases where governments consistently fail

---

[1] In 1961, for instance, the Conference Committee found that "the over-all percentage over the past two years was impressively high, i.e. 94 per cent" (45 R.P. 733).

to supply their reports are exceptional and singled out for special criticism. The Committee of Experts naturally lays stress on the first reports after ratification which must provide the starting point for its evaluation of a given case.

Year after year the Committee sums up prominently in its Report the credit and debit side of what might be called the balance sheet of reporting.[1] The Conference Committee likewise devotes several paragraphs to the supply of reports and gives pride of place in its special list to the countries which have failed to supply any reports.[2] Over the years, most governments have in fact acquired the habit of sending their reports regularly to Geneva and the absence of reports cannot thus be considered as a frequent or major obstacle to supervision.

The delays which occur in the receipt of the reports have, on the other hand, represented a more serious source of difficulty. The need for careful examination of the information supplied, well in advance of the Committee of Experts' session, renders this time element especially important. Although governments are asked to send their reports by 15 October, i.e. about five months before the Committee meets, only around 20 per cent of those due are usually available at that time.

As the number of reports to be examined has continued to increase the demand for stricter observance of the deadline has become more insistent, on the part not only of the Committee of Experts but of the Conference Committee as well. It was the employers' members in the latter body who asked in 1956 that the Committee of Experts indicate in future the percentage of reports received by the date requested, so that the results could be compared from year to year.[3] These statistics are now available on a current basis and for as far back as 1948-49, but their publication seems to have had little effect. In an effort to draw attention to individual cases where governments have been particularly slow in reporting, the Committee of Experts has, in recent years, addressed a "general observation" to each of the countries concerned, urging them to send reports on time.[4] It is too early to tell whether this more individualized approach will lead to any improvements.

For many years, as noted in Chapter One, a subcommittee of the Conference Committee considered reports received too late for examination by the Experts, so as to avoid any loss of time in the process of supervision. Although its increasing workload has forced the Conference Committee to abandon this practice, the postponement of the examination for a year has become less important, due to the introduction of the biennial system of reporting. In dispensing with its examination of late reports, the Conference Committee warned that this might lead to a double standard under which governments would be free from criticism precisely because they had failed to send their reports on time or even omitted reporting at all.

---

[1] Cf. the chapter entitled "Reports Submitted by Governments on Ratified Conventions" in the Committee's General Report, e.g. 1964 R.C.E. 10-12.

[2] Cf., for instance, 48 R.P. 648-649.

[3] 39 R.P. 649 and doc. C.App.C./PV.3 (roneoed), p. 3.

[4] In 1963, e.g., remarks of this kind were addressed to fourteen countries (1963 R.C.E. 27-34).

This danger is obviated to some extent, however, because the Committee of Experts regularly repeats its previous comments whenever no new information has been supplied by a government. It also refers to this need for repetitions in its "general observations" to the defaulting countries.

*Possible Remedies*

A proposal by the Committee of Experts in 1949 to introduce a sort of informal sanction for consistent failures to report won little support in the Governing Body or the Conference.[1] The observations of the two supervisory bodies, coupled with the Conference Committee's special list, thus remain the principal means of pressure available. Fortunately these attempts to rely on publicity have proved sufficient in the great majority of cases. Moreover, the Governing Body would always be free, in extreme circumstances, to resort to the complaints procedure "of its own motion", on the ground that "it is not satisfied", in the absence of reports, that a ratified Convention is effectively observed.[2] The fact that this has never been done would seem to indicate that the habit of supplying reports is best acquired and strengthened with the passage of time and the accumulation of experience. The need to report on certain unratified Conventions may also help to develop this habit, even prior to ratification.

If failure to report is due not to a government's unwillingness but to a lack of familiarity with the obligations and procedures involved–i.e. to lack of trained staff–technical help by the International Labour Office should prove useful. This was recognized by the Conference Committee already in 1934 when it urged countries experiencing "difficulty in filling up the forms (of report) for the first time", to inform the Director so that he could "arrange for advice to be given as to the exact nature of the obligation and as to the lines on which it should be met".[3] The possibility was referred to again by the same Committee two decades later when technical assistance had begun to be provided on a much larger scale.[4]

Such assistance usually takes the form of fellowships to government officials for visits to Geneva.[5] In other cases it is I.L.O. officials who are sent "to help in particular the new members of the Organization to familiarize themselves with these obligations and thus to develop their relations with the International Labour Organization on a concrete and regular basis".[6] The special needs of the newly independent countries, in this

---

[1] Cf. p. 27 above.

[2] Article 26, paragraphs 1 and 4, of the Constitution.

[3] 18 R.P. 537.

[4] "Assistance might profitably be given to help governments at their request to comply with their reporting obligations" (37 R.P. 497).

[5] In 1956, the Conference Committee recorded a statement by one government member that, "thanks to a period of study spent in the International Labour Office by an official from the Ministry of Labour of his country, the department concerned had been able to make a thorough examination of the action to be taken on the decisions of the Conference. The representative of another State submitted to the Committee a formal request for the wider use of technical assistance designed to achieve a similar purpose" (39 R.P. 646).

[6] As also noted by the Conference Committee in 1957 (40 R.P. 655).

respect, were recognized by the Committee of Experts in 1962 and 1963 when it referred to "difficulties and delays" in reporting which may result from recent accession to independence and from the administrative changes involved. Here also the availability of I.L.O. assistance was repeatedly emphasized.[1] At the same time bilateral help continues to be given by the countries which formerly ruled the new States, such as France and the United Kingdom. Naturally, the administrative and staff problems involved take time to overcome, and much depends also on the degree of priority given to the fulfilment of I.L.O. obligations.

*Failure to Provide Legislative Information*

The mere making of a report is of course not sufficient. Since international supervision must rely primarily on the information supplied by the governments themselves, it cannot function effectively unless all the necessary data are made available. This need for information led the Committee of Experts to suggest a number of improvements in the questionnaires, including the special question asking for the supply of information in response to requests or observations made by the Committee of Experts or the Conference Committee.

The report forms ask for information on the legislation and the practice in a country. If the Committee of Experts requires fuller particulars regarding laws and regulations giving effect to a Convention, it usually asks for this in a request addressed directly to the government. Failure to reply to such a request naturally complicates the task of supervision.

The two Committees have become increasingly preoccupied with this danger, as the number of member States and of ratifications has expanded and as the two-yearly reporting cycle has come into operation. To "obviate or reduce the difficulties" caused by failure to reply to observations and requests, the Committee of Experts asked the International Labour Office in 1961 to verify upon receipt of the reports whether they contain the necessary replies. If they do not, the Office is under instruction "to request the government to supply the information without delay".[2]

This system of reminders has so far proved only partly successful. In 1962, 12 of the 30 governments which were asked to supply further information responded to the reminder.[3] When in 1963 half the governments again failed to react, the Committee published a list of the States concerned[4] and also included special references to such cases in its general observations regarding particular countries. The Conference Committee pointed out in the same connection that "persistent failure by a government to deal fully in its reports with comments made by the Committee of Experts or by the present Committee impedes the work of supervision no less than failure to submit the reports".[5]

---

[1] 1962 R.C.E. 9; 1963 R.C.E. 18-19. In 1964 an African regional training course on "national and international labour standards" was held in Nairobi (Kenya) for labour administration officers (49 D.R. (Part II) 20-21).

[2] 1961 R.C.E. 7-8.

[3] 1962 R.C.E. 7.

[4] 1963 R.C.E. 6.

[5] 47 R.P. 516.

*Other Sources of Information*

The letters of reminder sent by the International Labour Office since 1961, on behalf of the Committee of Experts, constitute a major innovation aimed at preventing the process of supervision from being stifled at a crucial point. Whatever else may be attempted, the Committees must rely primarily on the co-operation of the governments. Nonetheless other avenues are open. Information on a country's legislation can usually be found in official gazettes and similar publications where laws and regulations are printed. The Committee of Experts is not limited in its examination to the data received from governments and has maintained the right to "seek out... and examine a very wide variety of texts" [1] insofar as they have a bearing on the implementation of a particular Convention. In some cases the necessary information has been published by the Office itself but not mentioned by the government in its reports, perhaps by inadvertence.[2]

Studies published by other United Nations agencies also provide useful sources of documentation. Thus, while there may be delays in obtaining a full picture of the position in law, no decisive obstacle to I.L.O. supervision usually exists in this sphere.

*Failure to Report on Practical Application*

To assess the degree of legislative conformity with a ratified Convention and to supervise its day-to-day application are two quite different problems. Compliance in law constitutes the first essential step, of course,[3] and much of the supervisory comment concentrates therefore on questions of legislation. The census of observations in Chapter Two is primarily based on the success or failure of this type of comment. The two Committees have been aware, since the beginning, however, that their examination cannot stop there and that they must also concern themselves with the factual, as distinct from the legal, position.

This desire to gain a fuller picture of "the extent to which the legislative measures corresponding to the provisions of a given Convention are effectively applied"[4] was at the origin of most of the suggestions made to the

---

[1] 1962 R.C.E. 196. As explained by the Committee in the introduction to its comprehensive survey of the effect given to the I.L.O. standards on forced labour. When criticism was voiced in the Conference Committee that the Committee of Experts had referred "to legislation which... was not relevant or which had not been mentioned by governments in their reports", it was pointed out in reply that "all too often the reports... are not sufficiently detailed" and that "while the reports supplied by governments constitute the essential basis of the Experts' work, the latter would fail in their task if they did not examine all legislation at their disposal which may be relevant to the application of Conventions" (46 R.P. 685).

[2] In 1962 an observation referred to an act, and to a notification of the Central Council of Trade Unions, both issued in Czechoslovakia in 1959 and which had "come to the attention of the Committee by reason of their publication in the *Legislative Series* of the I.L.O., although they were not mentioned in the government's reports" (1962 R.C.E. 66). The Committee was consequently able to note that effect was given to the Holidays with Pay Convention, 1936 (No. 52) in regard to a point raised by it "for several years".

[3] This is true even of the so-called "machinery Conventions" which call for the establishment of employment offices, minimum wage fixing boards, labour inspectorates, etc., usually on the basis of legislative (and budgetary) authorizations.

[4] As stressed by the Committee of Experts at its first session in 1927 (1927 R.C.E. 415).

Governing Body to revise and expand the report forms, in order to gain a maximum of useful information. The Committee of Experts also realized from the beginning that this was no easy task[1] and that it was necessary to remind some governments again and again.[2] There even seemed to be a feeling, during the first decade of supervision, that "with the passage of time the centre of gravity in regard to the application of Conventions is gradually shifting from the question of the harmony between national legislation and the Conventions to the question of the practical application of the national legislation".[3] That this expectation was somewhat premature became clear during the post-war period, when the Committee of Experts complained that it was "faced... with almost a complete lack" of information on effective application.[4]

The information called for in the report forms consists mainly of statistical data designed to throw light on the scope of application of the labour laws (the number of workers covered by a Convention and therefore by the legislation giving effect to it) and on the extent of compliance (number and nature of violations, accidents, etc.). A special study made by the Committee of Experts in 1963 brought out that 30 per cent of the reports contained such statistics,[5] a considerable improvement over the position a decade earlier.

Clearly, compliance with labour legislation is difficult to imagine without the existence of administrative machinery to enforce it and the need for efficient labour inspectorates was included as one of the basic principles enumerated in an appendix to the original Constitution of the I.L.O.[6] In addition to the statistics on the results of inspection, the report forms also ask for information on its organization and working. A Recommendation on this subject had been adopted in 1923, but the Committee of Experts left little doubt during its early years that more was required. It originated the idea of regional meetings of labour inspectors[7] and welcomed the Governing Body's decision to frame a Convention on inspection;[8] because

---

[1] In 1931, for instance, the Committee of Experts noted that it was "very difficult to obtain authentic information" on "the actual enforcement" of legislation (1931 R.C.E. 453).

[2] In 1933 the Committee of Experts listed, under each Convention, the governments which had failed to include this information in their reports (1933 R.C.E. 488-497).

[3] As indicated in the Report of the Conference Committee in 1935 (19 R.P. 752). The following year the Dutch workers' representative made the perceptive suggestion that "there might be room here for a possible division of labour between the Committee of Experts and the Conference Committee. Let the Committee of Experts examine carefully all questions of legislative application and let our (Conference) Committee deal primarily with effective application" (20 R.P. 510).

[4] 1951 R.C.E. 3.

[5] 1963 R.C.E. 8-16.

[6] During the discussions in the Commission on International Labour Legislation in 1919, M. Fontaine of France "urged that it was useless to adopt a programme of international labour legislation if there was nobody charged with supervising its application. It would in fact be to the detriment of those States who applied such legislation in a loyal spirit" (I O.B. 209-210).

[7] In its Report in 1933 (1933 R.C.E. 486). Such a meeting was held in the Netherlands in 1935 with 12 European countries represented (1936 R.C.E. 4).

[8] 1937 R.C.E. 4. The Conference Committee also strongly supported the need for such a Convention (24 R.P. 490).

of the war this instrument could only be completed a decade later. The Labour Inspection Convention of 1947 contains detailed provisions on the organization, functioning, powers and responsibilities of inspection services for work places in industry and commerce.[1] One of its most important requirements, from the point of view of international supervision, is the publication of "an annual general report" by the "central inspection authority" (article 20 of the Convention), to deal with a number of specified subjects including the staff of the service, statistics of work places and workers liable to inspection, inspection visits, violations and penalties, etc. (article 21). This inspection report must be published within 12 months after the year it covers and must be transmitted to the International Labour Office within three months of its publication. Ratification and observance of this Convention thus help to promote the supply of much of the information on practical application which I.L.O. supervision requires.[2]

The existence of an efficient labour inspectorate therefore emerges as the key to the problem of securing data on day-to-day implementation [3] and the fact that about half the member States as well as over 20 non-metropolitan countries are bound by this instrument shows that the I.L.O. has the means to come to grips with this problem.[4]

The supervisory Committees are not totally lacking in other sources of information, either within the framework of, or outside, the governments' reports. For instance, decisions of courts dealing with labour cases can afford an interesting insight into concrete problems of implementation. As the forms of report ask for the supply of such decisions only if there are "questions of principle" involved, the number made available is usually small.[5] Official documents may throw light on practical application [6] and

---

[1] A companion Convention on labour inspectorates in non-metropolitan territories, also adopted in 1947, contains less exacting requirements but can be applied to agricultural undertakings as well.

[2] A number of individual Conventions also call for statistical information (e.g. Nos. 2, 13, 102) or for the organization of inspection (e.g. Nos. 30, 32, 33, 79, 94, 106) or both (e.g. Nos. 26, 62, 99, 101) but these provisions are much less detailed than those of the 1947 Convention.

[3] In 1957 the Committee of Experts pointed out that "its examination of the effect given to ratified Conventions is greatly facilitated when the reporting countries apply the Labour Inspection Convention, 1947" (1957 R.C.E. 159). Although the Committee insists that it is concerned with the application, not the ratification, of I.L.O. standards, it made a significant exception to this rule when it expressed the hope in 1953 that "the great majority of countries will, before long, find it possible so to organize their systems of labour inspection as to enable them to ratify this Convention" (1953 R.C.E. 4).

[4] The survey shows (cf. Table 1) that in 33 of the 69 cases examined, observations were made on the Labour Inspection Convention and that during the decade covered full action had been taken in five cases and partial action in 11 others.

[5] In 1963, 2.5 per cent of the reports contained court decisions. The interest of this type of information is illustrated by two observations which the Committee of Experts made to France. In one case the government had quoted judgments pronounced by the "Cour de Cassation" which gave a broad interpretation of the concept of injuries suffered by seamen (1957 R.C.E. 68). On another occasion the Committee referred to a judgment by the same Court which it had found in a case law publication (*Recueil Dalloz*) and which showed that a provision of the Labour Code, previously termed obsolete by the government, was in fact still applied in practice (1959 R.C.E. 37).

[6] In 1958 the Committee of Experts pointed out in an observation that, according to the Report of the Department of Labour of Northern Rhodesia, no information on the

the terms of collective agreements also constitute a potential source of information, for instance in relation to wage levels.[1] Newspaper reports have been mentioned in the Conference Committee to illustrate violations of labour laws.[2]

Finally, reference must be made to the possibility of pooling the knowledge and experience of several international organizations. Arrangements to this effect have been formalized in the case of one instrument, the Indigenous and Tribal Populations Convention, 1957 (No. 107), which deals not only with conditions of employment and other matters for which the I.L.O. is particularly responsible but also with problems such as land tenure, health and education.[3] Since 1961 the four other organizations with recognized competence in these matters have been associated by the Committee of Experts in assessing the degree of compliance with this instrument. They examine the governments' reports and can put their views to the Committee of Experts.[4]

What can be concluded from this necessarily rapid survey of the means available to obtain as accurate and complete a picture of day-to-day application as can reasonably be expected in an international system of supervision? It is fair to say that full utilization of the sources tapped by the Governing Body in expanding the scope of the information called for in the report forms would go a long way toward bridging the gap between national and international supervision. But the two Committees already find it difficult to cope with all the questions of legislative conformity. Moreover, even if the fullest possible data were available from all governments, this would still leave doubts as to the reliability of the data supplied. Nor is the existence of a well-organized labour inspectorate sufficient to guarantee full enforcement, unless the workers (and, in certain cases, the employers) are able and willing to appeal to this inspectorate, to the courts and even to public opinion itself.

---

number of persons actually recruited was available, whereas the government had indicated that labour recruiters must provide such data to the authorities (1958 R.C.E. 78).

[1] In an observation to Italy regarding the Equal Remuneration Convention, the Committee of Experts indicated that it has "been able to refer to the texts of collective agreements in the tobacco industry" and in three food industries, which showed substantial wage differentials between men and women workers (1959 R.C.E. 56-57).

[2] In 1934 the Report of the Conference Committee recorded a statement by one of its members that, according to Rumanian press reports, hours considerably in excess of those permitted by the 48-hour week Convention were being worked in Bucharest, and "that it was impossible for the inspectors to secure the strict application of the law". The government representative in the Committee denied the accuracy of the reports (18 R.P. 540).

[3] The Convention notes in its preamble that it has been framed with the co-operation of the United Nations, the Food and Agriculture Organization of the United Nations, the United Nations Educational, Scientific and Cultural Organization and the World Health Organization and that "it is proposed to seek their continuing co-operation in promoting and securing the application of these standards."

[4] When it inaugurated this joint examination the Committee referred to the other Organizations, emphasizing that it "was indeed glad to have their views regarding those aspects of the governments' reports of interest to them, and to welcome to one of its sittings representatives of three of these Organizations" (1961 R.C.E. 104).

Viewed from this angle, the supervision of practical application depends on the quality rather than the quantity of the data available. An element of doubt remains, in other words, which even the strictest compliance with all the details of the reporting obligation might not remove. The Conference Committee's Report in 1947 called this a "feeling of uneasiness" caused by the fact that the "mechanism of supervision... is based solely on written documents and on a succession of acts of confidence which do not always bring out the facts in their full reality".[1] It is no coincidence that at the same session there was a proposal aimed at carrying supervision a step beyond the limits of written documentation.

### International Labour Inspection and Its Alternatives

The idea of giving international inspectors an opportunity to examine working conditions on the spot goes of course back much further than 1947 and was broached long before the I.L.O. was established.[2] Its attraction lies in its apparent reasonableness and simplicity: once the principle of international supervision has been accepted and has begun to be implemented, why should it not be carried to its logical conclusion by securing information on application directly in the countries themselves? Why should it not be possible to establish a direct link between those bound by an international labour Convention and those assessing the degree of compliance?

The realities of international life soon reduced this idea to its proper perspective. Although it was brought up from time to time in various forms, both during the early days of the I.L.O.[3] and during the "remodelling and re-equipping" phase (1944-1946),[4] there was no serious question of translating the idea into action.

---

[1] 30 R.P. 545.

[2] In 1889 the Socialist International included in a resolution asking for "international labour legislation" a request that "there shall be appointed national and international inspectors chosen by the workers and paid by the State" and that these inspectors "shall have authority to enter at all times every shop, mill, factory, yard, etc., to ascertain violations, make official reports and bring offenders to justice" (U.S. Department of Labor, Bulletin No. 268 of the United States Bureau of Labor Statistics, *Historical Survey of International Action Affecting Labor* (August 1920), p. 214).

[3] Albert Thomas' proposals in 1920 for the structure of the International Labour Office included a "Diplomatic Division" which was *inter alia* to "organize an Inspection Branch" (2 G.B. 27). The Governing Body did not object to this suggestion (3 G.B. 16) which however was never carried out.

[4] The possibility of instituting an "international labour inspectorate" was dealt with in some detail in the Report on "Future Policy, Programme and Status" placed before the Conference in 1944 (26 Report I, 102-104) and in the Report of the Conference Delegation on Constitutional Questions, placed before the Conference in 1946 (29 Report II(1), 57-60). Reference was also made to this possibility in the Report of the Application Committee set up at the 1945 Session of the Conference (27 R.P. 441) and support for the suggestion was voiced by the government delegates of Italy and Poland (27 R.P. 202, 287) and by an Indian workers' representative (27 R.P. 204); the Italian delegate indicated that his government "would be glad if, as soon as this corps of inspectors is established, one of its members would come to our country in order to examine on the spot the conditions under which our production is carried on, and the conditions of work and life of our working classes".

The obstacles to be overcome were readily apparent in 1947 when the less far-reaching proposal alluded to above was put forward in the Conference Committee by its reporter, Professor Georges Scelle. Speaking in his capacity as French government member, he suggested that "in order to strengthen the supervision of the application of Conventions, and to facilitate the work of the Committee of Experts", the Office should "have at its disposal in the various States or groups of States representatives who could keep in permanent touch with the national labour inspectorates and could keep the relevant section of the International Labour Office periodically informed of their observations on the application of Conventions".[1] While Professor Scelle considered such an innovation merely "a first timid but necessary step", the vast majority of the Committee thought otherwise.[2] The main objections to the proposal, as summed up in the Committee's Report, were as follows: it was premature and the new possibilities afforded by the communication of copies of the governments' reports to the representative workers' and employers' organizations should first be given a full trial; it contained "the nucleus of a system of international inspection" and might consequently encroach on State sovereignty as well as "retard the progress of international labour legislation"; finally, the information secured through Office representatives would lack "any formal official value". Among these arguments the second was the most weighty one, although it had apparently not been voiced when a somewhat similar proposal was made by the Committee of Experts, and endorsed by the Conference Committee, in 1939.[3] International inspection, on a routine basis, is thus clearly not within the realm of possibility in the I.L.O. It is worth recalling, however, that visits on the spot by Commissions of Inquiry set up under article 26 of the Constitution are by no means inconceivable and that a precedent to this effect has been established.[4] The machinery set up by

---

[1] 30 R.P. 545.

[2] The vote was 8 in favour and 29 against, with 4 abstentions. All the affirmative votes came from the workers' side and even in this group the Indian, Netherlands and United Kingdom members went on record as opposing the proposal (doc. XXX/C.App.C./ P.V.10 (roneoed), p. 2). Commenting on the Committee's reaction, Professor Scelle conceded that "while he fully expected certain objections to his proposal, he was somewhat surprised to see them coming from the employers' and workers' side" (doc. XXX/ C.App.C./P.V.7 (roneoed), p. 4). He added, just before the vote, that "he was primarily interested in ascertaining the attitude at this Conference in regard to the question of national sovereignty. Any progress in international organization necessarily involved a limitation of sovereignty" (doc. XXX/C.App.C./P.V.10 (roneoed), p. 1.)
The U.S.S.R. was not a member of the I.L.O. in 1947, but it is clear from an article published a decade later that it would have joined the other governments in opposing the Scelle proposal: "International supervision of the application of Conventions... can be improved, but the necessary condition for this must be respect for sovereignty", (S.A. Ivanov, "Application of International Labour Conventions, *Soviet Yearbook of International Law, 1958*, pp. 437-451).

[3] "The Committee of Experts would welcome steps which might be taken for establishing contact between the inspection services of the members of the Organization and between each of them and the technical staff of the International Labour Office" (1939 R.C.E. 5). The Conference Committee placed on record "its entire approval" of this suggestion (25 R.P. 415).

[4] The Commission appointed in 1961 to examine Ghana's complaint against Portugal, spent 13 days in Angola and Mozambique, visiting portions of the interior of each territory (*Commission of Inquiry Report (Ghana-Portugal) op. cit.*, pp. 22-30). The Commis-

the Organization to deal with alleged violations of the right of association has also on several occasions involved the despatch of fact-finding missions to the countries concerned.[1]

In addition to these rather exceptional cases, the objective of the 1947 proposal is now being achieved to an increasing extent through the I.L.O.'s external activities and, occasionally, in other ways. The incidental role of technical assistance in obtaining "far more reliable data than have been available hitherto regarding the practical application of Conventions" was foreshadowed by the Conference Delegation on Constitutional Questions in 1946 when it rejected international inspection as "neither politically possible nor practically feasible under present conditions".[2] Advisory services had been provided to governments on a limited scale before the war,[3] but the spectacular expansion of technical assistance has greatly increased the body of first-hand knowledge of conditions in the member countries.[4] The Reports on the results of advisory missions and related

---

sion stressed the fact that "one of the main objects of the... visits on the spot was to speak directly to African workers. The greater part of the Commission's activities was devoted to this end."

The Commission appointed in 1962 to examine Portugal's complaint against Liberia decided that a visit would "not be appropriate at the present time", adding, however, that "(a)ny failure to give effect to the recommendations of the Commission would raise the question of the desirability of further inquiry, including inquiry on the spot, but this would be a matter for consideration by the Governing Body in the unhappy, and it is hoped improbable, event of any such contingency arising" (*Commission of Inquiry Report (Portugal-Liberia)*, *op. cit.*, pp. 169-170).

[1] Fuller reference to this machinery is made on pp. 176-177 below. Two countries, one in North Africa, the other in Central America, suggested that allegations made against them be investigated on the spot. As reported by the Governing Body Committee on Freedom of Association which examines such complaints in the first instance, Lord Forster of Harraby, a former President of the Industrial Court of the United Kingdom and a member of the I.L.O. Fact-Finding and Conciliation Commission on Freedom of Association, paid a short visit to Libya in 1962 (XLV O.B. No. 2, Supplement I, pp. 46-60). Also in 1962, Professor H. S. Kirkaldy of Cambridge, who served for many years as reporter of the I.L.O. Committee of Experts, spent two weeks in Costa Rica (XLVI O.B. No. 1, Supplement pp. 15-30). In both cases the Governing Body Committee drew heavily on the findings of these missions. More recently, the Fact-Finding and Conciliation Commission itself visited Japan, as indicated on p. 145 above.

[2] 29 Report II(1), 58. The Delegation therefore proceeded to suggest the insertion in the revised Constitution of the reference to direct assistance (article 10, paragraph 2(b)), quoted on p. 130 above.

[3] Cf. *Technical Assistance* (Report submitted to the 37th Session of the International Labour Conference (1954)), pp. 4-5.

[4] In addition the I.L.O. has also extended its network of Branch Offices (to 12 countries) and National Correspondents (to over 30 countries). Attention was drawn to the potential value of this source of information during the discussion of Professor Scelle's proposal. The Mexican government member explained that "to the best of his knowledge it was the function of the Office's national correspondents to make monthly reports which included a section on the application of ratified Conventions. These reports were not only based on official information but also on additional sources" (doc. XXX/C.App.C./P.V.6 (roneoed), p. 2). The Brazilian government member pointed out that this process could be carried a step further: "It was... known that Office correspondents had in the past been able to intervene indirectly and discreetly with national governments and had thus succeeded in obtaining improvement in the conformity of national legislation and in the methods of application" (doc. XXX/C.App.C./P.V.8, p. 3).

activities contain not only detailed findings but also a wealth of concrete information on which the Office's recommendations are based.[1] Information of this kind can therefore be as useful and revealing as the data contained in national inspection reports and in the governments' reports to the I.L.O. on the effect given to ratified Conventions.

The second method whereby the I.L.O. can obtain more direct knowledge is through survey missions carried out, at the request of governments, by members of the Office staff, usually organized as a team. Such missions provide an opportunity to undertake a comprehensive examination of national conditions and problems on the spot. The number of surveys of this kind has been limited, but the information made available has been of great value.[2]

While international labour inspection appears thus at present not to offer concrete prospects as a source of direct information on the practical application of Conventions, definite progress has recently been made in obtaining data of this kind by other means: the same year when a rather modest first step toward on-the-spot verification failed to secure any significant support in the International Labour Conference, the Conference adopted a comprehensive instrument on national labour inspection, including a requirement that the results of inspection be published and sent to the I.L.O. Shortly afterwards technical assistance activities began to expand as part of the concerted effort undertaken in this field by the whole United Nations family. The findings and results which emerged have become available to the supervisory bodies of the I.L.O.[3] It cannot be said therefore that the absence of information on practical application constitutes a major obstacle to supervision. It may be assumed, in fact, that in the very cases

---

[1] Two examples from the Middle Eastern region illustrate this point. A Report on employment service organization in Iraq indicated that "although in theory certain... labour offices in the (provinces) are supposed to carry out employment activity, no instructions existed for the operation of these offices, nor was there any active control from headquarters" (*Report to the Government of Iraq on the Reorganization and Development of the National Employment Service*, I.L.O., Geneva, 1962, doc. ILO/TAP/Iraq/R.7 (roneoed), p. 4). Iraq is bound by the Employment Service Convention.

A Report on labour inspection training in four States stressed that two of these, Iraq and Syria, have ratified the Labour Inspection Convention and that certain measures needed to be taken to give fuller effect to the instrument in these countries (*Report on an I.L.O. Contribution to Training Programmes for Labour Administration Officers in Iraq, Jordan, Libya and Syria; Training for Labour Inspection*, I.L.O., Geneva, 1963, doc. OIT/TAP/NME/R.4 (roneoed), pp. 4, 16, 22-23, 26).

[2] Among the studies published during the post-war period figure *Labour Problems in Greece* (1949), *Freedom of Association and Conditions of Work in Venezuela* (1950), *Conditions in Ships Flying the Panama Flag* (1950), *Labour Conditions in the Oil Industry in Iran* (1950) and *Labour Problems in Turkey* (1950).

In more recent years a series of factual surveys relating to freedom of association was carried out between 1959 and 1961. Reports on the "Trade Union Situation" in the United States (1960), the U.S.S.R. (1960), the United Kingdom (1961), Sweden (1961), Malaya (1962) and Burma (1962) were issued as a result by the Office on the dates indicated.

[3] In 1955, for instance, the Committee of Experts referred to the "Report of the I.L.O. Labour Survey Mission on Labour Problems in Pakistan" (this Report was published by the government of Pakistan, as document LB-33, in 1954) as an indication that labour contractors and other recruiting agents, falling within the scope of the Fee-Charging Employment Agencies Convention (Revised), 1949 (No. 96), existed in the country (1955 R.C.E. 75).

where compliance has proved to be difficult, technical assistance has been envisaged as a possible means of facilitating application,[1] so that fuller data on the actual circumstances of a case should be forthcoming in due course.

It seems possible to conclude then that the problem of gaining a complete and accurate picture of the state of national law and practice in a ratifying country, though never fully solved, has not impeded I.L.O. supervision to any serious extent. Sooner or later a sufficient amount of information becomes available to enable the Committees to make a reliable evaluation of the position and to ask, where necessary, for additional measures of implementation. It is at this stage, rather, that the major problems of international supervision are usually encountered.

## II. The Problem of Promoting Action

Once the supervisory bodies have established to their own satisfaction that a ratified Convention is not fully complied with, their efforts must concentrate on promoting governmental action to eliminate the divergencies which have been noted. A government's attitude may range all the way from simple indifference to an actively negative stance and it is not always easy to pinpoint the motives which characterize most accurately the facts of a given case.

### Governmental Attitudes

Indifference to supervisory criticism may often be due to the kind of administrative difficulties already discussed. As noted, inadequate co-ordination between various departments dealing with I.L.O. affairs can seriously delay application. In some countries, the Foreign Affairs Ministries insist on maintaining exclusive control over all contacts,[2] so that supervision often becomes impossible. Ignorance of the terms of ratified Conventions, of the need for their implementation and of the supervisory procedures in general, is bound to stifle any initiative at home or any constructive participation in the work of the Conference Committee.

This type of barrier is encountered less often than in former years, but it may well account for some of the most intractable cases of non-compliance where the comments of the two Committees have to be repeated from year to year. Although improved administrative machinery and practices

---

[1] Cf. pp. 129-131 above.

[2] A candid account of Ecuador's relations with the I.L.O. describes in detail the controversy between the Ministry of External Relations and the Ministry of Social Welfare and Labour over the former's monopoly on all communications with Geneva. The matter had to be settled by the President who decided in 1960 (26 years after Ecuador joined the I.L.O.) that the Ministry of Social Welfare and Labour could henceforth correspond directly with the International Labour Office on "technical, routine questions". The account emphasizes that the practice previously followed was the cause of "considerable delays and incompetence in acknowledging and transmitting the technical correspondence of the I.L.O., thus preventing its timely examination and the intelligent participation of delegates in the meetings". Cf. Fernando Pavón Egas, "El Ecuador en la Organización Internacional del Trabajo", *Revista del Instituto de Derecho del Trabajo y Investigaciones Sociales* (Quito, Ecuador), Vol. II, No. 3 (January-June 1962), pp. 45-73.

offer the best hope for breaking down this barrier, sudden changes can hardly be expected and any ground gained in a given case may be lost again with a change of personnel or of administration. Patience and persistence are essential.[1]

Matters become more complicated if the passive attitude of a government is due not so much to a lack of familiarity with I.L.O. standards as to a deliberate policy of ignoring supervisory comment. This is not readily apparent, as a rule, and the general impression may well differ little from that given in the circumstances discussed above. Any government would be reluctant to acknowledge that it had decided to disregard its international obligations, unless it was prepared to face the possible consequences. Instead it will prefer to play for time and to give somewhat vague promises of future action. In the last analysis there will be less hope for improvement here than in cases of administrative inertia, and a patient approach will not have much chance of success.

### The Task of Persuasion

The problem in such cases is to stimulate action without unduly provoking the susceptibilities or sentivities of those to whom the Committee's comments are addressed. The practical dimensions of the problem differ of course depending on whether these comments are made in writing, i.e. by the Experts, or orally, i.e. in the Conference Committee. In the former case it is a matter of presentation and drafting so that the facts of a given case are clearly stated and provide a logical basis for the Committee's call for action. It is in this final summing up–in the peroration so to speak–that the Experts must attempt to strike the right note. To find fault is never a pleasant task,[2] which is hardly rendered any easier when it falls on an international body examining the performance of obligations by governments. In such circumstances the rather abstract notion of sovereignty becomes very concrete indeed.[3]

The Committee of Experts is of course well aware that its sole aim can be to persuade. This process usually involves two stages. It is necessary, in the first place, to demonstrate that the legal and factual position is not in conformity with the terms of a Convention. This may require time,

---

[1] As noted in footnote 2, p. 139, and footnote 4, p. 161 above, the Office may be able on occasion to discuss informally with governments the need and the methods for complying more fully with ratified Conventions.

[2] The Committee squarely recognized in 1952 that its "essential function" was "that of criticism", adding that "it would not desire concentration on criticism to obscure the real merits of many of the reports received" (1952 R.C.E. 4).

[3] "The great difficulty is not to reject the general and abstract notion of sovereignty", said a French jurist in 1950, "it is to gain acceptance for the practical consequences of this rejection every time that feelings or interests will be injured in the process. There are many people in public opinion who take pride in their internationalism and who acclaim international solidarity when it is presented to them as a general principle, but who will get their backs up when the principle has to be put into practice, every time this involves a material or moral sacrifice for them" (Emile Giraud, "Le Rejet de l'Idée de Souveraineté. L'Aspect Juridique et l'Aspect Politique de la Question" in Etudes en l'Honneur de Georges Scelle (Paris: Librairie Générale de Droit et de Jurisprudence, 1950), pp. 258-259).

either because the facts themselves are not clearly established or because the government disagrees with the Committee's conclusions. Clarity of presentation is an essential element, so that the findings may almost speak for themselves. Unless the position and the need for additional measures are made very explicit to the government concerned, as well as to the Conference Committee, there is little hope of securing action.[1]

The next, and most crucial, aim is to build up a desire for action without going beyond the limits set by the Committee of Experts' competence and by its objectives. This requires a sense of diplomacy in finding the right approach and in choosing the right tone.[2] It also involves persistence, a readiness to repeat and repeat again until compliance has been achieved.[3] Because governments are required to report periodically, this opportunity for reiteration, for a gradually rising degree of urgency is fully exploited by the Committee. The transition from annual to two-yearly reporting has not introduced any material change in this pattern and may even have increased its practical chances of success because governments have a longer period of time to decide on the necessary measures. The Committee now has the possibility, moreover, to make its comments somewhat more emphatic by asking for the next report immediately, rather than two years hence, whenever its previous attempts at persuasion have proved ineffective.

Over the years, the Committee of Experts has thus developed a technique which not merely requires skilful drafting but can almost be called psychological. Through its collective judgment and experience it has learned to gauge a given situation, in order to use just the right degree of emphasis. The fact that the procedure of supervision has been operating for over 30 years and that some of the Committee members have been engaged in this type of activity for two decades, greatly facilitates the choice of method and adds to the uniformity of approach.

As a result, the technical examination of the Experts may, by itself, have the desired effect. The record shows that progress has sometimes been secured in recent years solely through the requests the Experts have addressed directly to governments,[4] so that the intervention of the Conference was not needed. This is doubly fortunate since the Conference Committee's

---

[1] This need for fully motivated findings was stressed in Kaasik's pioneering study of international supervision: "A finding made by a supervisory organ must be convincing in itself. It does not have the material strength of the States to back it up; it must create the conviction that a mistake has been made which needs to be rectified. To create this conviction, the finding must be based on the convincing strength of legal arguments, it must be motivated like a judicial decision" (*Le Contrôle en Droit International, op. cit.*, p. 385).

[2] "The Committee of Experts is obliged to take certain precautions of a diplomatic order, not because it is diplomatic itself but because it is obliged in relation to certain countries to use tact if it wants to obtain something; it must act with a certain adroitness" (Georges Scelle, *Cours de Droit International Public* (1947-1948) (Paris, roneoed), p. 383).

[3] Professor Haas finds that "(t)he Committee's persistence in demanding full implementation of ratified Conventions is extraordinary" (*Beyond the Nation-State, op. cit.*, p. 257).

[4] The references listed in Appendix II contain a number of examples of action taken following direct requests.

time hardly suffices to deal with all the cases of non-application which come before it.

The problems encountered by the Conference Committee differ considerably from those faced by the Experts. This is due not only to its political, rather than technical, character but to the direct participation of the governments, which are brought face to face with tripartite supervision. In this confrontation, the advantages enjoyed by the Committee of Experts –time for reflection, anonymity, a unified approach–do not exist. It is far easier to deliberate and to reach conclusions in private than to engage in delicate discussions in a public forum which is at the same time intergovernmental and interoccupational.

The Conference Committee's methods and procedures have been reviewed in Chapter One; attention can now be focused on the specific problem of persuading governments to act. The Committee likes to refer to its task in terms of assisting and encouraging member States to give effect to their obligations. Yet it was probably inevitable that even a promotional, educational effort of this kind should hurt the susceptibilities of certain delegates, especially during the earlier years. The attempt at oral persuasion involves two stages: a clarification of the facts of a given case and an appeal to the government to eliminate shortcomings. The first stage presupposes a readiness on the part of governments to co-operate with the Conference Committee by supplying additional information and explaining obstacles to full compliance.

It is this participation of a government in the discussion that usually represents the most delicate phase of the proceedings, because of the "difficulties of a psychological nature" [1] which may arise. A government delegate may find it disconcerting to have to answer critical comments leveled at his country and his response may simply be to plead good faith.[2] If this plea is not accepted and if a prolonged technical discussion takes place, the government spokesman inevitably finds himself in a defensive posture. His response will vary, depending on his degree of familiarity with the points at issue, depending perhaps also on his temperament.[3] As for the Committee, it usually has little choice but to carry the discussion of each case through to a conclusion, although it does not particularly relish an assignment of this kind. More than once its reporters have emphasized the point: "The task of the Committee... is not always a pleasant one... But... it has a very clear duty–that is, to review the situation

---

[1] This phrase was used by a Belgian government representative in 1951 (34 R.P. 456).

[2] In 1947 the Colombian government member of the Application Committee asked the workers' vice-chairman "to accept the words of the delegate of Colombia as sufficient evidence and an expression of good faith" (doc. XXX/C.App.C./P.V.3 (roneoed), p. 5).

[3] Two examples, drawn from the discussion in the plenary in 1960, are typical in this respect. A Liberian government delegate explained: "With my short experience in the Committee I have observed that member States are defendants in the Committee" (44 R.P. 445). A government adviser from the United Arab Republic also referred to the "cross-examination" by the workers' and employers' vice-chairmen but added: "Our discussions, which lasted for an hour and a half, are a true example of the goodwill and objectivity of all parties concerned. Such a peaceful exchange of views, without resentment or retaliation, is most needed in such a delicate Committee in order to facilitate this work" (44 R.P. 432).

from year to year and to remind you of what must be done if we wish the work of the Conference not to be useless".[1]

The basic problem thus facing the Conference Committee when it discusses the Experts' observations with government representatives, is to sense almost intuitively just how far it should go in its efforts at persuasion. This sort of choice is delicate even in discussions or negotiations between individuals. Finding the proper approach and discerning the limits to which it can usefully be carried are tasks which the tripartite and public setting of the debate render more complex yet. In such a setting, it is essential to draw the line between persuasion and reprobation, and to resort to the latter only when all else fails.

Persuasion is central to the whole concept of international supervision. In the case of the I.L.O. it has been laid down as a basic tenet and recognized as the only realistic method of promoting governmental action, especially when coupled with a certain reliance on publicity. This idea was spelled out clearly when the Organization was established.[2] It was given further recognition and substance when the two supervisory Committees were set up a few years later.[3]

What, then, contributes to these appeals being heard and answered? What, in other words, causes national authorities to be responsive to international supervision? While it is possible to list the main elements which help to determine success or failure,[4] it is difficult to define with precision which element has played the decisive role in a given instance.

Such evidence as is available points to certain general conclusions regarding the persuasiveness of I.L.O. supervision. There can be little doubt, first of all, that the public character of the proceedings provides an important stimulus.[5] As just noted, this reliance on discussion is by no

---

[1] Professor Roberto Ago of Italy, speaking in the plenary in 1949 (32 R.P. 356-357). In 1955 another reporter spoke in a similar vein: "It is often a thankless task, and (it has brought us) in the past some accusations more violent than well thought-out" (38 R.P. 430).

[2] In presenting the Report of the Commission on International Labour Legislation to the Paris Peace Conference, the British member, Mr. Barnes, explained that the scheme was designed "to rely mainly upon the goodwill of States to accept advice and guidance which might be given to them... It is not coercion so much that is wanted in most things; it is more, I think, knowledge and goodwill... The effective idea in our scheme (is) the creation and mobilization of healthy public opinion" (I O.B. 288-289).

[3] In his speech supporting this innovation, the Australian government delegate, Sir Joseph Cook, likened the I.L.O. to "an international conciliation court in which both sides could compose their differences and reach conclusions fair to all. It was never intended that it should be a court to wield a big stick and go about with a blackthorn to flagellate nations which were recalcitrant. It was intended to be an Organization where reason and persuasion and public opinion should be enthroned" (8 R.P. 252).

[4] C. Wilfred Jenks writes that "responsiveness... to international criticism is of course a function of general political conditions. It depends upon the value attached to the pledged word and the keenness of the sense of international responsibility and interdependence in the country concerned, upon the prestige enjoyed there by the international body which has formulated the criticism, and upon the extent to which, under the conditions which prevail there, international criticism tends to reinforce or to silence national criticism of official policy "(*The International Protection of Trade Union Freedom, op. cit.*, p. 493).

[5] Professor Scelle pointed out that "the effectiveness (of I.L.O. supervision) resides less in the threat of sanctions than in the publicity which can be given to infractions". (*L'Organisation Internationale du Travail et le B.I.T., op cit.*, p. 193).

means incidental. It has been a mainstay of international organization since its very infancy.[1] The persuasive effect of publicity depends, of course, to a great extent on the existence of an informed public opinion at home and this condition is far from being fulfilled in many cases. Censorship, illiteracy or mere lack of interest often act as inhibiting factors.[2] On the other hand, even a government that has no internal comment to fear may be all the more eager to avoid international criticism. Countries particularly concerned to protect and promote their status as sovereign nations–because they desire to consolidate their recently achieved independence, their political system or simply their world image as law-abiding States–are often most sensitive to critical remarks from an international body. The results of observations, as tabulated in Appendix III, tend to confirm the existence of this type of motivation. The value of public discussion has moreover been expressly recognized both by students of international supervision as such [3] and by observers with personal experience of the I.L.O.'s procedures in this sphere.[4]

Another element which facilitates the task of persuasion is the continuous and repetitive character of the procedure. The fact that its previous explanations or measures have not satisfied the two Committees may help, in the end, to convince a government that full compliance alone will put an end to international criticism.[5] Institutionalized discussion and follow-up have thus become major factors in advancing the more technical types

---

[1] In a study of the Rhine Navigation Commission and of other international commissions which functioned in the second half of the 19th century, Professor Hans Wehberg pointed out that "the moral and political significance of a discussion within the framework of an international commission can exercise an important indirect influence on the readiness of States to conform to their treaty obligations. The effect is particularly clear when supervision is concerned with purely technical questions which are scarcely influenced by power politics" ("Entwicklungsstufen der Internationalen Organisation" (Stages of Development of International Organization), *Die Friedenswarte*, Vol. 52 (1954), No. 3, p. 199).

[2] For the special case of the developing countries, cf. Benjamin Akzin, *New States and International Organizations* (Paris: International Political Science Association, 1955), pp. 158-159.

[3] "Sociological sanctions, such as the reaction of the world press or of a politically interested public to the report of an international organ which is merely entrusted with fact-finding tasks, will exercise an influence on the conduct of the State concerned, which could not have been achieved through legal means due to the individualistic character of international law" (Hugo J. Hahn, "Internationale Kontrollen", *op. cit.*, p. 90).

[4] During a discussion in the Belgian Senate, in 1953, Mr. L.-E. Troclet explained to a questioner that "the sanction in the international field is still, in the present circumstances, a moral sanction to which the States are very sensitive. I can assure you of this since I had the honour to preside, last year, over the International Labour Conference Committee entrusted with the supervision of the application of Conventions; delegates from all the States came before this Committee to explain the divergencies which had been observed" (Belgian Senate, *Parliamentary Record*, Ordinary Session 1952-1953, p. 1255).

[5] "I.L.O. hopes that the mere act of investigation and possible verbal condemnation will prove sufficient to bring about a change... In the short run, the moral impact of recommendations is minimal. Still the essence of international organization is its permanence and continuity. Decisions are more in accordance with procedures which do not vary from year to year but follow an institutionalized pattern representing a minimum consensus of the member States" (Ernst B. Haas and Allan S. Whiting, *Dynamics of International Relations* (New York: McGraw-Hill, 1956), pp. 439-440).

of international co-operation, especially in the economic field.[1]  Closely related to this almost mechanical element is the effect which government spokesmen regularly attending I.L.O. Conference sessions may sometimes achieve on decision-making at home.  Their status as specialists in the field of international labour affairs, their success in pleading the cause of their country in the Application Committee, give them a certain prestige which may, in turn, help them to persuade the executive and legislative authorities to respond to international prompting.  Thus civil servants can wield real influence at home, especially if they represent, and are closely identified with, the ruling groups whose main desire is internal and external stability.[2]  Concrete evidence is hard to come by, but the results seem to confirm this hypothesis and semi-official pronouncements also point occasionally in the same direction.[3]

Discussion in the Conference Committee becomes impossible, of course, if a government does not participate in its work.  While refusals to respond to the Committee's invitation are very exceptional, absence from the Conference can create real difficulties, especially if it repeats itself several years in succession.[4]  The problem is by no means negligible and the Application Committee points out regularly in its Reports that it was "unfortunately unable to discuss the observations of the Committee of Experts regarding... States which were not represented at... the Conference.[5]  In some cases the fact that a country's delegation is incomplete, i.e. contains only government representatives, may also be detrimental to full discussion.

It is necessary, at this stage, to consider what other means are available to the Conference Committee, when repeated efforts at persuasion have proved ineffective.  A mere reiteration of arguments and appeals tends in the long run to weaken the impact of the annual discussions of the more serious cases, nor is it always possible for those outside the Conference Committee to distinguish between routine observations and those dealing with major violations.  For both these reasons the Committee came to the conclusion that action might be promoted if its Report were to "bring into sharper relief" [6] cases where the regular methods of persuasion had been employed to no avail.

---

[1] "If (an organization) becomes repeatedly utilized for reaching inter-governmental agreements in a given field, it may acquire a certain institutional weight and momentum. Certain substitutes for real political sanctions can then gradually be built up" (Gunnar Myrdal, *Realities and Illusions in Regard to Inter-Governmental Organizations, op. cit.*, p. 8),

[2] "Implementation (of international law) depends on the aims and attitudes of the elites concerned...  The only sanction remains the desire of all elites for some order, stability and predictability of conduct" (Haas and Whiting, *op. cit.*, p. 394).

[3] "The competent Polish authorities, in close collaboration with the trade union movement, see to it that internal legislation and practice in the sphere of social protection comply strictly with the requirements of I.L.O. Conventions and examine with great attention any possible remarks made on this subject by the relevant organs of the International Labour Organization" (Jan Rosner, "Si vis pacem, cole justitiam", *Polish Trade Union Review*, 1957, No. 4, pp. 4-5).

[4] Nicaragua, for instance, had no representation at the Conference in 1960, 1961 and 1962.

[5] In 1962, when Bolivia, Costa Rica, Ecuador, Guinea, Haiti, Iceland, Nicaragua and Somalia fell into this category (46 R.P. 681).

[6] In the words of the Committee's reporter in 1957 (40 R.P. 525).

## Spotlighting Special Cases

It was probably inevitable that in a system principally based on publicity an attempt should be made to exploit this means of pressure to the full in order to induce governments to discharge their obligations. During a decade of operation after World War II a series of cases had accumulated on which little or no progress had been achieved so that the non-governmental members of the Committee in particular became convinced of the need for a type of initiative which, while falling short of the constitutional representation or complaint procedures, would nonetheless act as an indication to the governments involved, and to the Conference, that the Committee was seriously concerned. It was in these circumstances that the "special list" was instituted in 1957. As related in Chapter One, this device has since become a regular feature of the Conference Committee's Report and criteria and procedures have been laid down in selecting cases for inclusion in the list. What are the basic purposes of this innovation and to what extent have they been achieved?

The aim of the special list is simple: when other efforts at discussion and persuasion have had no apparent effect, the Committee decides to spotlight the situation in the hope of generating a sense of uneasiness and of urgency on the part of governments.[1] All indications point to the conclusion that the listing of serious cases has, at the least, led some governments to attempt to justify themselves. Both in the Committee and in the plenary their representatives have explained the circumstances involved and given assurances that steps towards fuller compliance will be taken. Even in those instances where the principle of drawing up a list came under fire,[2] the interest stirred during the process was preferable to the rather perfunctory manner in which certain cases had been disposed of in previous years.

To gauge the impact of this new method of promoting action, it is necessary to trace the results in the cases which have appeared on the list on one or more occasions since 1957. Those who wished to demonstrate the usefulness of the list sometimes emphasized that countries mentioned at the preceding Conference session no longer figured on it.[3] Because of the

---

[1] The employers' vice-chairman put it bluntly, in 1960, when he explained to the Conference that "the idea of this list is to induce some shame on the part of the governments which show a persistent lack of interest in their obligations" (44 R.P. 430). There is a similarity between this formulation and "the mobilization of shame", a phrase coined many years earlier by Sir Alfred Zimmern (*The League of Nations and the Rule of Law 1918-1935* (London: Macmillan, 1936), p. 460).

[2] In 1958 an Italian government delegate questioned "the principle, the criterion behind a list of this kind". He asked the plenary sitting to "read this list and think for a moment about the impression on an outside reader without access to the facts available to the Committee" (42 R.P. 489-490).

[3] In 1958 the reporter noted in the plenary that "this practice has proved effective inasmuch as seven countries have disappeared from the list, since definite progress has been made during the past year towards eliminating the discrepancies in question" (42 R.P. 472). In 1963 the employers' vice-chairman pointed out that "this year more countries than usual dropped out of the list... We in the Committee think that this way of enumerating cases has had some positive effect" (47 R.P. 435). And in 1965 the workers' members considered the recent progress towards application of Convention No. 11 in Chile an indication that "the placing of a country on the special list, combined with assistance from the I.L.O. technical services, could help in solving problems" (49 P.R. No. 33, p. XVI).

importance of the issues involved, several of the case histories reviewed in Chapters Four and Five were chosen among those which the Conference Committee had singled out, so that it is unnecessary to review these cases in detail. Instead, it should suffice at this point to determine to what extent the divergencies have been eliminated, once they had been highlighted.

Leaving aside three cases placed on the list in 1964, the over-all picture at that time was as follows: of the 22 cases where "a serious breach of one or several basic provisions of ratified Conventions" [1] had been found to exist by the Conference Committee, the divergencies were completely eliminated in two cases (Cuba: Convention No. 58; France: No. 81); partial action was noted in eight cases (Austria: No. 94; Colombia: No. 3; Czechoslovakia: No. 89; Greece: No. 1; Guatemala: No. 87; Hungary: No. 45; Italy: No. 59; Liberia: No. 29); in two cases the introduction of amending legislation seemed sufficiently promising to the Committee to warrant removal from the list (Mexico: No. 32; Philippines: No. 87); no measures had been taken by five countries (Chile: No. 11; Nicaragua and Uruguay: many Conventions; Mexico: No. 8; Pakistan: No. 96); three countries eventually decided to denounce the Convention (Albania: No. 4; Brazil: No. 3; Bulgaria: No. 4); finally, the accession of two territories to independence altered the whole position at a later stage (Ruanda-Urundi: No. 29; Singapore: No. 84).

Although only a relatively small number of test cases exists, their importance and the time span they cover illustrate the degree of impact of the special list. While full compliance could be achieved only rarely, the absence of any impact whatever is almost equally rare. In three-quarters of the cases the governments were prevailed upon to take some measures at least, where previously no concrete efforts had been noted for a number of years. Regardless of whether these efforts constituted major steps toward full application, [2] or merely a beginning of implementing action, or even a decision to terminate the international obligations, the phase of indifference or immobility has clearly ended and an impasse has been overcome. The significance of this attempt to secure action through publicity resides, therefore, not so much in the proportion of cases of effectiveness–which is close to the over-all results of the survey [3]–but in the fact that progress becomes possible precisely in those cases where little or no response had previously been obtained and that this reaction is clearly discernible after a country has been placed on the list. [4]

---

[1] This is the standard formula used by the Conference Committee to describe this category of cases (e.g. 47 R.P. 515).

[2] Austria, Greece, Hungary, Italy, Liberia.

[3] The general results indicate that in 37 per cent of the cases no concrete action had been taken in response to supervisory comments; the corresponding figure for the special list cases is 35 per cent.

[4] When the Colombian Minister of Labour urged Congress late in 1964 to approve new amendments to the Labour Code designed to implement a number of ratified Conventions, he not only referred to the bills introduced for this purpose in previous years (cf. p. 107 above) but he also informed the legislators that because of the long delays in taking action Colombia had been placed on the special list by the 1964 Conference. The pamphlet published by the Ministry of Labour to bring the new bill to the attention of a

The very timing of the implementing measures occasionally provides an insight into the sense of urgency surrounding their adoption. It can be assumed that if the legislative action was taken shortly before or even during the International Labour Conference in June, the impending discussions there loomed as an important factor in a government's decision. Examples of this kind are therefore of more than academic interest.[1]

In some instances the impact of the list may even be latent,[2] especially if the workers' members state formally that a case will be mentioned or mentioned again in the list unless it is "settled by next year".[3] The device can therefore be made use of in a flexible manner, depending on the information and assurances which a government is able to give.

The institution of the special list can be put down as a positive contribution, so far, to the basic purpose of the supervisory procedures. It is too early yet to determine its long-term value, since its effect might diminish with the passage of time, as repetition blunts its impact. Nonetheless, the significance of this experiment in moral pressure is undeniable. As has been seen, the governments' reaction provides an interesting indication that the desired psychological effect is usually achieved.[4] It is understandable, therefore, that the non-governmental members continue to be

---

wider public, recalled in the preface that "our country has been placed, and not unjustly, on a kind of 'blacklist' of the International Labour Organization... Our country cannot continue year after year, to suffer the indignity to the national honour resulting from the systematic supervision of the I.L.O." And the Minister concluded his message to Congress by saying that prompt action on the amendments "would give prestige to our country in the international sphere" (Ministerio del Trabajo, Sección Divulgación, Bogotá, November 1964).

[1] Three such cases, all connected with the special list, may be cited. In 1959 the Czechoslovak government adopted on 12 June a decree to ensure conformity with Convention No. 89 (43 R.P. 691). In 1963 the Conference Committee learned of a Royal Decree of 30 May designed to give fuller effect to Convention No. 1 (47 R.P. 524). Also in 1963, an Austrian government representative informed the Committee that new provisions on labour clauses in public contracts (Convention No. 94) "had been submitted to the Council of Ministers and had just been approved" (47 R.P. 538).

[2] An item in a Brazilian newspaper, under the title "There is confirmation that Brazil was on the point of being placed on the blacklist of the I.L.O." related that, according to information received from a Brazilian government representative, his country "only had escaped the blacklist as a result of the acceptance by the Committee on the Application of Conventions of the explanations he was able to give in the name of the Brazilian government." *O Globo* (Rio de Janeiro), 24 July 1962.

[3] Such a warning was voiced to the Greek government in 1962 (46 R.P. 692) and a major step forward ensued in 1963. The same year the Committee, in discussing the effect given to Convention No. 96 by Pakistan, noted a government statement that draft legislation had been prepared. The Committee decided that "in view of the action now taken by the government, it would be appropriate to defer until next year the question of placing this case on the special list" (46 R.P. 714). No legislation having been adopted, the Committee proceeded to include this case in the list in 1963.

[4] In 1962 an Albanian government delegate suggested that the list's stated object "to help and to encourage the governments concerned to carry out their obligations... could be achieved not only by apportioning blame but also by moral encouragement–perhaps even by another special list, a positive list" (46 R.P. 429). The Conference Committee has in fact taken pains in the past to emphasize that many "instances of progress" (46 R.P. 680-681) have also come to its attention and the Committee of Experts even began, in 1964, to list such cases in its General Report (1964 R.C.E. 7-8); the Committee's Report in 1965 contained a list of some 50 further cases of progress (1965 R.C.E. 11).

"strongly in favour" [1] of a device which provides them with an additional amount of leverage without resorting to the more formal and cumbersome procedures laid down in the Constitution. They have, on occasion, made pointed allusion to this alternative [2] which therefore requires consideration now as further potential means of pressure to induce governments to eliminate divergencies with ratified Conventions.

## The Combination of Periodic and Judicial Procedures

The tenor of the provisions regarding formal representations and complaints, particularly in the form in which they were originally adopted in 1919, shows that their authors considered them an essential part of the system for the "enforcement" of obligations. [3] A representation can be made by an employers' or workers' organization which considers that a ratifying State "has failed to secure... the effective observance within its jurisdiction of any Convention to which it is a party". The Governing Body has the right to publish this representation and the government's reply to it, if the latter "is not deemed to be satisfactory". [4] A complaint can be filed by a member State if it considers that another member fails to give effect to a Convention both have ratified. The Governing Body may refer a complaint to a Commission of Inquiry not only in the above circumstances but also "of its own motion or on receipt of a complaint from a delegate to the Conference". The Commission is to incorporate its findings and recommendations in a published report. A government which declines to accept these recommendations can refer the complaint to the International Court of Justice which "may affirm, vary or reverse any of the findings or recommendations of the Commission of Inquiry". [5]

During the I.L.O.'s first two decades attention was repeatedly called to these constitutional procedures and to their bearing on the less formal system of supervision, as instituted in 1926. An Office note submitted to the Conference that year described the functions of the Committee of Experts as "entirely technical and in no sense judicial... The system of examination now proposed is not in any way concerned with the machinery of inquiry and sanctions... and its action is not based upon complaints". [6]

---

[1] 44 R.P. 603.

[2] In 1960 the employers' vice-chairman called on the Conference to study the special list so that "the cases mentioned get as much publicity as possible. Otherwise it will be necessary to put into action the complaints machinery which exists under articles 24 to 34 of the Constitution" (44 R.P. 430).

[3] The word is used in the Labour Commission's Report to the Plenary Peace Conference. The Report explained that the "procedure has been carefully devised in order to avoid the imposition of penalties, except in the last resort, when a State has flagrantly and persistently refused to carry out its obligations under a convention. It can hardly be doubted that it will seldom, if ever, be necessary to bring these powers into operation, but the Commission considers that the fact of their existence is nevertheless a matter of almost vital importance to the success of the scheme" (I O.B. 266).

[4] These provisions remained, unchanged, in the Constitution when it was amended in 1946 (articles 24 and 25).

[5] Articles 26-29 and 31-32 of the Constitution, as amended in 1946.

[6] 8 R.P. 400. This point was re-emphasized in the Report of the 1926 Conference Committee which proposed the setting up of periodic supervision machinery: "The Com-

As the new periodic system began to operate and to acquire a momentum of its own, its potential value as an alternative to the constitutional machinery became increasingly apparent. Thus, in 1932, the Conference Committee raised the question whether the Governing Body should not set in motion the complaints procedure in regard to Cuba which had ratified 16 Conventions in 1928 but failed to report on them for three successive years. Last-minute intervention by a government delegate, with a statement in plenary that a draft labour code had just been submitted to Congress and a promise that the reports would be supplied in future, led the Committee to drop its suggestion "in the hope that next year no occasion for criticism will arise".[1] The impression gradually emerged, then, that the automatic supervision machinery was not only workable but also preferable since routine cases could be examined and followed up without setting special procedures in motion. By channeling attention away from the purely formal and negative aspects of supervision, it might be possible to keep it focused on the substance of each case.[2]

Did experience bear out this general impression? It is true that the representation provisions of the Constitution were invoked on only six occasions and that only one complaint was lodged during the inter-war period.[3] The reasons for this obvious reluctance to invoke the formal procedures are difficult to discover. There may have been an understandable hesitation on the part of governments to use a device which could be turned against them. A workers' organization also thought twice, no doubt, before taking a step sure to upset its national authorities,

---

mittee of Experts would have no judicial capacity... It could not therefore encroach upon the functions of the Commissions of Inquiry and of the Permanent Court of Justice in regard to complaints regarding the non-observance of ratified Conventions" (8 R.P. 405). In his comments on the first Report of the Experts, the following year, Albert Thomas called their comparison of the application of Conventions "only the beginning of real supervision. The discussions in the Conference itself have no immediate sanction behind them... The only methods which can be effective are the procedures of representation and complaint" (10 D.R. 100).

[1] 16 R.P. 674. In proposing this addition in the plenary sitting, the Chairman of the Application Committee noted that "the Cuban delegate did not come to our Committee when he was invited to do so, but he has now given us an explanation" (16 R.P. 332).

[2] "By persuasion, by discussion and by the questions they had asked, (the two Committees) had prevented a number of cases reaching the point where a complaint might otherwise have been lodged" (statement of the Director in the Governing Body in 1936, 74 G.B. 25). A similar conclusion was reached by Mr. Zarras of Greece (author of the pre-war study of I.L.O. supervision referred to repeatedly in these pages), speaking in 1938 as reporter of the Conference Committee: Through the procedure of mutual supervision "the States become aware of their obligations and attempt sincerely to comply with them. (The procedure) has undoubtedly contributed to rendering unnecessary, to a large extent, recourse to stricter measures such as the sanctions procedure provided for by... the Constitution. If use would have to be made of this (latter procedure) in each case, this would probably have caused difficulties for our Organization" (24 R.P. 303). For a more recent evaluation of the respective roles of the various procedures, cf. C. Wilfred Jenks, *The International Protection of Trade Union Freedom, op. cit.*, pp. 495-498.

[3] By the Indian workers' delegate to the Conference in 1934. The complaint concerned the application of the Hours of Work (Industry) Convention, 1919 (No. 1) to the Indian Railways and led to a formal promise by the government to extend the benefits of the Convention gradually to all railway workers in India "with the least possible delay" (XX O.B. 15).

and with success by no means guaranteed, to judge from experience. Perhaps the annual examination of reports did play a decisive role in this failure of the judicial enforcement procedures to materialize.[1] In any case the resulting emphasis on systematic supervision has served to promote the regular implementation of Conventions, with the more formal method remaining available in case of need.[2]

It is clear, therefore, that a combination of what has been called the "permanent" and the "occasional" methods tends in the long run to reinforce both.[3] The full implications of the interaction of the two methods have by now been realized by all concerned. As noted at the beginning of this section, the non-governmental members of the Conference Committee have been able to use the existence of the formal procedures as an added means of pressure to be kept in reserve for particularly intractable cases of non-compliance. The possibility of filing a representation or complaint provides them with additional room for manœuvre, should the special list fail to yield results. The most unambiguous statement to this effect was made by the workers' vice-chairman of the Conference Committee in the plenary in 1960. Speaking of Liberia's "clear violation" of the Forced Labour Convention, he told the meeting of the decision of "the workers' group of the Conference... that, if next year the Convention is not applied, it will have recourse to article 26... We hope that this solemn warning will suffice to inform the government that the time has come for the application of a Convention which it has ratified".[4] A complaint was in fact lodged the following year but not by the workers' group.

It was the struggle for decolonialization in Africa which, after 40 years, finally put an end to the governments' reluctance to make use of the constitutional procedure. Twice within six months, in 1961, the Director-General of the I.L.O. received formal complaints regarding the effect given to the two Forced Labour Conventions. The first, filed by Ghana, concerned the application of the 1957 Convention in the Portuguese territories of Angola, Guinea and Mozambique. The second, filed by Portugal as a calculated response to the first, was directed against Liberia.[5] Without going into the

---

[1] There is a touch of irony in the fact that it was the Minister of Labour of South Africa who wondered in 1951 "why, over this long period of years, the provisions of articles 24 to 34 of the Constitution have not been invoked" (34 R.P. 442).

[2] In 1933 Kaasik pointed out, in discussing I.L.O. Conventions, that "almost in all cases where international law institutes administrative and judicial supervision side by side, the administrative method prevails and becomes the only one in operation, to the almost entire exclusion of judicial supervision" (op. cit., p. 145).

[3] P. Berthoud concluded in 1946 that "the juxtaposition of the two methods of supervision offers incontrovertible advantages... It adds to the effectiveness of supervision by reinforcing so to speak the supervision which is exercised regularly with a safety device which is ready to function immediately and without restraint in case of need. It permits moreover not to weigh down the permanent supervision procedure which will be relieved of the rare cases of exceptional gravity possibly confronting it, which might risk at times to paralyze the whole system of supervision" (op. cit., p. 277).

[4] 44 R.P. 444.

[5] The evidence cited by the Portuguese government in support of its complaint relied heavily on the previous examination of the case by the two supervisory Committees: "Liberia has been mentioned several times in the special list, but has always ignored these appeals... The International Labour Organization already has in its possession full documentary evidence concerning the violation of the Convention" (Commission of Inquiry Report (Portugal-Liberia), op. cit., p. 2).

substance either of the complaints or of their examination by two Commissions of Inquiry, it is necessary to consider their bearing on the effectiveness of I.L.O. supervision in general.

Regardless of their origin as acts of political warfare, they instilled life into a hitherto unused and somewhat theoretical procedure. As a result, future warnings to resort to this procedure should have a somewhat less hollow ring. They may moreover carry added conviction because of the measures taken by the Portuguese and the Liberian governments, during and after the discussion of the complaints, to give fuller effect to the respective Conventions.[1] While in the case of Portugal's ratification, which only came into force in 1960, the regular examination had not yet begun to function, in the case of Liberia the judicial procedure led to governmental action which the automatic system of supervision had signally failed to secure over many years.[2]

The most significant consequence of this development resides in the attempt to rely on the automatic system of supervision in following up observance of recommendations by the two Commissions of Inquiry. They asked that the States concerned "should indicate regularly in (their) reports under article 22... the action taken during the period under review to give effect to the recommendations contained in the present Report". They also left it "to the discretion of the Committee of Experts on the Application of Conventions and Recommendations to indicate when it no longer considers any special information on all or some of these matters necessary".[3] In pursuance of these instructions, the Experts and Conference Committees have begun to assume responsibility for assessing the progress made from year to year.[4] It is too early to determine to what extent this integration of the two separate supervision procedures will add to their effectiveness. But it is not unreasonable to expect that the findings and conclusions which emerged from the two complaints are much less likely to be forgotten, even after their immediate impact on public opinion has disappeared.

The interaction of two separate procedures can also be discerned, finally, in relation to the special machinery set up by the I.L.O. to deal with allegations of infringements of the right of association for trade union purposes.[5]

---

[1] In the case of Portugal, the Commission of Inquiry noted that "important changes for the purpose of bringing the law and practice into full conformity with the requirements of the Convention have been made since the complaint was lodged" (*op. cit.*, p. 234). The substance and implication of these changes are summarized on pp. 235-236 of the Report. In the case of Liberia, the Commission noted that "major discrepancies between Liberian legislation and the requirements of the Convention were not eliminated until February and May 1962" (*op. cit.*, p. 179). The position is summarized on pp. 176-177 of the Report.

[2] For a more general review of the special characteristics of the two Commissions of Inquiry and of their work, cf. Daniel Vignes, "Procédures Internationales d'Enquête" in *Annuaire Français de Droit International*, Vol. IX (1963), pp. 438-459.

[3] The relevant passages are drawn up in identical terms and appear on p. 247 of the Ghana-Portugal Report and on p. 179 of the Portugal-Liberia Report.

[4] Speaking of the first case, the Conference Committee noted in 1962 that the effect given to the Abolition of Forced Labour Convention by Portugal "will require the closest scrutiny both by the Committee of Experts and by the Conference" (46 R.P. 682).

[5] For the genesis and functioning of this procedure, cf. C. Wilfred Jenks, *The International Protection of Trade Union Freedom, op. cit.*, pp. 180-200, 500-511, and doc. G.B.161/20/1 (roneoed).

The consideration of such allegations is not limited to cases where binding obligations exist under the international labour Conventions on freedom of association and the right to organize. Where one or several of these instruments have been ratified, however, the Committee on Freedom of Association set up by the Governing Body in 1951 to carry out a preliminary examination of alleged violations, stresses the relevant obligations in its Reports and makes use of any conclusions reached by the Experts and Conference Committees.[1] On the other hand, the Committee of Experts examines "carefully" any divergencies to which the Governing Body Committee has drawn attention [2] and asks the government to indicate "further developments" in future reports.[3] Although the number of cases coming simultaneously before the Governing Body Committee on Freedom of Association and before the Committees dealing with annual reports is relatively small, their co-ordinated consideration should prove mutually beneficial by giving added emphasis to the examination of important cases and by guaranteeing that they are followed up regularly until the required measures of compliance have been adopted.

The evidence available seems to suggest, therefore, that a combination of two parallel supervision procedures can help materially in promoting governmental action. Experience has demonstrated, moreover, that the informal but systematic approach which received little attention when the I.L.O. was established now overshadows the constitutional procedures on which so much reliance had been placed in the early days. On the other hand, the very fact that these procedures have largely remained in the background enables them to exercise a latent influence in cases of exceptional gravity. Formal representations and complaints can be held in reserve, so to speak, for possible use when the periodic procedure seems to be losing momentum.

There exists another alternative if the Conference Committee should feel disinclined to contemplate formal action under articles 24 to 34 of the Constitution, yet consider that the facts of a case warrant exhaustive inquiry. Under article 10, paragraph 1, of the Constitution, the functions of the International Labour Office include "the conduct of such special investigations as may be ordered by the Conference or by the Governing Body". It would thus be possible to call for an investigation of this kind which would presumably be undertaken by a body especially set up for the purpose.[4] The results and recommendations would perhaps be less

---

[1] Cf. the reference in 1957 to these conclusions as regards the non-application of the Right of Association (Agriculture) Convention, 1921 (No. 11) in Chile: "The (Governing Body) Committee considers that, as the question at issue is the application of a Convention ratified by Chile, it should endorse those conclusions" (XL O.B. 168).

[2] Cf. for instance the observation made in 1957 regarding the application of the Right to Organize and Collective Bargaining Convention, 1949 (No. 98) in the Dominican Republic (1957 R.C.E. 94). The Committee noted in 1958 that the government had acted on this observation.

[3] Cf. for instance the observation made in 1963 regarding the application of Convention No. 98 in the United Kingdom (1963 R.C.E. 112).

[4] The Director-General proposed to the Governing Body in June 1963, that a special commission of investigation be set up under article 10 in order "to examine the extent to which the law and practice in South Africa... violate the fundamental human rights

incisive than the findings of a formal inquiry, but this very fact might make them more acceptable. An investigation of this kind might thus strike a balance between the persuasive element of automatic supervision and the weight of more formal procedures.

There remains the largely theoretical question of what would happen if a country failed to accept the recommendations of a commission of inquiry and possibly even of the International Court of Justice, should the matter be referred to it. The Governing Body is empowered, in this case, to "recommend such action as it may deem wise and expedient to secure compliance".[1] It is clear from the wording of the original Constitution that its framers did not exclude the possibility of economic sanctions [2] against States which "flagrantly and persistently" violate ratified Conventions. No commissions of inquiry were set up during the I.L.O.'s first quarter-century, so that the question of sanctions did not arise,[3] but the present powers of the Governing Body, as quoted above, certainly enable it "to adapt its action to the circumstances of a particular case and permit it", should a member State fail

---

set forth" in the I.L.O.'s standards concerning forced labour, freedom of association and discrimination in respect of employment and occupation. It is significant that this proposal was made although none of the relevant Conventions had been ratified by South Africa. The commission was to be composed of three independent members serving in a personal capacity; it would take into account any information provided by the Office, by member States, by international non-governmental organizations or by employers' or workers' organizations in South Africa; the government of the Republic of South Africa would have an opportunity to comment on this information but "absence of such co-operation" would not prevent the commission from proceeding; the commission would include in its report "any recommendations which it may think proper concerning the modifications of the law and practice of South Africa necessary to give effect" to the above-mentioned I.L.O. standards (156 G.B. 43). The Governing Body decided, in the end, to place before the 1964 Session of the Conference proposals which led to the vote of the constitutional amendment mentioned in footnote 3 on the next page, as well as to the adoption of a "Declaration concerning the Policy of *Apartheid* of the Republic of South Africa" (XLVII O.B. No. 3, Supplement I, pp. 1-4). The Governing Body also decided to initiate an "I.L.O. Programme for the Elimination of *Apartheid* in Labour Matters in the Republic of South Africa" (157 G.B. 34; 158 G.B.57).

[1] Article 33 of the Constitution, as amended in 1946.

[2] Under the provisions originally adopted in 1919, both a Commission of Inquiry and the Permanent Court of International Justice could "indicate the measures, if any, of an economic character (in French "sanctions d'ordre economique") which it considers to be appropriate and which other governments would be justified in adopting against a defaulting government" (I O.B. 341). The types of measures envisaged were spelled out in the original British memorandum: "When a two-thirds majority of the Conference is satisfied that the terms of the Convention have not been carried out, the signatory States should discriminate against the articles produced under the conditions of unfair competition proved to exist unless those conditions were remedied within one year or such longer period as the Conference might decide" (Shotwell, *op. cit.*, Vol. II, p. 125).

In its Report to the Plenary Peace Conference, the Commission on International Labour Legislation, "while taking the view that it will in the long run be preferable as well as more effective to rely on the pressure of international public opinion rather than on economic measures, nevertheless consider(ed) it necessary to retain the possibility of the latter in the background" (I O.B. 266).

[3] It is true that in 1945 a workers' member of the Governing Body expressed the opinion that "sanctions... could be applied quite easily. In the shipping industry, for instance, if a country failed to apply Conventions... to which it was a party, it might be threatened with a refusal to supply the necessary coal or oil for its ships, or with higher charges in port, or with a refusal to load or unload the ships" (94 G.B. 44).

to carry out the recommendations of a commission, "to draw a case of such failure to the attention of the Security Council of the United Nations".[1]

Even in an extreme case, the menace of expulsion can hardly be considered a realistic approach; it would negate the principle of universality on which international organization must rely, especially in pursuing its technical, non-political objectives; it would moreover represent a solution of despair foreclosing any hope for gradual change.[2] It is perhaps conceivable, in the light of the action which the I.L.O. has taken regarding South Africa,[3] that a government, rather than a country, might be gradually suspended from participation in the work of the Organization.[4] But even such limited action seems unlikely to constitute a credible contingency in present circumstances [5] nor would a proposal of this kind secure the necessary support.[6] Among the somewhat less drastic steps which might nonetheless carry considerable conviction, in certain cases, would be the withholding of

---

[1] In the words of the Conference Delegation on Constitutional Questions (29 Report II (1), p. 56).

[2] Expulsion of a State from an international organization has been described as "merely an *alibi* for the failure of other States to devise effective means of enforcing the provisions which have been flouted" (C. Wilfred Jenks, "Some Constitutional Problems of International Organizations", *British Yearbook of International Law, 1945*, pp. 25-26).

[3] A constitutional amendment voted in July 1964 empowers the Conference, by a two-thirds majority (including two-thirds of the government delegates present and voting) to "suspend from participation" in the Conference any State member "which has been found by the United Nations to be flagrantly and persistently pursuing a declared policy of racial discrimination such as *apartheid*"; suspension would continue until the Conference has found, by a similar vote "that the member has changed its policy" (XLVII O.B. No. 3, Supplement I, pp. 8-10). This amendment has not yet entered into force. South Africa had already given notice of withdrawal from the I.L.O. in March 1964 (159 G.B. 146-147).

[4] Professor Sohn has suggested that "exclusion of a government, rather than a state, from a slowly growing range of international activities might in its cumulative effect be more chastening to that government than the swift cut of all ties through expulsion". Cf. Louis B. Sohn, "Expulsion or Forced Withdrawal from International Organizations", *Harvard Law Review*, Vol. 77, No. 8 (June 1964), pp. 1381-1425.

[5] Professor Friedmann considers however that "the day can be foreseen when the I.L.O. conventions and directives will attain. . . (universal authority), and when the stigma of non-compliance will mean exclusion from an international labour market" (*op. cit.*, p. 90).

[6] During the Governing Body discussions on South Africa, in 1963, the employers' group suggested an amendment to the Constitution enabling the Conference "to expel or to suspend from attendance at the Conference for a specified period, or through its credentials procedure to refuse to admit, the delegation nominated by any member State whose national policies constitute a persistent and flagrant disregard of the fundamental principles on which the International Labour Organization is based". The employers' vice-chairman explained that in the opinion of his group "States other than the Republic of South Africa were violating other fundamental I.L.O. principles". The U.S.S.R. government member announced his intention to vote against this proposal which he said "merely befogged the issue and diverted attention from the real problem. . . the adoption of effective measures" against South Africa. The French government member also considered it "wise to concentrate on that issue rather than adopt a formula so broad as to endanger the very principle of universality of the Organization". The workers' group agreed that "while many of its members saw the merit of the proposal, this was not the time to consider an amendment of this kind". The proposal was eventually rejected by 25 votes to 15, with 5 abstentions (156 G.B. 13-27).

technical aid when a country fails consistently to implement important Conventions.[1]

It seems reasonable to conclude, in summing up this rapid review of possible coercive action to enforce Conventions, that moral pressure still offers the best hope for encouraging compliance. Its effectiveness depends, in the last analysis, on the extent to which various parallel procedures are successively or jointly brought into play.[2] The resulting gradation of emphasis and flexibility of approach should afford sufficient scope for national and international influence to make itself felt in the long run. The participation of non-governmental elements can also lend an additional resonance to the whole system. It is this special function of the workers' and employers' representatives which now requires fuller consideration.

### III.  The Special Role of Workers and Employers in I.L.O. Supervision

The most distinctive feature of the I.L.O.'s supervision procedure, as compared with others pursuing similar objectives, is the full-scale participation of non-governmental interests. It seems hardly surprising, in retrospect at least, that the tripartite system, which gives such a special imprint to the Organization's activities, should have exercised a profound influence in a sector of its work where governmental action comes under scrutiny. The reluctance of governments to participate actively in supervising other governments helped to accentuate the role played by the workers and employers and their organizations, to which special powers were given from the start to make representations in cases of non-observance of a Convention.

Interest was focused in the early days on the organizations' share in formulating standards rather than on their possible role in promoting effective implementation. As the new machinery began to acquire a tradition of its own, a tendency to leave the main burden of mutual supervision to the workers and employers became increasingly apparent. This trend was recognized by the Governing Body in revising the forms of report and by the Conference in amending the Constitution.

---

[1] A suggestion to this effect was made by the Greek workers' delegate in 1963: "We consider that severe sanctions should be contemplated against member countries which, having ratified (the freedom of association) Conventions, refuse to apply them or in any way infringe their spirit and their content. Such sanctions might involve, for instance, refusal to give technical assistance for countries which do not respect their commitments in this way" (47 R.P. 324). A similar idea was expressed, though in much more muted terms, by a Vice-President of the A.F.L.-C.I.O., George M. Harrison: "Another factor to be considered by A.I.D. (Agency for International Development, a U.S. government agency providing foreign assistance) is the adherence of recipient governments to the Conventions of the International Labor Organization... The I.L.O. Conventions are an international bill of rights for workers and they ought to be endorsed by every free country" (Address delivered in 1963 to the Tenth Annual Meeting of the National Conference on International Economic and Social Development).

[2] C. Wilfred Jenks places this "coherent approach" in a broader perspective when he explains that "standard-setting work, informational functions, promotional and operational activities, industrial relations responsibilities, quasi-judicial duties and educational programmes have been conceived and are developed as mutually complementary to each other" (*Law, Freedom and Welfare, op. cit.*, p. 26).

*The Tripartite Tradition*

Although non-governmental participation in the I.L.O. has become completely institutionalized, it is well to remember that the tripartite system represents a unique development in international life and that it has been a source not only of strength but also of difficulties for the Organization.[1]

Regardless of any internal divisions that might exist within each group, it is clear that their recognized status leaves a profound imprint on the appearance [2] and conduct of I.L.O. meetings. As a result the outlook is no longer determined solely by national or political considerations and many questions can be approached from a broader, professional viewpoint.[3] Nor has the changed position resulting from the increased proportion of member countries where fully free and independent workers' and employers' organizations do not exist [4] altered the tradition of intragroup consultation and of collective action, so that many of the decisions reached within each group tend to give expression to "the wider interests of an evolving world community".[5]

As might be expected, such a unified group approach cannot be achieved on all issues, particularly when political factors are involved. It is all the more interesting, therefore, that within the specific sphere of supervision the workers' and the employers' groups have generally been able to achieve a considerable degree of cohesion and unity.[6] In the case of the workers the reasons for this are fairly obvious, since the improvement of social standards

---

[1] For a study of the origins and problems of tripartite representation cf. Bernard Béguin, "I.L.O. and the Tripartite System", *International Conciliation*, No. 523 (May 1959). The history and functioning of the workers' group was described in Alexandre Berenstein, *Les Organisations Ouvrières – Leurs Compétences et leur Rôle dans la Société des Nations et notamment dans l'Organisation internationale du Travail* (Paris: Pédone, 1936); cf. in particular pp. 134-143.

[2] In the Governing Body and in the various Committees of the Conference the members of each of the three groups sit together as separate units, much like party groups in a national parliament.

[3] Writing in 1934, F.G. Wilson referred to "this unity of group or class interest... represented in the three forms of associations which control the Organization, that is, governments or public organizations, employers or economic associations, and workers or trade union organizations" (*Labor in the League System, op. cit.*, p. 272).

[4] A committee set up by the Governing Body in 1955, usually referred to as the "McNair Committee", concluded that in at least 20 of the 70 countries which were then members of the I.L.O., the government was able to dominate and control the employers' and workers' organizations (*Report of the Committee on Freedom of Employers' and Workers' Organisations* (XXXIX O.B. 475-599); cf. in particular pp. 579-580 of the majority Report). The I.L.O. now has well over a hundred members and it may be assumed that the proportion of countries where the organizations lack "full freedom" (as defined in the Freedom of Association and Protection of the Right to Organize Convention) has increased, rather than diminished, since 1955.

[5] C. Wilfred Jenks, *The International Protection of Trade Union Freedom, op. cit.*; pp. 514-517 discuss the role of "non-territorial forces of integration" as represented by the employers and workers in the I.L.O.

[6] For a general evaluation of voting cohesion in the two groups, cf. Ernst B. Haas, "System and Process in the International Labor Organization", *World Politics*, Vol. XIV, No. 2 (January 1962), pp. 343-351. The author concludes from a statistical analysis of votes on a number of issues that group consensus has been disintegrating but that "unity remains strongest in the case of labor conventions".

both in their own countries and elsewhere constitutes their primary objective. This is particularly true when the objective can be secured more easily through legislative action than through direct negotiation with the employers, i.e., in the less developed countries.[1] In the case of the employers' group the motivation is more complex. Briefly, it results from the group's cautious attitude toward adopting a Convention, rather than a Recommendation, which cannot create binding obligations and is less likely to add to labour costs. The employers feel, therefore, that once a Convention has been ratified it should be fully implemented, both to counteract low-cost competition by other countries and to demonstrate to governments the full implications of adopting and ratifying Conventions. Despite the diversity of their motives, the two groups seem to agree that they have a convergent interest in promoting compliance. This conviction has in fact grown stronger in recent years, during a period when many issues have had a divisive influence on consensus formation within and among the groups.

### The Basis of Non-Governmental Supervision

Once the tripartite system of framing Conventions had been established, it was only logical to follow the same principle in dealing with their application.[2] It was thought in the beginning that the mere supply of reports would cause the application of Conventions to be discussed in the Conference. It was also thought that the representations and complaints procedures in the Constitution would be utilized whenever serious cases of non-observance came to the notice of workers, employers or governments. When these expectations failed to materialize and the two supervisory Committees were set up, the non-governmental representatives in the I.L.O. were for the first time able to discuss breaches of Conventions with the governments on a regular basis.

As already indicated, the main share of responsibility fell, from the start, on the representative organizations,[3] particularly in the Conference Committee where the non-government members take the initiative. The special stake of the representative organizations in supervision was formally

---

[1] According to William H. Knowles, some unionists in the British West Indies, for instance, held that "under the conditions prevailing... political action is a more fruitful avenue than collective bargaining, because it is easier to legislate gains for workers when labor is assured control of the government than it is to overcome employer opposition to collective bargaining when labor's economic position is weak" (*Labor and Economic Development, op. cit.*, p. 275).

[2] Suggestions to this effect were advanced when the I.L.O. was proposed during World War I. In a document which Léon Jouhaux, as secretary of the French General Confederation of Labour, submitted to an Allied Trade Unions Conference in 1916, the possibility of "international control" was discussed: "As it is chiefly the workers in each country who are most interested in the application of each international labour legislation one of the best international guarantees of its strict application would be to summon the national labour organizations of every country to participate actively in controlling the application" (Shotwell, *op. cit.*, Vol. II, pp. 16-19).

[3] In 1928 Msgr. Nolens, long the principal government delegate from the Netherlands, discussed the examination of the annual reports and referred to "the important part which the industrial organizations, particularly the workers' organizations, have to play in this procedure" (11 R.P. 291).

recognized in 1946, when the amended Constitution made it incumbent on governments to send them copies of reports.[1]

*The Right to Make Written Comments on Application*

In asking governments whether the "organizations of employers and workers concerned" have commented on the application of a Convention, the Governing Body has spelled out the rights and obligations involved. Although only the representative organizations are entitled to receive copies of a government's reports, any labour union or employers' association with a clear interest in the implementation of the relevant standards may submit "observations" on the matter to its government. The government is expected to report and to answer these observations; only very rarely has a government passed over observations in silence.[2]

If an organization is directly concerned and familiar with "the practical fulfilment of the conditions prescribed by (a) Convention or the application of the legislation or other measures implementing the stipulations of the Convention"–in the words of the forms of report–it will be qualified to express an opinion as to the extent of application. In theory, then, every *bona fide* workers' or employers' organization is in a position to submit its comments, and might be expected to do so especially if the supervisory Committees have previously commented on shortcomings. In practice, a surprisingly small proportion of the organizations avail themselves of this opportunity.

The special question regarding observations by the occupational organizations has figured in the forms of report since 1932, but the Committee of Experts did not begin to provide specific data on the matter until the early nineteenfifties when the amended Constitution introduced a new element. The Committee apparently expected that the receipt of copies of the reports by many organizations would stimulate interest in the application of Conventions and lead more of them to submit observations. Noting, in 1953, that workers' organizations in two countries had commented on their governments' reports, it stressed that it "would be glad to see the further development of the practice hereby inaugurated, as a means of enabling it to report with greater confidence to the Governing Body on the practical application of ratified Conventions".[3] During the next three years the Committee of Experts was mainly intent on ensuring that the governments did in fact comply with the new constitutional requirement to send copies of their reports to the representative organizations. But it was clear from the small number of countries listed as failing to comply that the paucity of

---

[1] The original suggestion for this constitutional provision was made by the Conference Committee on Application, in 1945 (27 R.P. 442).

[2] In 1936 the Rumanian government admitted in the Conference Committee that it had received protests from workers' organizations alleging infringements of the Hours of Work (Industry) Convention, 1919 (No. 1). The Committee indicated that "surprise was expressed" at the government's failure to mention this fact in its report (20 R.P. 568). In 1955 the workers' vice-chairman charged that "he was aware of cases in which observations had been made (by workers' organizations) but not transmitted to the I.L.O." (doc. C.App.C./PV.2 (roneoed), p. 5). He did not specify.

[3] 1953 R.C.E. 4.

comments could not be attributed to the organizations' inability to see the reports.[1]

Although the membership of the I.L.O. and the supply of reports have steadily increased in recent years, the largest number of comments by organizations, subsequently recorded by the Committee of Experts, was nine.[2] The Committee has repeatedly expressed its disappointment at such a limited response and declared itself "at a loss to understand why this should be so".[3] It has even suggested that "a useful service would be performed in the interests of international supervision if governments were to invite such observations from the organizations in question".[4] The organizations' failure to avail themselves more regularly of their right to make written comments was noted with obvious concern in the Conference, where workers' and employers' representatives participate directly in the supervision procedure. The Application Committee and especially its workers' members were clearly embarrassed by this situation. In 1947 the Conference Committee stressed that communication of the reports "puts at the disposal of the employers and workers an effective weapon for exercising supervision at the very outset of the procedure".[5] In 1950 the Committee's reporter referred to the employers' and workers' "duty of criticizing" their governments when a ratification is not implemented.[6] Yet the following year the Conference Committee was forced to recognize that "the organizations do not give sufficient attention to this question",[7] and in 1955 the workers' vice-chairman made "an admission of our own guilt" in not seizing the opportunity to participate more fully in the work of supervision.[8]

It was at this stage that certain practical suggestions were advanced in the Conference to make it easier for the organizations to understand and scrutinize their governments' reports. The aim was, principally, to familiarize them with the terms of Conventions, with the reporting procedures and with the results of the Committee of Experts' yearly examination.

---

[1] Cf. 1954 R.C.E. 4; 1955 R.C.E. 3; 1956 R.C.E. 3. The number of countries listed never exceeded six.

[2] In 1959. The Committee did not give any figures in 1961 and 1962, but the average number of comments for the decade ending 1963 was five per year. The Committee has also indicated that these comments come "principally" from the workers' organizations (1963 R.C.E. 13).

[3] 1958 R.C.E. 4. The Committee added, with a touch of irony, that "in the great majority of cases the absence of such observations no doubt results from the organizations concerned being fully satisfied with the conformity of national law and practice with ratified Conventions. The Committee finds it hard to believe, however, that that can be the reason in all cases".

[4] 1948 R.C.E. 8. Only one country, Australia, seems to have acted on this suggestion (1953 R.C.E. 4; 38 R.P. 584).

[5] 30 R.P. 545.

[6] 33 R.P. 375.

[7] 34 R.P. 552. In 1953 Professor Rappard, speaking as a Swiss government delegate and as a long-time member of the Committee of Experts, called on "the organizations (to) study the reports. Cases of infringement, or of deviation in the application of Conventions should be reported to Geneva and to our Committee" (36 R.P. 258).

[8] "Workers' organizations... thus neglect an important tool of co-operation in the application of Conventions" (38 R.P. 433).

Thus the employers' vice-chairman suggested that the report forms be sent to the organizations with the copies of the reports.[1] Some workers' members also asked that the Report of the Experts be made available to the organizations as quickly after publication as possible.[2] A request by the workers' members that the governments send their reports to the organizations in draft form did not get any support from the other groups, which feared that it might cause delays.[3]

While measures such as these might help union and employer representatives to grasp the meaning of I.L.O. standards within their national context, it is clear that these measures would at best constitute a first step toward getting the responsible leaders in the two camps actively and permanently interested in the opportunities which international supervision might offer them in the pursuit of their objectives.

More will have to be said about this crucial issue below when discussing the problems and prospects of fuller participation by non-governmental elements. It is worth noting now that some efforts were made, by the workers in any case, to remind their organizations of the need for written comment on the governments' reports. An appeal to this effect appeared in 1953 in the monthly review of the International Federation of Christian Trade Unions. An article entitled "The Task of the Trade Union Movement" emphasized that the I.L.O. Constitution does not require governments to communicate copies of their reports "for the purpose of increasing the paper supplies of the labour organizations, but to permit trade unions to take a part in supervision. Are the statements made by your government in its report on the application of a given Convention accurate? Such is in substance the question asked the trade union movement when communicating the reports".[4] In 1955 the workers' members informed the Application Committee that they had "drawn the attention of the workers' group of the Conference to the potential importance of the employers' and workers' organizations participating actively in the mutual supervision of the application of Conference decisions".[5] The figures mentioned above confirm that their appeals have failed to lead to any marked increase in the number of comments received.

Perhaps as a reaction to this state of affairs, the Committee of Experts has taken pains to consider in detail any comments by the representative organizations mentioned in the governments' reports. In some cases such comments have made the Committee aware of divergencies not noted previously.[6] In other cases the Committee has reached the conclusion that

---

[1] 38 R.P. 434. It is worth recalling that a similar request was made by the Belgian workers' member of the Governing Body in 1932 and that the Director had given his agreement, "on the understanding that it was done unofficially" (60 G.B. 78-79).

[2] 39 R.P. 646.

[3] 39 R.P. 646. One government, that of the Federal Republic of Germany, seems to have followed such a procedure without any apparent difficulty (39 R.P. 442).

[4] *Labor* (Utrecht, Netherlands), Vol. 25, No. 11 (May 1953), pp. 344-346.

[5] 38 R.P. 584.

[6] Cf. the observations made to France since 1956 as regards the Maternity Protection Convention, as described on p. 92 above.

there was no infringement.[1] It tries, if at all possible, to get the parties concerned to settle difficulties amongst themselves.[2] The Committee of Experts also follows closely the tripartite discussions on particular cases which take place in the Conference Committee and the views put forward there not only by the government representatives but also by the workers' and employers' members.

Because of the scarcity of written comments, the Conference constitutes the principal platform for non-governmental supervision.

*Tripartite Discussion as the Focal Point of I.L.O. Supervision*

Enough was said in Chapter One on the procedures and atmosphere of the Conference Committee to illustrate the crucial function performed by workers' and employers' representatives. Without their participation the discussions in the Committee would be quite different; indeed one might wonder whether in such a case there would be any discussions at all beyond those on procedural questions of reporting and on the meaning of specific provisions of certain Conventions. The obvious reticence to intervene, usually displayed by governments when the application of standards by other governments is under consideration, reinforces the impression that the whole system largely depends on the active interest of the non-governmental groups.

In a real sense, therefore, the deliberations in the Conference Committee turn as a rule into a dialogue between these groups and the governments which reply to the observations of the Committee of Experts. During this dialogue there is, first of all, an opportunity for the workers and employers to do orally what they might already have done through written comments to their governments–i.e., to criticize the state of application in their own countries. Although such criticism is heard at every Conference session, the record shows that it occurs no more frequently than the observations the organizations send to their governments in writing. How is it, then, that the discussions in the Application Committee become as full and as lively as they often are? The reason for this is that the statements made by the non-government members represent not so much personal and individual points of view as expressions of the collective opinion of their groups. It is the group system which emerges as the motive force for regular and effective supervision in the Conference Committee.

Because of the informal, caucus-like mode of operation of the groups, only the results appear on the record; the preparatory group meetings are

---

[1] In 1957, e.g., the Committee found "after careful consideration of the question", that criticism of the national legislation, made by the Austrian Assembly of Chambers of Labour in regard to the Protection of Wages Convention was not well founded (1957 R.C.E. 90).

[2] In 1958, e.g., it examined a claim made by the General Confederation of Italian Industry, the previous year, that the employers were not being given equal representation on certain joint advisory bodies, as provided for in the Employment Service Convention. The Committee concluded that the efficient working of these bodies requires "practical agreement among the parties concerned" (1957 R.C.E. 85; 1958 R.C.E. 58).

shrouded in secrecy.[1] It is clear, nonetheless, that the strategy of the discussions with governments is planned there,[2] so that each case can be considered on the basis of a concerted and, if possible, a unified approach. Because this groundwork is a precondition of effective group action, it has become a traditional, albeit an unofficial, part of the method of operation followed by the workers' and employers' members in the Application Committee. With the Committee functioning at every regular session, a pattern of behaviour has thus developed.

This institutionalization of non-governmental supervision, not only as a system but even as an accepted and ingrained operating procedure, explains its acceptance by the governments. It is difficult to call into question a method of discussion which has functioned for so long without being challenged in its essential purpose. In a sense the inquisitive attitude itself has come to be expected by the governments. The supervisors feel less inhibited by nationalist attitudes since they speak in an international capacity. The supervised find it more difficult merely to plead good faith.[3] It is from the substance of their replies and, ultimately, of their actions that the degree of their compliance will be gauged. Failure to reply has in fact become so exceptional in the Conference Committee as to be subject to even more severe criticism than failure to apply. All these elements testify to the special position the workers and employers have been able to secure for themselves in supervision.

The significance of this achievement should not obscure the serious obstacles which still confront them individually and collectively in their attempt to make an effective contribution to I.L.O. supervision.

### Problems Facing Non-Governmental Participation

The unusual context of workers' and employers' participation in supervising the application of Conventions has led to difficulties which, without being new in themselves, take on different forms because of the international setting in which they arise. These problems are largely the same regardless of whether the contribution of the non-governmental organizations consists of written comments at home or oral comments in the International Labour Conference. They are connected with the ability of the organizations to become fully familiar with I.L.O. standards and to discuss with a minimum

---

[1] The *Daily Bulletin* of the Conference announces not only the plenary sittings and the meetings of the various committees but also, under the heading "Notices for the Information of Delegates", the separate meetings held by the employers' and workers' members of these committees.

[2] In 1955 the workers' vice-chairman of the Application Committee referred in the plenary to the "fruitful work" accomplished during the session, adding that "this year the workers' group has given particular importance to this important Committee. The group meetings, which were always well attended, carefully prepared the discussions" (38 R.P. 432).

[3] C. Wilfred Jenks concludes from his analysis of I.L.O. supervision that it is "impossible for governments to take refuge behind the unimpeachable word of a sovereign State and thus to escape criticism as easily as they have sometimes been able to do in bodies of purely diplomatic composition" (*The International Protection of Trade Union Freedom, op. cit.*, p. 519).

of restraint the degree of their implementation at home and elsewhere.[1] These factors require consideration at this juncture.

The constructive participation of labour and employers' organizations in tripartite supervision implies their ability to speak their minds freely, i.e. to be reasonably independent of outside interference. The importance of freedom of expression as a guarantee of equality of partnership was recognized during the early stages of I.L.O. supervision [2] and the subsequent expansion in the membership of the Organization has further emphasized the significance of this factor.[3] With circumstances varying from country to country and often subject to rapid change, it would be unwise to generalize. Experience tends to indicate however that in certain cases spontaneous comment from those directly concerned might do much to promote compliance with I.L.O. standards. The same purpose is of course pursued, collectively, by the non-governmental members of the Conference Committee whenever they discuss the effect given to Conventions in individual countries, but even their insistence on the ratification and application of the freedom of association Conventions is not likely, by itself, to lead to much progress, since respect for these instruments "necessarily reflects the more general background of the civil and political liberties enjoyed by the inhabitants of a country".[4]

When there are no workers' or employers' organizations the situation is little different, in terms of I.L.O. supervision, from that just described. While this is rather exceptional nowadays, the organizations in many countries are so rudimentary that they cannot be expected to participate actively in international supervision because at this stage of their development they necessarily concentrate their attention and resources on maintaining and strengthening their internal position. They may send representatives to the International Labour Conference and these may even on

---

[1] The Committee of Experts included among the possible reasons why the number of observations from the organizations was so small, "the still insufficient development of employers' and workers' organizations in certain countries, the shortage of qualified staff to undertake the examination of these questions, the fact that these organizations are not always fully aware of the possibilities afforded by the procedure for the examination of the application of ratified Conventions (and) their greater or more limited independence from the governmental authorities of their countries" (1963 R.C.E. 14).

[2] Already in 1934 the Conference Committee stressed that "a well-organized trade union movement may be of paramount importance as a guarantee of strict execution" (18 R.P. 538). Writing two years later, Professor Scelle recognized that the Constitution of the I.L.O. conceived "workers' and employers' associations as an autonomous social power in the Liberal State. There is no doubt that this conception and the very functioning of the International Labour Organization have been distorted by the evolution which has occurred in the countries with a dictatorial or totalitarian regime" (preface to Alexandre Berenstein, *Les Organisations Ouvrières, op. cit.,* p. X).

[3] The McNair Committee concluded in 1956 that "in the leading industrial States, in spite of the increase of government participation in the economic field, there is not much opportunity for government domination and control... In the countries which are less advanced industrially it seems that organizations of workers and employers are not so strong vis-à-vis their governments as in the leading industrial countries, and the material summarized in this report shows that in many of the less advanced countries restrictions and limitations exist which would afford opportunities of domination and control to a government desirous of using them" (XXX O.B. 581).

[4] As emphasized by the Committee of Experts in 1959 in its conclusions on the effect given to these Conventions in ratifying and non-ratifying countries (1959 R.C.E. 128).

occasion try to state their case, mostly through their group spokesmen, but such activities will usually be episodic. Yet from the point of view of effective action it is precisely by its regularity that non-governmental participation can hope to have the most visible impact over the long run.

Plainly, the institutionalization of tripartite supervision needs to be matched by a similar trend within the national organizations themselves. The questions raised by the application of ratified Conventions are too specialized and often too complex to be followed up and dealt with by the organizational leadership, unless its secretariat includes persons with some experience in legal matters and in international affairs. Even when this type of expertise is available, sufficient time must be spared from routine tasks at home to keep abreast of application questions not only in connection with I.L.O. meetings but throughout the year. All this is unlikely to happen, however, unless the organizations' role in I.L.O. supervision becomes recognized as constituting a routine function of no less importance and urgency than the other business with which the organizations must cope on a continuing basis.

From all indications, even the most highly developed and best staffed organizations in the advanced countries are seldom able or willing to attach sufficiently high priority to their supervisory tasks in order to fulfil these minimum requirements. Although no language problems arise in the case of many of these organizations, they seem to find it difficult to spare the persons needed, even on a part-time basis.[1] Yet without such a sustained follow-up at the national level and by the representative organizations themselves, the "grass roots" element of I.L.O. supervision cannot be exploited. As noted earlier, the non-governmental interests in the Conference are by no means unaware of this. As recently as 1963, the workers' members in the Application Committee, in direct response to the Experts' "surprise... that so few... comments are received each year from (the) organizations", requested assistance "in informing trade union organizations in all countries of their rights and obligations in connection with the... reports supplied by the governments on the effect given to I.L.O. standards".[2] But knowledge of these rights and obligations is

---

[1] The I.F.C.T.U. article, mentioned on p. 185 above, suggested in conclusion that each trade union should "free a permanent official to deal with international activities. For it is impossible to carry out the functions of delegate or technical adviser 'besides' (quotes in original text) the national activities and when the latter permit, and to carry out the said functions in a proper way; this will be even less possible in cases where the national language is not one of the official languages of the I.L.O. On the other hand all the questions treated have a very pronounced legal character" (*Labor, op. cit.*, p. 346).

[2] 47 R.P. 513. This initiative is similar to the one taken, also by the workers' members of the Conference Committee, in 1955. In 1963 the spokesman for these members used his speech in the plenary to address a request for help to the Workers' Relations Division of the Office (47 R.P. 421). According to the monthly news-letter of the International Federation of Petroleum and Chemical Workers, a "circular letter dealing with the role of workers' and employers' organizations in promoting the implementation of I.L.O. Conventions" was sent by the above Division "to trade-union centres of I.L.O. member countries". In addition to this circular the news-letter also contains an appeal on the same subject from the International Confederation of Free Trade Unions, stressing "the great importance which the international free trade union movement attaches to the activities of the I.L.O. in the field of establishing international labor standards and our great concern for their adequate implementation" (*Union Builder* (Denver, Colorado) (roneoed), March 1964).

only a first step and insufficient by itself unless coupled with adequate means to persevere. What counts, ultimately, is the readiness of the workers and employers to use this knowledge on a regular basis. Active participation in I.L.O. supervision thus constitutes a sort of index of their interest in the Organization and in its standards.[1]

Another important factor which may have an inhibiting influence on non-governmental supervision is an unduly nationalist outlook on the part of the workers and employers associated with it. At a time when the struggle for national entity and self-determination has set its stamp on contemporary history, it would be absurd to expect national considerations to be wholly absent from any part of international life. In the I.L.O. it is, of course, the government representatives who are directly responsible for defending their countries; and it is possible for non-government representatives to come to their support, especially when they feel that fundamental national or political interests are involved. As a rule, however, the attitude the workers and employers take in the Conference Committee is, in accordance with the tradition noted above, almost automatically one of doubtful questioning. The fact that this role is generally assumed by the groups as a whole rather than by the worker or the employer from the country under discussion, only confirms that tripartite supervision tends to submerge nationalist feelings in the vast majority of cases. Unless expressed in votes, such mental reservations or tacit dissents cannot influence the findings of the Committee. With each case of non-application considered on its merits, it is the occupational point of view which has so far prevailed in the Application Committee, more consistently perhaps than in any other body of the Conference.

In a Committee where national pride and susceptibilities might be expected, at first sight, to be particularly strong,[2] this predominance of the "non-territorial forces of integration" is of considerable significance. It shows that in this forum, at any rate, national interests do not usually carry greater weight than the collective aims and purposes of the non-government groups.[3] Those who consider the relative rareness of written comments by the workers' organizations a sign that "the trade unions act towards the I.L.O. in accordance with national criteria rather than in

---

[1] In 1922 Albert Thomas reminded the Congress of the International Federation of Trade Unions that the I.L.O. "is nothing else but a great international thermometer. If there is ardour and activity in the labour movement, its action expands. If, on the contrary, activity of the labour movement slows down and stagnates, our work too contracts" (Albert Thomas, *op. cit.*, p. 29).

[2] The Report of the Peruvian workers' delegation on the 1960 session of the Conference relates that there were "difficult moments for the workers' delegate, participating in the Conventions Committee, when confronted with criticism which, although addressed to the (Peruvian) government, affected us as trade union leaders" (*Peru ante el Mundo del Trabajo*, *op. cit.*, p. 37).

[3] Speaking of developments in the international labour movement, Lewis L. Lorwin concludes that they are "determined by the interaction of national interests and international aims and ideals with changing economic and social conditions. The purposes which brought the international labor movement into being... have come and continue to come into conflict with ideas of national interest and with nationalist attitudes in the different countries" (*The International Labor Movement* (New York: Harper, 1953), p. 333).

accordance with class interests",[1] tend to overlook the other, and perhaps more important, side of the coin: only in exceptional cases do the organizations fail to acquiesce in the critical comments which a tripartite international body publicly addresses to their governments. Nationalist attitudes are not likely to endanger the I.L.O.'s system of supervision so long as they are neutralized by the highly vocal expressions of group opinion which usually dominate and determine the proceedings of the Conference Committee. These expressions gain in weight because the workers and employers have a common interest in effective supervision which transcends, in this particular sphere, their tendency to act as countervailing forces in national and I.L.O. affairs.

*The Prospects For Strengthening Tripartite Supervision*

What are the prospects for bringing the workers' and employers' organizations and their representatives into closer association with I.L.O. supervision? It would go beyond the limits of this study to attempt to discuss the far-reaching political and structural changes required before government-dominated or weak organizations could contribute to the task. The improvements to be explored here are those within the province and the practical possibilities of the organizations themselves. Following the pattern adopted above, remedial action might be envisaged at the national and international levels.

To exploit more fully the opportunities for social progress at home requires an active interest in the effect given to Conventions, so that critical comments can be made at the appropriate moment and in a form which will enable the Committee of Experts and the Conference Committee to become aware of alleged divergencies in national law and practice. It is here that the need for greater institutionalization becomes fully apparent. Unless persons who are already acquainted with the I.L.O. assume responsibility for following up such divergencies, the prospects for more extensive non-governmental participation are unlikely to improve. Several organizations might conceivably pool their resources in order to achieve continuity of interest and follow-up.[2] Repeated appeals by the workers' members of the Conference Committee to their national organizations for regular comment on their governments' reports will find little response until these organizations are better equipped to examine the reports, to formulate their observations and to alert public opinion at home.

Is it reasonable to expect that measures of this kind can in fact be taken, i.e., that persons can be found to assume the responsibilities involved? Even if an organization is awake to the opportunities opened up by I.L.O. supervision, does it have officials who would be competent to undertake

---

[1] Cf. Anisse Salah-Bey, *L'Organisation Internationale du Travail et le Syndicalisme Mondial (1945-1960)* (Ambilly-Annemasse: Imprimerie Franco-Suisse, 1963), p. 60). The author adds that "the organizations apparently wish to avoid anything which might be considered as an accusation made against their government".

[2] The I.F.C.T.U. article quoted above, mentioned the possibility of "setting up a joint service with other confederations" (*Labor, op. cit.*, p. 346) but there is no evidence that such an attempt has actually been made.

such tasks? In the case of small or less developed countries the answer is often in the negative, so that effective participation is stifled from the start. In such cases there usually exists a broader problem of leadership training in all the phases of collective action. On the trade union side efforts are being made to deal with this problem through workers' education activities. The universities, international and national labour organizations, the International Labour Office itself,[1] have recognized the need for giving both the leaders and the rank and file a better understanding of their role in industrial and public life. Once it is realized that greater participation in I.L.O. supervision can help in promoting and achieving the objectives of an organization, those responsible for workers' education courses will perhaps make I.L.O. standards and supervision a more regular part of their curricula. Any national organizations which are deterred by language difficulties, by lack of familiarity with legal questions, etc. might turn to their international federations for advice and assistance.

Because of their special status in the I.L.O. and their experience of international questions, the world associations of workers' and employers' organizations are probably better prepared than most of their affiliates to exploit the potentialities of tripartite supervision. They should be well able, first of all, to advise their member organizations on how to draw application difficulties to the attention of their governments. This role of the world associations would resemble, in some respects, that of the legal aid societies which exist in many countries for the purpose of helping people of limited means and experience to safeguard their rights under the law. The national organizations could avail themselves of this specialized advice throughout the year, but they are most in need of assistance just before and during the annual sessions of the I.L.O. Conference when infringements of ratified Conventions can be discussed directly with governments.

In order to prepare these discussions, the world associations of workers' or employers' organizations could utilize any background information received from their affiliated organizations.[2] Their function would thus be first of all to secure such data. The repeated appeals to the national organizations, made by the workers' members of the Conference Committee and supported by the I.C.F.T.U. and the I.F.C.T.U., confirm the need for additional first-hand information. But the principal opportunity for strengthening tripartite supervision lies in the use made of this information during the discussions in the Conference Committee.

---

[1] In his Report to the 1963 session of the Conference, the Director-General proposed that "the I.L.O. should lay greater stress upon long-term workers' education activities under its own auspices" and referred especially to the training of trade union leaders (47 D.R. 79-81). For a review of the I.L.O.'s workers' education programme cf. doc. G.B.154/O.P./D.4/5 (roneoed).

[2] During the inter-war period the International Federation of Trade Unions urged its national organizations not only to send observations to their governments but also to inform the I.F.T.U. itself of "the general situation in their countries as regards the application of international labour Conventions, and to submit to us any suggestions they may deem useful for our report to the workers' group". In quoting from this I.F.T.U. circular, Zarras adds that the Federation published a yearly report on the application of Conventions in the various countries "based on the information received from the affiliated trade union centres" (*op. cit.*, p. 203).

Because the workers and employers in the Committee take the lead in these discussions, much depends on the extent to which they can prepare their stand and their arguments in advance. As noted, group meetings are regularly held for this purpose, but the participants may not always be familiar with the questions to be discussed or even with I.L.O. supervision as such. The prospects of tripartite supervision would improve if the non-governmental groups could rely on some sort of regular assistance both before and during the meetings of the Conference Committee, in order to prepare the discussions and in order to carry them through. It would of course be for the workers' and employers' members themselves to decide on the specific forms which such assistance might take. But it would not be contrary to their independence and autonomy if they would call on their own international confederations to lend a helping hand in this connection. An arrangement of this kind would moreover give an added degree of continuity to the yearly efforts of the two groups to participate effectively in mutual supervision.

While this continuity could never match that of the Committee of Experts, a year-to-year thread might emerge in the deliberations of the Conference Committee which would add to its cumulative impact over the long term. To achieve this, however, the workers and employers need to plan and pursue their collective action on a more systematic basis. Their interest, their knowledge and their skill are the determining factors in exploiting the unique opportunities which I.L.O. supervision offers to the non-governmental elements associated with it.

## IV. The Emergence of Political Problems

More than three decades after its establishment, the I.L.O.'s machinery of supervision came face to face with a new problem. The governments of Eastern Europe began to challenge the objectivity and validity of the findings of the Committee of Experts on the effect given in their countries to the three freedom of association Conventions. Although disagreement with the technical conclusions and suggestions of this Committee was by no means unprecedented, it was not until 1959 that its competence and impartiality were specifically called in question.

This development coincided with the Committee of Experts' examination and evaluation of the first reports by the U.S.S.R. on the application of Conventions Nos. 11, 87 and 98, ratified in 1956. In its response [1] the government questioned the Committee's ability to understand the social and economic context within which the Conventions were being implemented in the countries concerned. In subsequent years an attempt was also made to question the Committee's traditional mode of operation and principles. On the other hand, the findings of the Committee of Experts regarding the many other instruments devoid of such political significance were not only accepted but acted upon by the Eastern European countries, as noted in Chapter Three.

---

[1] The points raised by the Committee and the arguments put forward in reply are summed up on pp. 94-96 above.

For the first time in 1959, Soviet representatives in the plenary Conference openly warned the Committee of Experts "against going along the wrong road"[1] and expressed doubts that it was "an entirely objective and impartial organ".[2] In the years that followed the Committee was criticized for its "purely abstract juridical approach"[3] and its work was described as "one-sided, tendentious and formalistic".[4]

In 1963 the U.S.S.R. government member proposed to the Conference Committee that rules defining the composition and organization of the Committee of Experts be framed and that these rules incorporate certain basic principles such as "an objective appraisal of formal and actual facts", the taking into consideration of "the economic and social conditions of each country", the "equitable representation in the Committee of Experts of different social and economic systems and geographic regions as well as the replacement of its members at regular intervals".[5] This proposal gave rise to a lively discussion, first in the Conference Committee and then in the plenary. As summed up in the Conference Committee's Report, "a large number of government members, the employers' members and the great majority of the workers' members did not agree on the need to establish such formal rules", since they had "faith in the impartiality, objectivity and integrity of the Committee of Experts... Objectivity could not be guaranteed by rules of procedure but depended upon the personal qualities of the members of the Committee; detailed rules might, on the contrary, lead to subjective appraisals".[4]

Similar arguments were put forward in the plenary, by both the opponents and the supporters of the Soviet proposal. A United States government adviser emphasized the "heart-warming fact that the conclusions in the Experts' Report, with the exception of that portion dealing with Convention No. 87, were arrived at unanimously".[6] A Venezuelian workers' adviser called the proposal "unnecessary, dangerous and vexatious".[7] A Canadian employers' adviser expressed the view that to interpret I.L.O. Conventions "in different ways depending upon the economic and social structure of the countries concerned" would lead to "a double standard".[8] The author of the proposal, on the other hand, reiterated his contention that "the present system of supervision of application is ill-adjusted to the new conditions" and called on those opposing his suggestions to make counterproposals.[9] No formal vote was taken on the matter, but there was evidence that in addition to the delegates from Eastern Europe some from Africa agreed with the idea of imposing restraints on a Committee which had called on their governments to bring their law and practice into

---

[1] In the words of a U.S.S.R. government representative (43 R.P. 545).

[2] In the words of a U.S.S.R. workers' representative (43 R.P. 543).

[3] By a Polish government representative (46 R.P. 414).

[4] During the discussions in the Conference Committee in 1962 (46 R.P. 679).

[5] 47 R.P. 514.

[6] This point was made by Representative James Roosevelt of California (47 R.P. 419).

[7] 47 R.P. 431.

[8] 47 R.P. 421.

[9] 47 R.P. 426.

line with the I.L.O. standards on freedom of association and on forced labour.[1]

While it would clearly be premature to attempt an assessment of the significance of these proposals, it may be useful to recall certain pertinent facts. Firstly, the general idea of precise rules of procedure for a supervisory organ of the I.L.O. is not wholly new, although it had never been put forward in relation to the Committee of Experts. [2] Secondly, the appointments to the Committee made by the Governing Body in recent years have resulted in a pattern of regional distribution which reflects fairly closely the extent to which ratifications have been received from the various parts of the world. If purely arithmetical criteria are applied,[3] Asia, South America and Eastern Europe are found to be somewhat over-represented, whereas the African continent has less than its theoretical share. The presence in the Committee of persons from every part of the world naturally facilitates the task of examination because their familiarity with local laws and conditions adds to the sum total of knowledge and experience available. During the discussion in the Conference Committee one member pointed out in this connection that since the Committee of Experts was "required to act in a quasi-judicial capacity... long experience of its work was necessary to its proper functioning. Moreover, as shown by recent appointments..., there was no danger that membership would become static".[4]

Thirdly, the need for objectivity lies at the heart of the Committee of Experts' traditions. When the Committee used the occasion of its 30th anniversary to sum up those traditions in its Report, it described its functions as "pointing out in a spirit of complete independence and entire objectivity" to what extent the member States comply with their obligations and as "avoiding all political considerations in the technical and juridical examina-

---

[1] Mr. Borna, the Minister of Finance and Labour of Dahomey, suggested in a speech to the plenary that "the composition of the Committee of Experts (be) reconsidered, to avoid having our States judged by experts who, valuable though they may be, do not know anything at all about the facts of Africa and think that Algiers is the capital of Tanganyika and Dahomey the capital of Nigeria" (47 R.P. 81). At the time this statement was made, the Chief Justices of Nigeria and Senegal were both members of the Committee.

[2] As indicated in footnote 5, p. 48 above, a Mexican government delegate suggested in 1951 that the Standing Orders of the Conference Committee should be revised, so as to give it "precise terms of reference". No action was taken on this suggestion.

[3] Expressed in percentages, the respective shares of each region in the total number of ratifications and in the total membership of the Committee of Experts were as follows on 30 June 1964:

| Region | Per cent of Ratifications | Per cent of Committee Members |
| --- | --- | --- |
| Western Europe | 27 | 27 |
| Eastern Europe | 12 | 16 |
| Africa | 23 | 10 |
| Middle East | 6 | 5 |
| Asia | 10 | 16 |
| North and Central America (including Caribbean) | 11 | 10 |
| South America | 11 | 16 |

[4] Statement of the British government member (doc. C.App.C./PV.6, 47th Session of the Conference (roneoed), p. 10).

tion" entrusted to it. It concluded that "impartiality and objectivity are the fundamental rules of conduct which the Committee has set itself in performing its work".[1]

As regards, finally, the bearing of the social and economic conditions or system of a country on the application of any I.L.O. Convention, the Nigerian government member in the Conference Committee recalled that such conditions "did not fall within the Committee of Experts' terms of reference".[2] While the Committee has never questioned the right of certain countries to avail themselves of the flexibility clauses introduced in a Convention under article 19, paragraph 3, of the I.L.O. Constitution in order to meet the climatic, industrial or other special circumstances of these countries[3] and has shown understanding for the economic and social difficulties which may determine the pace at which full compliance can be achieved,[4] it has also stressed that from a legal point of view nothing short of full compliance can be accepted, especially in the case of the fundamental human rights standards. The Committee has moreover insisted that it must treat all ratifying States alike. To attempt to "express any view concerning the systems of different countries" would, in the words it used in 1963, constitute a "violation of its mandate".[5] It is in the Conference, rather than the Committee of Experts, that such extra-legal considerations can and do find expression.

While it is futile to speculate at this point on the possible consequences of such political difficulties for I.L.O. supervision, it hardly seems possible that anyone would wish to stake the existence of the whole system on a particular issue, basic though it may be. The resolution of these difficulties may be facilitated by the passage of time and may well depend, ultimately, on what happens in East-West relations, rather than on any developments within the I.L.O. itself.

---

[1] 1957 R.C.E. 3.

[2] Doc. C.App.C./PV.3, 47th Session of the Conference (roneoed), p. 8.

[3] Cf. p. 123 above.

[4] Cf. pp. 121 and 131 above.

[5] 1963 R.C.E. 85. The Committee replied here to the opinion voiced by the members from Poland and the U.S.S.R. that its observations on the freedom of association Conventions distorted "the aspects of social reality and may lead to erroneous conclusions". Cf. footnote 1, p. 96 above.

# Chapter Seven

# SOME CONCLUSIONS

The introductory pages of this study pointed to the possible role of international supervision as a stabilizing factor in the increasingly complex and close-knit world of today. Any such role is inconceivable, however, unless the supervisory arrangements can operate with some degree of success and the present inquiry was principally conceived as an attempt to measure and assess the extent of such impact, on the basis of a working model. It is now possible to put forward some tentative conclusions, in order to sum up the results of the inquiry, to bring out the lessons which have emerged and to determine whether the I.L.O.'s experience can be of value to other spheres of international organization.

## I. The Statistical Findings

The degree of effectiveness of international norms or procedures can be assessed either by selecting a set of typical case histories or by trying to survey the over-all influence of a system on as comprehensive a basis as possible. The present study uses these two methods together in the hope that the practical experience gained in a series of typical cases will help to illustrate and explain the over-all results, as expressed in purely statistical terms.

This combined approach seems preferable because any mere accumulation of figures, even when based on a very large number of formal international undertakings, must be interpreted with some circumspection lest too much be read into the results. Two factors, in particular, justify this note of caution: firstly, the critical comments of the supervisory organs are more concerned with legislative compliance than with the practical effect given to Conventions; secondly, the points raised in these comments are necessarily of varying seriousness.

Even when these limitations are taken into account, the total figures can provide a significant insight into the need for I.L.O. supervision and into its results. They show that, out of the nearly 3,500 ratifications and declarations of application subject to systematic follow-up, the supervisory committees have not felt it necessary to make any critical observations in close to 2,500 cases. For almost three-quarters of the formal undertakings subject to supervision no evidence of infringements has thus been brought to light, presumably because many governments had taken care to accept only those international obligations to which they could give effect. Perhaps, as discussed below, the existence of a regular system of supervision discouraged some governments from assuming such obligations. In any event, the relatively high proportion of cases where no evidence of violation has ever been turned up tends to confirm that the so-called "paper ratifications" represent the exception rather than the rule, as has been claimed at times.

The results of the observations also permit some general conclusions. All in all, the comments of the Committee of Experts and of the Conference Committee have not succeeded, in somewhat more than one-third of the one thousand cases of non-compliance, in inducing the States concerned to initiate the necessary implementing action. The analysis of the results in Chapter Three has, moreover, disclosed some interesting variations as between groups of Conventions and of countries. In particular, the economic and administrative difficulties which confront the developing countries are clearly reflected in their record of compliance and in the time required before action is taken.

Does the sum total of the statistical findings provide a clear-cut answer as to the degree of success or failure of I.L.O. supervision? In purely quantitative terms the results leave little doubt that the supervisory procedures have made the vast majority of States aware of the need for discharging their treaty obligations to the full. On the whole, the fact-finding function of international supervision has therefore had the desired effect. When it comes to the second function, that of promoting governmental action, the results are rather less conclusive: in some 63 per cent of the cases, systematic follow-up did lead to implementing action in the form of full or partial measures of compliance or even of a denunciation. Although this leaves over one-third of the cases where no impact is noticeable, such a degree of response must be regarded as sufficient evidence that I.L.O. supervision has proved its powers of persuasion in relation to a sizable proportion of the violations with which it has had to deal.[1] To what reasons can this degree of persuasiveness be attributed?

## II. The Sources of Strength of I.L.O. Supervision

The elements of strength and of weakness in I.L.O. supervision fall, broadly, under two headings, depending on whether they can be traced to the structure of the system or to its operation. The factors in the first category are connected with the fundamental origin and powers of the system, and might therefore be called "organic". The factors in the second category have emerged gradually over the years as the system has developed, and might therefore be called "operational". This distinction between the intrinsic and acquired features of I.L.O. supervision seems to be significant not only in exploring its effectiveness but also in assessing its relevance to other systems of international supervision.

Foremost among the inherent elements which give strength to the system are the legal obligations on which its structure and operation depend. Ratification of an international labour Convention not only represents an

---

[1] Professor Haas concludes, in summing up the working and results of I.L.O. supervision, that it has "a record of which any international agency can be intensely proud". Cf. *Beyond the Nation-State, op. cit.,* p. 258.

undertaking to carry out its terms over a specified and lengthy period of time but also involves the supply of reports at regular intervals and in accordance with a searching questionnaire. This questionnaire moreover requires the governments to answer the queries and comments made by the I.L.O.'s Committees, so that the supervisory process can proceed on the basis of up-to-date authoritative information.

Another organic source of strength is the combination of technical and political stages in the machinery of supervision. Every year, the examination by independent experts is followed by tripartite discussion, so that the task assigned to each Committee is facilitated by the division of labour between them. This institutional integration of two distinct and well-defined phases of supervision has clearly added to the over-all impact of the system.

In addition to the periodic supervision procedure involving the two Committees, there also exists the possibility of representations and complaints lodged in virtue of the I.L.O. Constitution. Much was expected in the early days of the simultaneous existence of two parallel systems, which might make it possible to apply pressure on a progressive scale, according to the circumstances of a given case. This potential organic asset proved, however, to be of limited practical value, as discussed more fully below.

The final element of intrinsic strength in I.L.O. supervision is the organic participation of non-governmental elements in the examination of reports and particularly in the discussions at the Conference. Ingrained diplomatic traditions and attitudes make it unusual for one State to criticize the conduct of another, unless major political questions are at issue. The burden of supervision in the Conference Committee falls, therefore, on its workers' and employers' members and the persistent intervention of their spokesmen provides its greatest source of strength. The initiative taken by the two non-government groups in drawing up a special list of serious cases illustrates the potentialities of tripartite supervision but here also certain operational weaknesses have emerged which require mention in the next section.

In the course of its evolution over the years certain additional elements have reinforced I.L.O. supervision. Foremost among these is the growing interdependence of the two Committees. As noted above, each was conceived as a separate organ serving a well-defined purpose but with the passage of time their operation has become fully co-ordinated: the Conference Committee relies more and more on the preliminary fact-finding carried out by the Committee of Experts and the latter benefits in turn from the deliberations and prestige of the Conference, as the supreme body of the Organization. It is in fact difficult to conceive the system, in retrospect, in any other form than with the two organs sharing their different but equally essential tasks. This crystallization of tasks requires fuller analysis.

The main burden has been carried from the beginning by the Committee of Experts whose responsibility for a thorough and objective technical examination has made it the pivot of the whole system. If the I.L.O.'s supervisory activities have not only managed to cope with the steady expansion in the network of treaty obligations but have in fact done so through improved and apparently more effective methods, the main credit must undoubtedly go to the Committee of Experts. In addition to the eminence of its individual members, the Committee has acquired a collective personality and tradition of its own, thereby enhancing the prestige of I.L.O. supervision as a whole.

The authority of such a body resides to no small degree in the independence of its members. Not only are they chosen because they do not represent any national or occupational interests, but the Director-General acts on his own initiative and responsibility in submitting their names to the Governing Body for appointment. This method of selection, though still exceptional in present-day international organization,[1] seems particularly well-suited for a quasi-judicial body whose functions are essentially international in character.

The nature of its functions leads the Committee of Experts to question governments on a multitude of detailed points and, where necessary, to indicate the shortcomings it has discovered. It is a measure of the confidence which the Committee has been able to generate that governments have, with very rare exceptions, come to accept these critical comments and have never thought of joining forces to oppose the Committee's findings. The tact and courtesy with which the Committee places its views on record have thus been conducive to securing the governments' trust and co-operation. Because its members have no responsibility for their own countries, the Committee of Experts submits the results of its annual examination as an expression of its collective opinion and judgment. If this collective technical approach were ever to be seriously challenged, the supervision procedure would certainly lose a major element of strength.

The practical evolution of the system seems to confirm the pivotal role of the Committee of Experts. As the network of obligations has expanded, the burden of supervision has had to be shouldered more and more by this technical organ in order to clear the way for meaningful tripartite examination. As a result, the Conference Committee now has the possibility of concentrating its attention on the really major cases of non-observance. The acceptance of broader responsibilities by the Committee of Experts constitutes concrete evidence of how indispensable and crucial its contribution to I.L.O. supervision has become over the years.

Such a shift of duties to the technical organ might well have upset the whole balance of the system, had the political organ of supervision not possessed a decisive weight of its own. This stability is due basically to the fact that the Conference Committee on Application is a tripartite organ which functions within the framework of the supreme assembly of the I.L.O. But here again an organic element of strength has acquired further

---

[1] As a rule governments are asked to propose names for a panel from which the members of the supervisory bodies are selected. In the case of the European Social Charter, e.g., the Committee of Experts which is to examine the reports on the effect given to the charter is selected from a list of persons nominated by the Contracting Parties (article 25, paragraph 1, of the Charter, *European Treaty Series*, No. 35).

Similarly, the draft Covenant on Civil and Political Rights which the Commission on Human Rights submitted to the Economic and Social Council in 1954 provided for the establishment of a "Human Rights Committee" to which charges of non-compliance with the Covenant might be submitted. Under article 28 of the draft Covenant the members of this Committee would be elected from a list of persons nominated by the States Parties to the Covenant (United Nations, Economic and Social Council, Official Records of the 18th Session, Supplement No. 7 (doc. E/CN.4/705), p. 69).

validity through the practical operation of the system. The prestige of the Conference Committee is certainly even greater today than it was in its early years.

Uniformity of approach is another element which has gradually tended to strengthen supervision. A network of treaty obligations as vast and varied as the I.L.O.'s requires a maximum of cohesion and homogeneity in its administration. Although neither the Committee of Experts nor even the Conference have been given any powers of interpretation, the rulings which have emerged from many years of supervision make up a sort of "case law" which in turn embodies consistent criteria applicable to all countries and added to from year to year.

Uniformity of appreciation in defining violations of a ratified treaty and in specifying the measures required for fuller compliance does not prevent the supervisory organs, on the other hand, from being realistic in regard to the speed with which they expect a country to reach the ultimate objective of full application. Some flexibility of approach becomes a necessity when economic difficulties have to be overcome, and a certain degree of latitude must be left to the government in reaching a decision as to the practical methods and the speed of implementation. Insistence on faithful discharge of obligations, combined with realism in appraising the rate of progress towards this goal, produce the kind of governmental response which helps supervision even in those cases where the existing obstacles seem, at first sight, to be insurmountable.

This mixture of firmness and realism has been found, over the years, to be more effective than undue criticism and censure. The two Committees attempt to include in their observations concrete suggestions designed to assist a government in eliminating infractions. The experience gained by other countries in similar circumstances, the clarification of the bearing of a Convention, the availability of technical aid, are mentioned as incentives in securing more satisfactory implementation. This constructive, promotional method represents a useful tool in seeking a positive response from governments. It helps to improve the observance of standards far more than a mere recital of neglected obligations.

This realistic approach in promoting governmental action is coupled with a similar approach in the definition of objectives. Without disregarding the need for practical measures of implementation, the supervisory organs have always been aware that their first and principal aim must be the achievement of legislative compliance with I.L.O. standards. By placing their main emphasis on this clearly defined and attainable goal, the Committees have enhanced their chances of success in the short term and left open the possibility of obtaining a maximum of practical compliance in the long run.


### III. The Weak Points of I.L.O. Supervision

Here also, a distinction can be drawn between organic flaws on the one hand and operational weaknesses on the other. As will be seen, the principal weakness of I.L.O. supervision may well be due to its apparent failure to benefit fully from certain of its greatest organic assets.

There would be little point to dwell here at any length on one of the basic weaknesses of almost all contemporary efforts at international supervision, i.e. its reliance on what has been called "sociological sanctions".[1] At the present stage of international relations and world order it would be illusory to expect any global system to possess powers of compulsion, combined with sanctions which would go beyond the limits of public censure.

A related inhibiting factor is that I.L.O. supervision cannot operate effectively without the collaboration of the offending State. Technical examination depends on the supply of a report. Mutual supervision is seriously impeded if the government concerned fails to participate in the work of the Conference Committee or, worse yet, of the Conference. Although such refusals to co-operate have been rather exceptional, the possibility of their occurring can never be excluded.

Of more far-reaching practical importance has been the obvious reluctance to make use of the formal representations and complaints procedure in cases where the periodic system of supervision has failed for a number of years to secure any improvements in the observance of a Convention. To some extent the very development of the regular system has rendered recourse to the judicial procedures less necessary than originally contemplated. But it seems surprising that the Conference Committee which has increasingly spotlighted the most serious cases should not have considered on occasion, when faced with a particularly unyielding situation, to bring the procedure under article 26 of the Constitution into play or to notify its intention of invoking this article unless there is early evidence of progress. The rarity of such an initiative would be likely to produce the kind of psychological impact which prolonged repetition of the same critical comments can no longer achieve. The case of Liberia provides an instructive example of this stimulating effect of a complaint and of the progress which can be obtained when the two parallel systems of supervision are used in conjunction.

Another area where only partial benefit has so far been derived from a potential asset is in connection with tripartite supervision. The crucial role of the workers and employers, both in securing fuller information and in persuading governments to take action, clearly places a special responsibility on their organizations. Much has been said in these pages about the unique character of non-governmental supervision and about its theoretical and practical implications. If the workers and employers minimize the importance of international standards and of their implementation, the impact of I.L.O. supervision will inevitably be weakened. The system is not so potent in its means of action that tripartite leverage can easily be dispensed with. To the contrary, the possibility of such leverage may tip the balance in precisely those cases where other means of influence have proved largely ineffective.

Despite the positive contribution which the employers' and the workers' groups already make to the success of the Conference Committee's work, as noted above, both groups have recognized that much could be done inside the individual countries to acquaint the representative organizations

---

[1] Hugo J. Hahn, "Internationale Kontrollen", *op. cit.*, p. 90.

further with their rights and responsibilities under the I.L.O. Constitution and ratified Conventions. Even in the Conference itself such action could be placed on a more solid and more continuous basis. Unless these possibilities are more generally understood by those directly concerned and unless the organizations are sufficiently developed and sufficiently free to exploit them, I.L.O. supervision will lack strength in the one area where it is best equipped, in theory, to operate effectively.

## IV. Has I.L.O. Supervision Stimulated or Discouraged Ratification?

When systematic supervision was first proposed in the I.L.O., a frequent argument in favour was the hesitation of some governments to ratify a Convention unless its application in other countries was followed up systematically. The British resolution of 1926 cited as one of the aims of the proposed procedure "to further... general ratification" of Conventions. But a totally different line of reasoning was also put forward, then and in later years, by those who argued that strict supervision would, on the contrary, discourage ratification.[1]

It would be idle to speculate at length about the precise nature of this interrelationship between ratification and supervision. From a legal and political point of view, a ratification motivated by the absence of strict supervisory measures gives less promise of implementation than one which is based on the prospect of close follow-up. The argument that supervision impedes ratification may therefore undermine what is most tangible and constructive in international standards and organization.

Leaving aside these rather abstract considerations, the question seems to have received a fairly clear practical answer during the three decades of I.L.O. supervision. Over a period when the technical and mutual examination procedures have noticeably gained in strictness, the rate of ratification has accelerated rather than slowed down. It is obvious, then, that governments have not refrained from assuming additional obligations because they thereby subjected themselves to international scrutiny and perhaps to criticism.

There is always a possibility, of course, that certain governments either were not aware of the extent of this scrutiny or decided deliberately, in advance, to ignore it. Neither of these alternatives seems very plausible however. Few States which attend the yearly sessions of the International Labour Conference can remain ignorant for very long of the operation and

---

[1] In 1926 Professor Mahaim of Belgium, who had played a pioneering role in the establishment of the I.L.O., wondered whether "in the face of the small number of ratifications... this tightening up of supervision... is really opportune" (8 R.P. 249). Speaking in the Governing Body some ten years later, the French labour leader, Mr. Jouhaux, expressed the fear that if supervision was carried any further "governments might be still more cautious than at present in ratifying Conventions" (74 G.B. 16).

A very similar opinion was recently put forward in the United Nations by the U.S.S.R. government when commenting on proposals for supervising the implementation of the draft International Covenants on Human Rights : "The inclusion in the draft Covenants of any measures of implementation that would open the door to interference in the internal affairs of States... would not contribute to the ratification of the Covenants by the largest possible number of States" (General Assembly, 18th Session, doc. A/5411/Add.1, p. 4).

the implications of I.L.O. supervision. Fewer still would wish to invite the prospect of repeated and increasingly incisive censure in an international forum. One encounters here, once more, the problem of the "ratification of principle" which troubled the I.L.O. in its early days. It is hard to estimate how many of these have been received in more recent years. But the fact that only two per cent of the Committee's observations have so far led to the denunciation of a Convention certainly shows that governments are disinclined to terminate their obligations even though they may have been motivated in some cases by reasons of prestige or propaganda.

On balance, any negative and positive effects of supervision on ratification have probably cancelled each other out in the long run. In any case the early fears of a strongly discouraging influence have not materialized. It is probable therefore that the main significance of I.L.O. supervision lies not so much in its pre-ratification impact than in the constant emphasis on the need for implementation with which all governments are confronted once they have ratified.

## V. The Relevance of I.L.O. Experience to Other Fields of International Supervision

As noted above, both the organic and the operational features of I.L.O. supervision can be reflected in other spheres of international organization. Have there been any concrete attempts by other organizations where the I.L.O.'s experience was or could become a factor?

The example of the I.L.O. is of course most pertinent in those cases where standards of a similar character have been elaborated by other organizations, where there exists an obligation to report regularly on the implementation of these standards and where machinery has been set up to examine such reports. When the Council of Europe decided to adopt a European Social Charter, it asked the I.L.O. to assist in its preparation. The instrument which emerged in 1961 not only contains a number of provisions which are based on those of international labour Conventions and Recommendations but also institutes a system of expert and mutual supervision patterned to a considerable extent on that of the I.L.O.[1] This link will continue now that the Charter has entered into force, since an I.L.O. representative will participate in a consultative capacity in the deliberations of the committee of experts to which the technical examination of the reports on the application of the Charter is to be entrusted (article 26 of the Charter). Aside from the somewhat different method of selection of the members of this committee,[2] the second, political stage of the supervisory procedure instituted by the European Social Charter also differs in certain respects from the comparable phase in the I.L.O. The subcommittee of the Governmental Social Committee of the Council of

---

[1] As regards the influence of the I.L.O. system of supervision on the European system, cf. "The European Social Charter and International Labour Standards", *International Labour Review*, Vol. LXXXIV, Nos. 5-6 (November-December 1961), pp. 354-375, 462-477. For a comparison of the two systems, cf. also F.M. van Asbeck, "La Charte Sociale Européenne: Sa Portée Juridique, La Mise en Œuvre", *Mélanges Offerts à Henri Rollin* (Paris: Pédone, 1964), pp. 427-448.

[2] Cf. footnote 1, p. 200 above.

Europe, which is to perform the same function as the International Labour Conference Committee on Application, will meet in private and will be composed exclusively of representatives of States which have ratified the Charter. Employers and workers will participate in the meetings of this subcommittee in a purely consultative capacity, through two international organizations of employers and of trade unions, invited by the subcommittee, and these organizations will only have the status of observers (article 27). The conclusions of this subcommittee are to be placed before the Consultative Assembly and the Committee of Ministers of the Council where the representatives of States which have not ratified the Charter participate (articles 28 and 29), but the Committee of Ministers requires a majority of two-thirds to make "recommendations" to a State in regard to its application of the Charter.

Despite the definite resemblances between the two systems of supervision, that of the I.L.O. is clearly broader in scope, due in particular to the tripartite and unrestricted character of the membership of its Conference Committee.[1] Regardless of these understandable differences of emphasis, the fact remains that one system of international supervision has served as a general model for another. This process was, moreover, repeated again, more recently, when the European Code of Social Security was signed in April 1964.[2]

The supervisory arrangements of the I.L.O. were also kept in mind in devising a procedure to follow up the implementation of the U.N.E.S.C.O. Convention against Discrimination in Education, adopted in 1960. The General Conference of U.N.E.S.C.O. was asked in 1964 to take the necessary decisions which, in the words of its Director-General, would "have a considerable influence on the Organization's general policy and methods in all its activity relating to the establishment of standards".[3] The reliance on I.L.O. precedent in developing these proposals–which covered all the various aspects of supervision such as questionnaires, frequency of reporting, expert and conference examination–is made very clear in the document [4] and this transposition of experience is especially interesting when the association of "non-governmental authorities, groups or individuals" in the

---

[1] Professor van Asbeck concludes from his comparison that "the I.L.O. procedure seems to be stronger than that of the Council of Europe not only because of the cooperation of the occupational organizations on a basis of equality with the governments, but also because of the publicity which prevails during the final phase of the procedure in the International Labour Conference" ("La Charte Sociale Européenne: Sa Portée Juridique, La Mise en Oeuvre", *op. cit.*, p. 446).

[2] *European Treaty Series*, No. 48. Supervision is entrusted in this case to the Committee of Experts on Social Security, and to the Committee of Ministers of the Council of Europe. The governments' reports on the application of the Code are also submitted to the "appropriate body" of the I.L.O., i.e. presumably to its Committee of Experts on Application of Conventions and Recommendations.

[3] General Conference, 13th Session, doc. 13 C/12, p. 2.

[4] "International experience in this matter and, more especially, that of the International Labour Organization which, for more than forty years, has been developing procedures and machinery for consideration of States' reports, might be of service in solving the problems confronting Unesco... (T)he noteworthy service rendered by (the I.L.O.'s) Committee of Experts in the complex and continuing task of supervising international instruments in the social sector affords an example." (doc. 13 C/12, p. 10).

task of supervision is suggested. Thus it is proposed that the States' reports be transmitted to the National Commissions for U.N.E.S.C.O. for observation, before they are communicated to U.N.E.S.C.O. itself,[1] and that non-governmental organizations be also given the possibility "to submit their comments". The Director-General's proposals were approved by the General Conference in November 1964.[2]

Another sphere where measures of supervision have been under discussion for some time is in relation to the two draft International Covenants on Human Rights pending before the United Nations Assembly. In 1963 the Secretary-General submitted to the Assembly a paper designed to clarify "the main issues involved in the implementation" of the proposed Covenants.[3] As recalled in this document the drafts adopted in 1954 for different human rights contained different measures of implementation: the draft Covenant on Civil and Political Rights, which foresaw the immediate guarantee of a set of relatively precise liberties, envisaged the establishment both of a system of reports by governments and of a complaints procedure; the draft Covenant on Economic, Social and Cultural Rights, which was formulated in more general terms and which was to be applied progressively, merely called for the supply of periodical reports to be considered by the Economic and Social Council as well as, possibly, by the U.N. Commission on Human Rights. The Secretariat paper pointed out the advantages of a reporting system, describing it as "a common method for encouraging promotion and observance of human rights".[4] The I.L.O.'s procedures were repeatedly referred to in this context as well as in connection with the initiation of complaints for alleged breaches of the Covenant on Civil and Political Rights.[5] The role which non-governmental organizations play in I.L.O. supervision was also fully covered throughout the document.

Without giving a detailed account of the proposals pending since 1954 [6] or of the discussions which took place in the Third Committee of the General Assembly in 1963–particularly as no decision has yet been reached–some

---

[1] The analogy of such a procedure with the constitutional obligation in the I.L.O. to communicate copies of the reports to the representative organizations of employers and workers, is emphasized (doc. 13 C/12, p. 11).

[2] The Conference asked the Executive Board of U.N.E.S.C.O. to take appropriate measures for the implementation of the proposed plan (30th Plenary Meeting, doc. 13 C/VR.30 (roneoed), p. 19). During the discussion of the proposals in the Legal Committee the French, British and United States members supported the establishment of an "independent and objective committee of experts... similar to the one set up by the I.L.O."; the U.S.S.R. and Spanish members opposed it (doc. 13 C/LEG/S.R. 8 (roneoed), pp. 13-15).

[3] General Assembly, 18th Session, doc. A/5411, p. 4.

[4] Doc. A/5411, p. 8.

[5] This exchange of experience is likely to continue. Thus a resolution adopted by the Economic and Social Council in July 1965 calls on the executive heads of the United Nations, U.N.E.S.C.O. and the I.L.O. to prepare reports on "their respective existing organizational and procedural arrangements for the implementation of conventions and recommendations in the field of human rights, including information on past experience as appropriate" (doc. E/RES/1075 (XXXIX)). During the discussion the representatives of Czechoslovakia, Rumania and the U.S.S.R. spoke against this resolution which was finally adopted by 14 votes to none, with three abstentions (doc. E/SR.1392, pp. 5-9).

[6] Cf. Official Records of the 18th Session of the Economic and Social Council, Supplement No. 7 (doc. E/CN.4/705).

points seem worth noting in the light of I.L.O. experience. It is interesting first of all that an attempt had been made to draw a line between what might be called political and non-political rights and that this had led to a particularly clear-cut distinction in the field of implementation. Whereas a complaints procedure exists for all I.L.O. Conventions, it is provided for only in the draft Covenant on Civil and Political Rights. It is for this reason perhaps that during the discussions in the Third Committee in 1963 general agreement centred on the system of implementation proposed for the draft Covenant on Economic, Social and Cultural Rights.[1] Secondly, the periodical reports required under this latter system are not to be examined by independent technical experts but are to go directly to the Economic and Social Council, i.e. to a body composed of government representatives. The Italian member of the Third Committee called therefore for a decision "whether a group of experts should be appointed by the Economic and Social Council to undertake a first survey",[2] but there was apparently no immediate echo to this suggestion.[3] A third point concerns the absence from the draft Covenants of any provisions authorizing non-governmental organizations to comment on the fulfilment of these instruments. A proposal in 1954 to provide for such comments in the draft Covenant on Economic, Social and Cultural Rights proved unsuccessful [4] and does not seem to have been renewed during the Assembly discussions in 1963. While institutionalized non-governmental participation has been a regular element of I.L.O. supervision for many years and is also in the process of finding acceptance in U.N.E.S.C.O. and in the Council of Europe, the prospects for its introduction into the proposed human rights implementation measures thus seem rather slight at the present stage.

This slow progress in the field of human rights standards must be contrasted with the considerable role which United Nations supervision has played in relation to colonial questions. Acting on the basis of the reporting provisions written into articles 73 and 87 of the Charter, the Committee on Non-Self-Governing Territories and the Trusteeship Council, composed of government representatives, have functioned as political organs during a period when the process of decolonization has been in full swing. The setting up by the General Assembly, in 1961, of the Special Committee on the Situation with Regard to the Implementation of the Declaration on the Granting of Independence to Colonial Countries and Peoples has been a further interesting development in this process.[5] Perhaps the acceptance

---

[1] Cf. General Assembly, 17th Session, Report of the Third Committee (doc. A/5655), p. 28.

[2] General Assembly, 18th Session, doc. A/C.3/S.R.1277, p. 6.

[3] It is true that under article 17, paragraph 2(b), of the draft Covenant on Economic, Social and Cultural Rights a copy or relevant extracts of a government's report must be sent to a specialized agency of which it is a member, so that the expert supervisory organs of such agencies could presumably try to evaluate the degree of application. If such an indirect and partial method of technical supervision were in fact to emerge, it would merely point up the need for more generalized arrangements of this kind.

[4] Cf. doc. E/2573, pp. 12-13.

[5] Cf. Resolution 1654 (XVI) (General Assembly, *Official Records:* Sixteenth Session, Supplement No. 17 (A/5100)).

of international accountability in this sphere will eventually pave the way for a similar attitude in regard to human rights. Some evolution in this direction has in fact been noticeable over the past few years. The U.S.S.R., which a decade ago had rejected the proposed measures for implementing the draft Covenants as unlawful interference in a country's internal affairs, supported the system of periodical reports in 1963. Given a favourable political climate, further progress is by no means impossible.[1]

Even in the highly complex sphere of arms control and disarmament the I.L.O.'s experience may not be wholly irrelevant. When the League of Nations made its abortive attempt in this sphere, the machinery envisaged resembled, in some of its features, that adopted a few years earlier by the International Labour Conference:[2] a permanent commission of government representatives, responsible to the League Council, was to examine reports and complaints and might also set up expert bodies and carry out on-the-spot inquiries. The main emphasis was however on reporting, rather than on inspection.[3] The disarmament discussions and plans of the post-World War II era have grappled much more with the crucial problem of verifying compliance through physical inspection. But supervision and control of armaments can also be facilitated if a maximum of valid information is first secured by less direct means so as to pave the way for international inspection and enhance its chances of success. Reporting and expert examination are therefore likely to occupy a useful place in devising systems which would be based on phased and progressive measures of implementation.[4] This method is already being used extensively by two arms control agencies, perhaps the only ones in actual operation at this time. Thus the Armaments Control Agency of the Western European Union has instituted what it calls "control from documentary

---

[1] Professor Lauterpacht foreshadowed this development when he wrote, already in 1950, that the Soviet refusal to consent to international supervision "need not be considered as synonymous with a permanently negative attitude to the adoption, under the aegis of the United Nations, of international machinery for the implementation of an International Bill of Rights" (H. Lauterpacht, *International Law and Human Rights* (London: Stevens & Sons, 1950), p. 301).

[2] In 1932 Professor O'Rahilly of Ireland, speaking as chairman of the Application Committee, reminded the Conference that there was "another great event happening in Geneva–the Disarmament Conference. I hold that our Committee has given a lead, because disarmament without an annual and perpetual mechanism of inquiry and control is of no use" (16 R.P. 318).

[3] Secretary of State Stimson instructed the United States delegation to accept a permenent international agency whose role would be to "study and report,... the mobilization of public opinion and the co-ordination of information". Cf. Richard Dean Burns, "Origins of the United States' Inspection Policy: 1926-1946", *Disarmament and Arms Control* (Oxford), Vol. 2, No. 2, (Spring 1964), p. 162.

[4] "One method for facilitating inspection at all stages is to require the participants to prove their compliance with specific obligations. They may be in a position to produce convincing evidence of their action much more easily than inspectors could establish the facts without assistance. The making of reports of various kinds by the parties can serve a similar purpose of facilitating inspection. The early stages of a system should capitalize on such techniques by beginning with limitations for which they are especially helpful". Robert C. Bowie, "Basic Requirements of Arms Control" in *Arms Control, Disarmament and National Security*, edited by Donald E. Brennan (New York: George Braziller, 1961), p. 51.

sources", which precedes physical inspection.[1] Similarly the Euratom Commission undertakes a statistical analysis of the data submitted by governments before carrying out on-the-spot checks.[2] The reporting and examination techniques already developed through existing supervisory procedures should therefore prove useful in the organization of arms control and disarmament on a global basis.

The I.L.O.'s experience in giving non-governmental elements a role in supervision may, moreover, help to introduce a novel idea into the disarmament plans now under discussion. During the League of Nations Conference on this subject the Soviet Union had raised the possibility that the workers in the factories producing weapons should report violations of an arms limitation treaty.[3] Under even more far-reaching proposals, made in recent years in the United States, such infringements would have to be reported by the citizens of a ratifying country to the international control agency.[4] The practical merits and feasibility of these proposals cannot be discussed here. But if, as concluded above, the regular participation of labour and management representatives has helped to promote compliance with I.L.O. standards, then this technique of seeking a broader basis for international supervision might also be worth further exploration in the sphere of disarmament.

## VI. The Outlook for International Supervision

In assessing the relevance and the effectiveness of I.L.O. supervision, it must always be remembered that this system has benefited from a combi-

---

[1] Information is supplied on the basis of a standard questionnaire addressed to the national authorities. Cf. Raymond Fletcher, "Existing Arrangements for International Control of Warlike Material–Western European Union", *Disarmament and Arms Control*, Vol. 1, No. 2 (Autumn 1963), pp. 144-152.

[2] Cf. in the same series of articles in *Disarmament and Arms Control*, mentioned in footnote 1 above, the one on Euratom by Jacques van Helmont, Vol. 2, No. 1 (Winter 1963/64), pp. 43-54.

[3] In the words of the U.S.S.R. delegate, "no one could be better informed than the workers employed in the factories and no one had greater interest than they in preventing a war". Commenting on this suggestion, Professor Bourquin of Belgium, who acted as reporter on the question of supervision, pointed out that the Permanent Disarmament Commission, which was to function as the supervisory organ, "could examine information received, not only from governments, but from any other source". Cf. League of Nations, *Records of the Conference for the Reduction and Limitation of Armaments*, Series C, Vol. I, pp. 49-50.

[4] Under this suggestion each ratifying country "shall require in its code of law that every citizen of the country report to the (international) inspectorate any evidence of evasion of the disarmament agreement. Failure to report such information would be punishable under the law, national as well as international" (Seymour Melman, *The Peace Race* (New York: Ballantine Books, 1961), p. 119. This suggestion for "inspection by the people" was originally made in *Inspection for Disarmament* (New York: Columbia University Press, 1958), edited by the same author. A similar proposal stresses the need for widespread support of, and faith in, any control agreement, lest "substantial fractions of the population will support a violation and not report what they may learn of it to the international authorities. Real patriotism, in other words, must clearly consist in reporting violations" (Lewis C. Bohn, "Non-Physical Inspection Techniques" in *Arms Control, Disarmament and National Security, op. cit.*, p. 349).

nation of favourable circumstances which may not easily be encountered elsewhere. A solid constitutional foundation, an extensive network of precise obligations, an organizational tradition, an experienced secretariat, the institutionalized collaboration of non-governmental groups, all these factors have exerted a positive influence on the working and the results of the I.L.O. procedures. The lessons which have emerged from this venture cannot therefore be applied automatically to other procedures, present or future, and even less to international supervision as a whole. The best that can be done is to see which aspects of the I.L.O.'s experience are of sufficiently general validity to have a bearing on the broader outlook for international supervision.

The essential task of supervision is to determine with a maximum of accuracy to what extent the national law and, if possible also the national practice, correspond to the international obligations assumed by States. Supervision, whatever its detailed characteristics, can thus perform both a corrective and a preventive function. The discovery of violations should not only lead to their removal in the cases which have been noticed but should incite governments to avoid infringements in all the cases covered by a permanent supervisory system. This psychological effect of supervision is especially valuable in an international society whose degree of cohesion is still very loose.

The mere existence of supervisory arrangements operating automatically therefore tends to increase mutual confidence among the parties to a treaty and provides at the same time a ready sounding board for ventilating charges of non-application without having to go to the extreme of lodging a formal complaint. By thus channeling dissatisfaction, regular supervision can in addition improve the climate of international relations.

Viewed in this perspective, systematic supervision has a real contribution to make to what has been called the "technology of international politics".[1] Even if the methods used are still imperfect and the results leave much to be desired, mechanisms are emerging through which international organizations can exert some influence on the behaviour of States.[2] The way in which these mechanisms are developing is in itself indicative of the outlook for international supervision. Whatever the specific techniques adopted, the essential purpose of supervision will be the same: to promote fuller respect for the standards agreed upon by the society of nations and to strengthen through their observance the rule of law in international life.[3]

---

[1] Philip C. Jessup and Howard J. Taubenfeld, *Controls for Outer Space* (New York: Columbia University Press, 1959), pp. 133-134.

[2] These mechanisms constitute one specific type of what Professor Virally has called the "techniques of inducement" ("techniques d'incitation"). Cf. "Le Juriste et la Science du Droit", *Revue du Droit Public et de la Science Politique en France et à l'Etranger* (Paris), Vol. LXXX, No. 3 (May-June 1964), p. 602.

[3] A recent series of lectures at The Hague on the quasi-legislative activities of the United Nations specialized agencies concluded, with reference to the application of the standards they have adopted, that it is "an essential duty of the United Nations and the specialized agencies" to "establish and maintain the most extensive and effective supervision possible". Cf. H. Saba, "L'Activité Quasi-Législative des Institutions Spécialisées des Nations Unies", *Recueil des Cours de l'Académie de Droit International*, 1964, Vol. I, p. 686.

Much of the value of international supervision, and its future prospects in particular, depend on the contribution it can make in achieving this progressive co-ordination of the conduct and activities of States. Only some of the forms which such a contribution can take have been sketched out above. Though other forms exist inside the I.L.O. and elsewhere, the experience described in these pages seemed especially suitable for fuller treatment because the systematic and permanent character of this specific model fits in well with what has been aptly described as "the international law of co-operation".[1] And the law-making treaty now plays such a major role in our world of sovereign States that this particular type of supervision seems most relevant to the present stage of international organization.

Since the nature of the international standards and institutions involved must determine the precise form of any supervisory machinery as well as the methods for its operation, the experience of the I.L.O., as described and evaluated in the present study, serves primarily to illustrate the problems and potentialities of international supervision in a given set of circumstances. When similar studies of the working and effectiveness of other systems become available, it should be possible to reach more generally valid conclusions as to the prospects and the outlook for international super-vision. Perhaps it will then be possible to say more conclusively to what extent this novel tool of international organization really holds promise for the future. In a world where even the smallest step toward orderly procedures and co-operative institutions can affect the balance between existence and extinction, the further development of such a tool surely is an urgent necessity.

---

[1] Wolfgang Friedmann, *op. cit.*, pp. 61-62.

LIST OF INTERNATIONAL LABOUR CONVENTIONS, INDICATING
RATIFICATIONS AND DECLARATIONS
(as at 30 June 1964)

| No. | Title | Total Number of Ratifications | Declarations |
|---|---|---|---|
| 1. | Hours of Work (Industry) Convention, 1919 | 30 | 0 |
| 2. | Unemployment Convention, 1919 | 41 | 11 |
| * 3. | Maternity Protection Convention, 1919 | 24 | 12 |
| * 4. | Night Work (Women) Convention, 1919 | 55 | 9 |
| * 5. | Minimum Age (Industry) Convention, 1919 | 54 | 39 |
| * 6. | Night Work of Young Persons (Industry) Convention, 1919 | 50 | 11 |
| * 7. | Minimum Age (Sea) Convention, 1920 | 38 | 30 |
| 8. | Unemployment Indemnity (Shipwreck) Convention, 1920. | 35 | 27 |
| 9. | Placing of Seamen Convention, 1920 | 27 | 2 |
| 10. | Minimum Age (Agriculture) Convention, 1921 | 36 | 20 |
| 11. | Right of Association (Agriculture) Convention, 1921 | 75 | 48 |
| 12. | Workmen's Compensation (Agriculture) Convention, 1921 | 46 | 27 |
| 13. | White Lead (Painting) Convention, 1921 | 46 | 10 |
| 14. | Weekly Rest (Industry) Convention, 1921 | 68 | 31 |
| 15. | Minimum Age (Trimmers and Stokers) Convention, 1921 . | 52 | 26 |
| 16. | Medical Examination of Young Persons (Sea) Convention, 1921 | 50 | 23 |
| 17. | Workmen's Compensation (Accidents) Convention, 1925 | 46 | 36 |
| * 18. | Workmen's Compensation (Occupational Diseases) Convention, 1925 | 51 | 8 |
| 19. | Equality of Treatment (Accident Compensation) Convention 1925 | 73 | 43 |
| 20. | Night Work (Bakeries) Convention, 1925 | 14 | 0 |
| 21. | Inspection of Emigrants Convention, 1926 | 28 | 3 |
| 22. | Seamen's Articles of Agreement Convention, 1926 | 36 | 16 |
| 23. | Repatriation of Seamen Convention, 1926 | 23 | 1 |
| 24. | Sickness Insurance (Industry) Convention, 1927 | 21 | 4 |
| 25. | Sickness Insurance (Agriculture) Convention, 1927 | 16 | 4 |
| 26. | Minimum Wage-Fixing Machinery Convention, 1928 | 69 | 33 |
| 27. | Marking of Weight (Packages Transported by Vessels) Convention, 1929 | 43 | 7 |
| + 28. | Protection against Accidents (Dockers) Convention, 1929 | 4 | 0 |
| 29. | Forced Labour Convention, 1930 | 89 | 55 |
| 30. | Hours of Work (Commerce and Offices) Convention, 1930 | 21 | 0 |
| *° 31. | Hours of Work (Coal Mines) Convention, 1931 | 2 | 0 |

* Convention revised by a subsequent Convention.

+ Convention no longer open to ratification as a result of the entry into force of a revising Convention.

° Convention which has not yet received the required number of ratifications for entry into force.

Total Number of

| No. | Title | Ratifications | Declarations |
|-----|-------|:---:|:---:|
| 32. | Protection against Accidents (Dockers) Convention (Revised), 1932 . . . . . . . . . . . . . . . . . . | 26 | 6 |
| + 33. | Minimum Age (Non-Industrial Employment) Convention, 1932 . . . . . . . . . . . . . . . . . . . . | 23 | 6 |
| + 34. | Fee-Charging Employment Agencies Convention, 1933 . . | 10 | 0 |
| 35. | Old-Age Insurance (Industry, etc.) Convention, 1933 . . . | 10 | 6 |
| 36. | Old-Age Insurance (Agriculture) Convention, 1933 . . . | 9 | 5 |
| 37. | Invalidity Insurance (Industry, etc.) Convention, 1933 . . | 9 | 3 |
| 38. | Invalidity Insurance (Agriculture) Convention, 1933 . . . | 8 | 3 |
| 39. | Survivors' Insurance (Industry, etc.) Convention, 1933 . . | 7 | 5 |
| 40. | Survivors' Insurance (Agriculture) Convention, 1933 . . . | 6 | 4 |
| + 41. | Night Work (Women) Convention (Revised), 1934 . . . . | 36 | 10 |
| 42. | Workmen's Compensation (Occupational Diseases) Convention (Revised), 1934 . . . . . . . . . . . . . . | 40 | 19 |
| 43. | Sheet-Glass Works Convention, 1934 . . . . . . . . | 9 | 0 |
| 44. | Unemployment Provision Convention, 1934 . . . . . | 11 | 4 |
| 45. | Underground Work (Women) Convention, 1935 . . . . | 67 | 20 |
| ° 46. | Hours of Work (Coal Mines) Convention (Revised), 1935 | 2 | 0 |
| 47. | Forty-Hour Week Convention, 1935 . . . . . . . . . | 4 | 0 |
| 48. | Maintenance of Migrants' Pension Rights Convention, 1935 . . . . . . . . . . . . . . . . . . . . . | 8 | 0 |
| 49. | Reduction of Hours of Work (Glass-Bottle Works) Convention, 1935 . . . . . . . . . . . . . . . . . | 7 | 0 |
| 50. | Recruiting of Indigenous Workers Convention, 1936 . . | 20 | 31 |
| ° 51. | Reduction of Hours of Work (Public Works) Convention, 1936 . . . . . . . . . . . . . . . . . . . . . | 0 | 0 |
| 52. | Holidays with Pay Convention, 1936 . . . . . . . . | 41 | 1 |
| 53. | Officers' Competency Certificates Convention, 1936 . . . | 19 | 10 |
| *° 54. | Holidays with Pay (Sea) Convention, 1936 . . . . . . | 6 | 8 |
| 55. | Shipowners' Liability (Sick and Injured Seamen) Convention, 1936 . . . . . . . . . . . . . . . . . | 9 | 8 |
| 56. | Sickness Insurance (Sea) Convention, 1936 . . . . . . | 8 | 8 |
| *° 57. | Hours of Work and Manning (Sea) Convention, 1936 . . | 5 | 4 |
| 58. | Minimum Age (Sea) Convention (Revised), 1936 . . . . | 39 | 35 |
| 59. | Minimum Age (Industry) Convention (Revised), 1937 . . | 21 | 31 |
| 60. | Minimum Age (Non-Industrial Employment) Convention (Revised), 1937 . . . . . . . . . . . . . . . . | 9 | 0 |
| ° 61. | Reduction of Hours of Work (Textiles) Convention, 1937 | 1 | 0 |
| 62. | Safety Provisions (Building) Convention, 1937 . . . . . | 20 | 5 |
| 63. | Convention concerning Statistics of Wages and Hours of Work, 1938 . . . . . . . . . . . . . . . . . . | 28 | 10 |
| 64. | Contracts of Employment (Indigenous Workers) Convention, 1939 . . . . . . . . . . . . . . . . . . . | 16 | 30 |
| 65. | Penal Sanctions (Indigenous Workers) Convention, 1939 | 18 | 33 |
| +° 66. | Migration for Employment Convention, 1939 . . . . . | 0 | 0 |
| 67. | Hours of Work and Rest Periods (Road Transport) Convention, 1939 . . . . . . . . . . . . . . . . . | 4 | 0 |
| 68. | Food and Catering (Ships' Crews) Convention, 1946 . . . | 14 | 4 |
| 69. | Certification of Ships' Cooks Convention, 1946 . . . . . | 15 | 8 |
| ° 70. | Social Security (Seafarers) Convention, 1946 . . . . . . | 6 | 5 |
| 71. | Seafarers' Pensions Convention, 1946 . . . . . . . . . | 8 | 4 |
| *° 72. | Paid Vacations (Seafarers) Convention, 1946 . . . . . . | 5 | 4 |
| 73. | Medical Examination (Seafarers) Convention, 1946 . . . | 16 | 4 |
| 74. | Certification of Able Seamen Convention, 1946 . . . . . | 12 | 13 |
| +° 75. | Accommodation of Crews Convention, 1946 . . . . . . | 5 | 0 |

| No. | Title | Total Number of Ratifications | Total Number of Declarations |
|-----|-------|:---:|:---:|
| *° 76. | Wages, Hours of Work and Manning (Sea) Convention, 1946 | 1 | 0 |
| 77. | Medical Examination of Young Persons (Industry) Convention, 1946 | 20 | 0 |
| 78. | Medical Examination of Young Persons (Non-Industrial Occupations) Convention, 1946 | 20 | 0 |
| 79. | Night Work of Young Persons (Non-Industrial Occupations) Convention, 1946 | 14 | 0 |
| 80. | Final Articles Revision Convention, 1946 | 50 | 0 |
| 81. | Labour Inspection Convention, 1947 | 59 | 22 |
| 82. | Social Policy (Non-Metropolitan Territories) Convention 1947 | 4 | 39 |
| 83. | Labour Standards (Non-Metropolitan Territories) Convention, 1947 | 1 | 0 |
| 84. | Right of Association (Non-Metropolitan Territories) Convention, 1947 | 4 | 37 |
| 85. | Labour Inspectorates (Non-Metropolitan Territories) Convention, 1947 | 4 | 33 |
| 86. | Contracts of Employment (Indigenous Workers) Convention, 1947 | 8 | 31 |
| 87. | Freedom of Association and Protection of the Right to Organize Convention, 1948 | 66 | 40 |
| 88. | Employment Service Convention, 1948 | 44 | 9 |
| 89. | Night Work (Women) Convention (Revised), 1948 | 38 | 6 |
| 90. | Night Work of Young Persons (Industry) Convention (Revised), 1948 | 28 | 1 |
| ° 91. | Paid Vacations (Seafarers) Convention (Revised), 1949 | 12 | 4 |
| 92. | Accommodation of Crews Convention (Revised), 1949 | 15 | 6 |
| *° 93. | Wages, Hours of Work and Manning (Sea) Convention (Revised), 1949 | 4 | 0 |
| 94. | Labour Clauses (Public Contracts) Convention, 1949 | 36 | 28 |
| 95. | Protection of Wages Convention, 1949 | 57 | 29 |
| 96. | Fee-Charging Employment Agencies Convention (Revised), 1949 | 28 | 1 |
| 97. | Migration for Employment Convention (Revised), 1949 | 21 | 17 |
| 98. | Right to Organize and Collective Bargaining Convention, 1949 | 72 | 31 |
| 99. | Minimum Wage-Fixing Machinery (Agriculture) Convention, 1951 | 24 | 14 |
| 100. | Equal Remuneration Convention, 1951 | 47 | 4 |
| 101. | Holidays with Pay (Agriculture) Convention, 1952 | 30 | 13 |
| 102. | Social Security (Minimum Standards) Convention, 1952 | 15 | 1 |
| 103. | Maternity Protection Convention (Revised), 1952 | 8 | 0 |
| 104. | Abolition of Penal Sanctions (Indigenous Workers) Convention, 1955 | 15 | 2 |
| 105. | Abolition of Forced Labour Convention, 1957 | 67 | 43 |
| 106. | Weekly Rest (Commerce and Offices) Convention, 1957 | 21 | 2 |
| 107. | Indigenous and Tribal Populations Convention, 1957 | 17 | 0 |
| 108. | Seafarers' Identity Documents Convention, 1958 | 11 | 0 |
| ° 109. | Wages, Hours of Work and Manning (Sea) Convention (Revised), 1958 | 3 | 0 |
| 110. | Plantations Convention, 1958 | 5 | 0 |
| 111. | Discrimination (Employment and Occupation) Convention, 1958 | 48 | 0 |
| 112. | Minimum Age (Fishermen) Convention, 1959 | 18 | 0 |

| No. | Title | Total Number of Ratifications | Declarations |
|---|---|---|---|
| 113. | Medical Examination (Fishermen) Convention, 1959. . . | 10 | 0 |
| 114. | Fishermen's Articles of Agreement Convention, 1959 . . | 11 | 0 |
| 115. | Radiation Protection Convention, 1960 . . . . . . . . | 10 | 0 |
| 116. | Final Articles Revision Convention, 1961 . . . . . . . | 36 | 0 |
| 117. | Social Policy (Basic Aims and Standards) Convention, 1962 | 6 | 0 |
| 118. | Equality of Treatment (Social Security) Convention, 1962 | 6 | 1 |
| °119. | Guarding of Machinery Convention, 1963 . . . . . . . | 5 | 0 |
| | | 2,919 | 1,297 |

APPENDIX II

## LIST OF OBSERVATIONS, INDICATING REFERENCES
## TO THEIR ORIGIN AND TO THE ACTION TAKEN
(as at 30 June 1964)

### Explanatory Note

As indicated in Chapter Two, this Appendix is intended to provide all necessary references to the 1,003 observations on which the present inquiry is based. The documents used are the Reports of the two supervisory Committees and the Summary of the governments' annual reports which is placed before every general session of the International Labour Conference.

The citations refer in the most succinct way possible to the original observation or request, and to any action taken on it. The first two numbers indicate the *date* of the document, the figures 1 and 9 being omitted: 27 stands for 1927, 62 for 1962.[1]

The letters indicate the *document* itself, abbreviated as follows: E for *Report of the Committee of Experts*, C for *Report of the Conference Committee*, S for *Summary of Reports on Ratified Conventions*, SS for *Supplement to* this *Summary*.

The numbers after the letters indicate the *page* of the document; if the relevant passage covers more than one page, only the number of the starting page is given.

Thus pages 40-42 of the Report of the Committee of Experts on its 1937 Session are cited as "37E40"; page 532 of the Report of the Conference Committee in 1958 as "58C532"; pages 132-133 of the Supplement to the Summary of Reports submitted to the 1935 Session of the Conference as "35SS132", etc.

The letters RD in the last column indicate that the *ratification* was *denounced* in the year indicated.

The *Report of the Committee of Experts* was published from 1927 to 1931 inclusive as an appendix to Volume II ("Report of the Director") of the Record of Proceedings of the Conference. In 1932 the Report of the Committee of Experts was printed in the Record of Proceedings itself. In 1933, 1934 and 1935 the Report of the Committee of Experts formed an appendix of the "Summary of Annual Reports under Article 408". Since 1936 this Report is published as a separate document which since 1950 forms "Report III (Part IV))" to the relevant Conference Session. The title of the Committee of Experts has varied over the years. Until 1935 inclusive it was called the "Committee of Experts appointed to examine the annual reports made under article 408." From 1936 to 1948 it was known as the "Committee of Experts on the Application of Conventions". Since 1949 its title is "Committee of Experts on the Application of Conventions and Recommendations." From 1928 to 1932 inclusive the Report of the Committee of Experts also contained, in a special appendix, the text of the governments' replies to the Committee's observations.

The *Report of the Conference Committee* is included in the Record of Proceedings of the relevant Conference Session. The title of this Committee has also undergone several changes. In 1927, 1928 and 1929 it was called "Committee appointed to examine the

---

[1] For purposes of clarity it was thought preferable to indicate the dates rather than the numbers of the relevant sessions.

summary of reports under article 408." In 1930-1934 the title was "Committee appointed to examine the annual reports supplied under article 408." In 1935 it was known simply as the "Committee on the Enforcement of Conventions." During 1936-1947 it was called the "Committee on the Application of Conventions." Since 1948 its title is "Committee on the Application of Conventions and Recommendations." During 1933-1939 the Report of the Conference Committee contained, in a special appendix, the text of the governments' replies to the observations of the Committee of Experts.

The *Summary of Reports* formed, until 1931 inclusive, the Second Part of the "Report of the Director" to the relevant Conference session. Since then it is published as a separate document which constitutes, since 1950, "Report III (Part I)" to the relevant Conference session.

In the case of *countries or parts of countries which were formerly non-metropolitan territories*, the date of entry into force of a given Convention is the date when the instrument actually became binding. If this occurred prior to independence and if the observation and the implementing action also preceded independence, the case in question is listed among the non-metropolitan territories of the State formerly responsible for the international relations of the now independent country. The achievement of independence has at times involved the division of a territory into separate States, the combination of several territories into a new State and/or a change in the name of a country. Thus the successor States of French Equatorial Africa are the Central African Republic, Chad, Congo (Brazzaville) and Gabon; the successor States of French West Africa are Dahomey, the Republic of Guinea, Ivory Coast, the Republic of Mali, the Islamic Republic of Mauritania, Niger, Senegal and Upper Volta. Madagascar has become the Malagasy Republic. The States of Malaya, North Borneo and Sarawak now form Malaysia. British Somaliland has joined with the Trust Territory of Somaliland to become Somalia. Tanganyika and Zanzibar have combined into Tanzania. The Gold Coast is now known as Ghana, Northern Rhodesia has taken the name of Zambia and Nyasaland the name of Malawi.

| Country | Entry into Force | Direct Request | Initial Observation | Action Taken in part | in full |
|---------|:---:|:---:|:---:|:---:|:---:|

## 1. HOURS OF WORK (INDUSTRY), 1919

| Country | Entry into Force | Direct Request | Initial Observation | Action in part | Action in full |
|---------|:---:|:---:|:---:|:---:|:---:|
| Bulgaria | 1922 | | 34E223 | | 37S22 |
| Canada | 1935 | | 38E6 | 50E16 | |
| Chile | 1925 | | 27E402 | 32E605 | |
| Colombia | 1933 | | 51C559 | | |
| Cuba | 1934 | | 36E6 | | 47E11 |
| Czechoslovakia | 1921 | | 57E13 | | |
| Dominican Republic | 1933 | | 53E18 | 59E16 | |
| Greece | 1920 | | 27E402 49C453 | 38E7 61E27 64C658 | |
| Haiti | 1952 | | 54E14 | 59E17 | |
| India | 1921 | | 30E608 56E19 | 38E7 47C554 57E15 | |
| Israel | 1951 | | 54E14 | | 56E20 |
| Luxembourg | 1928 | | 30C642 | | 34E224 |
| Nicaragua | 1934 | | 36E6 | 55S6 | |
| Peru | 1945 | | 55C595 | | |
| Portugal | 1928 | | 30C643 | 35E276 | |
| Rumania | 1921 | | 27E403 56E21 | 29E521 | 33E488 |
| Spain | 1929 | | 57E17 | 62E27 64C658 | |

## 2. UNEMPLOYMENT, 1919

| Country | Entry into Force | Direct Request | Initial Observation | Action in part | Action in full |
|---------|:---:|:---:|:---:|:---:|:---:|
| Argentina | 1933 | | 36C573 | 47E11 51E12 | 53E19 |
| Austria | 1924 | | 56E21 | | |
| Bulgaria | 1922 | | 55E22 | | RD1960 |
| Chile | 1933 | | 50E17 | 61E30 | |
| Colombia | 1933 | | 36E7 | 37E7 54C502 | |
| Greece | 1920 | | 27E404 57E19 | 36C573 | 38E7 58E14 |
| India | 1921 | | 27E404 | | RD1938 |
| New Zealand | 1938 | | 39E8 | | 47C547 |
| Nicaragua | 1934 | | 36E7 | 55S11 | |
| Rumania | 1921 | | 56E22 | | |
| Sudan | 1957 | 1959 | 64E36 | | |
| Sweden | 1921 | | 29E521 | | 36E7 |
| Turkey | 1950 | | 52E16 | | 54C502 |

| Country | Entry into Force | Initial Direct Request | Initial Observation | Action Taken in part | Action Taken in full |
|---|---|---|---|---|---|
| **2. UNEMPLOYMENT, 1919 (continued)** | | | | | |
| Uruguay | 1933 | | 36C573 | 57E19 | |
| Venezuela | 1944 | | 47C554 | 50C465 51C560 | |
| **3. MATERNITY PROTECTION, 1919** | | | | | |
| Argentina | 1933 | | 61E31 | | |
| Brazil | 1934 | | 35E277 | 47C554 | |
| | | | 54E15 | | RD1961 |
| Bulgaria | 1922 | | 55E23 | 58E15 | |
| Chile | 1925 | | 27E405 47E12 | 33E489 52C494 53E20 | |
| Colombia | 1933 | | 36E8 55E23 | 39E8 63E41 | |
| Cuba | 1928 | | 30C641 | | 35SS9 |
| France | 1950 | | 56E23 | | |
| Fed. Rep. of Germany | 1927 | | 53E44 | | |
| Greece | 1921 | | 27E406 48E16 | 33E489 50E17 | |
| Hungary | 1928 | | 30E609 56E24 | 32C609 | |
| Italy | 1952 | | 54E16 | 63C526 | |
| Luxembourg | 1928 | | 31E457 | | 34E225 |
| Nicaragua | 1934 | | 36E8 | 55S18 58E16 | |
| Rumania | 1921 | | 27E406 56E25 | 57E22 59E20 | 34E225 |
| Spain | 1923 | | 27E406 57E22 | 30C650 | |
| Uruguay | 1933 | | 36C574 | 54C505 | RD1955 |
| Venezuela | 1944 | | 47E13 | 50C466 54E16 | |
| Yugoslavia | 1927 | | 32E610 | 36E8 | |
| *France* | | | | | |
| Overseas Departments | 1955 | | 57E106 | | |
| St-Pierre & Miquelon | 1954 | | 57E106 | | |
| **4. NIGHT WORK (WOMEN), 1919** | | | | | |
| Afghanistan | 1939 | | 50E17 | | |
| Albania | 1932 | | 34E225 58E17 | 37C578 59C679 | RD1964 |

| Country | Entry into Force | Direct Request | Observation | in part | in full |
|---|---|---|---|---|---|
| | | | *Initial* | *Action Taken* | |

**4. NIGHT WORK (WOMEN), 1919 (continued)**

| Country | Entry into Force | Direct Request | Observation | in part | in full |
|---|---|---|---|---|---|
| Argentina | 1933 | | 36C574 | | 51E13 |
| Austria | 1924 | | 48E17 | | |
| Belgium | 1924 | | 31C631 | | 33E489 |
| Brazil | 1934 | | 35E278 | | RD1937 |
| Bulgaria | 1922 | | 55E24 | | RD1960 |
| Ceylon | 1951 | | 53E21 | | RD1953 |
| Chile | 1931 | | 38E8 | | |
| Colombia | 1933 | | 36E8 | | |
| Cuba | 1928 | | 30C641 | | 35SS13 |
| Czechoslovakia | 1921 | | 49E19 | | |
| France | 1925 | | 49E19 | | RD1955 |
| Gabon | 1939 | 1960 | | | 64E41 |
| Hungary | 1928 | | 30E610 | | 32E610 |
| India | 1921 | | 31E457 | | 36E8 |
| Italy | 1923 | | 49E19 | 52E18 | 53E21 |
| Morocco | 1956 | 1960 | | | 62E31 |
| Nicaragua | 1934 | | 36E8 | | |
| Peru | 1945 | | 50E18 | | |
| Rumania | 1921 | | 27E407 | | 33E490 |
| Spain | 1932 | | 57E23 | | 62E32 |
| Togo | 1939 | | 58E72 | | 63E45 |
| Uruguay | 1933 | | 36C574 | | RD1955 |
| Yugoslavia | 1927 | | 36E9 | | RD1957 |

**5. MINIMUM AGE (INDUSTRY), 1919**

| Country | Entry into Force | Direct Request | Observation | in part | in full |
|---|---|---|---|---|---|
| Albania | 1932 | | 57E23 | | |
| Austria | 1936 | | 49E19 | | 52C496 |
| Bolivia | 1954 | | 56E26 | | |
| Brazil | 1934 | | 48C393 | | 54E17 |
| Bulgaria | 1922 | | 55E25 | | 61E33 |
| Chile | 1925 | | 27E407 | | 32E611 |
| Colombia | 1933 | | 35E278 | | |
| Cuba | 1928 | | 30C641 | | 35SS15 |
| Denmark | 1923 | | 56E27 | | |
| Dominican Republic | 1933 | | 47E13 | 53E21 | 54E18 |
| Haiti | 1957 | | 59E21 | 63E45 | |
| India | 1955 | | 57E24 | | |
| Israel | 1953 | | 55E26 | | 59E21 |

| Country | Entry into Force | Direct Request | Initial Observation | Action Taken in part | in full |
|---|---|---|---|---|---|

## 5. MINIMUM AGE (INDUSTRY), 1919 (continued)

| Country | Entry into Force | Direct Request | Observation | in part | in full |
|---|---|---|---|---|---|
| Nicaragua . . . . . . . | 1934 | | 36E9 | 55S23 | |
| Rumania . . . . . . . . | 1921 | | 27E407 | | 33E490 |
| | | | 56E27 | | |
| Spain . . . . . . . . . | 1932 | | 57E24 | | 58E18 |
| Uruguay . . . . . . | 1933 | | 36C574 | | RD1955 |
| Vietnam . . . . . . . . | 1953 | | 55E26 | | 61E34 |
| Yugoslavia . . . . . . | 1927 | | 32C680 | | 51C562 |
| *Denmark* | | | | | |
| Faroe Islands . . . . . . | 1923 | | 57E107 | | |
| *France* | | | | | |
| St-Pierre & Miquelon . . | 1954 | | 58E72 | 61E115 | |

## 6. NIGHT WORK OF YOUNG PERSONS (INDUSTRY), 1919

| Country | Entry into Force | Direct Request | Observation | in part | in full |
|---|---|---|---|---|---|
| Albania . . . . . . . . | 1932 | | 57E25 | 63E46 | |
| Argentina . . . . . . . | 1933 | | 37C579 | | 51E15 |
| Austria . . . . . . . . | 1924 | | 48E17 | | 49E20 |
| Brazil . . . . . . . . . | 1934 | | 35E278 | 47C554 | 54E18 |
| Bulgaria . . . . . . . . | 1922 | | 55E26 | | 60E24 |
| Cameroon . . . . . . . | 1940 | | 58E73 | | 64E42 |
| Chile . . . . . . . . . | 1925 | 1960 | 27E407 | 32E612 | 47E14 |
| | | | 62E33 | | |
| Cuba . . . . . . . . . | 1928 | | 30C641 | | 35SS16 |
| Denmark . . . . . . . | 1923 | | 56E28 | | 63E46 |
| France . . . . . . . . . | 1925 | | 28E460 | | 31E459 |
| | | | 56E28 | 62C694 | |
| Hungary . . . . . . . | 1928 | | 30E611 | | 34E226 |
| | | | 55E26 | | |
| India . . . . . . . . . | 1921 | | 31E459 | | 36E10 |
| | | | 54E18 | | 55E26 |
| Italy . . . . . . . . . . | 1923 | | 49E20 | 52E19 | 53E22 |
| Malagasy Republic . . . | 1940 | | 58E73 | 60E59 | |
| Mexico . . . . . . . . | 1937 | | 38E9 | | RD1956 |
| Netherlands . . . . . . | 1924 | | 28E460 | | 32E612 |
| Nicaragua . . . . . . . | 1934 | | 36E10 | | |
| Portugal . . . . . . . . | 1932 | | 35E279 | | 37E9 |
| Rumania . . . . . . . . | 1921 | | 57E26 | 64E42 | |
| Spain . . . . . . . . . | 1932 | | 57E26 | | 61E34 |
| Togo . . . . . . . . . | 1940 | | 58E73 | | |
| Uruguay . . . . . . . | 1933 | | 36C575 | 54C506 | RD1955 |

| Country | Entry into Force | Direct Request | Initial Observation | Action Taken in part | in full |
|---|---|---|---|---|---|

**6. NIGHT WORK OF YOUNG PERSONS (INDUSTRY), 1919 (continued)**

| | | | | | |
|---|---|---|---|---|---|
| Vietnam . . . . . . . | 1953 | | 55E26 | 59E22 64E43 | |
| Yugoslavia . . . . . | 1927 | | 29E522 51C563 | 32E612 56E29 | RD1957 |
| *Denmark* | | | | | |
| Faroe Islands . . . . . | 1923 | | 57E108 | | |
| Greenland . . . . . . | 1954 | | 55E86 | | |
| *France* | | | | | |
| Central African Rep. . . | 1940 | | 58E73 | | 60E58 |
| Congo . . . . . . . . | 1940 | | 58E73 | | 60E58 |
| French Somaliland . . . | 1940 | | 58E73 | | |
| Ivory Coast . . . . . | 1940 | 1960 | | | 61E34 |
| Overseas Departments . . | 1940 | | 56E96 | 62C719 | |
| St-Pierre & Miquelon . . | 1940 | | 58E73 | | 64E168 |

**7. MINIMUM AGE (SEA), 1920**

| | | | | | |
|---|---|---|---|---|---|
| Belgium . . . . . . . | 1925 | | 27E408 | | 29E825 |
| Bulgaria . . . . . . . | 1923 | | 55E27 | | 57E27 |
| China . . . . . . . . | 1936 | | 56E29 | 60E25 | |
| Colombia . . . . . . | 1933 | | 35E279 | | |
| Cuba . . . . . . . . | 1928 | | 30C641 | | 35SS19 |
| Dominican Republic . . | 1933 | | 38E9 | | 53S33 |
| Hungary . . . . . . | 1928 | | 32E613 | | 34E226 |
| Nicaragua . . . . . . | 1934 | | 36E10 | | |
| Rumania . . . . . . . | 1922 | | 27E408 | | 29E625 |
| Uruguay . . . . . . | 1933 | | 36C575 | | RD1955 |
| Venezuela . . . . . . | 1944 | 1960 | 63E47 | | |

**8. UNEMPLOYMENT INDEMNITY (SHIPWRECK), 1920**

| | | | | | |
|---|---|---|---|---|---|
| Argentina . . . . . . | 1933 | | 35E279 | | |
| Belgium . . . . . . . | 1925 | | 27E409 | | 29C826 |
| Colombia . . . . . . | 1933 | | 36E10 | | |
| Cuba . . . . . . . . | 1928 | | 30C641 | 35E279 | 54E19 |
| Finland . . . . . . . | 1950 | | 51E15 | | 52E20 |
| Greece . . . . . . . . | 1925 | | 27E409 | | 29C826 |
| Ireland . . . . . . . | 1930 | | 33E491 | | 34E226 |
| Mexico . . . . . . . | 1937 | | 38E10 | | |
| Nicaragua . . . . . . | 1934 | | 36E11 | | |
| Norway . . . . . . . | 1936 | | 55E28 | | 59E22 |

| Country | Entry into Force | Initial | | Action Taken | |
|---|---|---|---|---|---|
| | | Direct Request | Observation | in part | in full |

## 8. UNEMPLOYEMENT INDEMNITY (SHIPWRECK), 1920 (continued)

| Country | Entry into Force | Direct Request | Observation | in part | in full |
|---|---|---|---|---|---|
| Poland . . . . . . . . | 1924 | | 27E409 | | 34E226 |
| Rumania . . . . . . . . | 1930 | | 32E613 57E28 | | 34E226 |
| Spain . . . . . . . . | 1924 | | 32E613 57E28 | 63E49 | 36C594 |
| Sweden . . . . . . . | 1935 | | 54E19 | | 63E49 |
| Uruguay . . . . . . | 1933 | | 36C575 | | 47E15 |
| Yugoslavia . . . . . | 1929 | | 32E614 55E28 | | 36E11 56C662 |

## 9. PLACING OF SEAMEN, 1920

| Country | Entry into Force | Direct Request | Observation | in part | in full |
|---|---|---|---|---|---|
| Belgium . . . . . . . | 1925 | | 27E410 | | 29S403 |
| Bulgaria . . . . . . . | 1923 | | 57E29 | | |
| Colombia . . . . . . | 1933 | | 36E11 | | |
| Cuba . . . . . . . . | 1928 | | 30C641 | | 35SS22 |
| Mexico . . . . . . . | 1939 | | 47E15 | 57E29 | |
| Nicaragua . . . . . . | 1934 | | 36E11 | | |
| Rumania . . . . . . . | 1930 | | 32E615 | 33E492 | |
| Spain . . . . . . . . | 1931 | | 32E614 57E29 | 36C594 59E23 | |
| Yugoslavia . . . . . | 1929 | | 31E460 | | 39S82 |

## 10. MINIMUM AGE (AGRICULTURE), 1921

| Country | Entry into Force | Direct Request | Observation | in part | in full |
|---|---|---|---|---|---|
| Argentina . . . . . . | 1936 | | 37C579 | | 47E15 |
| Netherlands . . . . . | 1956 | 1958 | | | 60E25 |
| Nicaragua . . . . . . | 1934 | | 36E11 | 55S34 | |

## 11. RIGHT OF ASSOCIATION (AGRICULTURE), 1921

| Country | Entry into Force | Direct Request | Observation | in part | in full |
|---|---|---|---|---|---|
| Albania . . . . . . . | 1957 | 1961 | 63E50 | | |
| Brazil . . . . . . . . | 1957 | | 59E23 | | |
| Byelorussia . . . . . . | 1956 | | 58E22 | | |
| Chile . . . . . . . . | 1925 | | 48E18 | | |
| China . . . . . . . . | 1934 | | 48E18 | 57E30 | |
| Cuba . . . . . . . . | 1935 | | 39E11 | | 47E16 |
| Nicaragua . . . . . . | 1934 | | 58E23 | | |
| Peru . . . . . . . . . | 1945 | 1959 | 63E52 | | |
| Poland . . . . . . . | 1924 | 1959 | 63E52 | | |
| Rumania . . . . . . . | 1930 | 1959 | 63E52 | | |
| Ukraine . . . . . . . | 1956 | 1958 | 63E52 | | |

| Country | Entry into Force | Initial | | Action Taken | |
|---|---|---|---|---|---|
| | | Direct Request | Observation | in part | in full |

## 11. RIGHT OF ASSOCIATION (AGRICULTURE), 1921 (continued)

| Country | Entry into Force | Direct Request | Observation | in part | in full |
|---|---|---|---|---|---|
| U.S.S.R. | 1956 | | 58E23 | | |
| United Arab Republic | 1954 | | 56E32 | | |
| Venezuela | 1944 | 1960 | 63E52 | | |
| *Belgium* | | | | | |
| Ruanda-Urundi | 1955 | | 60E59 | | 62E144 |

## 12. WORKMEN'S COMPENSATION (AGRICULTURE), 1921

| Country | Entry into Force | Direct Request | Observation | in part | in full |
|---|---|---|---|---|---|
| Argentina | 1936 | | 37C579 58E23 | | 47E16 |
| Nicaragua | 1934 | | 36E12 | 55S36 57E31 | |
| El Salvador | 1955 | | 57E31 | | |

## 13. WHITE LEAD, 1921

| Country | Entry into Force | Direct Request | Observation | in part | in full |
|---|---|---|---|---|---|
| Afghanistan | 1939 | | 50E21 | | |
| Argentina | 1936 | | 37C579 | | |
| Austria | 1924 | | 27E412 | | 28E463 |
| Bulgaria | 1925 | 1959 | 27E412 62E37 | | 33E492 64E48 |
| Chile | 1925 | | 31C636 | | 47E16 |
| Colombia | 1933 | | 37E11 | | |
| Cuba | 1928 | | 30C641 | | 35SS26 |
| Gabon | 1939 | | 57E109 | 63E53 | |
| Greece | 1926 | | 30C661 | 34C541 | 38C494 |
| Guinea | 1939 | 1960 | 62E38 | | |
| Hungary | 1956 | 1959 | 64E49 | | |
| Italy | 1952 | | 54E20 | 62E38 | |
| Ivory Coast | 1939 | 1960 | | | 64E49 |
| Luxembourg | 1928 | | 31E461 | | 32E651 |
| Mexico | 1938 | | 47E17 | | |
| Nicaragua | 1934 | | 36E12 | 56E33 | |
| Poland | 1924 | | 27E412 | 32E617 | |
| Rumania | 1925 | | 27E412 | 30C662 | 33E493 |
| Spain | 1924 | | 29E523 | | 32E616 |
| Uruguay | 1933 | | 37E11 | 38E12 | 53E23 |
| Venezuela | 1933 | 1960 | 35E282 63E53 | 37E11 | |
| Yugoslavia | 1929 | | 51C565 | | 57E32 |

| Country | Entry into Force | Initial | | Action Taken | |
|---|---|---|---|---|---|
| | | Direct Request | Observation | in part | in full |

### 13. WHITE LEAD, 1921 (continued)

*France*

| | | | | | |
|---|---|---|---|---|---|
| Cameroon . . . . . . . | 1939 | | 55E87 | | 57E109 |
| Comoro Islands . . . . . | 1939 | 1958 | | | 62E144 |
| French Somaliland . . . | 1939 | | 55E87 | | 57E109 |
| French West Africa . . . | 1939 | | 55E87 | 59C698 | |
| St-Pierre & Miquelon . . | 1939 | | 54E50 | | |
| Togo . . . . . . . . . | 1939 | | 55E87 | | 58C690 |

*Netherlands*

| | | | | | |
|---|---|---|---|---|---|
| Surinam . . . . . . . . | 1957 | 1958 | 63E131 | | |

### 14. WEEKLY REST (INDUSTRY), 1921

| | | | | | |
|---|---|---|---|---|---|
| Afghanistan . . . . . . | 1939 | | 50E21 | | |
| Bolivia . . . . . . . . | 1954 | | 56E34 | | |
| Bulgaria . . . . . . . . | 1925 | | 55E30 | | 58E24 |
| Canada . . . . . . . . | 1935 | | 38E12 | 52E22 | |
| China . . . . . . . . . | 1934 | | 48E19 | | |
| Colombia . . . . . . . | 1933 | | 36E5 | | |
| Denmark . . . . . . . | 1935 | | 54E21 | | |
| Gabon . . . . . . . . . | 1954 | 1962 | | | 63E54 |
| Greece . . . . . . . . . | 1929 | | 54E21 | 63E54 | |
| India . . . . . . . . . | 1923 | | 27E413 | | 32S208 |
| Ireland . . . . . . . . | 1930 | | 31E461 | | 37S207 |
| Nicaragua . . . . . . . | 1934 | | 36E13 | | 55S41 |
| Poland . . . . . . . . | 1924 | 1958 | 63E55 | | |
| Turkey . . . . . . . . | 1946 | | 48E19 61E38 | 51E17 | 52C497 |
| Vietnam . . . . . . . | 1955 | | 57E34 | 63C529 | |
| Yugoslavia . . . . . . | 1927 | | 53E24 | 58C666 | |

### 15. MINIMUM AGE (TRIMMERS AND STOKERS), 1921

| | | | | | |
|---|---|---|---|---|---|
| Argentina . . . . . . . | 1936 | | 37C579 | | 50C468 |
| Ceylon . . . . . . . . | 1951 | | 54E21 | | |
| China . . . . . . . . . | 1936 | | 56E36 | | |
| Colombia . . . . . . . | 1933 | | 36E13 | | |
| Cuba . . . . . . . . . | 1928 | | 30C641 56E36 | 36E13 | 47E17 57E35 |
| Finland . . . . . . . . | 1925 | | 30E613 | | 31E471 |
| France . . . . . . . . . | 1928 | | 30E613 | | 31E471 |
| Hungary . . . . . . . | 1928 | | 32E618 | | 34E227 |

| Country | Entry into Force | Initial | | Action Taken | |
|---|---|---|---|---|---|
| | | Direct Request | Observation | in part | in full |

## 15. MINIMUM AGE (TRIMMERS AND STOKERS), 1921 (continued)

| | | | | | |
|---|---|---|---|---|---|
| India | 1922 | | 27E413 | 32E619 | 33E494 |
| Ireland | 1930 | | 33E494 | | 34E227 |
| Morocco | 1958 | | 61E39 | | |
| Nicaragua | 1934 | | 36E13 | | |
| Rumania | 1923 | | 27E414 | 29C829 | 33E494 |
| Spain | 1924 | | 57E35 | | 59E24 |
| Turkey | 1959 | 1961 | | 63E56 | |
| Ukraine | 1956 | 1958 | | | 61E39 |
| U.S.S.R. | 1956 | 1958 | | | 61E39 |

## 16. MEDICAL EXAMINATION OF YOUNG PERSONS (SEA), 1921

| | | | | | |
|---|---|---|---|---|---|
| Argentina | 1936 | | 37C579 | | 38C498 |
| Brazil | 1936 | | 38E12 54E22 | 50E22 | 61E39 |
| Ceylon | 1951 | 1959 | 62E39 | | |
| China | 1936 | | 57E37 | 60E26 | |
| Colombia | 1933 | | 36E13 | | |
| Cuba | 1928 | | 30C641 | | 35SS30 |
| Ghana | 1957 | 1962 | | | 64E51 |
| Hungary | 1928 | | 32E619 | | 34E227 |
| India | 1922 | | 27E414 | | 32E619 |
| Ireland | 1930 | | 33E494 | | 34E227 |
| Nicaragua | 1934 | | 36E14 | | |
| Rumania | 1923 | | 27E414 | | 30S526 |
| Sierra Leone | 1950 | 1962 | | | 64E51 |
| Yugoslavia | 1927 | | 29E523 | | 32S253 |
| *Denmark* Greenland | 1954 | | 55E88 | | |

## 17. WORKMEN'S COMPENSATION (ACCIDENTS), 1925

| | | | | | |
|---|---|---|---|---|---|
| Argentina | 1950 | | 51E17 | 58E25 59E25 | |
| Belgium | 1927 | | 29E523 | | 32S258 |
| Bulgaria | 1929 | | 48E20 | | 55E32 |
| Chile | 1931 | | 34E228 | | |
| Colombia | 1933 | | 36E14 | 62E40 | |
| Cuba | 1928 | | 30C641 | | 35SS32 |
| Greece | 1952 | | 54E22 | 55E32 58E25 | |

| Country | Entry into Force | Direct Request | Initial Observation | Action Taken in part | in full |
|---|---|---|---|---|---|
| **17. WORKMEN'S COMPENSATION (ACCIDENTS), 1925 (continued)** | | | | | |
| Haiti . . . . . . . . | 1955 | | 57E37 | | 62E42 |
| Malaysia [1] . . . . . . | 1957 | 1962 | 64E53 | | |
| Mexico . . . . . . . | 1934 | | 35C757 | 47E18 | 60E27 |
| Netherlands . . . . . | 1927 | | 52E22 | | 57C668 |
| New Zealand . . . . | 1928 | | 39E14 58E26 | 47C555 64E54 | 52E22 |
| Nicaragua . . . . . . | 1934 | | 36E14 | 56E38 58E26 | |
| Portugal . . . . . . . | 1929 | | 34E228 47E18 | | 37E12 53S56 |
| Spain . . . . . . . . | 1929 | | 31E463 | 33E494 | |
| Sweden . . . . . . . | 1927 | | 56E38 | | |
| United Kingdom . . . | 1949 | | 57E38 | | |
| Uruguay . . . . . . | 1933 | | 37E12 | 47E18 64E55 | |
| *Netherlands* | | | | | |
| Netherlands Antilles . . . | 1957 | | 58E75 | 59E67 | |
| **18. WORKMEN'S COMPENSATION (OCCUPATIONAL DISEASES), 1925** | | | | | |
| Belgium . . . . . . . | 1927 | | 32E620 | | 47S60 |
| Ceylon . . . . . . . | 1952 | | 58E27 | | |
| Chile . . . . . . . . | 1933 | | 58E27 | 59E26 | |
| Colombia . . . . . . | 1933 | | 36E14 | 55E33 | |
| Cuba . . . . . . . . | 1928 | | 30C641 | | 35SS34 |
| Ivory Coast . . . . . | 1935 | 1960 | | 64E56 | |
| Luxembourg . . . . . | 1928 | | 58E27 | | |
| Morocco . . . . . . . | 1956 | 1958 | | 62E44 | |
| Nicaragua . . . . . . | 1934 | | 36E14 | 56E39 58E27 | |
| Spain . . . . . . . . | 1932 | | 57E38 | | |
| Switzerland . . . . . | 1927 | | 57E38 | 62E44 | |
| Tunisia . . . . . . . | 1959 | 1961 | 64E57 | | |
| Uruguay . . . . . . | 1933 | | 37E13 | | 38E13 |
| Yugoslavia . . . . . | 1927 | | 29E523 58E28 | 60E28 | 29C830 |
| **19. EQUALITY OF TREATMENT (ACCIDENT COMPENSATION), 1925** | | | | | |
| Argentina . . . . . . | 1950 | | 51E18 | | 58E28 |
| Austria . . . . . . . | 1928 | | 49E23 59E26 | | 50E24 60E28 |

[1] States of Malaya.

| Country | Entry into Force | Initial Direct Request | Initial Observation | Action Taken in part | Action Taken in full |
|---|---|---|---|---|---|
| **19. EQUALITY OF TREATMENT (ACCIDENT COMPENSATION), 1925 (contd)** | | | | | |
| Bulgaria | 1929 | | 34E228 55E34 | | 38E13 59E26 |
| China | 1934 | 1959 | 64E58 | | |
| Cuba | 1928 | | 30C641 | | 35SS37 |
| Czechoslovakia | 1927 | 1958 | 64E58 | | |
| France | 1928 | 1960 | | | 64E59 |
| Federal Rep. of Germany | 1928 | | 55E34 | | 58E28 |
| Greece | 1936 | | 37E13 55E34 | 39E14 | 56C663 |
| Haiti | 1955 | | 59E26 | | 62E45 |
| Italy | 1928 | | 59E26 | | 62E45 |
| Luxembourg | 1928 | | 58E28 | 60E28 | |
| Nicaragua | 1934 | | 36E15 | | |
| Portugal | 1929 | | 31E463 | | 32E621 |
| Spain | 1929 | | 57E40 | | 62E45 |
| Sweden | 1926 | | 50E24 | 52C499 | 56C663 |
| United Kingdom | 1926 | | 55E35 | | 58E29 |
| *Denmark* | | | | | |
| Greenland | 1954 | | 55E89 | 64E169 | |
| *Netherlands* | | | | | |
| Surinam | 1951 | | 56E100 | | |
| **20. NIGHT WORK (BAKERIES), 1925** | | | | | |
| Argentina | 1955 | | 61E40 | | |
| Bulgaria | 1929 | | 57E41 | | 62C697 |
| Colombia | 1933 | | 36E15 | | |
| Cuba | 1928 | | 56E42 | | 57C669 |
| Finland | 1928 | | 57E41 | | 63E60 |
| Luxembourg | 1928 | | 31E464 | | 32C652 |
| Nicaragua | 1934 | | 36E15 | | RD1950 |
| Spain | 1932 | | 34E11 57E41 | 36E15 61E41 64C662 | |
| Sweden | 1940 | | 52E23 | | |
| Uruguay | 1933 | | 47E18 | | 50E24 |
| **21. INSPECTION OF EMIGRANTS, 1926** | | | | | |
| Japan | 1928 | | 55E36 | | |

| Country | Entry into Force | Initial | | | Action Taken | |
|---|---|---|---|---|---|---|
| | | Direct Request | Observation | in part | in full |

## 22. SEAMEN'S ARTICLES OF AGREEMENT, 1926

| Country | Entry into Force | Direct Request | Observation | in part | in full |
|---|---|---|---|---|---|
| Argentina | 1950 | | 51E18 | | |
| Australia | 1935 | | 56E42 | | 59E27 |
| Belgium | 1928 | | 54E24 | | 62E46 |
| Bulgaria | 1929 | | 55E36 | 60E29 | |
| China | 1936 | | 48E21 | 64E61 | |
| Colombia | 1933 | | 36E16 | 55E36 | |
| Cuba | 1928 | | 30C641 | | 35SS40 |
| Fed. Rep. of Germany | 1930 | | 59E28 | | |
| Mexico | 1934 | | 35C757 | | |
| Morocco | 1959 | 1960 | | 64E63 | |
| Nicaragua | 1934 | | 36E16 | 56E44 | |
| Pakistan | 1933 | 1958 | 64E64 | | |
| Poland | 1931 | | 49E23 | | 59E28 |
| Spain | 1931 | | 57E43 | 64E64 | |
| Uruguay | 1933 | | 38E14 | | |
| Yugoslavia | 1929 | | 32E623 | | 36E16 |

## 23. REPATRIATION OF SEAMEN, 1926

| Country | Entry into Force | Direct Request | Observation | in part | in full |
|---|---|---|---|---|---|
| Argentina | 1950 | | 51E19 | | |
| China | 1936 | | 56E45 | | 64E66 |
| Colombia | 1933 | | 36E16 | | |
| Cuba | 1928 | | 30C641 | | 35SS43 |
| Mexico | 1934 | | 37E14 | | 47E19 |
| Nicaragua | 1934 | | 36E16 | 56E45 | |
| Spain | 1931 | | 57E44 | | 59E28 |
| Uruguay | 1933 | | 36C577 | | |
| Yugoslavia | 1929 | | 32E623 | | 36E16 |

## 24. SICKNESS INSURANCE (INDUSTRY), 1927

| Country | Entry into Force | Direct Request | Observation | in part | in full |
|---|---|---|---|---|---|
| Austria | 1929 | 1960 | | | 62E49 |
| Bulgaria | 1931 | | 32E623 | 55E37 | |
| Chile | 1932 | | 34E229 | 38E15 53E26 | |
| Colombia | 1933 | | 36E16 | 62C698 | |
| Czechoslovakia | 1929 | | 55E38 | | |
| France | 1948 | 1959 | 62E49 | | |
| Haiti | 1955 | | 57E45 | 62E50 | |
| Luxembourg | 1928 | | 31E464 | | 48S107 |

| Country | Entry into Force | Direct Request | Initial Observation | Action Taken in part | in full |
|---|---|---|---|---|---|

**24. SICKNESS INSURANCE (INDUSTRY), 1927 (continued)**

| Country | Entry into Force | Direct Request | Observation | in part | in full |
|---|---|---|---|---|---|
| Nicaragua | 1934 | | 36E17 | 55S68 57E46 | |
| Peru | 1946 | | 50E25 | 54E24 | |
| Rumania | 1929 | 1959 | 31E464 62E51 | | 34E12 |
| Spain | 1932 | | 57E46 | 59C681 | |
| Uruguay | 1933 | | 36C577 | | |

**25. SICKNESS INSURANCE (AGRICULTURE), 1927**

| Country | Entry into Force | Direct Request | Observation | in part | in full |
|---|---|---|---|---|---|
| Austria | 1929 | 1960 | | | 62E52 |
| Bulgaria | 1931 | | 32E624 | 55E39 | |
| Chile | 1932 | | 34E229 | 38E16 53E27 | |
| Colombia | 1933 | | 36E17 | 62C698 | |
| Czechoslovakia | 1929 | | 55E39 | | |
| Haiti | 1955 | | 57E47 | 62E52 | |
| Luxembourg | 1928 | | 31E465 | | 48S110 |
| Nicaragua | 1934 | | 36E17 | 55S70 57E47 | |
| Spain | 1932 | | 57E47 | 59C681 | |
| Uruguay | 1933 | | 36C577 | | |

**26. MINIMUM WAGE-FIXING MACHINERY, 1928**

| Country | Entry into Force | Direct Request | Observation | in part | in full |
|---|---|---|---|---|---|
| Argentina | 1951 | | 58E33 | | |
| Bulgaria | 1936 | | 38E16 | | 39E16 |
| China | 1931 | | 36E17 57E47 | 37E15 | |
| Colombia | 1934 | | 37E15 | 53C382 | |
| Czechoslovakia | 1951 | 1958 | 63E63 | | |
| Ecuador | 1955 | | 57E48 | | |
| Hungary | 1933 | | 35E285 | 36E17 | 38E16 |
| Italy | 1931 | | 51E20 | | 59E30 |
| Nicaragua | 1935 | | 36E17 | 55S74 | |
| Spain | 1931 | | 32E625 57E48 | 36C577 | |
| Uruguay | 1934 | | 37E15 | | 47E20 |
| Venezuela | 1945 | | 51C569 | | |
| *United Kingdom* | | | | | |
| Guernsey | 1930 | | 56E101 | | 59E68 |

| Country | Entry into Force | Initial Direct Request | Initial Observation | Action Taken in part | Action Taken in full |
|---|---|---|---|---|---|
| **27. MARKING OF WEIGHT (PACKAGES TRANSPORTED BY VESSELS), 1929** | | | | | |
| Argentina | 1951 | 1958 | 51E21 63E64 | 54E27 | |
| Belgium | 1935 | | 47E20 | | 49E25 |
| Burma | 1932 | | 50E27 | | 52E25 |
| Chile | 1934 | | 37E15 | | 46S81 |
| Fed. Rep. of Germany | 1934 | | 55E41 | | 59E30 |
| Hungary | 1938 | | 56E48 | | 58E34 |
| India | 1932 | | 48E23 55E42 | 52E25 63E64 | |
| Indonesia | 1934 | 1958 | 63E64 | | |
| Ireland | 1931 | | 33E16 | | 35S239 |
| Nicaragua | 1935 | | 36E17 | | |
| Poland | 1933 | | 34C545 | | 36E18 |
| Uruguay | 1934 | | 38E17 | 39E17 | |
| Venezuela | 1933 | | 35E285 | | 46S81 |
| Yugoslavia | 1934 | | 36E18 52C501 | | 38C512 56E48 |
| **28. PROTECTION AGAINST ACCIDENTS (DOCKERS), 1929** | | | | | |
| Ireland | 1932 | | 35C757 | | 63S76 |
| Nicaragua | 1935 | | 36E18 | | |
| **29. FORCED LABOUR, 1930** | | | | | |
| Bulgaria | 1933 | | 57E50 | 58E34 | |
| Central African Rep. | 1938 | 1962 | 64E72 | | |
| Congo (Brazzaville) | 1938 | 1960 | 62E53 | | |
| Congo (Leopoldville) | 1960 | | 53E40 | 62E54 | |
| Czechoslovakia | 1958 | 1960 | | 64E73 | |
| Dominican Republic | 1957 | 1959 | 64E73 | | |
| Ecuador | 1955 | | 57E50 | | |
| Gabon | 1938 | 1962 | | 64E73 | |
| Greece | 1953 | | 56E49 | 61E44 | |
| Guinea | 1938 | 1960 | 62E54 | | |
| Honduras | 1958 | 1960 | 64E75 | | |
| Hungary | 1957 | | 61E44 | | |
| India | 1955 | | 57E51 | | |
| Israel | 1956 | 1958 | 64E75 | | |
| Ivory Coast | 1938 | 1962 | 64E77 | | |

| Country | Entry into Force | Direct Request | Initial Observation | Action Taken in part | in full |
|---|---|---|---|---|---|

### 29. FORCED LABOUR, 1930 (continued)

| Country | Entry into Force | Direct Request | Initial Observation | Action Taken in part | in full |
|---|---|---|---|---|---|
| Liberia [1] . . . . . . . . | 1932 | | 35E286 | 63E65 | |
| Malagasy Republic . . . | 1938 | 1962 | 64E79 | | |
| States of Malaya . . . . | 1931 | | 49E27 | 56E104 | 59E31 |
| Nicaragua . . . . . . . | 1935 | 1959 | 64E80 | | |
| Sweden . . . . . . . . | 1932 | | 54E29 | | |
| Ukraine . . . . . . . . | 1957 | 1959 | | 64E80 | |
| U.S.S.R. . . . . . . . | 1957 | 1959 | | 64E80 | |
| Venezuela . . . . . . . | 1945 | 1960 | 63E66 | | |
| Vietnam . . . . . . . | 1954 | | 57E53 | | |
| *Australia* | | | | | |
| Papua . . . . . . . . . | 1933 | | 35E285 | 55E89 58E76 | 62S287 |
| *Belgium* | | | | | |
| Ruanda-Urundi . . . . . | 1944 | | 53E40 | 62E145 | |
| *France* | | | | | |
| All non-metropolitan territories . . . . . . | 1938 | | 49E27 | 51E32 | 54E51 |
| *Netherlands* | | | | | |
| Netherlands Antilles . . . | 1934 | | 57E112 | | 60E62 |
| Netherlands East Indies . | 1934 | | 35E287 | 36E19 48E24 | 53C383 |
| Netherlands New Guinea . | 1934 | | 56E102 | | 57E112 |
| Surinam . . . . . . . . | 1934 | | 57E112 | | |
| *United Kingdom* | | | | | |
| Bechuanaland . . . . . | 1932 | | 50E43 | 64E170 | |
| British Honduras . . . . | 1932 | | 56E103 | | 63E133 |
| Fiji . . . . . . . . . . | 1932 | | 56E103 | 62E146 64E171 | |
| Gold Coast . . . . . . | 1932 | | 35E285 | 36E18 | |
| Kenya . . . . . . . . | 1932 | | 49E27 56E103 | 52E35 59E69 64E77 | |
| Nigeria . . . . . . . . | 1932 | | 55E8 | 57E113 | |
| North Borneo (Sabah) . | 1932 | | 55E91 | | 62E146 |
| Northern Rhodesia . . . | 1932 | 1959 | | 64E171 | |

---

[1] Information on the progress noted in 1963 will be found not in the Report of the Committee of Experts but in that of the Commission of Inquiry appointed to examine the complaint by Portugal concerning the observance of Convention No. 29 by Liberia *(Commission of Inquiry Report (Portugal-Liberia), op. cit.,* pp. 95-96 in particular).

| Country | Entry into Force | Initia | | Action Taken | |
| --- | --- | --- | --- | --- | --- |
| | | *Direct Request* | *Observation* | *in part* | *in full* |

### 29. FORCED LABOUR, 1930 (continued)

| Country | Entry into Force | Direct Request | Observation | in part | in full |
| --- | --- | --- | --- | --- | --- |
| Seychelles . . . . . . . | 1932 | | 54E52 | | 56E104 |
| Sierra Leone . . . . . . | 1932 | | 35E286 | 36E19 | |
| Singapore . . . . . . . | 1932 | | 54E52 | | 57E113 |
| Solomon Islands . . . . | 1932 | 1959 | | 64E171 | |
| Tanganyika . . . . . . | 1932 | | 33E497 49E28 | 34E230 62E55 | |
| Uganda . . . . . . . . | 1932 | | 55E91 | 62S290 | |
| Zanzibar . . . . . . . . | 1932 | | 49E28 | 58E77 | |

### 30. HOURS OF WORK (COMMERCE AND OFFICES), 1930

| Country | Entry into Force | Direct Request | Observation | in part | in full |
| --- | --- | --- | --- | --- | --- |
| Argentina . . . . . . . | 1951 | | 52E26 | | 55E45 |
| Bulgaria . . . . . . . . | 1933 | | 35E287 57E54 | 37E17 59E31 64C666 | |
| Haiti . . . . . . . . . | 1953 | | 57E54 | | |
| Israel . . . . . . . . . | 1952 | | 54E30 | | 56E52 |
| Nicaragua . . . . . . . | 1935 | | 36E20 | 56E52 | |
| Norway . . . . . . . . | 1954 | | 57E54 | | |
| Spain . . . . . . . . . | 1933 | | 58E35 | | |

### 32. PROTECTION AGAINST ACCIDENTS (DOCKERS) (Revised), 1932

| Country | Entry into Force | Direct Request | Observation | in part | in full |
| --- | --- | --- | --- | --- | --- |
| Argentina . . . . . . . | 1951 | | 52E26 | | |
| Belgium . . . . . . . . | 1953 | | 55E46 61E48 | | 58E36 |
| Bulgaria . . . . . . . . | 1950 | 1958 | | 61E48 64E83 | |
| Chile . . . . . . . . . | 1936 | | 38E19 | 47E21 | |
| China . . . . . . . . . | 1936 | | 57E55 | 63E68 | |
| Cuba . . . . . . . . . | 1955 | | 57E55 | | |
| Finland . . . . . . . . | 1950 | | 52E26 | | 54E30 |
| France . . . . . . . . . | 1956 | | 61E48 | | |
| India . . . . . . . . . | 1948 | | 49E28 | | 51E22 |
| Italy . . . . . . . . . . | 1934 | | 59E33 | 63E68 | |
| Mexico . . . . . . . . | 1935 | | 37E17 | | |
| New Zealand . . . . . | 1939 | | 56E52 | 58E36 | |
| Pakistan . . . . . . . . | 1948 | | 50E28 | | 52E27 |
| Spain . . . . . . . . . | 1935 | | 57E56 | 63E69 | |
| Uruguay . . . . . . . | 1934 | | 37E17 | 47E22 | |

| Country | Entry into Force | Initial Direct Request | Initial Observation | Action Taken in part | Action Taken in full |
|---|---|---|---|---|---|
| **33. MINIMUM AGE (NON-INDUSTRIAL EMPLOYMENT), 1932** | | | | | |
| Argentina | 1951 | | 51E22 | 58E37 | |
| Austria | 1937 | | 48E25 | 49E28 53E30 | 63E69 |
| Congo (Brazzaville) | 1954 | 1961 | | | 64E84 |
| Cuba | 1937 | | 38E20 | 54E31 | |
| France | 1940 | | 48E25 | 55E47 | |
| Ivory Coast | 1954 | 1961 | | | 63E69 |
| Malagasy Republic | 1954 | 1961 | | 63E70 | |
| Spain | 1935 | | 57E57 | 61E50 | |
| Togo | 1954 | | 57E113 | | 63E70 |
| Uruguay | 1935 | | 37E17 | | RD1954 |
| *France* | | | | | |
| Comoro Islands | 1954 | | 57E113 | | 63E133 |
| St-Pierre & Miquelon | 1954 | 1959 | 63E133 | | |
| **34. FEE-CHARGING EMPLOYMENT AGENCIES, 1933** | | | | | |
| Chile | 1936 | | 57E57 | 60C618 | |
| Mexico | 1939 | | 57E57 | | |
| Spain | 1936 | | 57E57 | | 60E33 |
| **35. OLD-AGE INSURANCE (INDUSTRY, ETC.), 1933** | | | | | |
| Argentina | 1956 | | 58E38 | | |
| Bulgaria | 1950 | | 61E50 | | |
| Chile | 1937 | | 51E22 | 53E30 | |
| Peru | 1946 | | 50E29 | 64E85 | |
| **36. OLD-AGE INSURANCE (AGRICULTURE), 1933** | | | | | |
| Argentina | 1956 | | 58E38 | | |
| Bulgaria | 1950 | | 61E51 | | |
| Chile | 1937 | | 51E24 | 53E31 | |
| **37. INVALIDITY INSURANCE (INDUSTRY, ETC.), 1933** | | | | | |
| Bulgaria | 1950 | | 55E48 | 58E38 | |
| Chile | 1937 | | 57E59 | | |
| Peru | 1946 | | 50E30 | 64E86 | |
| **38. INVALIDITY INSURANCE (AGRICULTURE), 1933** | | | | | |
| Bulgaria | 1950 | | 55E49 | 58E38 | |

| Country | Entry into Force | Direct Request | Observation | Action Taken in part | Action Taken in full |
|---------|:---:|:---:|:---:|:---:|:---:|

**39. SURVIVORS' INSURANCE (INDUSTRY, ETC.), 1933**

| Country | Entry into Force | Direct Request | Observation | in part | in full |
|---------|:---:|:---:|:---:|:---:|:---:|
| Bulgaria | 1950 | | 55E49 | 58E39 | |
| Peru | 1946 | | 50E30 | 64E86 | |

**40. SURVIVORS' INSURANCE (AGRICULTURE), 1933**

| Country | Entry into Force | Direct Request | Observation | in part | in full |
|---------|:---:|:---:|:---:|:---:|:---:|
| Bulgaria | 1950 | | 55E49 | 58E39 | |

**41. NIGHT WORK (WOMEN) (Revised), 1934**

| Country | Entry into Force | Direct Request | Observation | in part | in full |
|---------|:---:|:---:|:---:|:---:|:---:|
| Afghanistan | 1940 | | 50E30 | | |
| Brazil | 1937 | | 38E20 | 47C555 | 55E49 |
| Ceylon | 1951 | | 60E34 | | |
| Gabon | 1940 | | 54E50 | | 63E72 |
| Greece | 1937 | | 55E49 | 56E54 | RD1959 |
| Hungary | 1937 | | 55E50 | | |
| Iraq | 1939 | | 51E25 | | |
| New Zealand | 1939 | | 47E22 | | 50E31 |
| Peru | 1946 | | 50E31 | | |
| Switzerland | 1937 | | 49E30 | | 51E25 |

**42. WORKMEN'S COMPENSATION (OCCUPATIONAL DISEASES) (Revised), 1934**

| Country | Entry into Force | Direct Request | Observation | in part | in full |
|---------|:---:|:---:|:---:|:---:|:---:|
| Argentina | 1951 | 1959 | 64E87 | | |
| Austria | 1937 | | 57E60 | | 64E88 |
| Belgium | 1950 | 1959 | 52E29 64E88 | 54E32 | 57E60 |
| Bulgaria | 1950 | | 57E60 | 64C667 | |
| Czechoslovakia | 1950 | | 58E40 | | |
| Denmark | 1940 | 1960 | 64E89 | 64C667 | |
| France | 1949 | | 49E30 | 54E32 | |
| Fed. Rep. of Germany | 1956 | | 58E40 | 62E60 | 64E91 |
| Greece | 1953 | | 55E50 | 57E61 62E60 | |
| Haiti | 1956 | | 61E52 | | 64E91 |
| Hungary | 1936 | | 55E50 | | 59E35 |
| Mexico | 1938 | | 53C385 | 58E41 | |
| Morocco | 1958 | 1960 | 64E92 | | |
| New Zealand | 1939 | 1958 | 64E93 | | |
| Norway | 1936 | | 58E41 | 64E93 | |
| Poland | 1949 | | 56E56 | 57E61 | 62E62 |
| Rep. of South Africa | 1953 | 1959 | 63E74 | | |

| Country | Entry into Force | Initial Direct Request | Initial Observation | Action Taken in part | Action Taken in full |
|---|---|---|---|---|---|
| **42. WORKMEN'S COMPENSATION (OCCUPATIONAL DISEASES (Revised), 1934 (continued)** | | | | | |
| Sweden . . . . . . . | 1938 | | 56E56 | | |
| Uruguay . . . . . . | 1955 | | 57E62 | | |
| *Belgium* | | | | | |
| Belgian Congo and Ruanda-Urundi . . . . | 1957 | 1959 | | 60E62 | |
| *France* | | | | | |
| Overseas Departments . . | 1955 | | 56E106 | | |
| *Netherlands* | | | | | |
| Netherlands Antilles . . . | 1955 | | 57E114 | | |
| Surinam . . . . . . . | 1951 | | 57E114 | | |
| *Rep. of South Africa* | | | | | |
| South West Africa . . . | 1958 | 1959 | | 63E134 | |
| **43. SHEET-GLASS WORKS, 1934** | | | | | |
| Bulgaria . . . . . . . | 1950 | | 57E62 | | |
| Czechoslovakia . . . . . | 1939 | | 49E30 | | |
| France . . . . . . . . | 1939 | | 49E31 | | 55E51 |
| Mexico . . . . . . . | 1939 | | 50E31 | | |
| United Kingdom . . . . | 1938 | | 58E42 | | RD1958 |
| Uruguay . . . . . . | 1955 | | 57E63 | | |
| **44. UNEMPLOYMENT PROVISION, 1934** | | | | | |
| Bulgaria . . . . . . . | 1950 | | 55E51 | 58E42 | |
| Czechoslovakia . . . . . | 1951 | | 56E57 | | |
| **45. UNDERGROUND WORK (WOMEN), 1935** | | | | | |
| Afghanistan . . . . . . | 1938 | | 50E32 | | |
| Austria . . . . . . . | 1938 | | 51E26 | | 53E32 |
| Bulgaria . . . . . . . | 1950 | | 58E43 | | 60E35 |
| Chile . . . . . . . . | 1947 | 1962 | 64E97 | | |
| China . . . . . . . . | 1937 | | 58E43 | 64E97 | |
| Fed. Rep. of Germany . . | 1955 | | 57E63 | | |
| Greece . . . . . . . . | 1937 | 1962 | 64E98 | | |
| Hungary . . . . . . | 1939 | | 55E52 | 63E75 | |
| Poland . . . . . . . | 1958 | 1960 | | | 64E98 |
| United Arab Republic . . | 1948 | 1960 | | | 63E75 |
| Yugoslavia . . . . . . | 1953 | | 59E36 | 63E75 | |

| Country | Entry into Force | Initial Direct Request | Observation | Action Taken in part | in full |
|---------|------------------|------------------------|-------------|----------------------|---------|

**48. MAINTENANCE OF MIGRANTS' PENSION RIGHTS, 1935**

| Country | Entry into Force | Initial Direct Request | Observation | in part | in full |
|---------|------------------|------------------------|-------------|---------|---------|
| Czechoslovakia . . . . . | 1951 | | 55E52 | 56E58 | 57E64 |
| Hungary . . . . . . . | 1938 | | 55E53 | | |
| Netherlands . . . . . . | 1939 | | 51E26 | 53E32 | 59E36 |
| Spain . . . . . . . . . | 1938 | | 57E64 | | |

**49. REDUCTION OF HOURS OF WORK (GLASS-BOTTLE WORKS), 1935**

| Country | Entry into Force | Initial Direct Request | Observation | in part | in full |
|---------|------------------|------------------------|-------------|---------|---------|
| Bulgaria . . . . . . . . | 1950 | | 57E64 | | |
| Czechoslovakia . . . . . | 1939 | | 49E31 | | |
| France . . . . . . . . . | 1939 | | 49E31 | | 55E54 |
| Mexico . . . . . . . . | 1939 | | 56E59 | | |

**50. RECRUITING OF INDIGENOUS WORKERS, 1936**

| Country | Entry into Force | Initial Direct Request | Observation | in part | in full |
|---------|------------------|------------------------|-------------|---------|---------|
| Argentina . . . . . . . | 1951 | | 61E54 | | |
| *Belgium* | | | | | |
| Belgian Congo and | | | | | |
| Ruanda Urundi . . . . | 1948 | | 51E33 | 56E107 | |
| *United Kingdom* | | | | | |
| British Guiana . . . . . | 1940 | 1958 | 63E134 | | |
| Brunei . . . . . . . . . | 1940 | | 51E33 | | 56E107 |
| Hong Kong . . . . . . | 1940 | | 53E40 | | |
| Kenya . . . . . . . . | 1940 | | 57E115 | | 58E78 |
| Northern Rhodesia . . . | 1940 | | 57E115 | | |
| Sarawak . . . . . . . . | 1940 | | 51E33 | | 54E53 |
| Swaziland . . . . . . . | 1958 | | 52E36 | 63E134 | |
| Tanganyika . . . . . . | 1939 | | 52E36 | | 61E118 |

**52. HOLIDAYS WITH PAY, 1936**

| Country | Entry into Force | Initial Direct Request | Observation | in part | in full |
|---------|------------------|------------------------|-------------|---------|---------|
| Argentina . . . . . . . | 1951 | | 51E26 | | |
| Bulgaria . . . . . . . . | 1950 | | 55E54 | 58E44 59E37 | 62E65 |
| Burma . . . . . . . . . | 1955 | | 58E44 | | |
| Byelorussia . . . . . . | 1957 | | 60E36 | | |
| Cuba . . . . . . . . . | 1954 | | 56E59 | 59E37 | |
| Czechoslovakia . . . . . | 1951 | | 55E54 | | 62E66 |
| Finland . . . . . . . . | 1950 | | 52E30 | 61E55 | |
| France . . . . . . . . . | 1940 | | 57E66 | | |
| Greece . . . . . . . . | 1953 | | 55E55 | 62E66 | |
| Israel . . . . . . . . . | 1952 | | 54E34 | | 58E45 |

| Country | Entry into Force | Initial | | Action Taken | |
|---|---|---|---|---|---|
| | | Direct Request | Observation | in part | in full |

**52. HOLIDAYS WITH PAY, 1936 (continued)**

| Country | Entry into Force | Direct Request | Observation | in part | in full |
|---|---|---|---|---|---|
| Italy . . . . . . . . . | 1953 | | 55E56 | 60E36 | |
| Mexico . . . . . . . | 1939 | | 47E24 | 57E67 | |
| Morocco . . . . . . . | 1957 | 1959 | | | 62E67 |
| Tunisia . . . . . . . | 1957 | 1960 | | 64E102 | |
| Ukraine . . . . . . . | 1957 | | 59E38 | | |
| U.S.S.R. . . . . . . | 1957 | | 59E38 | | |
| United Arab Republic . . | 1955 | | 58E44 | 60E37 | |
| Uruguay . . . . . . | 1955 | | 57E67 | | |
| Vietnam . . . . . . . | 1954 | | 57E67 | 59E38 | 60E37 |
| Yugoslavia . . . . . | 1954 | | 56E61 | 59E38 | |

**53. OFFICERS' COMPETENCY CERTIFICATES, 1936**

| Country | Entry into Force | Direct Request | Observation | in part | in full |
|---|---|---|---|---|---|
| Bulgaria . . . . . . . | 1950 | | 59E39 | | |
| United Arab Republic . . | 1940 | | 49E31 | 51E26 | 57E68 |

**55. SHIPOWNERS' LIABILITY (SICK AND INJURED SEAMEN), 1936**

| Country | Entry into Force | Direct Request | Observation | in part | in full |
|---|---|---|---|---|---|
| Italy . . . . . . . . . | 1953 | | 55E57 | | 64E104 |
| Morocco . . . . . . . | 1959 | 1961 | | 62E69 | |

**58. MINIMUM AGE (SEA) (Revised), 1936**

| Country | Entry into Force | Direct Request | Observation | in part | in full |
|---|---|---|---|---|---|
| Albania . . . . . . . | 1958 | 1962 | | | 63E78 |
| Belgium . . . . . . . | 1939 | | 48E28 | | 62E70 |
| Cuba . . . . . . . . | 1954 | | 56E62 | | 59E39 |
| Uruguay . . . . . . | 1955 | | 57E68 | | |
| *Netherlands* | | | | | |
| Netherlands Antilles . . . | 1957 | 1958 | 63E135 | | |

**59. MINUMUM AGE (INDUSTRY) (Revised), 1937**

| Country | Entry into Force | Direct Request | Observation | in part | in full |
|---|---|---|---|---|---|
| Albania . . . . . . . | 1958 | | 62E70 | 63E78 | |
| China . . . . . . . . | 1941 | | 48E28 | | |
| Cuba . . . . . . . . | 1955 | | 57E68 | | 59E39 |
| Italy . . . . . . . . . | 1953 | | 55E57 | 62E71 | |
| New Zealand . . . . | 1948 | | 49E32 | 54E35 | 58E47 |
| Norway . . . . . . . | 1941 | | 48E28 | | 49E32 |
| Pakistan . . . . . . . | 1956 | 1958 | 63E78 | | |
| Uruguay . . . . . . | 1955 | | 57E69 | | |

| Country | Entry into Force | Initial Direct Request | Initial Observation | Action Taken in part | Action Taken in full |
|---|---|---|---|---|---|
| **60. MINIMUM AGE (NON-INDUSTRIAL EMPLOYMENT) (Revised), 1937** | | | | | |
| Bulgaria . . . . . . . . | 1950 | | 55E58 | 58E47 | 59E40 |
| Cuba . . . . . . . . . | 1955 | | 57E69 | 59E40 63E78 | |
| Italy . . . . . . . . . | 1953 | | 55E58 | 62E71 | |
| Luxembourg . . . . . . | 1959 | 1962 | | 63E79 | |
| New Zealand . . . . . | 1950 | | 49E32 | 59E40 | RD1961 |
| Uruguay . . . . . . . | 1955 | | 57E70 | | |
| **62. SAFETY PROVISIONS (BUILDING), 1937** | | | | | |
| Belgium . . . . . . . . | 1952 | | 54E35 | | 58E47 |
| Bulgaria . . . . . . . | 1950 | | 57E70 | | |
| Finland . . . . . . . . | 1948 | | 49E32 | 55E58 57E70 | |
| France . . . . . . . . | 1951 | | 53E34 | 62E71 | |
| Mexico . . . . . . . . | 1942 | | 47E25 | 63E79 | |
| Poland . . . . . . . . | 1951 | | 53E34 | 57E71 | |
| Switzerland . . . . . . | 1942 | | 47E25 | 50E33 | 52E31 |
| Uruguay . . . . . . . | 1955 | | 57E71 | | |
| *France* Overseas Departments . . | 1955 | | 56E108 | 62E147 | |
| *Netherlands* Surinam . . . . . . . | 1951 | | 57E116 | | |
| **63. STATISTICS OF WAGES AND HOURS OF WORK, 1938** | | | | | |
| Burma . . . . . . . . | 1962 | | 58E48 | 61E57 | |
| Ceylon . . . . . . . . | 1953 | | 55E59 | 57E71 | 59E41 |
| Cuba . . . . . . . . . | 1955 | | 57E72 | 62E72 | |
| Czechoslovakia . . . . . | 1951 | | 55E59 | 60E39 | |
| Denmark . . . . . . . | 1940 | 1959 | 50E33 64E106 | 53E34 | 56E64 |
| Finland . . . . . . . . | 1948 | | 50E33 | 59E41 60E39 | |
| France . . . . . . . . | 1952 | | 54E36 | 55E60 57E72 | 64E106 |
| Mexico . . . . . . . . | 1943 | | 47E25 | 56E64 58E49 59E41 | |
| Netherlands . . . . . . | 1941 | | 49E33 | 54E36 | 55E60 |
| Norway . . . . . . . . | 1941 | | 50E34 | 53E34 54E36 | 59E41 |

| Country | Entry into Force | Direct Request | Initial Observation | Action Taken In part | in full |
|---------|------------------|----------------|---------------------|-------------|---------|

### 63. STATISTICS OF WAGES AND HOURS OF WORK, 1938 (continued)

| Country | Entry into Force | Direct Request | Initial Observation | In part | in full |
|---------|------------------|----------------|---------------------|---------|---------|
| Sweden | 1940 | | 50E34 | 59E41 | |
| United Arab Republic | 1941 | | 49E33 | 53E34 59E41 | |
| Uruguay | 1955 | | 57E73 | | |

### 64. CONTRACTS OF EMPLOYMENT (INDIGENOUS WORKERS), 1939

*United Kingdom*

| Country | Entry into Force | Direct Request | Initial Observation | In part | in full |
|---------|------------------|----------------|---------------------|---------|---------|
| Basutoland | 1948 | | 56E109 | 58E79 | |
| Bechuanaland | 1948 | | 56E110 | 63C546 | |
| British Guiana | 1948 | | 57E117 | | |
| British Honduras | 1948 | 1958 | | | 63E136 |
| Brunei | 1948 | | 56E110 | 58E79 | 59E71 |
| Kenya | 1948 | | 57E117 | | |
| Northern Rhodesia | 1948 | | 57E117 | | |
| Seychelles | 1948 | | 55E94 | | |
| Sierra Leone | 1948 | | 54E53 | 57E118 64E107 | |

### 65. PENAL SANCTIONS (INDIGENOUS WORKERS), 1939

| Country | Entry into Force | Direct Request | Initial Observation | In part | in full |
|---------|------------------|----------------|---------------------|---------|---------|
| States of Malaya | 1943 | | 55E95 | | 59E42 |
| *New Zealand* | | | | | |
| Western Samoa [1] | 1947 | | 50E40 | 52E35 | 57E119 |
| *United Kingdom* | | | | | |
| Basutoland | 1944 | | 55E95 | 58E80 | |
| Bechuanaland | 1944 | | 55E95 | 64E173 | |
| British Guiana | 1944 | | 55E95 | | 62E148 |
| British Honduras | 1944 | | 56E111 | | 57C687 |
| Brunei | 1944 | | 50E40 | | 55E95 |
| Gilbert & Ellice Islands | 1944 | | 50E40 | | 53E41 |
| Kenya | 1944 | | 56E111 | 58E80 64E107 | |
| Mauritius | 1944 | 1962 | | 64E173 | |
| Northern Rhodesia | 1944 | | 55E95 | 64E173 | |
| Sierra Leone | 1944 | | 55E96 | | 57E119 |
| Singapore | 1944 | | 50E40 | | 52E36 |
| Swaziland | 1944 | | 55E96 | | 62E148 |

[1] Western Samoa became independent on 1 January 1962, but has not joined the I.L.O. thus far.

| Country | Entry into Force | Initial | | Action Taken | |
|---|---|---|---|---|---|
| | | Direct Request | Observation | in part | in full |

**65. PENAL SANCTIONS (INDIGENOUS WORKERS), 1939 (continued)**

| Country | Entry into Force | Direct Request | Observation | in part | in full |
|---|---|---|---|---|---|
| Tanganyika | 1944 | | 50E41 | 55E96 | 57E119 |
| Uganda | 1944 | | 50E41 | 55E96 56E111 | |
| Zanzibar | 1944 | | 55E96 | | 57E119 |

**67. HOURS OF WORK AND REST PERIODS (ROAD TRANSPORT), 1939**

| Country | Entry into Force | Direct Request | Observation | in part | in full |
|---|---|---|---|---|---|
| Cuba | 1955 | | 57E73 | | |
| Uruguay | 1955 | | 57E74 | | |

**68. FOOD AND CATERING (SHIPS' CREWS), 1946**

| Country | Entry into Force | Direct Request | Observation | in part | in full |
|---|---|---|---|---|---|
| Argentina | 1957 | | 61E58 | | |
| Portugal | 1957 | 1959 | | 61E58 | |

**69. CERTIFICATION OF SHIPS' COOKS, 1946**

| Country | Entry into Force | Direct Request | Observation | in part | in full |
|---|---|---|---|---|---|
| Belgium | 1953 | | 55E60 | 58E50 | 60E40 |
| Bulgaria | 1953 | | 57E74 | | 59E42 |
| Italy | 1953 | | 55E60 | 56E65 | 58E50 |
| Poland | 1954 | | 56E66 | 58E50 | 64E109 |
| Portugal | 1953 | | 55E61 | 59E42 | 64E109 |
| *Netherlands* | | | | | |
| Netherlands Antilles | 1953 | | 56E111 | | |

**73. MEDICAL EXAMINATION (SEAFARERS), 1946**

| Country | Entry into Force | Direct Request | Observation | in part | in full |
|---|---|---|---|---|---|
| Argentina | 1955 | | 60E40 | | |
| Belgium | 1955 | | 57E75 | | 59E42 |
| Bulgaria | 1955 | | 57E75 | | 59E42 |
| Finland | 1956 | 1958 | | | 60E40 |
| France | 1955 | | 57E75 | | 62E74 |
| Italy | 1955 | | 57E75 | | 64E109 |
| Poland | 1955 | | 57E75 | | 59E42 |
| Portugal | 1955 | | 57E75 | 59E42 | 64E109 |
| Uruguay | 1955 | | 57E76 | | |

**74. CERTIFICATION OF ABLE SEAMEN, 1946**

| Country | Entry into Force | Direct Request | Observation | in part | in full |
|---|---|---|---|---|---|
| Belgium | 1952 | | 54E37 | 58E50 | 60E40 |
| Poland | 1953 | | 55E76 | 58E51 59E43 | |
| Portugal | 1953 | | 57E61 | 59E43 | |

| Country | Entry Into Force | Direct Request | Initial Observation | Action Taken in part | in full |
|---|---|---|---|---|---|

## 77. MEDICAL EXAMINATION OF YOUNG PERSONS (INDUSTRY), 1946

| Country | Entry Into Force | Direct Request | Initial Observation | in part | in full |
|---|---|---|---|---|---|
| Argentina . . . . . . . | 1956 | | 58E51 | | |
| Cuba . . . . . . . . . | 1955 | | 57E76 | | 59E43 |
| France . . . . . . . . | 1952 | | 54E37 | 56E66 60E40 | |
| Guatemala . . . . . . | 1953 | | 57C675 | | |
| Hungary . . . . . . | 1957 | 1960 | 62E75 | | |
| Iraq . . . . . . . . | 1952 | | 54E37 | | |
| Israel . . . . . . . . | 1954 | | 56E66 | 64E111 | |
| Italy . . . . . . . . . | 1953 | | 55E62 | | |
| Luxembourg . . . . . | 1959 | 1961 | 64E111 | | |
| Uruguay . . . . . . | 1955 | | 57E77 | | |

## 78. MEDICAL EXAMINATION OF YOUNG PERSONS (NON-INDUSTRIAL OCCUPATIONS), 1946

| Country | Entry Into Force | Direct Request | Initial Observation | in part | in full |
|---|---|---|---|---|---|
| Argentina . . . . . . | 1956 | | 58E51 | | |
| Bulgaria . . . . . . . | 1950 | | 55E62 | 60E41 | |
| Cuba . . . . . . . . | 1955 | | 57E77 | | 59E43 |
| France . . . . . . . . | 1952 | | 54E37 | 56E67 | |
| Guatemala . . . . . . | 1953 | | 57C676 | | |
| Hungary . . . . . . | 1957 | 1960 | 64E112 | | |
| Israel . . . . . . . . | 1954 | | 56E67 | 64E112 | |
| Italy . . . . . . . . . | 1953 | | 55E62 | | |
| Luxembourg . . . . . | 1959 | 1963 | 64E112 | | |
| Poland . . . . . . . | 1950 | | 52E32 | 60E41 | |
| Uruguay . . . . . . | 1955 | | 58E52 | | |

## 79. NIGHT WORK OF YOUNG PERSONS (NON-INDUSTRIAL OCCUPATIONS) 1946

| Country | Entry Into Force | Direct Request | Initial Observation | in part | in full |
|---|---|---|---|---|---|
| Argentina . . . . . . | 1956 | | 58E52 | | |
| Bulgaria . . . . . . . | 1950 | | 55E63 | | |
| Cuba . . . . . . . . | 1955 | | 57E78 | 63E82 | |
| Dominican Republic . . | 1954 | | 56E67 | 57E78 59E44 | |
| Guatemala . . . . . . | 1953 | | 57C676 | 62E77 | |
| Israel . . . . . . . . | 1954 | | 56E68 | 59E44 64E113 | |
| Italy . . . . . . . . . | 1953 | | 55E63 | | |

| Country | Entry into Force | Initial | | Action Taken | |
|---------|:---:|:---:|:---:|:---:|:---:|
| | | Direct Request | Observation | in part | in full |

### 81. LABOUR INSPECTION, 1947

| Country | Entry into Force | Direct Request | Observation | in part | in full |
|---------|:---:|:---:|:---:|:---:|:---:|
| Argentina . . . . . . . | 1956 | | 60E41 | | |
| Austria . . . . . . . . | 1950 | | 53E35 | | 54E38 |
| Brazil . . . . . . . . . | 1958 | 1960 | 64E115 | 64C671 | |
| Bulgaria . . . . . . . . | 1950 | | 58E52 | 59E44 | |
| Ceylon . . . . . . . . | 1957 | | 60E42 | | |
| Cuba . . . . . . . . . | 1955 | | 57E79 | | |
| Dominican Republic . . | 1954 | | 56E69 | | |
| France . . . . . . . . . | 1951 | | 53E36 | | 59E44 |
| Fed. Rep. of Germany . . | 1956 | 1958 | | 62E80 | |
| Greece . . . . . . . . . | 1956 | | 60E42 . | | |
| Guatemala . . . . . . . | 1953 | | 57E79 | 62E80 | |
| Haiti . . . . . . . . . | 1953 | | 55E64 | 60E43 62E80 | |
| Iraq . . . . . . . . . | 1952 | | 54E38 | 62E81 | |
| Israel . . . . . . . . . | 1956 | 1958 | 62E81 | | |
| Italy . . . . . . . . . . | 1953 | | 56E69 | 57E80 | |
| Japan . . . . . . . . . | 1954 | | 57E80 | 58E53 | 62E81 |
| Morocco . . . . . . . . | 1959 | 1961 | | 62E81 | |
| Netherlands . . . . . | 1952 | | 55E65 | | 59E45 |
| Nigeria . . . . . . . . | 1958 | 1959 | 64E119 | | |
| Pakistan . . . . . . . . | 1954 | | 56E70 | | |
| Panama . . . . . . . . | 1959 | 1961 | 64E119 | | |
| Sierra Leone . . . . . . | 1958 | 1959 | 64E119 | | |
| Turkey . . . . . . . . | 1952 | | 54E38 | 59E45 | |
| United Arab Republic . . | 1957 | 1959 | 62E82 | | |

#### Netherlands

| Country | Entry into Force | Direct Request | Observation | in part | in full |
|---------|:---:|:---:|:---:|:---:|:---:|
| Netherlands Antilles . . . | 1952 | | 55E96 | | |
| Surinam . . . . . . . . | 1952 | | 57E120 | | |

#### United Kingdom

| Country | Entry into Force | Direct Request | Observation | in part | in full |
|---------|:---:|:---:|:---:|:---:|:---:|
| Barbados . . . . . . . | 1958 | 1959 | 63E137 | | |
| Grenada . . . . . . . . | 1958 | 1960 | 64E175 | | |
| Hong Kong . . . . . . | 1958 | 1959 | | 62E149 | |
| Jersey . . . . . . . . . | 1950 | | 56E113 | | 58E81 |
| Mauritius . . . . . . . | 1958 | 1959 | | 62E149 | |
| North Borneo (Sabah) . . | 1958 | 1959 | 62E150 | | |
| Southern Rhodesia . . . | 1960 | 1961 | 64E175 | | |

| Country | Entry into Force | Direct Request | Initial Observation | Action Taken in part | in full |
|---|---|---|---|---|---|

## 82. SOCIAL POLICY (NON-METROPOLITAN TERRITORIES), 1947

*United Kingdom*

| Country | Entry into Force | Direct Request | Initial Observation | Action Taken in part | in full |
|---|---|---|---|---|---|
| Aden . . . . . . . . . | 1955 | 1958 | 64E175 | | |
| Antigua . . . . . . . | 1955 | 1958 | 64E176 | | |
| Bahamas . . . . . . . | 1955 | 1958 | 64E176 | | |
| Barbados . . . . . . | 1955 | | 61E120 | | |
| Bechuanaland . . . . | 1955 | 1958 | | 64E177 | |
| Bermuda . . . . . . . | 1955 | 1959 | 62E150 | | |
| British Guiana . . . . | 1955 | 1958 | 64E177 | | |
| British Virgin Islands . . | 1955 | 1959 | | | 61E120 |
| Mauritius . . . . . . | 1955 | 1958 | | 62E151 | |
| Montserrat . . . . . . | 1955 | | 62E151 | | 63E137 |
| Northern Rhodesia . . . | 1955 | 1959 | 62E151 | 64E178 | |
| Southern Rhodesia . . . | 1955 | 1958 | | 62E151 | |
| Swaziland . . . . . . | 1955 | 1958 | | 62E115 | |

## 84. RIGHT OF ASSOCIATION (NON-METROPOLITAN TERRITORIES), 1947

*United Kingdom*

| Country | Entry into Force | Direct Request | Initial Observation | Action Taken in part | in full |
|---|---|---|---|---|---|
| Fiji . . . . . . . . . . | 1953 | | 55E97 | | |
| Jamaica . . . . . . . | 1950 | 1958 | | | 61E121 |
| Hong Kong . . . . . . | 1953 | | 56E114 | 63E138 | |
| Nyasaland . . . . . . | 1953 | | 58E82 | | |
| Southern Rhodesia . . . | 1953 | | 57E121 | 61E122 | |

## 85. LABOUR INSPECTION (NON-METROPOLITAN TERRITORIES), 1947

*United Kingdom*

| Country | Entry into Force | Direct Request | Initial Observation | Action Taken in part | in full |
|---|---|---|---|---|---|
| Bahamas . . . . . . . | 1955 | | 57E123 | | |
| British Virgin Islands . . | 1955 | 1962 | | | 64E179 |
| Dominica . . . . . . . | 1955 | | 59E75 | | |
| Gambia . . . . . . . | 1955 | | 60E65 | | |
| Malta . . . . . . . . | 1955 | | 58E84 | | |
| Montserrat . . . . . . | 1955 | | 58E84 | | |
| Northern Rhodesia . . . | 1955 | | 59E75 | 60E65 64E179 | |
| Nyasaland . . . . . . | 1955 | | 57E124 | 59E75 | 64E179 |
| St. Christopher-Nevis-Anguilla . . . . . . . | 1955 | | 58E84 | | |
| St. Helena . . . . . . | 1955 | | 58E85 | | |
| St. Lucia . . . . . . . | 1955 | | 58E85 | 62E154 | |
| Southern Rhodesia . . . | 1955 | | 58E85 | | |

| Country | Entry into Force | Direct Request | Initial / Observation | Action Taken / in part | in full |
|---|---|---|---|---|---|

### 86. CONTRACTS OF EMPLOYMENT (INDIGENOUS WORKERS), 1947

*United Kingdom*

| | | | | | |
|---|---|---|---|---|---|
| British Guiana . . . . . | 1953 | | 57E126 | | |
| Northern Rhodesia . . . | 1953 | | 57E126 | | |
| Seychelles . . . . . . . | 1953 | | 55E98 | | 57E126 |
| Sierre Leone . . . . . . | 1950 | | 55E98 | | 57E126 |
| Southern Rhodesia . . . | 1953 | | 55E98 | | |
| Zanzibar . . . . . . . . | 1953 | | 55E99 | | 58E86 |

### 87. FREEDOM OF ASSOCIATION AND PROTECTION OF THE RIGHT TO ORGANIZE, 1948

| | | | | | |
|---|---|---|---|---|---|
| Albania . . . . . . . . | 1958 | | 61E60 | | |
| Burma . . . . . . . . . | 1956 | 1961 | 62E83 | | |
| Byelorussia . . . . . . . | 1957 | | 59E46 | | |
| Cameroon . . . . . . . | 1954 | 1963 | 64E123 | | |
| Central African Rep. . . | 1954 | 1961 | 63E88 | | |
| Cuba . . . . . . . . . | 1953 | | 55E65 | | |
| Dahomey . . . . . . . | 1954 | | 63E91 | 64C673 | |
| Denmark . . . . . . . | 1952 | | 57E82 | | 61E69 |
| Dominican Republic . . | 1957 | | 61E69 | | |
| France . . . . . . . . . | 1952 | | 55E66 | | 57E82 |
| Guatemala . . . . . . . | 1953 | | 57E82 | 62E91 64C674 | |
| Honduras . . . . . . . | 1957 | | 61E69 | | |
| Hungary . . . . . . . | 1958 | 1960 | 62E92 | | |
| Malagasy Republic . . . | 1954 | 1961 | 63E95 | | |
| Mexico . . . . . . . . | 1951 | | 58E55 | | |
| Netherlands . . . . . . | 1951 | | 59E48 | | |
| Niger . . . . . . . . . | 1954 | | 61E75 | | |
| Pakistan . . . . . . . . | 1952 | | 54E39 | | |
| Philippines . . . . . . . | 1954 | | 57E84 | | |
| Poland . . . . . . . . | 1958 | | 59E49 | | |
| Rumania . . . . . . . . | 1958 | 1959 | 62E99 | | |
| Senegal . . . . . . . . | 1954 | | 61E77 | | |
| Sierra Leone . . . . . . | 1958 | 1959 | | | 64E132 |
| Ukraine . . . . . . . . | 1957 | | 59E49 | | |
| U.S.S.R. . . . . . . . | 1957 | | 59E50 | | |
| United Arab Republic . . | 1958 | | 60E46 | 64C674 | |
| *United Kingdom* | | | | | |
| Nyasaland . . . . . . . | 1959 | 1960 | | | 64E180 |
| Swaziland . . . . . . . | 1959 | | 61E123 | 63E140 | |

| Country | Entry Into Force | Direct Request | Initial Observation | Action Taken in part | in full |
|---|---|---|---|---|---|
| **88. EMPLOYMENT SERVICE, 1948** | | | | | |
| Argentina . . . . . . | 1957 | 1960 | 62E113 | | |
| Australia . . . . . . . | 1950 | | 54E39 | | |
| Brazil . . . . . . . . | 1958 | | 60E47 | | |
| Bulgaria . . . . . . . | 1950 | | 55E67 | | RD1961 |
| Cuba . . . . . . . . | 1953 | | 55E67 | | |
| Dominican Republic . . | 1954 | | 56E73 | | 62E114 |
| Guatemala . . . . . . | 1953 | | 57C677 | 59E51 | |
| Iraq . . . . . . . . | 1952 | | 54E40 | 62C712 | |
| Italy . . . . . . . . . | 1953 | | 55E68 | | |
| Philippines . . . . . . | 1954 | | 57E85 | 64E135 | |
| Sierra Leone . . . . . | 1958 | 1959 | 64E135 | | |
| Turkey . . . . . . . | 1951 | | 54E40 | 55E69 | |
| United Arab Republic . . | 1955 | | 58E57 | 59C691 | |
| *Netherlands* | | | | | |
| Netherlands Antilles . . . | 1951 | | 56E114 | | |
| Surinam . . . . . . . | 1951 | | 56E114 | | |
| **89. NIGHT WORK (WOMEN) (Revised), 1948** | | | | | |
| Austria . . . . . . . | 1951 | | 53E36 | | |
| Czechoslovakia . . . . . | 1951 | | 55E69 | 60E48 | |
| Dominican Republic . . | 1954 | | 56E75 | 59E52 | |
| France . . . . . . . . | 1954 | | 56E75 | | |
| Guatemala . . . . . . | 1953 | | 57E87 | 62E116 | |
| India . . . . . . . . | 1951 | | 52E34 | | 55E69 |
| Netherlands . . . . . . | 1955 | | 57E87 | 62E116 | |
| Pakistan . . . . . . . | 1952 | | 54E40 | | |
| Philippines . . . . . . | 1954 | | 56E76 | | |
| Rumania . . . . . . . | 1958 | | 59E52 | | 64E137 |
| Rep. of South Africa . . | 1951 | | 60E48 | | |
| Syrian Arab Republic . . | 1950 | | 54E41 | | 55E70 |
| Tunisia . . . . . . . | 1958 | 1960 | | | 62E117 |
| Uruguay . . . . . . | 1955 | | 57E87 | | |
| *France* | | | | | |
| Overseas Departments . . | 1955 | | 56E115 | | |
| *Netherlands* | | | | | |
| Netherlands Antilles . . . | 1955 | | 57E128 | | 62E155 |
| *Rep. of South Africa* | | | | | |
| South West Africa . . . | 1958 | | 59E76 | | |

| Country | Entry into Force | Initial | | Action Taken | |
|---|---|---|---|---|---|
| | | Direct Request | Observation | in part | in full |

## 90. NIGHT WORK OF YOUNG PERSONS (INDUSTRY) (Revised), 1948

| Country | Entry into Force | Direct Request | Observation | in part | in full |
|---|---|---|---|---|---|
| Argentina | 1957 | | 61E94 | | |
| Czechoslovakia | 1951 | | 55E70 | | |
| Dominican Republic | 1958 | 1960 | 64E138 | | |
| Guatemala | 1953 | | 57C679 | 62E118 | |
| Haiti | 1958 | | 60E49 | | |
| India | 1951 | | 53E37 | | 55E71 |
| Israel | 1954 | | 56E77 | 57E88 | 59E53 |
| Italy | 1953 | | 55E71 | | |
| Luxembourg | 1959 | 1961 | 64E139 | | |
| Mexico | 1957 | | 58E60 | 62E118 64E139 | |
| Netherlands | 1955 | | 57E88 | 62E119 | |
| Pakistan | 1952 | | 54E41 | | |
| Philippines | 1954 | | 56E78 | | |
| Ukraine | 1957 | | 61E94 | | |
| Uruguay | 1955 | | 57E89 | | |
| *Netherlands* | | | | | |
| Netherlands Antilles | 1955 | | 57E128 | 62E156 | |

## 92. ACCOMMODATION OF CREWS (Revised), 1949

| Country | Entry into Force | Direct Request | Observation | in part | in full |
|---|---|---|---|---|---|
| Brazil | 1954 | | 56E78 | 60E50 | |
| Cuba | 1953 | | 55E72 | | |
| Poland | 1955 | | 56E79 | | |
| Portugal | 1953 | | 55E72 | 61E94 | |

## 94. LABOUR CLAUSES (PUBLIC CONTRACTS), 1949

| Country | Entry into Force | Direct Request | Observation | in part | in full |
|---|---|---|---|---|---|
| Austria | 1952 | | 54E41 | 63C538 | |
| Belgium | 1953 | | 55E72 | 57E89 | |
| Bulgaria | 1956 | | 60E50 | | |
| Cuba | 1953 | | 55E72 | | |
| Denmark | 1956 | | 58E61 | | |
| Finland | 1952 | | 54E42 | 57E90 62E123 | |
| Guatemala | 1953 | 1958 | 64E142 | | |
| Israel | 1954 | | 57E90 | | 64E142 |
| Morocco | 1957 | | 62E123 | 62C714 | |
| Netherlands | 1953 | | 55E73 | | 57E90 |
| Philippines | 1954 | | 56E81 | | |

| Country | Entry into Force | Direct Request | Initial Observation | Action Request in part | in full |
|---|---|---|---|---|---|

**94. LABOUR CLAUSES (PUBLIC CONTRACTS), 1949 (continued)**

| Country | Entry into Force | Direct Request | Initial Observation | Action Request in part | in full |
|---|---|---|---|---|---|
| United Arab Republic . . | 1961 | 1962 | 64E143 | | |
| Uruguay . . . . . . . | 1955 | | 58E61 | | |
| *Netherlands* | | | | | |
| Netherlands Antilles . . . | 1955 | | 56E116 | 58E87 | |
| Surinam . . . . . . . | 1955 | | 56E116 | 62E156 | |
| *United Kingdom* | | | | | |
| Bermuda . . . . . . . | 1958 | 1959 | | 64E182 | |
| Fiji . . . . . . . . . | 1960 | 1963 | | 64E183 | |
| Grenada . . . . . . . | 1958 | 1961 | | 63E141 | |
| Guernsey . . . . . . . | 1952 | | 56E116 | | 59E77 |
| Kenya . . . . . . . | 1958 | 1959 | | | 64E143 |
| St. Lucia . . . . . . . | 1958 | 1959 | | 62E157 | |

**95. PROTECTION OF WAGES, 1949**

| Country | Entry into Force | Direct Request | Initial Observation | Action Request in part | in full |
|---|---|---|---|---|---|
| Afghanistan . . . . . | 1958 | | 61E96 | | |
| Ecuador . . . . . . . | 1955 | | 57E91 | | |
| Greece . . . . . . . . | 1956 | 1960 | 62E124 | | |
| Guatemala . . . . . . | 1953 | | 57E91 | | |
| Philippines . . . . . . | 1954 | | 56E83 | | |
| Poland . . . . . . . | 1955 | | 57E91 | | |
| Sierra Leone . . . . . | 1958 | 1959 | | 64E145 | |
| Uruguay . . . . . . . | 1955 | | 57E92 | | |
| *Netherlands* | | | | | |
| Netherlands Antilles . . . | 1955 | | 56E117 | 60E67 | |
| Surinam . . . . . . . | 1955 | | 56E117 | | |
| *United Kingdom* | | | | | |
| Grenada . . . . . . . | 1958 | 1961 | 62E157 | | |
| Jersey . . . . . . . . | 1956 | | 57E130 | | |
| Mauritius . . . . . . | 1958 | 1960 | | 62E158 | |
| Tanganyika . . . . . | 1958 | 1959 | | 62E125 64E145 | |
| Zanzibar . . . . . . . | 1958 | 1961 | | 62E158 | |

**96. FEE-CHARGING EMPLOYMENT AGENCIES (Revised), 1949**

| Country | Entry into Force | Direct Request | Initial Observation | Action Request in part | in full |
|---|---|---|---|---|---|
| Brazil . . . . . . . . | 1958 | 1960 | 64E145 | | |
| France . . . . . . . . | 1954 | | 56E83 | | |
| Fed. Rep. of Germany . . | 1955 | | 57E93 | 62E126 | |

| Country | Entry into Force | Direct Request | Initial Observation | Action Taken in part | in full |
|---------|:---:|:---:|:---:|:---:|:---:|

**96. FEE-CHARGING EMPLOYMENT AGENCIES (Revised), 1949 (continued)**

| | | | | | |
|---|:---:|:---:|:---:|:---:|:---:|
| Guatemala . . . . . . . | 1954 | | 57C680 | | |
| Italy . . . . . . . . . . | 1954 | | 56E83 | | 59E55 |
| Pakistan . . . . . . . . | 1953 | | 55E75 | | |
| Sweden . . . . . . . . | 1951 | | 54E42 | | 57E93 |
| Turkey . . . . . . . . | 1953 | | 55E75 | | |
| *Netherlands* | | | | | |
| Surinam . . . . . . . . | 1955 | | 56E117 | | |

**97. MIGRATION FOR EMPLOYMENT (Revised), 1949**

| | | | | | |
|---|:---:|:---:|:---:|:---:|:---:|
| France . . . . . . . . . | 1955 | | 58E62 | | |
| Guatemala . . . . . . . | 1953 | | 58E63 | | |

**98. RIGHT TO ORGANIZE AND COLLECTIVE BARGAINING, 1949**

| | | | | | |
|---|:---:|:---:|:---:|:---:|:---:|
| Brazil . . . . . . . . . | 1953 | | 56E85 | | |
| Byelorussia . . . . . . | 1957 | | 61E97 | | |
| Cuba . . . . . . . . . | 1953 | | 62E128 | | |
| Dominican Republic . . | 1954 | | 56E85 | 58E63 61E97 | |
| France . . . . . . . . . | 1952 | | 55E77 | | 57E94 |
| Guatemala . . . . . . . | 1953 | | 57E94 | | |
| Japan . . . . . . . . . | 1954 | | 59E56 | | |
| Morocco . . . . . . . . | 1958 | 1959 | | 61E98 | |
| Pakistan . . . . . . . . | 1953 | | 55E77 | 61E98 | |
| Poland . . . . . . . . | 1958 | | 62E128 | | |
| Rumania . . . . . . . . | 1959 | 1961 | 62E128 | | |
| Turkey . . . . . . . . | 1953 | | 56E85 | | |
| Ukraine . . . . . . . . | 1957 | | 61E99 | | |
| U.S.S.R. . . . . . . . | 1957 | | 61E99 | | |
| United Arab Republic . . | 1955 | | 57E94 | 61E99 | |
| United Kingdom . . . . | 1951 | | 61E99 | | |
| *United Kingdom* | | | | | |
| St. Lucia . . . . . . . . | 1958 | 1960 | | 61E125 | |

**100. EQUAL REMUNERATION, 1951**

| | | | | | |
|---|:---:|:---:|:---:|:---:|:---:|
| Austria . . . . . . . . | 1954 | | 57E96 | | |
| Belgium . . . . . . . . | 1953 | | 55E77 | 58E64 | |
| Italy . . . . . . . . . . | 1957 | | 59E56 | 61E100 63E114 | |
| Philippines . . . . . . | 1954 | | 59E57 | | |

| Country | Entry into Force | Initial | | Action Taken | |
|---------|------------------|---------|---|--------------|---|
| | | Direct Request | Observation | in part | in full |

**101. HOLIDAYS WITH PAY (AGRICULTURE), 1952**

| Country | Entry into Force | Direct Request | Observation | in part | in full |
|---------|------------------|----------------|-------------|---------|---------|
| Cuba . . . . . . . . . | 1955 | | 57E97 | | 59E57 |
| France . . . . . . . . | 1955 | | 59E57 | | |
| Fed. Rep. of Germany . . | 1956 | 1959 | 62E129 | | |
| Poland . . . . . . . | 1957 | | 61E101 | | |
| United Kingdom . . . . | 1957 | 1960 | | | 62E129 |
| Yugoslavia . . . . . . | 1956 | | 58E64 | 59E57 | |
| *United Kingdom* | | | | | |
| Tanganyika . . . . . . | 1959 | 1960 | | | 62E129 |

**102. SOCIAL SECURITY (MINIMUM STANDARDS), 1952**

| Country | Entry into Force | Direct Request | Observation | in part | in full |
|---------|------------------|----------------|-------------|---------|---------|
| Denmark . . . . . . . | 1956 | | 58E64 | 61E101 | |
| Greece . . . . . . . . | 1956 | | 59E57 | | |
| Norway . . . . . . . | 1955 | | 57E97 | 58E65 | |
| Sweden . . . . . . . | 1955 | | 57E98 | | |
| Yugoslavia . . . . . . | 1955 | | 58E65 | 64E151 | |

**103. MATERNITY PROTECTION (Revised), 1952**

| Country | Entry into Force | Direct Request | Observation | in part | in full |
|---------|------------------|----------------|-------------|---------|---------|
| Cuba . . . . . . . . | 1955 | | 57E100 | 63C541 | |
| Uruguay . . . . . . | 1955 | | 57E100 | 64E151 | |

**105. ABOLITION OF FORCED LABOUR, 1957**

| Country | Entry into Force | Direct Request | Observation | in part | in full |
|---------|------------------|----------------|-------------|---------|---------|
| Canada . . . . . . . | 1960 | 1962 | | 64E152 | |
| Dominican Republic . . | 1959 | 1961 | 64E152 | | |
| Israel . . . . . . . . | 1959 | 1961 | 64E152 | | |
| Portugal . . . . . . . | 1960 | | 62E131 | 63E116 | |
| El Salvador . . . . . | 1959 | 1961 | | 64E154 | |
| *United Kingdom* | | | | | |
| Bechuanaland . . . . . | 1958 | 1963 | 64E184 | | |
| Hong Kong . . . . . . | 1959 | 1961 | | 62E159 64E184 | |
| Solomon Islands . . . . | 1960 | 1963 | | 64E184 | |
| Southern Rhodesia . . . | 1959 | 1961 | 64E184 | | |
| Swaziland . . . . . . | 1958 | 1962 | | 64E187 | |

**106. WEEKLY REST (COMMERCE AND OFFICES), 1957**

| Country | Entry into Force | Direct Request | Observation | in part | in full |
|---------|------------------|----------------|-------------|---------|---------|
| Ghana . . . . . . . . | 1959 | 1961 | 63E118 | | |

**111. DISCRIMINATION (EMPLOYMENT AND OCCUPATION), 1958**

| Country | Entry into Force | Direct Request | Observation | in part | in full |
|---------|------------------|----------------|-------------|---------|---------|
| Portugal . . . . . . . | 1960 | 1962 | 64E155 | | |

## Appendix III

### OBSERVATIONS MADE AND ACTION TAKEN IN RESPONSE, TABULATED BY COUNTRIES

#### (as at 30 June 1964)

| | Formal Undertakings Covered | No Operative Observations | First Series | Second Series | Action in Full | Action in Part | Denunciations | No Action Taken |
|---|---|---|---|---|---|---|---|---|
| | | | of Observations | | | | | |
| **Africa** | | | | | | | | |
| Algeria | 41 | 41 | — | — | — | — | — | — |
| Burundi | 16 | 16 | — | — | — | — | — | — |
| Cameroon | 21 | 19 | 2 | — | 1 | — | — | 1 |
| Central African Republic | 12 | 10 | 2 | — | — | — | — | 2 |
| Chad | 14 | 14 | — | — | — | — | — | — |
| Congo (Brazzaville) | 12 | 10 | 2 | — | 1 | — | — | 1 |
| Congo (Leopoldville) | 16 | 15 | 1 | — | — | 1 | — | — |
| Dahomey | 15 | 14 | 1 | — | — | 1 | — | — |
| Gabon | 25 | 20 | 5 | — | 3 | 2 | — | — |
| Ghana | 22 | 20 | 2 | — | 1 | — | — | 1 |
| Guinea | 15 | 13 | 2 | — | — | — | — | 2 |
| Ivory Coast | 21 | 17 | 4 | — | 2 | 1 | — | 1 |
| Liberia | 4 | 3 | 1 | — | — | 1 | — | — |
| Libya | 2 | 2 | — | — | — | — | — | — |
| Malagasy Republic | 15 | 11 | 4 | — | — | 2 | — | 2 |
| Mali | 13 | 13 | — | — | — | — | — | — |
| Mauritania | 13 | 13 | — | — | — | — | — | — |
| Morocco | 25 | 15 | 10 | — | 2 | 6 | — | 2 |
| Niger | 13 | 12 | 1 | — | — | — | — | 1 |
| Nigeria | 18 | 17 | 1 | — | — | — | — | 1 |
| Rwanda | 14 | 14 | — | — | — | — | — | — |
| Senegal | 22 | 21 | 1 | — | — | — | — | 1 |
| Sierra Leone | 28 | 23 | 5 | — | 1 | 2 | — | 2 |
| Somalia | 14 | 14 | — | — | — | — | — | — |
| Republic of South Africa | 10 | 8 | 2 | — | — | 1 | — | 1 |
| Sudan | 5 | 4 | 1 | — | — | — | — | 1 |
| Tanganyika | 24 | 24 | — | — | — | — | — | — |
| Togo | 12 | 9 | 3 | — | 2 | — | — | 1 |
| Tunisia | 25 | 22 | 3 | — | 1 | 1 | — | 1 |
| Uganda | 15 | 15 | — | — | — | — | — | — |
| Upper Volta | 16 | 16 | — | — | — | — | — | — |
| **America–South, Central & Caribbean** | | | | | | | | |
| Argentina | 54 | 21 | 33 | 2 | 9 | 3 | — | 23 |
| Bolivia | 6 | 4 | 2 | — | — | — | — | 2 |
| Brazil | 28 | 16 | 12 | 1 | 4 | 3 | 2 | 4 |
| Chile | 35 | 16 | 19 | 2 | 4 | 11 | — | 6 |
| Colombia | 24 | 4 | 20 | 1 | — | 9 | — | 12 |
| Costa Rica | 3 | 3 | — | — | — | — | — | — |

| | Formal Undertakings Covered | No Operative Observations | First Series | Second Series | Action in Full | Action in Part | Denunciations | No Action Taken |
|---|---|---|---|---|---|---|---|---|
| | | | of Observations | | | | | |

### America–South, Central & Caribbean (continued)

| | | | | | | | | |
|---|---|---|---|---|---|---|---|---|
| Cuba | 59 | 22 | 37 | 1 | 24 | 6 | — | 8 |
| Dominican Republic | 21 | 9 | 12 | — | 3 | 4 | — | 5 |
| Ecuador | 6 | 3 | 3 | — | — | — | — | 3 |
| Guatemala | 16 | 3 | 13 | — | — | 6 | — | 7 |
| Haiti | 21 | 11 | 10 | — | 3 | 5 | — | 2 |
| Honduras | 7 | 5 | 2 | — | — | — | — | 2 |
| Jamaica | 17 | 17 | — | — | — | — | — | — |
| Mexico | 42 | 25 | 17 | — | 2 | 6 | 1 | 8 |
| Nicaragua | 30 | 1 | 29 | — | 1 | 15 | 1 | 12 |
| Panama | 1 | — | 1 | — | — | — | — | — |
| Peru | 16 | 8 | 8 | — | — | 4 | — | 4 |
| Trinidad and Tobago | 10 | 10 | — | — | — | — | — | — |
| El Salvador | 4 | 2 | 2 | — | — | 1 | — | 1 |
| Uruguay | 54 | 18 | 36 | — | 5 | 5 | 6 | 20 |
| Venezuela | 18 | 10 | 8 | 1 | 1 | 3 | — | 5 |

### America–North

| | | | | | | | | |
|---|---|---|---|---|---|---|---|---|
| Canada | 18 | 15 | 3 | — | — | 3 | — | — |
| United States of America | 4 | 4 | — | — | — | — | — | — |

### Asia & Far East

| | | | | | | | | |
|---|---|---|---|---|---|---|---|---|
| Afghanistan | 6 | — | 6 | — | — | — | — | 6 |
| Burma | 21 | 17 | 4 | — | 1 | 1 | — | 2 |
| Ceylon | 18 | 11 | 7 | — | 1 | — | 1 | 5 |
| China | 15 | 3 | 12 | 1 | 1 | 7 | — | 5 |
| India | 25 | 12 | 13 | 3 | 9 | 4 | 1 | 2 |
| Indonesia | 6 | 5 | 1 | — | — | — | — | 1 |
| Japan | 23 | 20 | 3 | — | 1 | — | — | 2 |
| States of Malaya | 12 | 9 | 3 | — | 2 | — | — | 1 |
| Pakistan | 26 | 17 | 9 | — | 1 | 1 | — | 7 |
| Philippines | 15 | 8 | 7 | — | — | 1 | — | 6 |
| Vietnam | 11 | 6 | 5 | — | 2 | 2 | — | 1 |

### Europe–West

| | | | | | | | | |
|---|---|---|---|---|---|---|---|---|
| Austria | 31 | 16 | 15 | 1 | 11 | 1 | — | 4 |
| Belgium | 57 | 40 | 17 | 2 | 15 | 2 | — | 2 |
| Denmark | 30 | 22 | 8 | 1 | 3 | 2 | — | 4 |
| Finland | 35 | 26 | 9 | — | 5 | 4 | — | — |
| France | 65 | 41 | 24 | 1 | 11 | 5 | 1 | 8 |
| Federal Republic of Germany | 36 | 27 | 9 | — | 3 | 2 | — | 4 |
| Greece | 29 | 13 | 16 | 4 | 5 | 10 | 1 | 4 |
| Iceland | 9 | 9 | — | — | — | — | — | — |
| Ireland | 39 | 33 | 6 | — | 6 | — | — | — |
| Italy | 58 | 37 | 21 | — | 8 | 8 | — | 5 |
| Luxembourg | 43 | 31 | 12 | — | 6 | 2 | — | 4 |
| Netherlands | 48 | 38 | 10 | — | 7 | 2 | — | 1 |
| Norway | 48 | 42 | 6 | — | 3 | 2 | — | 1 |
| Portugal | 22 | 11 | 11 | 1 | 6 | 5 | — | 1 |
| Spain | 43 | 20 | 23 | 5 | 9 | 14 | — | 5 |
| Sweden | 26 | 36 | 10 | — | 4 | 1 | — | 5 |
| Switzerland | 26 | 23 | 3 | — | 2 | 1 | — | — |
| United Kingdom | 54 | 49 | 5 | — | 2 | — | 1 | 2 |

| | Formal Undertakings Covered | No Operative Observations | First Series | Second Series | Action in Full | Action in Part | Denunciations | No Action Taken |
|---|---|---|---|---|---|---|---|---|
| | | | \|\_\_\_ of Observations \_\_\_\| | | | | | |

*Europe–East*

| | | | | | | | | |
|---|---|---|---|---|---|---|---|---|
| Albania | 16 | 9 | 7 | 1 | 1 | 3 | 1 | 3 |
| Bulgaria | 67 | 25 | 42 | 3 | 17 | 16 | 3 | 9 |
| Byelorussia | 21 | 17 | 4 | — | — | — | — | 4 |
| Czechoslovakia | 36 | 20 | 16 | — | 2 | 3 | — | 11 |
| Hungary | 33 | 16 | 17 | 2 | 8 | 2 | — | 9 |
| Poland | 47 | 29 | 18 | — | 7 | 4 | — | 7 |
| Rumania | 22 | 5 | 17 | 5 | 11 | 3 | — | 8 |
| Ukraine | 22 | 15 | 7 | — | 1 | 1 | — | 5 |
| U.S.S.R. | 22 | 16 | 6 | — | 1 | 1 | — | 4 |
| Yugoslavia | 44 | 27 | 17 | 4 | 11 | 8 | 2 | — |

*Middle East*

| | | | | | | | | |
|---|---|---|---|---|---|---|---|---|
| Cyprus | 11 | 11 | — | — | — | — | — | — |
| Iran | 3 | 3 | — | — | — | — | — | — |
| Iraq | 16 | 12 | 4 | — | — | 2 | — | 2 |
| Israel | 26 | 14 | 12 | — | 6 | 3 | — | 3 |
| Jordan | 1 | 1 | — | — | — | — | — | — |
| Kuwait | 6 | 6 | — | — | — | — | — | — |
| Syrian Arab Republic | 27 | 26 | 1 | — | 1 | — | — | — |
| Turkey | 14 | 7 | 7 | 1 | 2 | 3 | — | 3 |
| United Arab Republic | 30 | 20 | 10 | — | 2 | 5 | — | 3 |

*Oceania*

| | | | | | | | | |
|---|---|---|---|---|---|---|---|---|
| Australia | 21 | 19 | 2 | — | 1 | — | — | 1 |
| New Zealand | 42 | 35 | 7 | 1 | 4 | 2 | 1 | 1 |

*Non-Metropolitan Territories*

*Australia*

| | | | | | | | | |
|---|---|---|---|---|---|---|---|---|
| Nauru | 6 | 6 | — | — | — | — | — | — |
| New Guinea | 12 | 12 | — | — | — | — | — | — |
| Norfolk Islands | 5 | 5 | — | — | — | — | — | — |
| Papua | 12 | 11 | 1 | — | 1 | — | — | — |

*Belgium*
*Former Territories*

| | | | | | | | | |
|---|---|---|---|---|---|---|---|---|
| Congo & Ruanda-Urundi | 2 | — | 2 | — | — | 2 | — | — |
| Ruanda-Urundi | 2 | — | 2 | — | 1 | 1 | — | — |

*Denmark*

| | | | | | | | | |
|---|---|---|---|---|---|---|---|---|
| Faroe Islands | 21 | 19 | 2 | — | — | — | — | 2 |
| Greenland | 12 | 9 | 3 | — | — | 1 | — | 2 |

*France*

| | | | | | | | | |
|---|---|---|---|---|---|---|---|---|
| Comoro Islands | 16 | 14 | 2 | — | 2 | — | — | — |
| French Polynesia | 16 | 16 | — | — | — | — | — | — |

| | Formal Undertakings Covered | No Operative Observations | First Series of Observations | Second Series | Action in Full | Action in Part | Denunciations | No Action Taken |
|---|---|---|---|---|---|---|---|---|
| **Non-Metropolitan Territories** (continued) | | | | | | | | |
| French Somaliland . . . . . | 16 | 14 | 2 | — | 1 | — | — | 1 |
| New Caledonia . . . . . . . | 16 | 16 | — | — | — | — | — | — |
| Overseas Departments . . . . | 35 | 30 | 5 | — | — | 2 | — | 3 |
| St-Pierre & Miquelon . . . . | 16 | 11 | 5 | — | 1 | 1 | — | 3 |
| **Former Territories** | | | | | | | | |
| All territories . . . . . . . . | 1 | — | 1 | — | 1 | — | — | — |
| Cameroon . . . . . . . . . | 1 | — | 1 | — | 1 | — | — | — |
| Central African Republic . . | 1 | — | 1 | — | 1 | — | — | — |
| Congo . . . . . . . . . . . | 1 | — | 1 | — | 1 | — | — | — |
| Ivory Coast . . . . . . . . | 1 | — | 1 | — | 1 | — | — | — |
| French West Africa . . . . . | 1 | — | 1 | — | — | 1 | — | — |
| Togo . . . . . . . . . . . | 1 | — | 1 | — | 1 | — | — | — |
| **Netherlands** | | | | | | | | |
| Netherlands Antilles . . . . . | 25 | 14 | 11 | — | 2 | 4 | — | 5 |
| Surinam . . . . . . . . . . | 18 | 8 | 10 | — | — | — | — | 10 |
| **Former Territories** | | | | | | | | |
| Netherlands East Indies . . . | 1 | — | 1 | — | 1 | — | — | — |
| Netherlands New Guinea . . | 1 | — | 1 | — | 1 | — | — | — |
| **New Zealand** | | | | | | | | |
| Cook Islands & Niue . . . . | 10 | 10 | — | — | — | — | — | — |
| Tokelau Islands . . . . . . . | 4 | 4 | — | — | — | — | — | — |
| **Former Territory** | | | | | | | | |
| Western Samoa . . . . . . | 1 | — | 1 | — | 1 | — | — | — |
| **Republic of South Africa** | | | | | | | | |
| South West Africa . . . . . | 4 | 2 | 2 | — | — | 1 | — | 1 |
| **United Kingdom** | | | | | | | | |
| Aden . . . . . . . . . . . | 12 | 11 | 1 | — | — | — | — | 1 |
| Antigua . . . . . . . . . . | 18 | 17 | 1 | — | — | — | — | 1 |
| Bahamas . . . . . . . . . . | 20 | 18 | 2 | — | — | — | — | 2 |
| Barbados . . . . . . . . . | 26 | 24 | 2 | — | — | — | — | 2 |
| Basutoland . . . . . . . . . | 12 | 10 | 2 | — | — | 2 | — | — |
| Bechuanaland . . . . . . . . | 10 | 5 | 5 | — | — | 4 | — | 1 |
| Bermuda . . . . . . . . . . | 11 | 9 | 2 | — | — | 1 | — | 1 |
| British Guiana . . . . . . . | 22 | 17 | 5 | — | 1 | — | — | 4 |
| British Honduras . . . . . . | 22 | 19 | 3 | — | 3 | — | — | — |

|  | Formal Undertakings Covered | No Operative Observations | First Series of Observations | Second Series | Action in Full | Action in Part | Denunciations | No Action Taken |
|---|---|---|---|---|---|---|---|---|

### United Kingdom (continued)

| | | | | | | | | |
|---|---|---|---|---|---|---|---|---|
| British Virgin Islands . . . . | 11 | 9 | 2 | — | 2 | — | — | — |
| Brunei . . . . . . . . . . . | 13 | 10 | 3 | — | 3 | — | — | — |
| Dominica . . . . . . . . | 19 | 18 | 1 | — | — | — | — | 1 |
| Falkland Islands . . . . . . | 13 | 13 | — | — | — | — | — | — |
| Fiji . . . . . . . . . . . | 16 | 13 | 3 | — | — | 2 | — | 1 |
| Gambia . . . . . . . . . | 16 | 15 | 1 | — | — | — | — | 1 |
| Gibraltar . . . . . . . . | 20 | 20 | — | — | — | — | — | — |
| Gilbert & Ellice Islands . . . | 13 | 12 | 1 | — | 1 | — | — | — |
| Grenada . . . . . . . . . | 20 | 17 | 3 | — | — | 1 | — | 2 |
| Guernsey . . . . . . . . | 42 | 40 | 2 | — | 2 | — | — | — |
| Hong Kong . . . . . . . | 18 | 14 | 4 | — | — | 3 | — | 1 |
| Jersey . . . . . . . . . . | 42 | 40 | 2 | — | 1 | — | — | 1 |
| Malta . . . . . . . . . . | 20 | 19 | 1 | — | — | — | — | 1 |
| Isle of Man . . . . . . . | 42 | 42 | — | — | — | — | — | — |
| Mauritius . . . . . . . . | 19 | 15 | 4 | — | — | 4 | — | — |
| Monserrat . . . . . . . . | 13 | 11 | 2 | — | 1 | — | — | 1 |
| Northern Rhodesia . . . . . | 11 | 4 | 7 | — | — | 4 | — | 3 |
| Nyasaland . . . . . . . . | 14 | 11 | 3 | — | 1 | 1 | — | 1 |
| St. Christopher-Nevis-Anguilla | 11 | 10 | 1 | — | — | — | — | 1 |
| St. Helena . . . . . . . . | 10 | 9 | 1 | — | — | — | — | 1 |
| St. Lucia . . . . . . . . | 19 | 16 | 3 | — | — | 3 | — | — |
| St. Vincent . . . . . . . . | 18 | 18 | — | — | — | — | — | — |
| Seychelles . . . . . . . . | 11 | 8 | 3 | — | 2 | — | — | 1 |
| Solomon Islands . . . . . | 11 | 9 | 2 | — | — | 2 | — | — |
| Southern Rhodesia . . . . . | 8 | 2 | 6 | — | — | 2 | — | 4 |
| Swaziland . . . . . . . . | 11 | 6 | 5 | — | 1 | 4 | — | — |

### Former Territories

| | | | | | | | | |
|---|---|---|---|---|---|---|---|---|
| Gold Coast . . . . . . . | 1 | — | 1 | — | — | 1 | — | — |
| Jamaica . . . . . . . . . | 1 | — | 1 | — | 1 | — | — | — |
| Kenya . . . . . . . . . | 20 | 15 | 5 | 1 | 2 | 3 | — | 1 |
| Nigeria . . . . . . . . . | 1 | — | 1 | — | — | 1 | — | — |
| North Borneo (Sabah) . . . . | 16 | 14 | 2 | — | 1 | — | — | 1 |
| Sarawak . . . . . . . . . | 17 | 16 | 1 | — | 1 | — | — | — |
| Sierra Leone . . . . . . . | 4 | — | 4 | — | 2 | 2 | — | — |
| Singapore . . . . . . . . | 19 | 17 | 2 | — | 2 | — | — | — |
| Tanganyika . . . . . . . | 5 | — | 5 | 1 | 3 | 3 | — | — |
| Uganda . . . . . . . . . | 2 | — | 2 | — | — | 2 | — | — |
| Zanzibar . . . . . . . . . | 21 | 17 | 4 | — | 2 | 2 | — | — |

### United States of America

| | | | | | | | | |
|---|---|---|---|---|---|---|---|---|
| American Samoa . . . . . . | 3 | 3 | — | — | — | — | — | — |
| Guam . . . . . . . . . . | 3 | 3 | — | — | — | — | — | — |
| Panama Canal Zone . . . . . | 4 | 4 | — | — | — | — | — | — |
| Puerto Rico . . . . . . . | 3 | 3 | — | — | — | — | — | — |
| Trust Territory of Pacific Islands. . . . . . . . . | 1 | 1 | — | — | — | — | — | — |
| Virgin Islands . . . . . . | 3 | 3 | — | — | — | — | — | — |

# BIBLIOGRAPHY

## I. *I.L.O. Documents*

Constitution
Official Bulletin.
Records of Proceedings of the International Labour Conference.
Reports submitted to the International Labour Conference.
Minutes of the Governing Body.
Roneoed Documents submitted to the Governing Body and to its Committees.

## II. *Books*

Akzin, Benjamin, *New States and International Organizations* (Paris: International Political Science Association, 1955).

Bahramy, Ahmad-Ali, *La Législation Internationale du Travail et son Influence sur le Droit Iranien — Aspects Internationaux du Problème du Développement Economique et Social* (Geneva: Librairie Droz, 1963).

Berenstein, Alexandre, *Les Organisations Ouvrières - Leur Compétences et leur Rôle dans la Société des Nations et Notamment dans l'Organisation Internationale du Travail* (Paris: Pédone, 1936).

Bernath, Erwin, *Die Internationale Kontrolle* (Zurich: Ernst Lang, 1935).

Berthoud, Paul, *Le Contrôle International de l'Exécution des Conventions Collectives* (Geneva: Imprimerie de Saint-Gervais, 1946).

Bowett, D.W., *The Law of International Institutions* (London: Methuen, 1964).

Brennan, Donald E. (editor), *Arms Control, Disarmament and National Security* (New York: George Braziller, 1961).

Brierly, J.L., *The Law of Nations*, Sixth Edition (Oxford: Clarendon Press, 1963).

Follows, John W., *Antecedents of the International Labour Organization* (Oxford: Clarendon Press, 1951).

Friedmann Wolfgang, *The Changing Structure of International Law* (London: Stevens & Sons, 1964).

Galenson, Walter (editor), *Labor and Economic Development* (New York: John Wiley & Sons, 1959).

Guggenheim, Paul, *Traité de Droit International Public* (Geneva: Librairie de l'Université, 1954).

Haas, Ernst B., *Beyond the Nation-State, Functionalism and International Organization* (Stanford: Stanford University Press, 1964).

– and Whiting, Allan S., *Dynamics of International Relations* (New York: McGraw-Hill, 1956).

Hudson, Manley O., *International Legislation*, Vol. I, 1919-1921 (Washington: Carnegie Endowment for International Peace, 1931).

International Labour Office, *The International Labour Organization. The First Decade* (London: Allen & Unwin, 1931).

- *The International Labour Code 1951* (Geneva: 1952).
- *Lasting Peace the I.L.O. Way. The Story of the International Labour Organization* (Geneva: 1953).
- *The Trade Union Situation in the U.S.S.R.* (Geneva: 1960).
- *International Labour Standards, Their Nature—Their Working—Their Value* (Geneva: 1964).

Jenks, C. Wilfred, *The International Protection of Trade Union Freedom* (London: Stevens & Sons, 1957).
- *The Common Law of Mankind* (London: Stevens & Sons, 1958).
- *Human Rights and International Labour Standards* (London: Stevens & Sons, 1960).
- *Law, Freedom and Welfare* (London: Stevens & Sons, 1963).

Jessup, Philip C. and Taubenfeld, Howard J., *Controls for Outer Space* (New York: Columbia University Press, 1959).

Kaasik, V.N., *Le Contrôle en Droit International* (Paris: Pédone, 1933).

Kelsen, Hans, *Théorie Pure du Droit* (Paris: Dalloz, 1962).

Labeyrie-Ménahem, C., *Des Institutions Spécialisées — Problèmes Juridiques et Diplomatiques de l'Administration Internationale* (Paris: Pédone, 1953).

Lauterpacht, H., *International Law and Human Rights* (London: Stevens & Sons, 1950).

Lorwin, Lewis L., *The International Labor Movement* (New York: Harper, 1953).

Maclure, Stuart, *"If you wish Peace, cultivate Justice". The International Labour Organization after Forty Years* (Geneva: World Federation of United Nations Associations, 1960).

McNair, Lord Arnold, *The Law of Treaties* (Oxford: Clarendon Press, 1961).

Melman, Seymour (editor), *Inspection for Disarmament* (New York: Columbia University Press, 1951).

Oppenheim, L., *International Law*, Eighth Edition (Edited by H. Lauterpacht) (London: Longmans, 1955), Vol. I.

Phelan, E.J., *Yes and Albert Thomas* (New York: Columbia University Press, 1949).

Puri, Madan Mohan, *India in the International Labour Organization* (The Hague: Institute of Social Studies, 1958).

Salah-Bey, Anisse, *L'Organisation Internationale du Travail et le Syndicalisme Mondial (1945-1960)* (Ambilly-Annemasse: Imprimerie Franco-Suisse, 1963).

Scelle, Georges, *L'Organisation Internationale du Travail et le B.I.T.* (Paris: Marcel Rivière, 1930).
- *Cours de Droit International Public* (1947-1948) (Paris, roneoed).

Schnorr, Gerhard, *Das Arbeitsrecht als Gegenstand internationaler Rechtsetzung* (Munich and Berlin: C.H. Beck, 1960).

Shotwell, James T. (editor), *The Origins of the International Labor Organization* (New York: Columbia University Press, 1934).

Thomas, Albert, *International Social Policy* (Geneva: International Labour Office, 1948).

Troclet, Léon-Eli, *Législation Sociale Internationale* (Brussels: Cahiers de l'Institut de Sociologie Solvay, Editions de la Librairie Encyclopédique, 1952).

U.S. Department of Labor, *Historical Survey of International Action Affecting Labor*, (Bulletin No. 268 of the United States Bureau of Labor Statistics) (Washington, August 1920).

Virally, Michel, *La Pensée Juridique* (Paris: Librairie Générale de Droit et de Jurisprudence, 1960).

Visseur, Pierre-Arthur, *L'Evolution du Contrôle International sur l'Application de la Protection Ouvrière jusqu'à la Constitution de l'O.I.T. à Genève* (Bar-le-Duc: Imprimerie du Barrois, 1950).

Zarras, Jean, *Le Contrôle de l'Application des Conventions Internationales du Travail* (Paris: Librairie Sirey, 1937).

Zimmern, Sir Alfred, *The League of Nations and the Rule of Law 1918-1935* (London: Macmillan, 1936).

## III. *Articles*

Anon., " La Tâche du Mouvement Syndical ", *Labor* (Utrecht), Vol. 25, No. 11 (May 1953), pp. 344-346.

Anon., "The European Social Charter and International Labour Standards", *International Labour Review*, Vol. LXXXIV Nos. 5-6 (November-December 1961), pages 354-375, 462-477.

Anon., "The Influence of I.L.O. Standards", *Eastern Worker* (Karachi), Vol. III No. 1 (January 1963).

van Asbeck, Frederik M., "Une Commission d'Experts", *Symbolae Verzijl* (The Hague: Martinus Nijhoff, 1958, pp. 9-21).

- "Quelques aspects du contrôle international non-judiciaire de l'application par les gouvernements de conventions internationales", *Netherlands International Law Review*, Volume en l'honneur du professeur François (Leyde: A.W. Sijthoff's, 1959, pp. 27-41).

- "La Charte Sociale Européenne : Sa Portée Juridique, La Mise en Œuvre", *Mélanges Offerts à Henri Rollin* (Paris: Pédone, 1964).

Béguin, Bernard, "I.L.O. and the Tripartite System", *International Conciliation*, No. 523 (May 1959).

Berenstein, A., "The Influence of International Labour Conventions on Swiss Legislation", *International Labour Review*, Vol. LXXVII, No. 6 (June 1958), pp. 495-528.

- "L'Activité de l'Organisation internationale du Travail et ses Résultats ", *Rivista di diritto internazionale e comparato del lavoro* (Bologna), Vol. II, No. III, pp. 379-395.

Burns, Richard Dean, "Origins of the United States' Inspection Policy: 1926-1946 ", *Disarmament and Arms Control* (Oxford), Vol. 2, No. 2 (Spring 1964).

Chamberlain, Joseph P., "Legislation in a Changing Economic World ", *Annals of the American Academy of Political and Social Science*, Vol. 166, (1933).

Charak, H. Leo, "Auf absteigenden Pfaden. Vor Sanktionen der I.A.O. gegen Österreich", *Arbeit und Wirtschaft* (Vienna), Vol. 14, No. 10 (October 1960).

Chatterjee, Sir Atul C., "Federalism and Labour Legislation in India", *International Labour Review*, Vol. XLIX, Nos. 4-5, (April-May 1944).

Douty, H.M., "The International Labor Conference of 1962", *Monthly Labor Review* (United States Department of Labor), Vol. 85, No. 9 (September 1962).

Evans, Alona E., "Some Aspects of the Problem of Self-Executing Treaties", *Proceedings, American Society of International Law, 1951*.

Faupl, Rudolph, "International Labor Organization", *Labor Law Journal*, Vol. 13, No. 7 (July 1962).

Feis, Herbert, "International Labour Legislation in the Light of Economic Theory", *International Labour Review*, Vol. XV, No. 4 (April 1927).

Fletcher, Raymond, "Existing Arrangements for International Control of Warlike Material–Western European Union", *Disarmament and Arms Control*, Vol. 1, No. 2 (Autumn 1963).

Giraud, Emile, "Le Rejet de l'Idée de Souveraineté. L'Aspect juridique et l'Aspect Politique de la Question", *Etudes en l'Honneur de Georges Scelle* (Paris: Librairie Générale de Droit et de Jurisprudence, 1950).

Haas, Ernst B., "System and Process in the International Labor Organization", *World Politics*, Vol. XIV, No. 2 (January 1962), pp. 343-351.

Hahn, Hugo, J., "Internationale Kontrollen", *Archiv des Völkerrechts*, Vol. 7 (1958), pp. 88-112.

van Helmont, Jacques, "Existing Arrangements for International Control of Warlike Material - Euratom", *Disarmament and Arms Control*, Vol. 2, No. 1 (Winter 1963/64).

Higgins, Rosalyn, "Technical Assistance for Human Rights", *The World Today* (Chatham House), Vol. 19, Nos. 3 and 5 (April and May 1963), pp. 174-180, 219-224.

Ivanov S.A., "Application of International Labour Conventions", *Soviet Yearbook of International Law*, 1958, pp. 437-451.

Jenks, C. Wilfred, "The Interpretation of International Labour Conventions by the International Labour Office", *British Yearbook of International Law 1939*, pp. 132-141.

– "Some Constitutional Problems of International Organizations", *British Yearbook of International Law, 1945*, pp. 25-26.

– "The Application of International Labour Conventions by Means of Collective Agreements", *Zeitschrift für Ausländisches Öffentliches Recht und Völkerrecht*, Vol. 19, Nos. 1-3 (August 1958), pp. 197-224.

Kopelmanas, L., "Le Contrôle International", *Recueil des Cours de l'Académie de Droit International* (The Hague), 1950, Vol. II, pp. 59-149.

Linares, Francisco Walker, "Trade Unionism among Agricultural Workers in Chile", *International Labour Review*, Vol. LXVIII, No. 6 (December 1953), pp. 509-523.

Looper, Robert B., " 'Federal State' Clauses in Multilateral Instruments", *British Yearbook of International Law, 1955-56*, pp. 162-203.

Menon, V.K.R., "The Influence of International Labour Conventions on Indian Labour Legislation", *International Labour Review*, Vol. LXXIII, No. 6 (June 1956).

Merle, Marcel, "Le Contrôle Exercé par les Organisations Internationales sur les Activités des Etats Membres", *Annuaire Français de Droit International*, Vol. V (1959), pp. 411-431.

Myrdal, Gunnar, *Realities and Illusions in Regard to Inter-Governmental Organizations*, L. T. Hobhouse Memorial Trust Lecture No. 24, Bedford College, London, 1954 (Oxford: Oxford University Press, 1955).

Pavón Egas, Fernando, "El Ecuador en la Organización Internacional del Trabajo", *Revista del Instituto de Derecho del Trabajo y Investigaciones Sociales* (Quito, Ecuador), Vol. II, No. 3 (January-June 1962), pp. 45-73.

Rosner, Jan, "Si vis pacem, cole justitiam", *Polish Trade Union Review*, 1957, No. 4.

Saba, H., "L'Activité Quasi-Législative des Institutions Spécialisées des Nations Unies", *Recueil des Cours de l'Académie de Droit International* (The Hague), 1964, Vol. I.

Schaaf, C. Hart, "The Role of Resident Representatives of the U.N. Technical Assistance Board", *International Organization*, Vol. 14, No. 4 (Autumn 1960).

Scheer, Otto, "Die Internationale Arbeitskonferenz 1962", *Das Recht der Arbeit* (Vienna), Vol. 12, No. 4 (September 1962).

Siotis, Jean, "The Secretariat of the United Nations Economic Commission for Europe: The First Ten Years", *International Organization*, Vol. XIX, No. 2 (Spring 1965).

Sohn, Louis B., "Expulsion or Forced Withdrawal from International Organizations", *Harvard Law Review*, Vol. 77, No. 8 (June 1964), pp. 1381-1425.

Sørensen, Max, "The Quest for Equality", *International Conciliation*, No. 507 (March 1956).

Valticos, Nicolas, " Conventions internationales du travail et droit interne", *Revue Critique de droit international privé* (Paris), 1955, No 2, pp. 251-288.

– "Aperçu de certains grands problèmes du contrôle international (spécialement à propos des Conventions internationales du Travail)", *Eranion en l'honneur de G. S. Maridakis* (Athens: Klissiounis, 1964, Vol. III) pp. 543-586.

Vignes, Daniel, "Procédures Internationales d'Enquête", *Annuaire Français de Droit International*, Vol. IX (1963), pp. 438-459.

Virally, Michel, " Le Juriste et la Science du Droit", *Revue du Droit Public et de la Science Politique en France et à l'Etranger* (Paris), Vol. LXXX, No. 3 (May-June 1964).

Wehberg, Hans, " Entwicklungsstufen der Internationalen Organisation", *Die Friedenswarte*, Vol. 52 (1954), No 3, pp. 193-218.

Wolf, Francis, " Les Conventions internationales du Travail et la succession d'états", *Annuaire Français de Droit International*, Vol. VII (1961), pp. 742-751.

# INDEX [1]

---

[1] The abbreviations G.R., E.R. and W.R. indicate that the person in question was a government, employers' or workers' representative of the country mentioned. Index entries regarding countries identify all pages where reference is made, directly or indirectly, to the implementation of I.L.O. Conventions in the countries concerned.

Swaziland, 238, 241, 245, 246, 251
Sweden, 88, 162, 219, 224, 228, 229, 233, 237, 241, 250, 251
Switzerland, 6, 59, 85, 88, 108, 109, 110, 113, 149, 228, 236, 240
Syria, 162, 247

TABULATION, METHOD OF, 62-63
Tanganyika, former, 234, 238, 242, 249, 251
Tanzania, 15
Taubenfeld, Howard J., 210
Thailand, 13, 123
Thomas, Albert, 9, 17, 21, 84, 120, 137, 159, 190
Togo, 15, 137, 221, 222, 226, 235
Torres Cereceda, I. (G.R., Chile), 101
Trinidad and Tobago, 15
Tripartism, 181-182
Troclet, L.-E. (G.R., Belgium), 5, 9, 49, 126, 168
Tunisia, 6, 15, 228, 239, 247
Turkey, 162, 219, 226, 227, 244, 247, 250

UGANDA, 15, 234, 242
Ukraine, 224, 227, 233, 239, 246, 248, 250
U.N.E.S.C.O., 158, 205-206
United Arab Republic, 48, 51, 225, 237, 239, 241, 244, 246, 247, 249, 250
United Kingdom, 13, 72, 162, 177, 228, 229, 237, 250, 251
United Nations, 2, 26, 84, 94, 127. 131-133, 141, 155, 158, 179, 206-208
United States of America, 13, 71, 104, 108, 109, 147, 162
Upper Volta, 15

Uruguay, 13, 62, 71, 84, 106, 131, 135-136, 171, 220, 221, 222, 223, 224, 225, 228, 229, 230, 231, 232, 234, 235, 237, 239, 240, 241, 242, 243, 247, 248, 249, 251
U.S.S.R., 94-96, 162, 193-194, 225, 227, 233, 239, 246, 250

VALTICOS, NICOLAS, 3, 103, 108
Venezuela, 130, 162, 220, 223, 225, 231, 232, 233
Vietnam, 123, 222, 223, 226, 233, 239
Vignes, Daniel, 176
Virally, Michel, 108, 210
Visits on the Spot, 96, 145, 160, 162, 208
Visseur, Pierre-Arthur, 9

WEAVER, G. L.-P. (G.R., United States), 50
Wehberg, Hans, 168
Western European Union, 208-209
Western New Guinea, former, 61
Western Samoa, 61, 241
Whiting, Allan S., 168, 169
W.H.O., 158
Wilson, Francis Graham, 9, 120, 181
Withdrawal from I.L.O., 60
Wolf, Francis, 15
Wolfe, H. (G.R., United Kingdom), 18

YUGOSLAVIA, 62, 71, 108, 220, 221, 222, 223, 224, 225, 226, 227, 228, 230, 232, 237, 239, 251

ZANZIBAR, 234, 242, 246, 249
Zarras, Jean, 9, 19, 43, 83, 174, 192
Zimmern, Sir Alfred, 170